Graphic Design, Print Culture, and the Eighteenth-Century Novel

The uniformity of the eighteenth-century novel in today's paperbacks and critical editions no longer conveys the early novel's visual exuberance. Janine Barchas explains how, during the genre's formation in the first half of the eighteenth century, the novel's material embodiment as printed book rivalled its narrative content in diversity and creativity. Innovations in layout, ornamentation, and even punctuation found in, for example, the novels of Samuel Richardson, an author who printed his own books, helped shape a tradition of early visual ingenuity. From the beginning of the novel's emergence in Britain, prose writers including Daniel Defoe, Jonathan Swift, and Henry and Sarah Fielding experimented with the novel's appearance. Lavishly illustrated with more than 100 graphic features found in eighteenth-century editions, this important study aims to recover the visual context in which the eighteenth-century novel was produced and read.

JANINE BARCHAS is Assistant Professor in the Department of English at the University of Texas at Austin. She is the editor of *The Annotations in Lady Bradshaigh's Copy of* Clarissa (1998), and has contributed to *Essays on Eighteenth-Century Genre and Culture* (2001), as well as various journals in the field of eighteenth-century studies.

Among other Errors, the Reader is desired to excuse this: That in the Second Volume, Mr. *Adams*, is, by Mistake, mentioned to have sat up two subsequent Nights; when in reality, a Night of Rest intervened.

– From Henry Fielding's first edition of *Joseph Andrews* (1742).

Graphic Design, Print Culture, and the Eighteenth-Century Novel

JANINE BARCHAS

CAMBRIDGE UNIVERSITY PRESS
Cambridge, New York, Melbourne, Madrid, Cape Town, Singapore, São Paulo, Delhi

Cambridge University Press
The Edinburgh Building, Cambridge CB2 8RU, UK

Published in the United States of America by Cambridge University Press, New York

www.cambridge.org
Information on this title: www.cambridge.org/9780521819084

© Janine Barchas 2003

This publication is in copyright. Subject to statutory exception
and to the provisions of relevant collective licensing agreements,
no reproduction of any part may take place without the written
permission of Cambridge University Press.

First published 2003
Reprinted 2004
This digitally printed version 2008

A catalogue record for this publication is available from the British Library

ISBN 978-0-521-81908-4 hardback
ISBN 978-0-521-09057-5 paperback

Contents

Errata		*page* ii
List of figures		vi
Acknowledgments		xiii
Note on the text		xvi
1	**Expanding the literary text**	1
	a textual studies approach	
2	**The frontispiece**	19
	counterfeit authority and the author portrait	
3	**The title page**	60
	advertisement, identity, and deceit	
4	***Clarissa*'s musical score**	92
	a novel's politics engraved on copper plate	
5	**The space of time**	118
	graphic design and temporal distortion	
6	**Sarah Fielding's *David Simple***	153
	a case study in the interpretive significance of punctuation	
7	**The list and index**	173
	a culture of collecting imprints upon the novel	
	Coda	214
	Notes	218
	Works cited	271
	Index	290

Figures

	Frontispiece "Errata," from Henry Fielding's first edition of *Joseph Andrews* (1742). Annenberg Rare Book & Manuscript Library, University of Pennsylvania.	*frontispiece*
1.1	Recto of the original *Tatler No. 238*, published in half-sheets on 17 October 1710. Special Collections Research Center, the University of Chicago Library.	2
1.2	Verso of the original *Tatler No. 238*, published in half-sheets on 17 October 1710. Special Collections Research Center, the University of Chicago Library.	3
1.3	From a posthumous two-volume edition of Sterne's complete *Tristram Shandy* (London: Printed for T. Caddel, 1780), 1, 195. Special Collections Research Center, the University of Chicago Library.	17
2.1	Frontispiece portrait of Eliza Haywood by George Vertue found in her *Works* (1723–24) and her *Secret Histories, Novels, and Poems* (1724–25). Huntington Library, San Marino, California.	23
2.2	Frontispiece portrait of Henry Fielding by William Hogarth from Fielding's *Works* (London: Printed for A. Millar, 1762). Special Collections Research Center, the University of Chicago Library.	25
2.3	Frontispiece portrait of Samuel Richardson by Charles Grignion from the sixth edition of *The History of Sir Charles Grandison*, 7 vols. (London: Printed for J. and F. Rivington, 1770). Private Collection.	26
2.4	First state of the frontispiece portrait of Capt. Lemuel Gulliver from the first issue of the first edition of Swift's *Travels* (London: Printed for Benj. Motte, 1726). The Newberry Library, Chicago.	28
2.5	Second state of the frontispiece portrait of Capt. Lemuel Gulliver from a later issue of the first edition of Swift's *Travels* (London: Printed for Benj. Motte, 1726). The Newberry Library, Chicago.	29

FIGURES vii

2.6 Frontispiece portrait of Capt. Lemuel Gulliver from the third volume in the octavo edition of Swift's *Works*, 4 vols. (Dublin: Printed by and for George Faulkner, 1735). Special Collections Research Center, the University of Chicago Library. 32

2.7 Frontispiece portrait of Capt. Lemiuel [*sic*] Gulliver from the third volume in the duodecimo edition of Swift's *Works*, 4 vols. (Dublin: Printed by and for George Faulkner, 1735). Special Collections Research Center, the University of Chicago Library. 33

2.8 Frontispiece portrait of Dr. Swift found in the first volumes of both the octavo and duodecimo editions of Swift's *Works*, 4 vols. (Dublin: Printed by and for George Faulkner, 1735). Special Collections Research Center, the University of Chicago Library. 34

2.9 Full-length frontispiece portrait of Hannah Snell in riding habit from the book-length version of *The Female Soldier* (London: Printed for and sold by R. Walker, 1750). Thomas Fisher Rare Book Library, University of Toronto. 38

2.10 Frontispiece bust-portrait of Hannah Snell in martial costume from the book-length version of *The Female Soldier* (London: Printed for and sold by R. Walker, 1750). The William Andrews Clark Memorial Library, University of California, Los Angeles. 39

2.11 Frontispiece portrait and title to the second edition of *The History of the Life and Adventures of Mr. Duncan Campbell* (1720). Annenberg Rare Book & Manuscript Library, University of Pennsylvania. 40

2.12 Frontispiece portrait from Daniel Defoe's *Robinson Crusoe* (1719). Annenberg Rare Book & Manuscript Library, University of Pennsylvania. 43

2.13 Frontispiece portrait from Daniel Defoe's *Roxana* (1724). Special Collections Research Center, the University of Chicago Library. 44

2.14 Frontispiece portrait from an unidentified "early edition" of Daniel Defoe's *Moll Flanders*. Beinecke Rare Book & Manuscript Library, Yale University. 45

2.15 Frontispiece portrait from a pirated edition of Daniel Defoe's *Jure Divino* (1706). Annenberg Rare Book & Manuscript Library, University of Pennsylvania. 46

2.16 Frontispiece portrait and title to Edward Kimber's *The Life and Adventures of Joe Thompson* (1750). Annenberg Rare Book & Manuscript Library, University of Pennsylvania. 49

2.17 Frontispiece portrait from Francis Coventry's *The History of Pompey the Little* (1751). Special Collections Research Center, the University of Chicago Library. 51

FIGURES

2.18	Frontispiece and title page to John Kidgell's *The Card* (1755). Private Collection.	52
2.19	George Bickham's pastiche of anti-Jacobite propaganda, *The Highlanders Medley, or the Duke Triumphant* (1746). The Lewis Walpole Library, Yale University.	54
2.20	Frontispiece to Sarah Scott's *Millenium Hall* (1762). Special Collections Research Center, the University of Chicago Library.	55
2.21	Frontispiece and title to Delarivier Manley's *The Adventures of Rivella* (1714). Annenberg Rare Book & Manuscript Library, University of Pennsylvania.	57
3.1	Title page to Daniel Defoe's *Robinson Crusoe* (1719). Annenberg Rare Book & Manuscript Library, University of Pennsylvania.	63
3.2	Title page to Daniel Defoe's *Moll Flanders* (1722). Annenberg Rare Book & Manuscript Library, University of Pennsylvania.	64
3.3	Title page to Delarivier Manley's *A Secret History of Queen Zarah* (1705). Annenberg Rare Book & Manuscript Library, University of Pennsylvania.	68
3.4	Title page to Eliza Haywood's *A Spy Upon the Conjurer* (1724). Annenberg Rare Book & Manuscript Library, University of Pennsylvania.	69
3.5	Title page to Robert Hooke's *Micrographia* (1667). Private Collection.	73
3.6	Advertisement pages attached to Edmund Curll's edition of *Love and Artifice* (1734), attributed to William Fitzmaurice Kelly. Annenberg Rare Book & Manuscript Library, University of Pennsylvania.	75
3.7	Title page to Richardson's first edition of *Pamela* (1740). Special Collections Research Center, the University of Chicago Library.	78
3.8	Title page to Hannah Snell's *The Female Soldier* (1750). Princeton University Library.	81
3.9	Title page to *The Life and Memoirs of Ephraim Tristram Bates* (1756). Annenberg Rare Book & Manuscript Library, University of Pennsylvania.	82
3.10	Title page to John Kidgell's *The Card* (1755). Private Collection.	84
3.11	Title page to Henry Fielding's *Tom Jones* (1749). Private Collection.	86
3.12	Title page to second edition of Tobias Smollett's *Roderick Random* (1748). Annenberg Rare Book & Manuscript Library, University of Pennsylvania.	87
3.13	Title page to Sarah Fielding and Jane Collier's *The Cry* (1754). Private Collection.	88

4.1	Musical score folded closed (a) and opened out (b) from the first edition of Samuel Richardson's *Clarissa*, 7 vols. (1748), II, 50. Special Collections Research Center, the University of Chicago Library.	95
4.2	From *A Collection of the Choicest Songs and Dialogues* (London, 174?). Special Collections Research Center, the University of Chicago Library.	102
4.3	From *A Collection of the Choicest Songs and Dialogues* (London, 174?). Special Collections Research Center, the University of Chicago Library.	103
4.4	From a 1965 facsimile reprint (New York: Broude Bros.) of *The Musical Entertainer... Engraved by George Bickham, Junr.*, 2 vols. (London: Printed for and sold by Charles Corbett Bookseller, 1740), II, 11. Special Collections Research Center, the University of Chicago Library.	104
4.5	From *An Antidote against Melancholy. Being a Collection of Fourscore Merry Songs, Wherein Those of the Same Subject and Key Are Placed in Agreeable Succession in Relation to the Different Measures of Time, after the Manner of Suits of Lessons* (London: Printed for Daniel Brown, 1749), 32–33. Special Collections Research Center, the University of Chicago Library.	105
4.6	From *The Gentleman's Magazine* 19 (1749), 84, detail.	106
4.7	From Richard Griffith's *Something New*, 2 vols. (1772), II, 253–[255]. Annenberg Rare Book & Manuscript Library, University of Pennsylvania.	113
4.8	From John Kidgell's *The Card*, 2 vols. (1755), I, 12. Private Collection.	114
4.9	From John Kidgell's *The Card*, 2 vols. (1755), II, 295–96. Private Collection.	115
5.1	From the first edition of Samuel Richardson's *Clarissa*, 7 vols. (1748), II, 232. Special Collections Research Center, the University of Chicago Library.	121
5.2	From the first edition of *Clarissa*, 7 vols. (1748), II, 304. Special Collections Research Center, the University of Chicago Library.	122
5.3	From the first edition of *Clarissa*, 7 vols. (1748), IV, 18. Special Collections Research Center, the University of Chicago Library.	123
5.4	From the first edition of *Clarissa*, 7 vols. (1748), IV, 124. Special Collections Research Center, the University of Chicago Library.	124
5.5	From the first edition of *Pamela*, 2 vols. (1740), I, 17. Special Collections Research Center, the University of Chicago Library.	126
5.6	From the first edition of *Pamela*, 2 vols. (1740), I, 55. Special Collections Research Center, the University of Chicago Library.	127

5.7(a)	From the first edition of *Clarissa*, 7 vols. (1748), IV, 328 and V, 239. Special Collections Research Center, the University of Chicago Library.	130
5.7(b)	From the first edition of *Clarissa*, 7 vols. (1748), VII, 198 and 309. Special Collections Research Center, the University of Chicago Library.	131
5.8	From the second edition of Samuel Richardson's *Sir Charles Grandison*, 6 vols. (1754), VI, 265. Private Collection.	138
5.9	From the first edition of *Clarissa*, 7 vols. (1748), IV, 316. Special Collections Research Center, the University of Chicago Library.	139
5.10	From the third edition of *Clarissa*, 8 vols. (1751), II, 246–47. Private Collection.	140
5.11	From the third edition of *Clarissa*, 8 vols. (1751), II, 6. Private Collection.	141
5.12	From the third edition of *Clarissa*, 8 vols. (1751), VII, 90 and VIII, 9. Private Collection.	142
5.13	From the third edition of *Clarissa*, 8 vols. (1751), III, 30. Private Collection.	143
5.14	From the first edition of *Clarissa*, 7 vols. (1748), III, 55. Special Collections Research Center, the University of Chicago Library.	144
5.15	From a 1741 edition of Jonathan Swift's *A Tale of a Tub* (1704), 224. Private Collection.	145
5.16	From the second edition of Sterne's *Tristram Shandy* (1761), III, 73. Private Collection.	146
5.17	From the anonymous *The Life and Memoirs of Ephraim Tristram Bates* (1756), 60. Annenberg Rare Book & Manuscript Library, University of Pennsylvania.	147
5.18	From the third edition of *Clarissa*, 8 vols. (1751), II, [3]; III, [3]; and IV, 375. Private Collection.	150
5.19	Tailpiece to Volume V in the third edition of *Clarissa*, 8 vols. (1751). Private Collection.	151
6.1	Page 298, Volume II, as it appears in the first (left) and second (right) editions of Sarah Fielding's *The Adventures of David Simple*, 2 vols. (London: Printed by A. Millar, 1744). Private Collection (1st edn.) and Special Collections Research Center, the University of Chicago Library (2nd edn.).	158
6.2	Page 260, Volume II, as it appears in the first (left) and second (right) editions of Sarah Fielding's *The Adventures of David Simple*, 2 vols. (London: Printed by A. Millar, 1744). Private Collection (1st edn.) and Special Collections Research Center, the University of Chicago Library (2nd edn.).	161

6.3	From a microfilm reproduction of John Dunton's *A Voyage Round the World: Or, a Pocket-Library, Divided into Several Volumes. The First of Which Contains the Rare Adventures of Don Kainophilus* (London: Printed for Richard Newcome, [1691]), I, 26–27. University Microfilms, Ann Arbor, Michigan.	167
6.4	From Laurence Sterne's *Tristram Shandy*, second edition (1761), III, 28–29. Private Collection.	168
7.1	From Defoe's *Moll Flanders* (1722), 199–201. Annenberg Rare Book & Manuscript Library, University of Pennsylvania.	178
7.2	From Henry Fielding's *Joseph Andrews*, 2 vols. (1742), I, 265 and from the second edition of Tobias Smollett's *Roderick Random*, 2 vols. (1748), I, 71. Annenberg Rare Book & Manuscript Library, University of Pennsylvania.	180
7.3	From Sarah Fielding's *Familiar Letters*, 2 vols. (1747), II, 312. Annenberg Rare Book & Manuscript Library, University of Pennsylvania.	181
7.4	From Henry Fielding's *Joseph Andrews*, 2 vols. (1742), II, 34. Annenberg Rare Book & Manuscript Library, University of Pennsylvania.	182
7.5	From the first edition of Samuel Richardson's *Pamela*, 2 vols. (1740), I, 250–52. Special Collections Research Center, the University of Chicago Library.	183
7.6	From the fifth edition of *The Attorney's Compleat Pocket-Book*, 2 vols. (1764), II, 56–57 (left) and II, 255 (right).	185
7.7	From Richardson Head's *The English Rogue Described in the Life of Meriton Latroon* (1672). Annenberg Rare Book & Manuscript Library, University of Pennsylvania.	187
7.8	From the second octavo edition (published simultaneously with the first in duodecimo) of Samuel Richardson's *The History of Sir Charles Grandison*, 6 vols. (1754), I, [viii] and [1]. Private Collection.	188
7.9	From William Hawkins's play *Henry and Rosamond* (London, 1749). Special Collections Research Center, the University of Chicago Library.	189
7.10	From Edward Young's play *The Brothers. A Tragedy.* (London, 1753). Special Collections Research Center, the University of Chicago Library.	190
7.11	From the third edition of *Clarissa*, 8 vols. (1751), IV, 162–63. Private Collection.	191
7.12	From the first volume of Sarah Fielding and Jane Collier's *The Cry*, 3 vols. (London: Printed for R. and J. Dodsley, 1754). Private Collection.	192

7.13(a)	From Samuel Richardson's first edition of *Clarissa*, 7 vols. (1748), I, ix–x. Special Collections Research Center, the University of Chicago Library.	194
7.13(b)	From Samuel Richardson's first edition of *Clarissa*, 7 vols. (1748), I, xi–xii. Special Collections Research Center, the University of Chicago Library.	195
7.14	From Samuel Richardson's second edition of *Clarissa*, 7 vols. (1749), I, v. Private Collection.	196
7.15	From the third edition of *Clarissa*, 8 vols. (1751), I, [xii] and [1].	197
7.16	First page of the subscription list to Alexander Pope's *The Works of Shakespear* (London: Printed for Jacob Tonson, 1725). Special Collections Research Center, the University of Chicago Library.	199
7.17	The first page of the index found in the second edition of Samuel Richardson's *The History of Sir Charles Grandison*, 6 vols. (1754), VI, 305. Private Collection.	201
7.18	Title page and first page of index from an edition of Daniel Defoe's *A Tour Thro' the Whole Island of Great Britain* printed on Richardson's press, 4 vols. (London, 1742), I, title and [357]. Annenberg Rare Book & Manuscript Library, University of Pennsylvania.	210
7.19	From Richardson's edition of Defoe's *Tour* (1742), II, 150 and 152. Annenberg Rare Book & Manuscript Library, University of Pennsylvania.	211
7.20	From Richardson's edition of Defoe's *Tour* (1742), IV, 316–17. Annenberg Rare Book & Manuscript Library, University of Pennsylvania.	212

Acknowledgments

Book acknowledgments are not just frank tallies of debts. For better or worse, acknowledgments – like other paratexts placed conventionally at the threshold of a book – mediate the book's relationship with the reader. Modern readers tend to read such an opening inventory of names as a coded shortcut to a book's authority – as brand. Authors tend to name people for whose association or help they are proud as well as grateful. Johnson and Pope were right: every such public thank you is a feeble boast, a veiled declaration of intimacy with those talented or powerful enough to have been in a position to lend assistance. Unlike them, I cannot upend this custom and declare that I did this on my own merit. Instead, I may brag of having benefited from the teachings, kindnesses, and advice of some of the very best. Yet, in acknowledging my debts to the following people I disavow all credit that might otherwise accrue to me by association. I was not always worthy of the help and tutelage I received. In most cases, I should really have learned far more than I did and taken better notes!

My greatest debt is to my teachers. During my time as a graduate student at the University of Chicago, an all-star team of dissertation advisors coached me in matters eighteenth-century: J. Paul Hunter, Bruce Redford, and Stuart Sherman. I could not have asked for better. This team's expertise was supplemented by that of two very special mentors on the emeritus faculty, Edward Rosenheim and Gwin Kolb. In matters bibliographical I received additional instruction from Alice Schreyer, who witnessed my early fumblings among the University of Chicago's rare materials and subsequently took me under her wing, and Terry Bellanger, whose summer course at the Virginia Rare Books School was truly fundamental.

The bulk of this book was written during four happy years as a Lecturer and Senior Lecturer at the University of Auckland in New Zealand. The Arts Faculty supported my research with a grant and a period of leave while the English Department provided a hospitable environment in which to think and work. The visual acuity of my Kiwi students also repeatedly proved a boon. I am particularly grateful to colleagues at Auckland and elsewhere who read portions of this project during various stages of gestation: Brian Boyd, for a palimpsest of annotations and Nabokov anecdotes; Ken Larsen, for tireless translations of Latin; Shef Rogers, for countless updates on matters bibliographical; Stuart Sherman, for spending his own research time teaching a "former" pupil lessons in rhetoric she should have learned years prior; Patricia Brückmann, for steering an argument in a more suitable direction and, also, for walking to the Fisher Library during a Toronto winter just to check a data point; Mac Jackson for his saintly reading of a chapter during the first frantic week of a term; and – most particularly – Sebastian Black, for potent editorial inkings on all seven chapters. Jocelyn Harris did not merely pen improving marginalia on several chapters, but kept up my spirits with numerous encouragements and a flow of "FYI" brown-paper parcels. With the two anonymous Cambridge University Press readers the manuscript fell into expert and charitable hands. These readers' detailed lists of improving "corrigenda" constituted acts of pure kindness that polished the book to a finer patina. In thanking my colleagues I should not forget: Don Smith and his unexpected gift of a stray volume of an old edition of *Clarissa* that proved a missing link; Joanne Wilkes, for her reactions to bits on Austen; and Sophie Tomlinson, who graciously endured many lunchtime queries.

The final phase of this project was completed at The University of Texas at Austin, where students and colleagues, and especially the Department Chair, James Garrison, have made the project and its author feel very much at home.

Along the way, many scholars, librarians, curators, booksellers, bibliophiles, and collectors shared their expertise, their resources, and their treasures. A very special thanks is due to Mary Kisler, of the Auckland Art Gallery; the Kolbs; Bruce Whiteman, of the William Andrews Clark Memorial Library; and Stephen Weissman, of Ximenes Books. The long-distance help of Jerry Beasley, Alex Pettit, Patrick Spedding, and Stephen Tabor was invaluable in resolving several Haywood conundrums. With the same generosity, P. N. Furbank, David Goldthorpe, and Vincent Giroud shared their expertise when I was stumped by a *Moll Flanders* riddle. A partial artifact of my years of residence in the southern hemisphere was that I hardly ever saw, except at the occasional conference, those friends and mentors who eased my entrance into the profession, and to whom this book and its author owe much goodwill – particularly Kevin Cope, Kenney Mencher, Albert J. Rivero, Elizabeth Scala, and Howard Weinbrot.

The illustrations in this book form an essential element of my argument. I am deeply grateful to all the institutions and individuals who not only granted permission to reproduce works held in their collections but who assisted me in the swift gathering of bibliographical information, slides, photographs, and electronic scans. Two people who have been exceptionally heroic in this respect are Alice Schreyer, Curator of the Special Collections Research Center, the University of Chicago Library, and Michael Ryan, Director of the Walter H. and Leonore Annenberg Rare Book & Manuscript Library, University of Pennsylvania. Their respective staff, particularly Debra Levine at Chicago and John Pollack and Greg Bear at Penn, proved no mere mortals, tackling daunting chores with Herculean ease. Sincere thanks are also due to Linda Bree, my point of contact with the Press, for first taking on this illustration-heavy project and subsequently for insuring the quality of the book's own graphics. A University Cooperative Society Subvention Grant awarded by the University of Texas at Austin helped to significantly defray the illustrations' production costs.

With the respective publishers' kind permission, sections of this book rework material that previously appeared in *Studies in the Novel*, *Eighteenth-Century Life*, *ELH*, and *Eighteenth-Century Fiction*. The publisher has used its best endeavors to ensure that the URLs for external websites referred to in this book are correct and active at the time of going to press. However, the publisher has no responsibility for the websites and can make no guarantee that a site will remain live or that the content is or will remain appropriate.

Finally, I would like to thank my family, whose systemic contributions to this project are difficult to isolate. My parents, Jan Duijvestein and Hanny Van Leeuwen, instilled in me a Dutch appreciation of visual presentation – an inheritance I share with my architect-brother Arjan and my artist-sister Mylène. When I subsequently married into a family of academics and book collectors they beguiled me with a passion for rare books that spanned at least three generations. Jack Barchas and the late Patricia Barchas gave me my first first edition; Cecile Barchas and the late Samuel Barchas offered inspiration; and – in recent years – Rosemary Stevens has enriched this family legacy with her friendship and bibliophilic spirit.

To my husband, Isaac Barchas, whose faith in this project never once wavered, and our daughter Madison Cecile Barchas, whose own love of books is just beginning, I dedicate this effort.

Note on the text

The two main sources for Samuel Richardson's correspondence cited in the text are abbreviated throughout the book as follows:

Barbauld   *Correspondence of Samuel Richardson*, ed. Anna Laetitia Barbauld, 6 vols. (London: R. Phillips, 1804).

Carroll   *Selected Letters of Samuel Richardson*, ed. John Carroll (Oxford: Clarendon Press, 1964).

CHAPTER 1

Expanding the literary text

a textual studies approach

> *Now from all Parts the swelling Kennels flow;*
> *And bear their Trophies with them as they go:*
> *Filth of all Hues and Odours seem to tell*
> *What Street they sail'd from, by their Sight and Smell.*
> *They, as each Torrent drives, with rapid Force*
> *From* Smithfield *or St.* Pulchre's *shape their Course,*
> *And in huge Confluent join'd at* Snow-Hill *Ridge,*
> *Fall from the* Conduit *prone to* Holborn-Bridge.
> *Sweepings from Butchers Stalls, Dung, Guts, and Blood,*
> *Drown'd Puppies, stinking Sprats, all drench'd in Mud,*   }
> *Dead Cats and Turnip-Tops come tumbling down the Flood.*

It is generally accepted that Jonathan Swift concludes his *Description of a City Shower* (1710) with this stanza and its closing triplet, a triplet that tops with a graphic flourish and the rhythmical excess of an alexandrine a poem comically devoted to the piquancy of observed details and to notions of material excess and overflowings. Thus the bathos of "*the Flood*" offers a fitting close to this mock georgic. These final lines, suffused with onomatopoetic trickery, simultaneously ridicule and display the eighteenth-century penchant for triplets and the related affectation that sound must echo sense.[1] Yet this standard reading may be incomplete. In point of fact, Swift's literary text does not end with these lines. This is not because a long-lost fragment torn from Swift's original holograph can be brought to light. Nor is there a neglected closing gloss by Steele-as-Bickerstaff found in the original half-sheet of that issue of *The Tatler* in which this poem first appeared in print on 17 October 1710, namely *No. 238*.[2] Bickerstaff does not expand upon his opening introduction, remaining, in fact, uncharacteristically silent, even absent, at the periodical's close. Yet the printed half-sheet of the original *Tatler* offers more text. That text, in turn, offers a

FIGURE 1.1
Recto of the original *Tatler No. 238*, published in half-sheets on 17 October 1710.

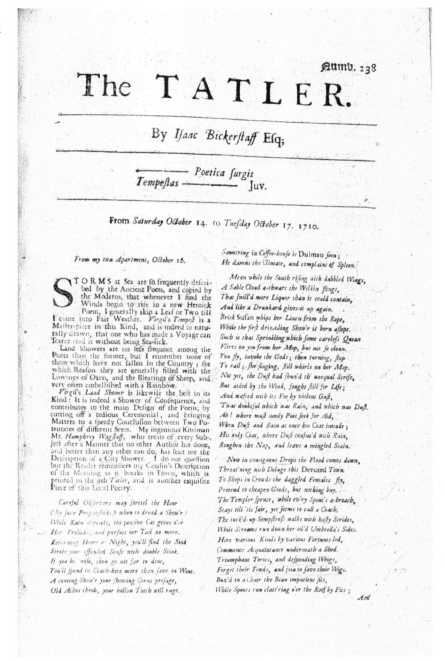

graphic context for the poem as a whole, and one that expands upon Swift's alexandrine in its continuation, imitation, and elaboration of the poem's comically expressed aspersions of urban materialism. By the light of that "missing" text, we can see that Swift's *Shower* resists just the type of closure which, as a result of being lifted out of its original visual context, is usually attributed to it.

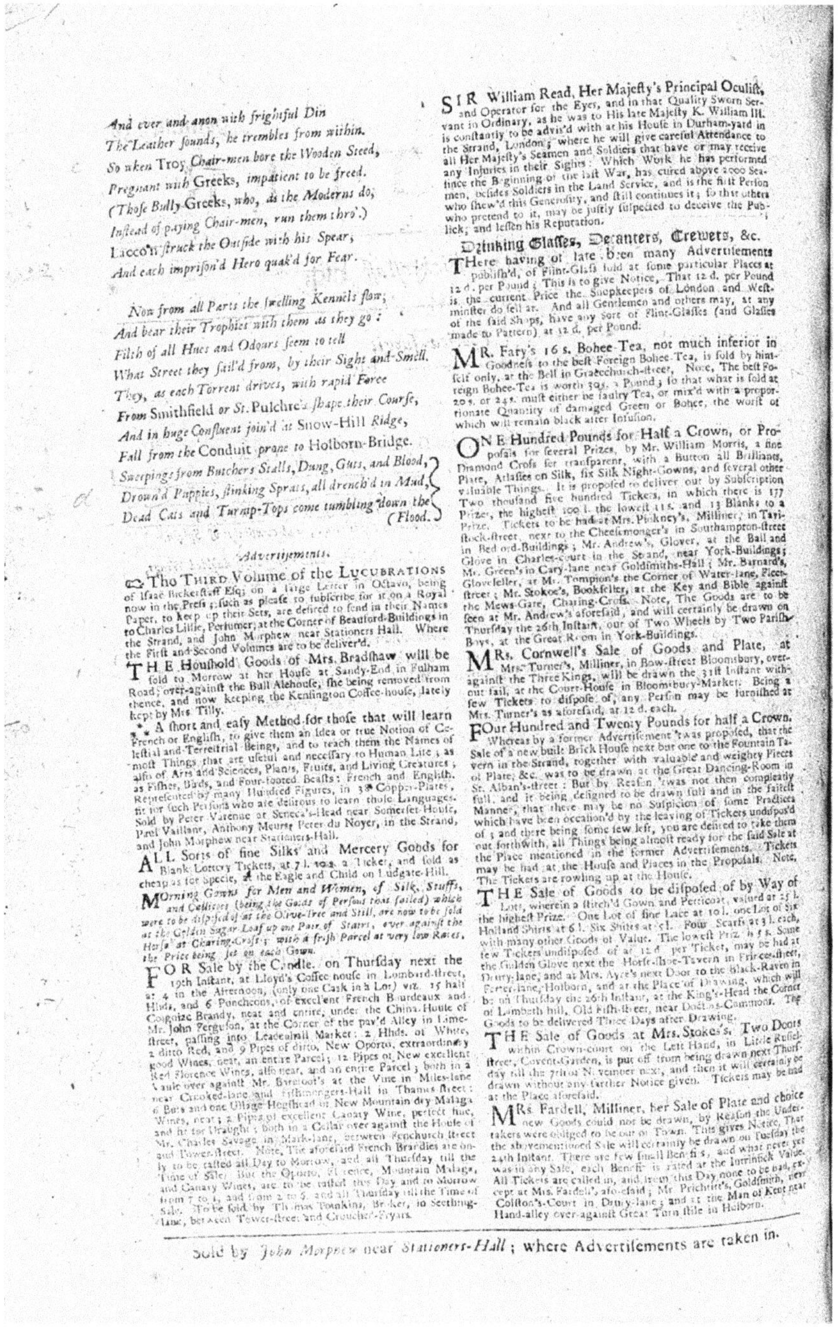

And ever and anon with frightful Din
The Leather ſounds, he trembles from within.
So when Troy *Chair-men bore the Wooden Steed,*
Pregnant with Greeks, *impatient to be freed.*
(Thoſe Bully Greeks, *who, as the Moderns do,*
Inſtead of paying Chair-men, run them thro'.)
Laocoon *ſtruck the Outſide with his Spear,*
And each impriſon'd Hero quak'd for Fear.

Now from all Parts the ſwelling Kennels flow,
And bear their Trophies with them as they go:
Filth of all Hues and Odours ſeem to tell
What Street they ſail'd from, by their Sight and Smell.
They, as each Torrent drives, with rapid Force
From Smithfield *or* St. Pulchre's *ſhape their Courſe,*
And in huge Confluent join'd at Snow-Hill *Ridge,*
Fall from the Conduit *prone to* Holborn-Bridge.
Sweepings from Butchers Stalls, Dung, Guts, and Blood,
Drown'd Puppies, ſtinking Sprats, all drench'd in Mud,
Dead Cats and Turnip-Tops come tumbling down the
(Flood.

Advertiſements.

☞ The THIRD Volume of the LUCUBRATIONS of Iſaac Bickerſtaff Eſq; on a large Letter in Octavo, being now in the Preſs; ſuch as pleaſe to ſubſcribe for it on a Royal Paper, to keep up their Sets, are deſired to ſend in their Names to Charles Lillie, Perfumer, at the Corner of Beauford-Buildings in the Strand, and John Morphew near Stationers Hall. Where the Firſt and Second Volumes are to be deliver'd.

THE Houſhold Goods of Mrs. Bradſhaw will be ſold to Morrow at her Houſe at Sandy-End in Fulham Road, over-againſt the Bull Alehouſe, ſhe being removed from thence, and now keeping the Kenſington Coffee-houſe, lately kept by Mrs Tilly.

** A ſhort and eaſy Method for thoſe that will learn French or Engliſh, to give them an Idea or true Notion of Celeſtial and Terreſtrial Beings, and to teach them the Names of moſt Things that are uſeful and neceſſary to Human Life; as alſo of Arts and Sciences, Plants, Fruits, and Living Creatures, as Fiſhes, Birds, and Four-footed Beaſts: French and Engliſh. Repreſented by many Hundred Figures, in 38 Copper-Plates, fit for ſuch Perſons who are deſirous to learn thoſe Languages. Sold by Peter Varenne at Seneca's-Head near Somerſet-Houſe, Paul Vaillant, Anthony Meurſe, Peter du Noyer, in the Strand, and John Morphew near Stationers-Hall.

ALL Sorts of fine Silks and Mercery Goods for Blank Lottery Tickets, at 7 l. 10 s. a Ticket, and ſold as cheap as for Specie, at the Eagle and Child on Ludgate-Hill.

MOrning Gowns *for Men and Women, of Silk, Stuffs, and Calicoes (being the Goods of Perſons that failed) which were to be diſpoſed of at the Olive-Tree and Still, are now to be ſold at the Golden Sugar-Loaf up one Pair of Stairs, over againſt the Horſe at Charing-Croſs; with a freſh Parcel at very low Rates, the Price being ſet on each Gown.*

FOR Sale by the Candle, on Thurſday next the 19th Inſtant, at Lloyd's Coffee-houſe in Lombard-ſtreet, at 4 in the Afternoon, (only one Cask in a Lot) viz. 15 half Hhds. and 6 Puncheons, of excellent French Bourdeaux and Cogniac Brandy, neat and entire, under the China-Houſe of Mr. John Ferguſon, at the Corner of the pav'd Alley in Lime-ſtreet, paſſing into Leadenhall Market: 2 Hhds. of White, 2 ditto Red, and 9 Pipes of ditto, New Oporto, extraordinary good Wines, neat, an entire Parcel; 12 Pipes of New excellent Red Florence Wines, alſo neat, and an entire Parcel; both in a Vault over againſt Mr. Barefoot's at the Vine in Miles-lane near Crooked-lane and Fiſhmongers-Hall in Thames-ſtreet: 6 Butts and one Ullage Hogſhead of New Mountain dry Malaga Wines, neat; 2 Pipes of excellent Canary Wine, perfect fine, and fit for Draught; both in a Cellar over againſt the Houſe of Mr. Charles Savage in Mark-lane, between Fenchurch-ſtreet and Tower-ſtreet. Note, The aforeſaid French Brandies are only to be taſted all Day to Morrow, and all Thurſday till the Time of Sale: But the Oporto, Florence, Mountain Malaga, and Canary Wines, are to be taſted this Day and to Morrow from 7 to 1, and from 2 to 5, and all Thurſday till the Time of Sale. To be ſold by Thomas Tomkins, Broker, in Seething-lane, between Tower-ſtreet and Crouched-Fryars.

SIR William Read, Her Majeſty's Principal Oculiſt, and Operator for the Eyes, and in that Quality Sworn Servant in Ordinary, as he was to His late Majeſty K. William III. is conſtantly to be adviſ'd with at his Houſe in Durham-yard in the Strand, London; where he will give careful Attendance to all Her Majeſty's Seamen and Soldiers that have or may receive any Injuries in their Sights: Which Work he has performed ſince the Beginning of the laſt War, has cured above 2000 Seamen, beſides Soldiers in the Land Service, and is the firſt Perſon who ſhew'd this Generoſity, and ſtill continues it; ſo that others who pretend to it, may be juſtly ſuſpected to deceive the Publick, and leſſen his Reputation.

Drinking Glaſſes, Decanters, Crewets, &c.

THere having of late been many Advertiſements publiſh'd, of Flint-Glaſs ſold at ſome particular Places at 12 d. per Pound; This is to give Notice, That 12 d. per Pound is the current Price the Shopkeepers of London and Weſtminſter do ſell at. And all Gentlemen and others may, at any of the ſaid Shops, have any ſort of Flint-Glaſſes (and Glaſſes made to Pattern) at 12 d. per Pound.

MR. Fary's 16 s. Bohee-Tea, not much inferior in Goodneſs to the beſt Foreign Bohee-Tea, is ſold by himſelf only, at the Bell in Gracechurch-ſtreet. Note, The beſt Foreign Bohee-Tea is worth 30 s. a Pound; ſo that what is ſold at 20 s. or 24 s. muſt either be faulty Tea, or mix'd with a proportionate Quantity of damaged Green or Bohee, the worſt of which will remain black after Infuſion.

ONE Hundred Pounds for Half a Crown, or Propoſals for ſeveral Prizes, by Mr. William Morris, a fine Diamond Croſs ſet tranſparent, with a Button all Brilliants, Plate, Atlaſſes on Silk, ſix Silk Night-Gowns, and ſeveral other valuable Things. It is propoſed to deliver out by Subſcription Two thouſand five hundred Tickets, in which there is 177 Prizes, the higheſt 100 l. the loweſt 11 s. and 13 Blanks to a Prize. Tickets to be had at Mrs. Pinkney's, Milliner, in Taviſtock-ſtreet, next to the Cheeſmonger's in Southampton-ſtreet in Bedford-Buildings; Mr. Andrew's, Glover, at the Ball and Glove in Charles-court in the Strand, near York-Buildings; Mr. Green's in Cary-lane near Goldſmiths-Hall; Mr. Barnard's, Gloveſeller, at Mr. Tompion's the Corner of Water-lane, Fleet-ſtreet; Mr. Stokoe's, Bookſeller, at the Key and Bible againſt the Mews-Gate, Charing-Croſs. Note, The Goods are to be ſeen at Mr. Andrew's aforeſaid, and will certainly be drawn on Thurſday the 26th Inſtant, out of Two Wheels by Two Pariſh-Boys, at the Great Room in York-Buildings.

MRs. Cornwell's Sale of Goods and Plate, at Mrs. Turner's, Milliner, in Bow-ſtreet Bloomsbury, over-againſt the Three Kings, will be drawn the 31ſt Inſtant without fail, at the Court-Houſe in Bloomsbury-Market. Being a few Tickets to diſpoſe of, any Perſon may be furniſhed at Mrs. Turner's as aforeſaid, at 12 d. each.

FOur Hundred and Twenty Pounds for half a Crown. Whereas by a former Advertiſement 'twas propoſed, that the Sale of a new built Brick Houſe next but one to the Fountain Tavern in the Strand, together with valuable and weighty Pieces of Plate, &c. was to be drawn at the Great Dancing-Room in St. Alban's-ſtreet: But by Reaſon 'twas not then compleatly full, and it being deſigned to be drawn full and in the faireſt Manner, that there may be no Suſpicion of ſome Practices which have been occaſion'd by the leaving of Tickets undiſpos'd of; and there being ſome few left, you are deſired to take them out forthwith, all Things being almoſt ready for the ſaid Sale at the Place mentioned in the former Advertiſements. Note, Tickets may be had at the Houſe and Places in the Propoſals. The Tickets are rowling up at the Houſe.

THE Sale of Goods to be diſpoſed of by Way of Lots, wherein a ſtitch'd Gown and Petticoat, valued at 25 l. the higheſt Prize. One Lot of fine Lace at 10 l. one Lot of Six Holland Shirts at 6 l. Six Suites at 5 l. Four Scarfs at 3 l. each, with many other Goods of Value. The loweſt Prize is 5 s. Some few Tickets undiſpoſed of at 12 d. per Ticket, may be had at the Golden Glove next the Horſe-ſhoe-Tavern in Princes-ſtreet, Drury-lane, and at Mrs. Ayre's next Door to the Black-Raven in Fetter-lane, Holborn, and at the Place of Drawing, which will be on Thurſday the 26th Inſtant, at the King's-Head the Corner of Lambeth hill, Old Fiſh-ſtreet, near Doctors-Commons. The Goods to be delivered Three Days after Drawing.

THE Sale of Goods at Mrs. Stokes's, Two Doors within Crown-court on the Left Hand, in Little Ruſſel-ſtreet, Covent-Garden, is put off from being drawn next Thurſday till the 7th of November next, and then it will certainly be drawn without any farther Notice given. Tickets may be had at the Place aforeſaid.

MRs. Fardell, Milliner, her Sale of Plate and choice new Goods could not be drawn, by Reaſon the Undertakers were obliged to be out of Town. This gives Notice, That the abovementioned Sale will certainly be drawn on Tueſday the 24th Inſtant. There are few ſmall Benefits, and what never yet was in any Sale, each Benefit is rated at the Intrinſick Value. All Tickets are called in, and from this Day none to be had, except at Mrs. Fardell's aforeſaid; Mr. Prichtite's, Goldſmith, near Colſton's-Court in Drury-lane; and at the Man of Kent near Hand-alley over-againſt Great Turn ſtile in Holborn.

Sold by John Morphew near Stationers-Hall; where Advertiſements are taken in.

FIGURE 1.2
Verso of the original *Tatler No. 238*, published in half-sheets on 17 October 1710.

I refer, of course, to the text of the advertisements that crowd the remainder of *Tatler No. 238* in the original half-sheet (Figures 1.1 and 1.2). From these concluding advertisements emerges London's bustling materiality in a manner that deftly transfers Swift's indulgent critique of urban living onto the space of the real-world reader. In the "*frightful Din*"(line 45) of the page's typographical cacophony and the range of goods it cries for sale, a reader is offered the spoils of empire – from the services of "**Her Majesty's Principal Oculist**" to "Holland shirts at 6 l.," from flint "𝔇𝔯𝔦𝔫𝔨𝔦𝔫𝔤 𝔊𝔩𝔞𝔰𝔰𝔢𝔰" to "Foreign Bohee-Tea," and from "All Sorts of Fine Silks" to "excellent French Bourdeaux and Coigniac Brandy, neat and entire." Just as the poem shows the fare of the countryside ending up as decaying urban garbage, these advertisements record the domestic fates of the realm's grand commercial harvests. The lack of moral order that plagues Swift's poetic world also distresses the language of commerce found in the ads. For example, Mr. Fary, in his attempts to declare the inferiority of teas sold by others, unwittingly incriminates his own:

> MR. **Fary's 16s. Bohee-Tea**, not much inferior in Goodness to the best Foreign Bohee-Tea, is sold by himself only, at the Bell in Gracechurch-street. Note, The best Foreign Bohee-Tea is worth 30*s.* a Pound; so that what is sold at 20*s.* or 24*s.* must either be faulty Tea, or mix'd with a proportionate Quantity of damaged Green or Bohee, the worst of which will remain black after Infusion.

The bargain-priced, foreign Bohee-Tea – that coveted luxury of empire which distastefully blackens in the Londoner's China cup – becomes as potent a symbol of eighteenth-century decay, of the follies of commercial materialism, and of Swift's peculiar aesthetic as the poem's "*Dead Cats and Turnip-Tops.*" Likewise a Mrs. Bradshaw, Mrs. Cornwell, and Mrs. Fardell, Milliner, feature in the ads, like the poem's "*Brisk Susan*" and "*tuck'd-up Sempstress*," only through the material objects they briefly wield (lines 17 and 37). As a result of financial distresses that expose these real-world women to the double indignity of an impending sale of their personal possessions and the reader's voyeuristic gaze, their very lives and identities emerge before us in the form of their "Goods and Plate."

The juxtaposition of poem and advertisement on the printed page enhances and extends a reading of the *Shower*, irrespective of authorial control – or even intent. An attentive reader sees the materiality of the poem's rushing tributary of London offal flow directly into the sea of advertisements below. As a result, the comic critique of humanity's waste and physicality that saturates the poem also irrigates the advertisements. The poem, in turn, is enriched and expanded by its embodiment on the printed page and its nearness to the commercial narratives of the ads. A reading of a poem that humorously evokes the chaos of the physical world must consider the work's own materiality and the original circumstances of its publication.

Although authorial intent need not be a prerequisite for textual authority, Swift and Steele had co-authored an earlier *Tatler*, namely *No. 21*, in which they explicitly reflected upon the periodical's printed appearance and its advertisements.³ In *Tatler No. 21*, Swift (in the guise of Bickerstaff's cousin Ephraim Bedfast) interrupts Steele to comment upon the expansion and upward encroachment of the periodical's advertisements. Swift's meta-writing invokes the metaphor of the textual body for the printed page, likening the encroaching ads to the "Dose of Poison" that Athenians were obliged to take when condemned to death: "which made them die upwards, seizing first upon their Feet, making them cold and insensible, and so ascending gradually, till it reached the Vital Parts."⁴ Swift-as-Bedfast warns Steele-as-Bickerstaff to cure his newspaper of such a fatal distemper:

> The lower Part of you, that is, the *Advertisements*, is dead; and these have risen for these Ten Days last past, so that they now take up almost a whole Paragraph. Pray, Sir, do your Endeavour to drive this Distemper as much as possible to the extreme Parts, and keep it there, as wise Folks do the Gout; for if it once gets into your Stomach, it will soon fly up into your Head, and you are a dead Man.⁵

By Bedfast's diagnosis, the later *Tatler No. 238* has virtually succumbed to textual rigor mortis. In issue *No. 238* the ads equal, if not exceed, the space devoted to the periodical's central offerings. The images of death and decay running through the *Shower*'s rhyming triplet are thus reinforced by the ensuing material death of *The Tatler* itself — as witnessed in the abundance of ads that in one full column of text have already flown up to the "Head" of the page. Yet the juxtaposition of poem and advertisement offers the failing patient a possible cure. Perhaps in an effort at textual resuscitation, this issue appropriates the advertisements at the foot of the half-sheet as part of *The Tatler*'s textual body on the printed page, making it an extension of the poem. Out of the juxtaposition of verse and advertisement Swift co-opts the language of the ads to further his own interpretive ends in the *Shower*. At the very least, Swift's comments as Bedfast confirm an environment of production that is deeply self-conscious of *The Tatler*'s embodiment as print object. Swift and Steele's documented awareness of *The Tatler*'s physicality in *No. 21* improves the possibility that when Swift and Steele reunite in the construction of *No. 238* they anticipate the workings of the book trade in that issue's graphic layout. Even if unaided by Steele, Swift would have known that the poem was to be followed by advertisements identical in kind to those that had supported the periodical's publication from its inception. Although such rationale beats a circuitous path back to authorial intention, the text's resulting visual self-consciousness must be considered a combination of print culture's happenstance and Swift's deliberate authorial design, possibly with Steele's approval or complicity.

I open with this brief glance at Swift's *Description of a City Shower*, because the rewards of a textual studies approach that resituates that short poem within its original visual context are transparent and transparently rich. The suggestion that *The Tatler*, or a poem printed therein, deserves reconsideration within the context of its initial appearance into print will not shake the foundations of established scholarly practice. For poetry, at least, has always been historically attentive to its manifestations on the printed page – and that long before Dickinson's dashes and Blake's illuminated *Songs* entered academic vogue. Yet the rewards in the case of Swift's poem may also appear deceptively self-evident and may sketch a misleadingly unproblematic picture of what a textual studies approach has to offer when applied to the novel. While the *Shower*'s example is a representative instance of the rambunctious materiality of eighteenth-century texts and demonstrates how attention to that materiality can breathe new life into a literary reading, my argument that the poem's material embodiment resists closure and continues the literary "text" even past the alexandrine's full stop adds only a footnote to the poem itself and a corollary to our traditional understanding of Swift's project. Unlike the turn of an English sonnet, the language of the advertisements does not alter the direction of the poem's argument. Thus the excision of *The Tatler*'s closing text from history's consideration of the poem has not resulted in a gross misunderstanding of Swift's description.

The novel's original packaging is not entirely as transparent or, indeed, as easy to reconstruct. First of all, when it comes to modern editions and reprints of the eighteenth-century novel, editorial practice has not been attentive to the genre's original appearance as a printed book, ignoring its layout, prefatory puffs, end matter, and graphic design and dismissing its punctuation and ornamentation as "accidentals." I do not wish to overstate my claim: the gains derived from modernized editions are many and obvious – especially in a classroom context. Yet standard editorial practice has, in the name of "modernization," systematically eradicated innovations in the genre's graphic design from book to book. As a result, the insipid uniformity of modern paperback editions of eighteenth-century fiction so distorts and diminishes the early novel's graphic diversity that it is difficult to resurrect the genre's lost visual dynamism. When, piece by piece, some of the novel's original physical attributes are reinstated, the resulting schematic of the impact of graphic design is more complex than is the case in Swift's *Shower*. An "anatomically correct" study of the novel's appearance as a printed book discloses the interpretive function of, to tweak Swift's metaphor, a mass of neglected organs and appendages, forcing an expanded redefinition of the genre's textual body. A formal study of the novel as book also impacts on our understanding of the genre's evolution writ large and, as I intend to demonstrate with a series of case studies, may even wholly reshape our local interpretations of specific narratives.

Yet this study does not offer an exhaustive anatomy of the eighteenth-century novel. Although a detailed graphic anatomy was my initial ambition, I came to realize that the eighteenth-century novel's many printed appendages and digits are too numerous, too unwieldy, or too prone to mutations from book to book and author to author, to allow anyone to draw a static picture of the ancestral appearance of the modern novel. Instead, I have tried to isolate some elements of the genre's graphic genomics. To this end, the ensuing chapters trace across the eighteenth century a few of the novel's principal adaptations of the printed features of other books as well as explore several remarkable experiments in the early novel's graphic design. The chapters on the novel's physicality focus upon six significant graphic features and expressions that served the early novel's original audience as visual guides to both generic ambition and local story: frontispieces, title pages, non-pictorial illustrations, ornamentation, punctuation, and catalogues. All these elements of the eighteenth-century novel's "text" have ceased to make regular appearances in modern editions of those fictions in which they originally played a key role. Thus the pages or features of a novel that I discuss, whether it be the ornaments and musical score in *Clarissa*, the punctuation in *David Simple*, or the author portraits in Swift's *Travels* and Defoe's *Crusoe*, may not be familiar to contemporary readers as part of the literary "text" of those novels with which they had cause to think they were thoroughly familiar. Our unfamiliarity with these elements of the early novel's text is part of my point.

Not only may readers be surprised at the presence of the unknown but also they may, conversely, object to the absence of the familiar. There are no accounts of such obvious graphics as attendant pictorial illustrations. The fact is that the lack of a satisfactorily "literary" language for the elements of book design forces me to adopt a rubric (that of the "graphic") that sets up the false expectation of a pictorial approach. Similarly, some elements treated in this study, such as the novel's punctuation or its propensity to deploy lists, may, at first, not strike my reader as befitting the mandate of "graphic design." Yet, the interpretive role of the dash or those lists which package some early novels defy traditional narrative categories and demand a special visual–verbal consideration. However, even when taken on its own terms, this book is not a complete inventory of those physical elements that feature in the novel's design as a printed book. The absence of any sustained discussion of, for example, typeface or footnotes in the novel's printed "look" may cast doubt upon my invocation of the metaphor of the novel's textual body – a body that lies before you grossly butchered, a faceless amputee. In spite of these limitations, I hope the early novel's assembled graphic parts are recognizable as belonging to the early genre's remains and that this recognition will disclose the extent to which the early novel depends for its literary effects upon its graphic appearance as a printed book.

Although its choice of terrain is "novel," my approach to literary texts is by no means new – not even within eighteenth-century studies. This book combines the cultural studies interest in the dynamic interaction and mutual reshaping of texts and contexts with both traditional literary criticism and the evolving theoretical vocabulary of textual studies. The study of eighteenth-century literature is increasingly informed by an appreciation of the interaction between authors, readers, and the complex social, economic, and technological machinery that mediated the space between them – what today we use the shorthand of "print culture" to describe. Indeed this book makes grateful use of decades of advances in the field of print culture. In the late 1970s Elizabeth Eisenstein added to the historical landscape sketched by Marshall McLuhan and the team of Lucien Febvre and Henri-Jean Martin (whose work only then appeared in English translation) new insights about the manner in which the material reality of print technology affects social change.[6] At the very heart of such studies about the emergence of a European "print culture" sits the basic assumption that presentation affects interpretation. Eisenstein's work, for example, asserts that the new duplication of knowledge in the form of a printed book not only affected the dissemination of fact but acted as an agent of verification and legitimization within the culture. In the wake of this pioneering work, literary scholars cultivated within their own historical specialties various interests in print technology. In eighteenth-century studies, the 1980s witnessed a veritable explosion of bibliographically oriented histories of the eighteenth-century book trade, offering new and detailed information on how commercial print culture shaped literary production in preindustrial Britain.[7] As a result, literary scholars began to make use of this new material by exploring the ways in which individual authors adapted available print conventions for the presentation of their work.[8] In the ensuing watershed in the field of eighteenth-century authorship and printing, the book itself has been recognized as a material artifact whose physical features – in addition to its narrative content – interact with and reveal history, culture, and ideology. In effect, the study of print culture has already forced literary scholars to expand their definition of "text" to include a work's visual makeup and graphic design.

This literary expansion of text has, in the area of eighteenth-century studies, focussed on a narrow band of authors whose work manifests a conspicuous preoccupation with textuality and print, most notably Pope, Sterne, and Blake. The illustrated poetry of printer-author William Blake was one of the first works to be scrutinized through the lens of book design and, as a result, has become one of the most familiar eighteenth-century examples of the overlap between image and text.[9] In addition, literary scholars were quick to recognize Alexander Pope's footnotes in *The Dunciad*[10] and Laurence Sterne's marbled and black pages in *Tristram Shandy*[11] as instances of authors deliberately eliding the distinction between verbal text and visual context. Yet, as subsequent scholarship has shown, the works of Pope and Sterne include a far wider variety of graphic designs (for example, ornamentation and punctuation) which the scholarly community is just beginning to recognize as textual phenomena with interpretive impact.[12]

An essay collection entitled *Ma(r)king the Text: The Presentation of Meaning on the Literary Page* (2000) has virtually guaranteed that the circumscribed canon of authors who have hitherto enjoyed the graphic spotlight will soon be subject to expansion – if not explosion.[13] This vibrant collection bundles together essays on such diverse "graphic" concerns as punctuation, footnotes, white space, annotation, typography, and the electronic text. As its contributors deftly range across minor and major works in poetry, prose, and drama, covering territory from Spenser to Stendhal and from sixteenth-century metrical practices to an early translation of *Tristram Shandy* in Portuguese, *Ma(r)king the Text* bears witness to a burgeoning field – a field so young that it is, like the emerging novel in the eighteenth century, defined by a collective self-consciousness and a shared investigational approach rather than a common vocabulary or unified subject. For, in addition to needing to locate authors whose works have not yet been examined in the light of this new graphic awareness, the scholarly community (which has hitherto relied heavily upon the vocabulary of traditional bibliography to talk about the graphic elements of a text) faces unmet challenges in defining the relationship between author and reader when the "old" distinction between visual context and verbal text erodes.

In recent times there have been three notable developments across the related areas of textual studies and print culture that impact upon my study: the first concerns an emerging theoretical sensitivity towards paratexts; the second a reorientation of editorial theory; and the third a querying of some of the pioneering assumptions of *print culture*. First, the 1997 English translation of Gérard Genette's *Seuils* (1987) as *Paratexts* made accessible to more scholars a fresh perspective on the physical dimensions of a book.[14] Evidencing a new sensitivity to those liminal devices and conventions that mediate the book to the reader, theorists such as Genette have invigorated the "old" language of descriptive bibliography by interrogating tacit distinctions between text and paratext, between a book and its packaging. Although Genette does not consider the graphics of *mise en page* as such, his work directly engages with the scholarly attention that is currently focussing on the degree to which a work's self-presentation as a printed book should be accorded "literary" status.

Genette maintains that a printed text's presentation of itself (its dust jacket, title page, notes, preface, even the author's name) is "always the conveyor of a commentary that is authorial or more or less legitimated by the author."[15] Thus he convincingly argues that these framing materials, or "paratexts," constitute an integral part of a literary text, providing loci of interpretation that complement and complicate the narratives they physically contain.[16]

Secondly, Genette's phrase "more or less" encapsulates the critical reorientation of editorial practice that took place just prior to the initial publication of *Seuils* in 1987, namely the equivocation of authorial intention. As a direct result of this equivocation, editorial theory has, ironically, placed increasingly less emphasis on the original appearance of a printed text, even though the shifting sands of editorial practice were, in part, disturbed by the storm of textual studies. Instead, under the mid-1980s influence of Deconstruction, editorial practice slowly shed its reverence for "initial" and "final" intention, a reverence that had traditionally placed an unrelenting emphasis upon first and so-called "authoritative" editions. Jerome McGann's *Critique of Modern Textual Criticism* (1983) questioned the dominant role assigned to "authorial intention" and "final intention" in the textual editing of modern English texts.[17] McGann's critique was essentially directed at editors such as G. Thomas Tanselle who had articulated the process of the selection of a copy-text in terms of a high textuality, demanding that a modern critical edition aim to create the "ideal" text that its author had intended to produce.[18] McGann declared such intentionality irretrievably lost, and his resignation to the irrecoverability of the ideal text opened the door for Hans Walter Gabler to propose his model of the "synoptic edition" – an edition that took a shape (from a confident collation of a text's various historical manifestations) never witnessed in its actual publication history. Thus, while McGann had continued to share with Tanselle the "observance of the public form of the work and the intentionality implied in the act of publication," Gabler argued that "a critical edition *qua* edition may legitimately claim the privilege of bringing into focus a form or forms of the work not attained in publication."[19] Thus Gabler's edition of *Ulysses* (1984), although a *tour de force* as a record of Joyce's multilayered revisions, looks nothing like the printed book of early editions. Reminiscent of the "variorum" editions of old, the synoptic *Ulysses* aims to show in its parallel display the evolution of the text through subsequent layers of alterations from manuscript to print and edition to edition.[20] Gabler's synoptic text leaps the problematics of authorial intention and editorial mimesis in one stride, offering a redefinition ("text" is replaced by "work") that elides manuscript and published text, initial and final intention, and allocates equal privilege to a work's various historical manifestations – be it on paper or in print, penned by the author or emended perfunctorily by an editor.

Although standard editorial practice has not adopted the synoptic model of textual editing, finding it both unwieldy and impractical for most books, the net effect of Gabler's well-deserved influence on book editing has been a change in emphasis from "recovery" to something akin to textual "renovation." Modern editions no longer need to resemble in "looks" the books whose experiences they claim to offer. It is here that this study intersects with editorial theory and the problematics of initial or authorial intention. I have already stated that my study is a project of recovery: this book aims to contextualize the manner in which the novel genre's original audience read and experienced the new species of writing. Yet my literary excavation of the novel's fossilized remains aims to reconstruct the "lost world" of the novel genre as a printed book – and only occasionally does this merge with what we might call the lost intentionality of the individual author. Indeed, an interpretive reaction to a book's appearance may not always have been sanctioned or anticipated by its original designer. Printer-author Samuel Richardson's ineffectual struggles to channel interpretation through graphic design are a case in point. This study also acknowledges the impact of printing practices upon the novelist's published product and thus corrodes authorial intention with the acid of print culture.

Yet my argument repeatedly stumbles into the quagmire of intentionality. Sometimes the circumstances of eighteenth-century publication practices demand that I eliminate or acknowledge other sources of control and intentionality in a book's design or self-presentation (the role of an engraver, publisher, or compositor, for example) in the creation of a book's graphic embellishment or its title page. Thus, with each example of graphic design, this study seeks to explore and define the various influences on the novel's appearance (from market practices to authorial control) as well as its literary effects. Sometimes I do, as in the case of Swift's *Shower*, find myself plodding a return course to the author in order to validate the interpretive implications of a graphic design with reference to authorial control, self-consciousness, or intention. While this study treads softly on the notion of an "authoritative" edition in its discussion of generic forms, it registers a graphic design as "literary" only if the author was involved in, or cognizant of, its production. On the whole I avoid considerations of scurrilous or pirated editions of early fiction even though such productions may impact or refract generic trends. Yet authorial intention, even in the *Shower* example, is more tangential and off-center in my discussion than it might have been some years ago. In this sense, this study aligns itself with Genette's "more or less" philosophy towards consideration of authorial intention. Novelists, by virtue of their participation in the emerging culture of eighteenth-century print and the growing professionalization of the author, tacitly sanctioned the shapes that their books took on when a printer, bookseller, or publisher helped to usher their work into print. Yet the trouble begins when the emerging genre of the novel shows signs of manipulating or querying the very print conventions that bring it into being. Then the violation of print convention demands that the extent of the author's involvement in a text's self-consciousness be established – and this can only be done on a case-by-case basis.

Thirdly, with the 1998 publication of Adrian Johns's *The Nature of the Book*, some of the fundamental assumptions at the base of "print culture" have come under pressure. Johns argues that the culture, stability, and credibility of the printed book did not emerge fully formed from Gutenberg's press, but that throughout the hand-press period the publishing industry (particularly the Stationer's Company) exerted enormous effort and expense to regulate and control the troublesome mutability of the printed book. Johns "brutally" sums up such regulatory practices as evidence "that Eisenstein's print culture does not exist."[21] Elaborate rhetorical and legal campaigns to restrain piracy, assert ownership to titles, and proclaim print's veracity paved the rough road towards the printed book's modern reputation as a stable vehicle for the dissemination of fact. Johns warns that the notion that the early printed book was a stable emblem of "veracious knowledge in modern society" is "substantially false."[22] If, as Johns argues, even publishers of science books at the turn of the eighteenth century still relied upon an intricate network of professional practices and rhetorical strategies for insurance against the reputational instability of print, emerging literary forms such as the novel faced enormous obstacles in their attempts to establish a stable genre. Of course, readers of early novels did not set out to "trust" a fiction in the manner that they approached scientific works, yet the nature of their relationship to the emerging genre did have to be built on their fragile confidence in the printed book. In fact, it is the early novelists themselves (such as Swift with the *Travels* and Defoe with *Crusoe*) who align the emerging novel with problems of veracity. While Johns focusses on the "rhetorical procedures to project authenticity" in the "newest literary forms," I look at the manner in which the printed shape of the novel attempted to lock in appearances of authenticity or veracity.[23] To combat the mutability that Johns defines, the novel selects out of the emerging culture of print the formal graphic features of established genres that had already fought and won print's reputational battle.

This is not to say that the novel combats the printed book's mutability through a uniformity of design. The contrary is true, for the genre plays its own games of havoc with the form and meaning of the printed word. Unfortunately, the uniformity of the eighteenth-century novel in today's paperback series and modern critical editions no longer conveys its extraordinary visual diversity. Particularly during the early decades of the genre's formation, the English novel's material embodiments as printed books rivaled its narrative contents in diversity and creativity. This parallel between formal and stylistic fluctuation is unsurprising: novels were the new species of writing, with the opportunity to redefine both audience expectation and print convention. As a result, writers of prose fiction during roughly the first half of the eighteenth century experimented broadly (and, broadly speaking, every publication was an experiment) with the material presentation of the novel as well as its narrative content. The fluidity of publishing practices in the eighteenth century enabled this formal experimentation. Even for the majority of writers who were not, like Samuel Richardson, printer, publisher, and author of their own work, the printer's trade and writer's art were by no means as distanced from one another as now. As witnessed in both the general fascination with Grubstreet and the specific references to print in the literature from Dryden to Defoe and Swift to Johnson, whether printers or not, the writers of the time seem smeared with printer's ink. A great variety of authors, differently assisted by different printers and publishers, enthusiastically mined print culture for forms that could give shape to the new genre, the novelty of which would earn it the label "the novel."

The publishing practices of eighteenth-century booksellers and printers associated with the new brand of fiction not only confirm the mutability and instability of the early printed book, but they warn us not to make anachronistic starting assumptions about authorial control or intention behind a book's physical appearance. The notorious publishing practices of bookseller Edmund Curll may serve as an example, albeit an extreme one, of the Protean qualities of even the ostensibly "finished" book at the time that the novel appears on the scene:

> He seems to have sold whole editions to other booksellers when he became tired of stacking them in his shop, and he bought old sheets which were given no more than a fresh title-page to become what on the face of it seem to be entirely new books. He would announce a book for publication "next week," and . . . that would be the end of it. He would publish old books as new, delightfully disguised in the advertisement.[24]

In addition to manipulating title pages, Curll was a master of the graphic packaging and repackaging of new and old books, enthusiastically seizing upon any graphic gimmick or illustration that might promote sales. In many cases it is impossible to determine whether an author even knew of (let alone sanctioned or controlled) a graphic Curllicism inserted into a version of their text touted on its scurrilous title page as "corrected by the author." Yet, although Edmund Curll occasionally crosses the career paths of Daniel Defoe, Delarivier Manley, and Eliza Haywood, the eighteenth-century novel was by no means forged exclusively in his Grubstreet smithy. In many cases, printers and authors left behind the fingerprints of consultation and collaboration in the pliable clay of a book's graphic form.

In addition to the shape-shifting forces of dubious publishing practices, a novel's "look" – even post-publication – might also be subject to the consumer's whim. In a sense, a scrutiny of graphic packaging and paratexts as "text" takes seriously the adage that readers, for better or worse, do judge books by their covers. Indeed, readers would seem to have done so long before publishers invented the modern printed cover in the early nineteenth century.[25] In the eighteenth century, however, publishers and authors rarely controlled the outside covers of their books. Consumers predominantly purchased works unbound, in gatherings or "folded quires (latterly stitched and with the intentionally temporary protection of wrappers or paper-covered boards)," and occasionally in cheap leather trade bindings "put on by or for the bookseller."[26] Prior to about 1825, these trade bindings and wrappers were mute and ephemeral.[27] Most eighteenth-century readers had their purchases bound or rebound in their own preferred style, often to match the rest of their library.[28] A consumer might even instruct that several short works be bound together in a single volume, in effect creating a unique book out of a miscellany of hand-picked pamphlets, poetry or ephemera. Thus the dominant paratextual packaging whereby a reader might judge a novel – or indeed any book – consisted, therefore, of those fringe texts and graphics that presented, named, identified, glossed, and framed their accompanying stories before being shipped off to an uncertain fate at the bindery.

The mutability of the novel's printed form (and its graphic borrowings from other genres) compounds rather than solves the recurrent problems of generic definition endemic to modern studies of the eighteenth-century novel, from the taxonomies of Northrop Frye and Ian Watt to the contextualizations of Benedict Anderson and Michael McKeon.[29] Unfortunately the early novel's graphic genetics do not offer the key to the genre's mutability or unlock those narrative strains that have proven so resistant to theoretical mapping. At the risk of engaging the unwoundable ogre of semantics, this study focusses on the graphic design of novelistic fictions published in Britain during, roughly, the first half of the eighteenth century. And although it acknowledges a long-standing tradition of visual novelty in books prior to the century's start (from the punctuation of illuminated manuscripts and *incunabula* to the list of *dramatis personae* in Restoration drama and the index in seventeenth-century manuals), it thus considers outside of its scope the graphic designs of those quasi-novelistic fictions published prior to 1700. In addition, this study holds that the consolidation of prose fiction into the mature *narrative* form of "the novel" (though still not yet called such) takes place with the late arrival of *Pamela* (1740), that sentimental hinge text between the exotics of Manley, Defoe, and Swift and the hyperrealism and colloquial color of the Fieldings and Sterne. I argue that the mature genre's *graphic* shape gels even later – in the ensuing decade of the 1750s.

Within the strict confines of the eighteenth century, I also consider fiction writers whom some contemporary critics might dismiss as minor or liminal (Edward Kimber and Francis Coventry) alongside the progenitors of the species' dominant lines of descent (Richardson and Fielding). Of course, because of master printer Richardson's indubitable control over almost every element of his work's production as well as his equally doubtless impact upon the genre writ large, his is the work awarded the most extensive consideration in this study. Although a reader may come across some unfamiliar names and many little-known experiments in the novelist's art, my study's scope (even the chapter devoted to Sarah Fielding) largely accepts the contemporary canon of the early genre, which has recently been expanded along gender lines. And although it recognizes the influence of late-seventeenth-century print traditions upon the nascent novel's graphic pilferings and, on the other end of the historical spectrum, tracks certain graphic trends to the eighteenth-century novel's nineteenth-century descendants, I do not, on the whole, overstep the marks of the study's "eighteenth-century novel" rubric.

Thus a relatively canonical inventory of novelists gives evidence of the need for a radically expanded redefinition of the novel as a genre. This redefinition includes consideration of the astounding graphic self-consciousness and experimentality that was common across much of the new species of writing, from "high" to "low" and peripheral to mainstream. Those fiction writers and publishers who, along with their respective printers, emerge as particularly prone to graphic experimentality include members of the cult of novelty seekers – such as Edmund Curll, Delarivier Manley, Eliza Haywood, and Daniel Defoe – as well as the Augustan traditionalists – such as Jonathan Swift and, to some extent, Henry Fielding (interestingly, he proved opposed to a certain kind of graphic gimmickry found in the novels of his sister Sarah). The novel genre's accommodation of graphic innovation was seized upon by B-grade authors and unknowns who depended upon demonstrable novelty for a sale, such as Hannah Snell and John Kidgell, as well as those whose literary ambitions were already on a secure footing after the success of prior fictions, such as Samuel Richardson and Tobias Smollett. Opportunities to engage in the novel's graphic dialogue thus cut across gender and class – at least to the extent that the general opportunities for publishing did – and involved printer-authors as well as those lacking direct access to the trade of print.

The apotheosis of this generic experimentation with form is, of course, Laurence Sterne's *Tristram Shandy* (1759–67). Sterne uses both graphic design and paratexts to test the boundaries of the emerging genre itself, rearranging the conventional ingredients of an eighteenth-century book to challenge readerly expectation. *Tristram Shandy*'s obvious preoccupation with graphic design has inoculated it against most of the editorial cancers plaguing the genre as a whole – though it has not proven entirely immune to textual mutation and intervention from edition to edition (see Figure 1.3). Although at least one early re-publication lacked the book's marbled pages and many more omit the ironic games played with, for example, the text's catchwords and layout, *Tristram Shandy*'s flamboyant bookishness is familiar to even a reader of modern editions. Even in modern paperbacks the oddly placed dedication in Volume IX, the Shandys' legalistic marriage articles, the untranslated French medical treatise labelled "Memoire presenté à Messieurs les Docteurs de Sorbonne," and the novel's famous marbled pages (the misplaced endpapers of a book) – all flaunt the genre's by then well-established talent for hijacking formal structure and manipulating the conventions of print. As J. Paul Hunter argues, Sterne "is not so much an inventor as a publicist" of the novel's liberal use of technological innovation and printing techniques.[30] He is, to use Richard Macksey's phrase, a "pioneer anatomist" rather than a forger of new forms.[31] In a sense, Sterne's work records how far the novel has progressed by the late 1750s and early 1760s; the success of *Tristram Shandy* may, in part, be attributed to the preexistence of a novel readership that had been schooled to "read" the visual components of the genre as part of its text. For example, the comical errata at the start of Fielding's *Joseph Andrews* (1742) and the pyrotechnics of the marginal "dots" in the 1751 edition of Richardson's *Clarissa* had been just as self-consciously suffused with bookishness and graphic design as *Tristram*'s special pages.[32] By the time that Sterne writes, the novel's reliance upon formal structures, including graphic design, is firmly enough established to be manipulated to comic effect, allowing a satire of form to become a bestseller. One has to look to the novelists (and pre-novelists) before Sterne, and to the established discourses in print culture with which they interacted, to trace the genre's visual evolution over the first half of the century and rebuild the visual toolkit of the eighteenth-century novel reader. This book takes such a look.

If novelists before Sterne considered the graphic designs of their texts, by implication the emerging novel's graphic vitality must have been a fundamental part of the eighteenth-century reader's encounter with the genre *qua* genre. If this is so, why then is there so little evidence of the genre's early graphic dimension in modern novels? Editorial practice alone is not to blame for the novel's eradication of its own printed image. As the novel matures it relies less and less on print to guide presentation, marketing, and the reader's interpretation. Over the course of the eighteenth century, the manner in which many early novels deploy graphic design charts a pattern of appropriation, subversion, and eventual desertion of the graphic markings of other literary genres co-opted by

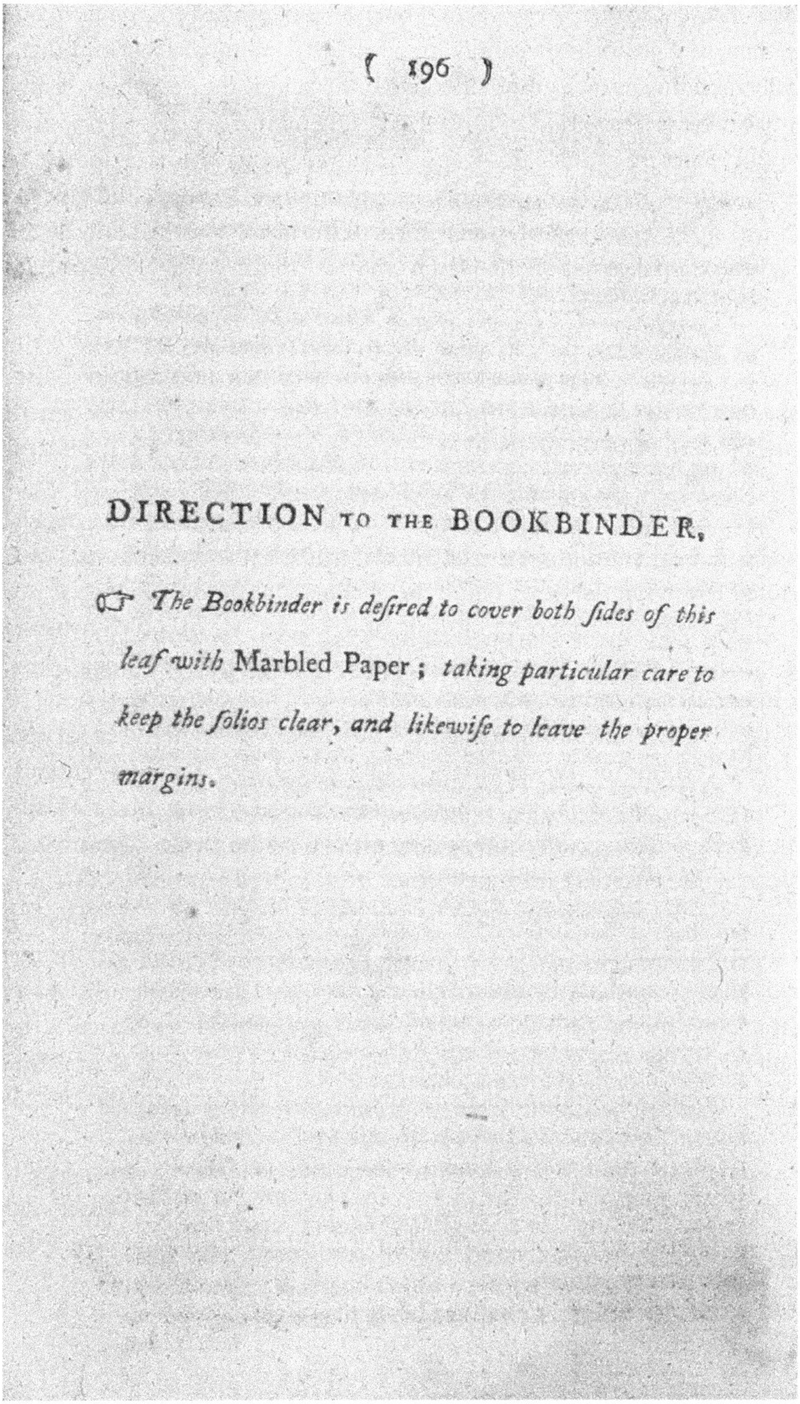

(196)

DIRECTION TO THE BOOKBINDER,

☞ *The Bookbinder is deſired to cover both ſides of this leaf with* Marbled Paper; *taking particular care to keep the folios clear, and likewiſe to leave the proper margins.*

FIGURE 1.3
From a posthumous two-volume edition of Sterne's complete *Tristram Shandy* (London: Printed for T. Caddel, 1780), I, 195.

the novel's nascent form. The novel first borrows the printed trappings of authority, then, as it grows more confident, it subverts and mocks that authority, eventually shedding its own graphic plagiarism. Tracking the novel historically, the genre's most active period of formal experimentation reaches a crescendo in the 1750s. Starting in the early 1760s, the novel begins a slow striptease of its graphic attire – its author portraits, cacophonous title pages, and graphic embellishments. It is the bare narrative form of the novel, adorned only by the figleaf of attendant illustration, that enters the next century, where as a printed book it dons the new costumes of serialization and machine printing.

To some extent, the functions of graphic design and the paratext in the early novel (during a time when book buyers had their books bound after purchase) has been replaced by the printed dust jacket, blurbs, and endorsement modes of modern publishing. Perhaps because much of this modern paratext is placed "outside" of the printed book-pages of text, and nearly always by other hands, the novelistic text nowadays tends to aspire to self-enclosedness: its self-advertising and orientation are already in the reader's possession in the form of a printed cover. On the other hand, the decline of authorial paratext is not only a consequence of modern publishing practices having found equivalents for the functions served by some eighteenth-century paratexts (book tours, author interviews, endorsements, and cover design), but also partly a result of the easy familiarity of the novel as a genre. The modern novel need not set up a series of expectations for a reader of the genre. In, for example, the twentieth-century novel, the self-contained sanctity and immediacy of the text are taken for granted. Because the convention of the novel is so thoroughly assimilated, we rush straight into these imagined other lives. Indeed, reminders that this is a printed book are felt to undermine the illusion – even in some cases to the point of eliminating chapters as artificial breaks, which, ironically, brings the form full circle back to the unbroken, chapterless narratives of early Defoe. Novelistic experiments with the printedness of the printed book are, in the twentieth century, comparatively rare outside of the avant-garde (Barthelme and others) or parodies of romances of yore (in, say, Barth's *Sot-Weed Factor* or Fowles's *French Lieutenant's Woman*).

In the first half of the eighteenth century, however, readers still needed to be lured over the threshold of the emerging genre. It was then that novelists used the developing novel's graphic presentation as printed book to entice readers and guide their interpretation.

CHAPTER 2

The frontispiece

counterfeit authority and the author portrait

> The foundation of [Isabel Archer's] knowledge was really laid in the idleness of her grandmother's house, where, as most of the other inmates were not reading people, she had uncontrolled use of a library full of books with frontispieces, which she used to climb upon a chair to take down. When she had found one to her taste – she was guided in the selection chiefly by the frontispiece – she carried it into a mysterious apartment which lay beyond the library and which was called, traditionally, no one knew why, the office.
> – Henry James, *The Portrait of a Lady* (1881)[1]

Seldom does a first edition of a Henry James novel carry a frontispiece.[2] By the late Victorian period the frontispiece was an anachronism, a signal of style over substance appropriate to an ornamental library in a house full of non-readers. In the narrative context of Isabel's plight, her willingness to be seduced by a book's packaging foreshadows her tragic seduction into Osmond's bower of aestheticism. Isabel's unexamined acceptance of the architecture of the printed book mirrors her larger failure to look beyond the world of appearances. Isabel will also fail to recognize, as the reader must, that the "imposing front" of Osmond's villa is, like a book's frontispiece, nothing but an architectural façade: "the mask, not the face of the house."[3]

Yet this is not to say that appearances, fronts, and façades do not matter. Indeed, in a Jamesian novel especially, architectural details such as the "pierced" and "massively cross-barred" front of Osmond's villa offer the attentive reader clues to the temperament of a building's inhabitant – even if the fictional characters themselves pay no heed to (or misinterpret) such visible evidence of soul.[4] Extending James's many architectural metaphors, if the books that young Isabel takes down include eighteenth-century novels, then the Palladian architecture of that "house of fiction" also offers observable proof of the nature of its occupant, in this case the early novel.[5] The fact is that the eighteenth-century novel to which James is heir relies heavily upon its own physical presentation as a printed book to guide the reader in interpretation. And whereas James's anecdote about Isabel's early reading postulates, at first glance, a distinction between a narrative and the presentation of that narrative – a distinction accepted by his contemporaries and most modern editors of eighteenth-century books – his own penchant for architectural metaphors to describe the novelist's art allows for his acknowledgment of a more complicated relationship between a book's graphic architecture and its narrative tenant.

Perhaps one could say that James's suspicion of the novel's architecture mirrors that of the novel's eighteenth-century forebears. The extra-narrative pages of graphic design that frame so many eighteenth-century novels – the "paratext" of frontispieces, subscription lists, tables of contents, title pages, indexes, dedications, so-called "puffs," and the like – reflect and refract deep tensions in the eighteenth century between appearances and reality, form and content, between generic assertions to authority and genuine truth claims. How, after all, does a new type of fiction, yet another brand of make-believe, stake out its claim to uphold basic human truths and manage the term "history" so prevalent on its title pages? It seems that many early novelists enlisted the role of graphic design to negotiate the tension between textual authority and fictional identity.

Perhaps the most prominent example of the graphic packaging of books – prominent, because always found at the very front of a work, prefacing even the title page – is the frontispiece. Frontispieces to eighteenth-century books come in a dizzying variety of styles, subjects, and shapes. I confine my discussion here to a consideration of the author portraits inserted as frontispieces to many pre- or early novels. For whereas the mere title of James's novel links the sister-art of portrait painting to novel writing, many earlier fictions physically contained a miniature portrait of the fiction's supposed author in the form of an engraved plate. Swift's *Travels*, for example, first appeared with a frontispiece portrait of its ostensible author Lemuel Gulliver, looking rather distinguished in long locks and a velvet cloak. Although such portraits brazenly counterfeit the status and authority that eighteenth-century print culture awarded to a text graced with a frontispiece of its author, their function was not to falsely convince a reader that Gulliver was the book's "real" author (although the portrait must have fooled some naïve readers). Rather, such author portraits are nearly always transparently counterfeit, filled with clues that draw attention to such packaging's problematic elision of identity and authority.

The so-called "Boggs Bills" of artist J. S. C. Boggs offer a contemporary parallel, of sorts, to the counterfeit authority fronting many eighteenth-century narratives. Boggs is an American artist who draws paper money, but not for the sake of counterfeiting (although the US Secret Service remains somewhat unconvinced and occasionally confiscates his work). Boggs's hand-drawn notes often include humorous textual deviations and mock mini-portraits, identifying them as "genuine fakes." Boggs is equally notorious for the faux-financial transactions he creates with his art, offering his dollar bills for goods and services in lieu of real money. He always reminds the other party that his notes are not "real" money. At the same time, he will only trade a five-dollar Boggs Bill for five dollars' worth of goods (as he has risen in the art world, he has been able to deploy ever larger denominations). When prosecuted for forgery, Boggs claimed that his work interrogates the true nature and value of money, exposing it as an abstraction open to manipulation.[6] Just so, the frontispieces found in early novels by Defoe, Swift, and others, are not merely caste labels of authority (although some authors deployed and readers perceived them as such). In many cases, the comical and puzzling details in the portraits, like the hidden clues in the portraiture on a Boggs Bill, assert the artistry of the imitation and call attention to the act of counterfeiting. Thus these frontispiece portraits query the authority that they have come to represent in contemporary print culture. As in one of Boggs's transactions, a purchaser of the novel is made aware of the joke – aware of the counterfeit – and nonetheless agrees to accept the face value of the authority thus counterfeited. In other words, the resulting "transaction" between the early novel and its reader not only points to the plasticity of print culture's authority but also suggests that counterfeit or faked authority has its own independent currency as a marketing device.

First some background on the genre of the frontispiece and its rhetorical status in the culture of eighteenth-century print is needed. The frontispiece portrait, a subgenre of the long-standing tradition of the author portrait, emerges as a feature of English book production in the seventeenth century.[7] Frontispieces commonly offered an engraved likeness of the book's author within a masonry frame, frequently accompanied by a Greek or Latin inscription. This model, which David Piper terms "the equivalent in engraving of the sculpted memorial bust in its niche," constitutes "a formula that repeats for the next two hundred years for hundreds of authors in their frontispieces, varying only in details of dress [and] inscription, but with of course each one individualized by the sitter's own face."[8] By the mid-seventeenth century "the frontispiece is a firmly enough established convention for it to be played about with."[9] Because in some cases engraved frontispiece portraits were Lilliputian copies of preexisting paintings, they conform to the visual conventions of the painted portrait, and share, in miniature, that genre's complexities of iconography and composition. A frontispiece might therefore convey the sitter's reputation with standard iconographic embellishments, such as a laurel crown, classical costume, or hovering muse.[10] Every frontispiece portrait offered a miniature surrogate of the book's absent author, a small private fetish that the book buyer could take home along with the text. Recent interest in parallels between eighteenth-century portraiture and literary innovation has not yet alighted on the frontispiece, a genre that offers a discreet overlap of these two disciplines within the compass of the printed book.[11]

The inclusion of a copper-plate engraving at the front of a work inevitably raised the price of a hand-press book, and hence seventeenth-century frontispiece portraits are almost exclusively found in the collected works of established writers, editions of classical authors, and, occasionally, high-profile biographies, histories, or travel narratives. For reasons both of custom and cost, the frontispiece portrait quickly evolved into a caste label: at the start of the eighteenth century, author portraits are largely absent from cheap Grubstreet productions or the works of unestablished writers in experimental genres.

Thus it comes as no great surprise that when, in the 1720s, several four-volume editions of Eliza Haywood's amatory works appear fronted by an engraved portrait of the author, such a premature attempt to garner this caste label for the nascent novel is received with unbridled derision (see Figure 2.1).[12] It is this portrait, which is possibly the first instance of a genuine author portrait being used as a frontispiece within the emerging genre, that sparks Pope's infamous description of "Eliza" in *The Dunciad* (1728).[13] Unfortunate for both Haywood's reputation and that of the emerging novel, Pope's barbed couplets fixed Haywood for posterity as the grotesque prize in Dulness's pissing contest:

> Fair as before her works she stands confess'd,
> In flow'r'd brocade by bounteous Kirkall dress'd.
> Pearls on her neck, and roses in her hair,
> And her fore-buttocks to the navel bare.
> The Goddes then: "Who best can send on high
> "The salient spout, fair-streaming to the sky;
> "His be yon Juno of majestic size,
> "With cow-like udders, and with ox-like eyes."[14]

The poem's machinery of footnotes augments the insult with bibliographical specificity: "*Kirkall*, the Name of a Graver. This Lady's Works were printed in four Volumes *duod*. with her picture thus dress'd up before them."[15] Pope's specificity has led to some scholarly confusion, which must be sorted before proceeding to gloss the engraving. The image reproduced in my Figure 2.1 is the only extant frontispiece portrait of Haywood and is signed "*Parmentier pinx*" and "*Vertue Sculp*."[16] It is not the work of an engraver named Kirkall, but that of George Vertue after an original design by Jacques Parmentier.[17] An

FIGURE 2.1 Frontispiece portrait of Eliza Haywood by George Vertue found in her *Works* (1723–24) and her *Secret Histories, Novels, and Poems* (1724–25).

engraver named Elisha Kirkall did execute and sign a frontispiece to the fourth edition of *Love in Excess* (published 24 February 1722); yet, that picture does not offer a portrait of Haywood but rather illustrates a dramatic scene from the accompanying story.[18] Present Haywood scholarship now concurs that, in the absence of any physical evidence of a portrait by Kirkall, it seems most likely that Pope conflated two separate frontispieces attached in the 1720s to works by Haywood.[19] This implies that Pope made a simple error of memory, naming Kirkall where he should have named Vertue (missing the opportune pun). Indeed, the physical features of the Vertue portrait match Pope's derisive description in all but the mentioned string of pearls. And here Pope may be accessorizing his verbal picture with a blazon-tradition cliché befitting his satirical mode. Yet, it seems more satisfactory to imagine that Pope's conflation of two frontispieces is intentional. I think it likely that Pope sacrifices the lesser-known "Kirkall" in order to avoid naming the better-known Vertue and risk tarring himself with the same brush. After all, it was George Vertue who engraved that "monument to vanity" that served as a frontispiece to Pope's own sumptuously produced 1717 *Works*.[20] The fact that the respectable Vertue was a fellow Roman Catholic may also have greased the way for Pope's slip-up. Whatever the cause or politics of Pope's misattribution, the double-barrelled *Dunciad* takes direct aim at this one-and-only Haywood portrait.

Pope's assault confirms the dubious status of the Haywood portrait as printed authority. Vertue's engraving deliberately titillates rather than authoritates. The flower tucked behind her ear; the brazen, direct gaze; the dramatically plunging neckline; the ruffled informality of what appears to be a dressing gown; and the unfastened locks of hair arranged suggestively over both shoulders – all these visual clues make abundantly clear to an Augustan audience that the nature of the accompanying writing is amatory.[21] In at least one state of Vertue's portrait, Haywood also sports, like Hogarth's harlot, a prominent beauty spot under one eye.[22] Like the epistolary conceit of the later novel, the engraving's cameo conceit (the likeness is framed as a private miniature on ivory and pinned to a background with a ribbon) licenses and enhances the intimate nature of the portrait. The result works as clever advertisement. In coarse language, it is a pin-up of the "Great Arbitress of Passion," promising another sensational bodice-ripper to the potential customer.[23] In conceptual terms, the portrait offers a personification of the accompanying text. In neither idiom can the nascent novel of the 1720s (both collections tentatively bundle Haywood's so-called novels with established genres) claim such a graphic gesture as a merited caste label. Attuned to the iconography of print culture, Pope ridicules the very gesture of adding a frontispiece portrait to an amatory *oeuvre* and savours this engraving of Haywood as a particularly ludicrous example of popular, print-culture kitsch.

Actually it is not until the early 1760s, and only after the novel (although not yet always called such) has successfully established itself as a durable literary genre, that frontispiece portraits of celebrated novelists begin to grace the reprintings of their fictions with some frequency and authority. Henry Fielding's posthumous *Works* (1762), for example, offers a smirking cartoon

FIGURE 2.2 Frontispiece portrait of Henry Fielding by William Hogarth from Fielding's *Works* (London: Printed for A. Millar, 1762).

profile of the author (complete with 5 o'clock shadow) designed by William Hogarth (Figure 2.2). The portrait is recognizably Hogarthian and perfectly in keeping with Fielding's own comic mode. Compare this with the engraved portrait of Samuel Richardson signed "C. Grignion sculp." that serves as the

FIGURE 2.3 Frontispiece portrait of Samuel Richardson by Charles Grignion from the sixth edition of *The History of Sir Charles Grandison*, 7 vols. (London: Printed for J. and F. Rivington, 1770).

frontispiece for many posthumous editions of his works (Figure 2.3).[24] The sobriety and simplicity of the Grignion engraving contrasts with the playful, rough profile of Fielding drawn by Hogarth. The artists who created these portraits adapted frontispiece conventions to suit both their own hallmark styles and those of their literary subjects. Even the chosen frames, the cluttered still-life in the Hogarth and the austere masonry of the Grignion, reflect differences in a designer's visual repertoire which, in turn, parallel differences in the narrative techniques of the books they front. Despite Hogarth's fun, his portrait does not make light of Fielding's status as novelist. It conforms to print convention as much as Grignion's. Both early-1760s frontispieces preface eminent works by then-well-established authors, bestowing the honor of such engraved portraiture to respected texts in established genres.

Yet, although Fielding and Richardson's collected works appeared with suitable frontispiece portraits *ex post*, after their literary status and that of the English novel was secure, earlier prose fictions had also appeared with frontispiece portraits, defying print convention in order to signal their literary status *ex ante*. The bulk of these frontispiece portraits in early novels do not, however, depict the work's genuine author (Haywood's portrait is a rare exception and one which illustrates the dangers of such a premature gesture). Because experimental prose fictions were largely published anonymously or pseudonymously, they fictionalized the author portrait, appropriating it for their fictional characters. From the beginning of the English novel's emergence, prose fictions by Delarivier Manley, Daniel Defoe, Jonathan Swift, Francis Coventry, and others were offered to the public with frontispiece portraits of the fiction's ostensible author and narrator. The function of these earlier "fictional" portraits is decidedly different from the later "real" portraits of Fielding and Richardson. While both sets of portraits elide identity and authority, the one (of the real author) confirms a value, the other (of the fictional author) claims it. Yet these early claims prove very different in kind from the hollow affectations of the sensual Haywood portrait.

As prefacing illustrations, these earlier frontispiece portraits provide interpretive guides to a fiction, supplying a local visual context for the accompanying verbal text. While historians of the book and material culture acknowledge the frontispiece as a cultural artifact of the printed book, literary scholars do not usually treat it as a part of the text, worthy of literary study.[25] Frontispieces found in eighteenth-century novels disappear and reappear, along with other less-studied paratexts and original print features of the hand-press period, in reprintings of those works. I will not concern myself here with novels (such as the posthumous editions of Fielding and Richardson) that acquired their frontispieces over time; those images belong to the history of attendant book illustration. Rather, I wish to examine frontispiece portraits produced as part of a novel's first appearance, or whose inclusion in a later authoritative edition appears to have been (as Genette says, "more or less") sanctioned or initiated by the original author of the work. Found in many early novels, these portraits (of the fictional, not real, author) assert literary status and generic preoccupations, while containing local interpretive clues.

FIGURE 2.4 First state of the frontispiece portrait of Capt. Lemuel Gulliver from the first issue of the first edition of Swift's *Travels* (London: Printed for Benj. Motte, 1726).

In addition, these frontispiece portraits partially negotiate the genre's triangulated relationship between the reader, the author, and the work's narrative persona.

Swift's *Travels* (1726), for example, participates in this visual dialogue through its use of the frontispiece portrait. The frontispiece plays a multilevel, ironic game with the reader: it draws on the tradition of author portraiture to claim narrative authority for Gulliver, yet it subverts that authority by destabilizing the identity of the portrayed subject. While the original maps in the *Travels* and the book's rich illustration history have received ample critical attention, this prominent graphic feature (a feature with equal or greater claim to Swift's involvement in its production) has garnered comparatively little critical notice.[26] In the portrait of Gulliver that appears in two states in the first edition of the *Travels* (1726) printed by Benjamin Motte, traditional frontispiece conventions promote Gulliver's stature and authority as author, presenting him in the velvet-cloaked guise of a distinguished statesman or scholar (Figures 2.4 and 2.5).[27] The abbreviated Latin inscription, "Ætat. fuae 58,"

FIGURE 2.5
Second state of the frontispiece portrait of Capt. Lemuel Gulliver from a later issue of the first edition of Swift's *Travels* (London: Printed for Benj. Motte, 1726).

discloses his age. The plate's second state relocates the original legend "*Captain Lemuel Gulliver, of* Redriff. Ætat. fuae 58" around the oval frame, altered only in the typographical sobriety of capital letters and Roman numerals. The new image also strengthens Gulliver's claim to authority and veracity with a more complex Latin inscription:

> *Compoſitum jus, faſque animi, ſanctoſque receſſus Mentis, et incoctum generoſo pectus honeſto.*[28]

The new quotation from the concluding lines of Persius' *Second Satire*, a poem that laments the want of the pure of heart, describes a genuinely honest man: "a heart rightly attuned towards God and man; a mind pure in its inner depths, and a soul steeped in nobleness and honour."[29] In both states, the sober portrait reinforces Gulliver's maturity and authority through text and image, simultaneously promoting his authority and that of "his" text.

Yet, unlike a frontispiece portrait in a traditional travel narrative, Gulliver's portrait participates in the satirical fiction it prefigures (or prefaces). Like Gulliver's own autobiographical portrait at the start of the *Travels*, the book's graphic self-promotion proves unreliable, even fraudulent. Although the text's narrator tells us "next to nothing about his personal appearance," this image and the text do not add up.[30] First, the portrait does not look like the Gulliver who at the end of the *Travels* is an impecunious and frustrated outcast, searching, like Diogenes, for reconciliation to humankind. It is difficult to imagine that the man who now finds human contact repulsive would sit for a portrait cloaked in the velvet trappings of the Yahoo culture he disdains. Moreover, the disclosure of Gulliver's age as "*58*" contradicts the data provided by Gulliver in his prefatory autobiography, a verbal complement to the visual portraiture of the frontispiece. According to Gulliver's account, he was at least 38 years old at the time of his first voyage in May of 1699.[31] This means that at the time of the *Travels*'s publication in the Fall of 1726, Gulliver has reached the age of 65.[32] It is Swift, born on 30 November 1667, who is 58 years of age when the *Travels* are published on 28 October 1726.[33] Thus, "Ætat. fuae *58*" proves an oblique reference to the age of the text's true author: Swift himself. In this manner the frontispiece discriminates between readers, as the anonymous publication of the politically explosive *Travels* made this encoded clue to Swift's age almost certainly inaccessible to everyone but a handful of the author's closest acquaintances.

In the Faulkner edition of 1735, Swift offers his readers two new portraits of Gulliver – portraits so unlike those found in the first edition and, more importantly, so unlike each other that they undermine the ability of the frontispiece portrait to signify identity. While it is known that Swift took a great interest in George Faulkner's publication of the 1735 edition, and collaborated with him on the text's editorial preparation, opinions differ as to the extent of his involvement in the details of production. The unconventional nature of the multiple Gulliver portraits, however, suggests that Swift masterminded their creation. Published simultaneously in octavo and duodecimo as part of Faulkner's edition of Swift's collected *Works*, the two 1735 versions of the *Travels* contain radically different portraits of Gulliver.[34] The octavo portrait depicts Gulliver as a youthful, energetic Everyman (see Figure 2.6). His partly unbuttoned seaman's jacket and the knotted kerchief around his neck project a professional confidence and youthful nonchalance. In contrast, the portrait in the duodecimo text presents the author as a weary and tattered indigent (see Figure 2.7).[35] Whereas dark, lush eyebrows lend distinction to the octavo

Gulliver, in the duodecimo portrait a menacing brow rims a pair of eyes that are strangely clouded – as if the onset of glaucoma hints at an impending blindness that carries moral overtones. Instead of projecting the authoritative images of Gulliver as a possible elder statesman or promising sea-bound surgeon, the duodecimo frontispiece confronts the reader with an untidy Yahoo who has just emerged from a sleepless night in the stables of the Houyhnhnms.[36] Although the duodecimo portrait is nearest to the narrative's closing portrayal of Gulliver, it is reputationally unsound: Gulliver's wild and disheveled appearance does not instill confidence in his narrative reliability. Compounding visual unreliability with typographical error, the cramped misspelling of "CAPT. LEMUEL GULLIVE^R" in the duodecimo portrait also highlights the portrait's instability as an artifact of print.

In both formats, Swift substitutes the complex lines from Persius found in the 1726 frontispiece with a more easily decoded epigraph: "*Splendide Mendax*," or "glittering liar." The new quotation contradicts the spirit of the old 1726 inscription and, instead, declares Gulliver's unreliability – his lack of authority – outright. And whereas the first edition's Latin quotation remained unidentified, the Faulkner edition labels the new epigraph as by "*Hor*[ace]." Yet the quotation's seeming simplicity and accessibility is itself a lie. For here the context of Horace's original ode from which this phrase is taken subverts the literal text. Horace tells the story of a young woman who refuses to obey her father's command to slay her husband, perjuring herself to save him.[37] He presents this perjury as noble and suggests that speaking "the thing that is not" can be the highest form of truthtelling. The passage, in context, thus opens the question of Gulliver's complicated moral reliability even as it impeaches his narrative veracity. The quotation also works to position Gulliver's actions within the framework of female virtue, which, of course, activates the gender ambiguity that reverberates throughout the *Travels*.

The fact that the octavo and duodecimo editions of the 1735 *Travels* contain distinct, though equally precarious, portraits of Gulliver raises the possibility that Swift aims the two images at separate audiences.[38] Yet, although the portraits seem to urge a different view of Gulliver from the book's subscription audience than from its general reading public, the primary impact of the multiple Gulliver portraits lies in their visual acknowledgment that a definitive "view" of the narrator is unattainable. Even the resemblances between the frontispiece portrait of Swift himself (included in both formats of the *Works*'s first volume) and the portrait of the younger Gulliver appear intended to elide the distinction between genuine and fictitious authorship (Figure 2.8).[39] In this sense, the frontispieces in both the Motte and Faulkner editions of the *Travels* deconstruct the tradition of the author portrait and, by extension, the persona of the author. Ironically then, the inclusion of an author portrait allows Swift

FIGURE 2.6
Frontispiece portrait of Capt. Lemuel Gulliver from the third volume in the octavo edition of Swift's *Works*, 4 vols. (Dublin: Printed by and for George Faulkner, 1735).

FIGURE 2.7
Frontispiece portrait of Capt. Lemiuel [sic] Gulliver from the third volume in the duodecimo edition of Swift's *Works*, 4 vols. (Dublin: Printed by and for George Faulkner, 1735).

to signal the generic authority of his text, while his particular execution of the frontispieces enables him to interrogate that authority. By fronting multiple editions with multiple Gullivers (and by confronting different readers with different Gullivers), Swift highlights the plasticity of his text and the problematic influence that the material conventions of book production can exert upon interpretation. Swift's appropriation of the frontispiece tradition, and the early novel's graphic borrowings in general, mutates print convention in the service of an emerging genre's unique demands. Tension among image, text, and tradition, both within the frontispiece portraits of Gulliver and within the variously formatted editions of the *Travels* more broadly, questions the expectation of textual reliability. The net effect of this tension is an assault on the reader,

FIGURE 2.8 Frontispiece portrait of Dr. Swift found in the first volumes of both the octavo and duodecimo editions of Swift's *Works*, 4 vols. (Dublin: Printed by and for George Faulkner, 1735).

who must read displaced print conventions such as the frontispiece in a new manner.

Although the interpretive impact of the author portrait is rarely as dramatic as in Swift's *Travels*, many other eighteenth-century prose fiction writers also deployed the frontispiece portrait to assert generic status, to guide interpretation, and even to instruct the reader in the problems of harnessing text and image. Swift's successful manipulation of the author portrait showed how, as an interpretive device that creates readers and readings, the frontispiece also functions as a literary element of a text. Yet this literariness – the ability of the frontispiece to shape a reader's encounter with the narrative it prefaces – reveals yet another facet of the relationship between text and graphic frame, namely the tension between authorial intent and the process of production. The inclusion of a frontispiece can prove problematic for authors who must turn its execution over to a third party. Such was apparently the case when Samuel Richardson commissioned William Hogarth to design two frontispiece portraits for his novel *Pamela* (1740).[40] When avid demand for the first edition of *Pamela* quickly prompted the planning of a second, Richardson seized upon the idea of adding two images of the heroine to distinguish the text and enhance the dignity of his creation.[41] Although the details of the commission are not known, T. C. Duncan Eaves and Ronald Paulson speculate that Hogarth was asked to sketch the heroine within specific scenes from the novel.[42] Whether the commission demanded a contextualized portrait or a traditional bust of Pamela, this elegant repackaging of the novel with portraits of its ostensible author appears to reflect Richardson's growing hopes that his new epistolary fiction would, as his friend Aaron Hill wrote, "live on, through posterity."[43] While the inclusion of an author portrait suits Richardson's ambitions for the epistolary novel, his choice of designer runs counter to his printerly reputation for austerity and cautious frugality. His investment in Hogarth suggests a decision to couple the artist's high-profile renown to the generic authority of the frontispiece portrait, thereby increasing the potential impact of the engraving as a marketing device.

Richardson, however, never used Hogarth's final designs. In the Preface to the second edition, Richardson unsatisfactorily blames an incompetent engraver and a rapid production schedule for the unadorned nature of the new edition:

> it was intended to prefix two neat Frontispieces to this Edition, (and to present them to the Purchasers of the first) and one was actually finished for that Purpose; but there not being Time for the other, from the Demand for the new Impression; and the Engraving Part of that which was done (tho' no Expence was spared) having fallen very short of the Spirit of the passages they were intended to represent, the Proprietors were advised to lay them aside.[44]

In his wording Richardson is careful to fault the engraver, not Hogarth. It is "the Engraving Part of that which was done," as opposed to the merit of the original Hogarth sketches, which has "fallen very short of the Spirit" of the illustrated passages. But if the engraver produced an unsatisfactory rendering of Hogarth's designs, why have the plates not been altered or re-engraved by someone else for use in the many subsequent unadorned editions? Since the unused plates do not survive, we are left with what T. C. Duncan Eaves calls the "tantalizing problem" of why Richardson rejected them.[45] Perhaps Hogarth offered readings of *Pamela* that conflicted with Richardson's own. Hogarth's success as an illustrator for his friend Fielding supports Eaves's assertion that the artist, "seeing Pamela with the eyes of a Fielding, confronted Richardson with a graphic 'Shamela.'"[46] Richardson's own description of the frontispieces as "having fallen very short of the Spirit of the passages they were intended to represent" comes close to disqualifying the illustrations on their visual inappropriateness for his fiction. The failed Hogarth commission confronted Richardson with the interpretive consequences of illustrating his text with an author portrait: the author-portrait genre, translated into a narrator portrait, exerts an independent hermeneutic authority when prefacing the new species of writing.[47] The unused Hogarth portraits, quite possibly, released a "misinterpretation" of *Pamela* that clashed with Richardson's desire for generic authority and interpretive cohesion.

The failed Hogarth commission, then, suggests that Richardson wanted to use frontispieces as marketing devices, but rejected this marketing strategy because it risked ceding interpretive control of the text. Other authors and printers had no such qualms. For example, Laurence Sterne enthusiastically wrote to Dodsley, his London publisher, "I would give both my Ears . . . for no more than ten Strokes of *Howgarth's* witty Chissel, to clap at the Front of my next Edition of *Shandy*."[48] Many earlier novelists similarly rejoiced in the commercial and comical possibilities of the frontispiece. Some used frontispiece portraits aggressively to attract and titillate a growing book-buying public to the novel, promoting the genre's reputation for sensationalism, voyeurism, and novelty. In particular, narratives that appealed to the age's voyeuristic fascination with (and anxiety about) sexual uncertainty enthusiastically deployed frontispiece portraiture to promote the gender ambiguity of their hero(in)es. A cult of celebrity, coupled with an insatiable curiosity for the "monstrous" and the "grotesque," had sustained a staggering early-eighteenth-century print market for first-person accounts of sexual transgression and gender ambiguity, from the 1726 textual barrage generated by "rabbit-woman" Mary Toft to Henry Fielding's *The Female Husband* (1746).[49] The new species of writing appealed, as J. Paul Hunter demonstrates in *Before Novels*, to this popular market as well as to a more sophisticated readership.[50] For example, the semi-autobiographical narrative of wife-turned-foot-soldier, *The Life and Adventures of Mrs. Christian Davies, Commonly Called Mother Ross* (1740), formerly attributed to Defoe, may be one of the better-known novelistic examples in this tradition. It, too, contains a frontispiece portrait of its British Amazon. This formal military portrait shows a boyish "Mother Ross" dressed in full regalia and posing, in the manner of the later portraits of Catherine the Great, atop a muscled horse.[51] Such portraits, like the literature they accompany, present their female heroines in the guise of handsome young men, "objects of passion to the women they met" and dangerous ciphers of individualism.[52]

Another participant in this tradition is Hannah Snell, whose novelesque autobiography (whether the text is a "fiction" or not is unclear) is entitled *The Female Soldier; Or, The Surprising Life and Adventures of Hannah Snell, Born in the City of Worchester, Who Took Upon Herself the Name of James Gray* (1750).[53] What makes Snell's *The Female Soldier* particularly noteworthy in its enthusiastic deployment of the author portrait is that it offers not just one but two portraits of its cross-dressing heroine at the book's threshold.[54] Both images of Snell adhere to the conventions of frontispiece portraiture, although in strict bibliographical terms only the full-length portrait qualifies as a frontispiece, since it alone faces the book's title page (Figure 2.9). Yet the formal bust portrait (Figure 2.10) is inserted just as if it were a second frontispiece, immediately after the title and facing the opening page of the book's narrative. Thus Snell's portraits evoke between the covers of the same book the narrative indeterminacy that Swift indicated across multiple editions of his variously formatted *Travels*.

Both the frontispiece portraits found in the octavo edition of *The Female Soldier* stimulate the reader with the juxtaposition between a "male" subject, outfitted in the masculine iconography of a country gentleman's riding habit or a martial costume, and the caption's assertion that the sitter is actually the work's female author-narrator. Both images entice by dressing the supposed female author in a costume that is, whether accessorized with crop or sword, gendered decidedly male. The fact that both these images of Snell resurface elsewhere in the print culture of 1750, one in a contemporary review and the other in a Dutch translation, suggest that such portraits enhanced the narrative's appeal.[55] True, these images are just marketing gimmicks, but they are rich ones, and ones that illuminate the relationship between text and frontispiece as brightly as do Richardson's missing Hogarths. The point of the pictures, the reason they work as marketing, is precisely that Hannah's true identity cannot be "seen" at a glance. The observer cannot penetrate her subjectivity – her "I" is inaccessible to our eye – and our comprehension requires exposure to her narrative. The promise of subjective understanding of a single character, a promise made to the potential purchasers of Snell's book by the opposition of frontispiece portrait and narrative text, is, of course, the impossible promise implicitly made by many early novels. The fact that the novel was issued with two entirely different portraits of Snell (it may or may not be the same person in both pictures) enhances, as did the multiple Gullivers, the tantalizing falsity of the novel's pledge.

The History of the Life and Adventures of Mr. Duncan Campbell (1720), another text traditionally attributed to Defoe, also makes this promise.[56] Written by a self-styled friend, it is an account of London's famous deaf-and-dumb soothsayer Duncan Campbell.[57] This account of Campbell's predictions, sign language, and natural magic enhances its exploration of the stability and transparency of personal identity through the addition of a biographical frontispiece (Figure 2.11).[58] As this text shows, the genetic link between biography and the novel becomes ever clearer during those early decades of the century. Sensational biographies such as this history of *Duncan Campbell* (and Snell's *Female Soldier*) were aimed at precisely that sector of the print market that would

FIGURE 2.9 Full-length frontispiece portrait of Hannah Snell in riding habit from the book-length version of *The Female Soldier* (London: Printed for and sold by R. Walker, 1750).

FIGURE 2.10
Frontispiece bust-portrait of Hannah Snell in martial costume from the book-length version of *The Female Soldier* (London: Printed for and sold by R. Walker, 1750).

eventually fall to the novel's share. In fact, the book's summary subtitle, "A Gentleman, who tho' Deaf and Dumb, writes down any Stranger's Name at first Sight: with their future Contingencies of Fortune," promises a story of "life and adventures" as fantastical as any novel. The double tragedy of Campbell's inability to hear and speak has mysteriously yielded a supernatural intensity of sight. The title page claims that with a single glance Campbell can both identify a stranger by name and see into their future. Yet any attempts by the reader to glean parallel insight into Campbell's identity from the accompanying portrait end in frustration: the engraving depicts a dignified, youngish gentleman, stout of mien and respectably attired in a well-groomed wig and cravat – a man utterly devoid of any extraordinary, or indeed distinguishing,

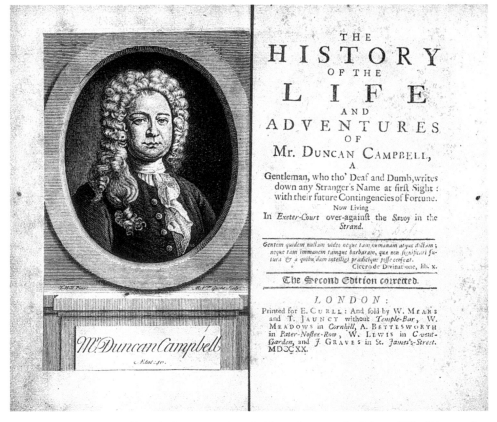

FIGURE 2.11 Frontispiece portrait and title to the second edition of *The History of the Life and Adventures of Mr. Duncan Campbell* (1720).

features. His ears, the site in which the accompanying text locates the mystery of his wondrous handicap-turned-gift, are inaccessible, concealed by the wig. Similarly, the eyes, that vehicle through which Campbell works the wonders of his insights, are distinctively without distinction. The central narrative and additional illustrations in the text enhance this portrait's reluctance to signify. For although the narrative contains an elaborate explanation of the concept of sign language, including an instructive plate detailing the hand signal for each letter of the alphabet, the frontispiece does not include a view of Mr. Campbell's hands.[59] The absence of his hands in the portrait thus renders the subject doubly mute and impenetrable.

The stories of *Snell* and *Campbell* deploy the same ironic strategy of visual self-presentation: in both books the frontispiece portrait normalizes the sitter by costuming him/her in what at first glance appears a conventional or unremarkable habit. Thus the portraits pun on the sensational and "invisible" habits or actions described on the facing title page as the focus of the book (these behaviors, of course, center on the very act of seeing or appearing). The multiplicity of meanings generated by the many visual–verbal puns ("first" and "second" sight/site/insight, I/eye, habit/habit, sign language/language of signs) deconstruct the traditional sign system of the author portrait. Instead, the juxtaposition of image and facing text queries the very generic authority that the author portrait's inclusion might generate for a book. Although perhaps not as transparently as the Gulliver portraits that show fiction-made-flesh and are inscribed "*Splendide Mendax*," the frontispieces of the real-world Duncan Campbell and Hannah Snell flagrantly counterfeit authority. Yet these obvious counterfeits also have currency. All three portraits do work as marketing tools, either because they dupe the reader into taking them at face value, or because they underscore the text's inquiry into the problematics of appearances with a graphic design that "teases" the potential buyer. They highlight the "freakish" nature of their title character by offering an image of the person which does not allow the viewer to experience that uniqueness. Together, text and image imply that to gain that experience readers must purchase the book. Thus, even before readers enter the narrative, they are attuned to (or victims of) the plasticity of authority and identity explored in the book's story.

With each such counterfeit appearance in a popular "lowbrow" fiction, the frontispiece portrait risks devaluation. As such frontispieces in Grubstreet productions became increasingly common, they risked demotion from caste label to – as Pope warned – popular kitsch. And, although the portraiture in the *Duncan Campbell* frontispiece still works as a clever visual tease in line with the narrative's dominant exploration of perception and personal identity, the enthusiasm of its putative author Defoe for fronts and paratexts as marketing devices elsewhere may occasionally have been less restrained – risking the loss of interpretive cohesion. For, whereas Samuel Richardson appears to have guarded his texts against the interpretive dissonance that can result from the process of illustration, there is no evidence that Defoe shared his concerns for maximum authorial control.[60] Defoe's graphic track record, in fact, suggests the contrary. From engraved illustrations and folding maps to lists, tables, and addenda of various quality, uses, and authority, the creative packaging of Defoe's books attests to an author who enthusiastically indulged print culture's appetite for graphic design and visual novelty. In so doing Defoe willingly relinquished his works into the hands of a great many illustrators, mapmakers, and publishers. He associated with a wide array of printers and booksellers, possibly even – if indeed he took part in the *Duncan Campbell* narrative – the "unspeakable" Edmund Curll, infamous for a marketing savvy and sensationalism that flew in the face of authorial intention.[61] Some of Defoe's publishers, even if not as unscrupulous as Curll, may very well have attached plates or paratexts into his books of their own accord, hoping this would make a text sell better.

Author portraits, in fact, are conspicuously numerous in Defoe's *oeuvre*. Not only does *The History of Mr. Duncan Campbell* (if it is his) come equipped with a frontispiece portrait of the title character, but so also do *Robinson Crusoe* (1719), *Roxana* (1724),[62] and *Moll Flanders* (1722) – though there the frontispiece appears in a later edition (Figures 2.12, 2.13, and 2.14).[63] Among the extensive portrait gallery found in Defoe's writings hangs an image of the author himself, attached to scurrilous editions of his satirical poem (note that it is not a fiction that bears his own portrait) *Jure Divino* (1706) (Figure 2.15). Originally engraved by Michiel Van der Gucht for use in Defoe's earlier 1703 *Works*, the coarsened copy of the Defoe portrait appears in various versions (of varying quality and likeness) attached to pirated and chap book editions of *Jure Divino* – not, interestingly, to his own legitimate folio edition.[64] Cost, it seems, does not always inhibit Grubstreet's appropriation of the frontispiece portrait. Benjamin Bragg's pirated edition of *Jure Divino*, complete with a copper-plate likeness of Defoe (see Figure 2.15), was offered for sale at five shillings, "half the price of the non-portrait, legitimate folio edition."[65] In reflecting on the "tributes" of such piracies, Paula Backscheider explains that in 1706 "*Jure Divino* was a poem on a highly charged current issue by one of the most notorious political criminals in England."[66] Ironically then, the author's own criminality makes the pirated portrait of Defoe appear even more of a piece with the gallery of rogues and outcasts that front (presumably with his approbation) his many subsequent criminal biographies and sensational fictions. Appropriated by high and low, by pirates and legitimate printers, for both fiction and fact, frontispieces could hardly serve the novel as straightforward authority. In the case of Defoe's graphically promiscuous fictions, his frontispieces of fictional characters are as various and variously authoritative as the proliferated images of the author himself. Drawn by different artists under the direction of different publishers, the author portraits of his later fictions also do not always participate in the iconography of print culture self-consciously, nor do they equally facilitate interpretation.

For example, David Blewett has declared that what may justifiably be hailed as the eighteenth-century novel's best-known frontispiece portrait, namely the full-length portrait of the supposed author-narrator of *Crusoe*, "poses several problems of interpretation."[67] In fact, the Crusoe portrait, a portrait "continually reprinted in all authorized editions for the next sixty years" and one that exerts a "lasting influence" on the manner in which illustrators and readers continue to imagine the central character, perpetuates interpretive dissonance.[68] First, and perhaps least problematically, the pictorial rendering of Crusoe's garb and armament does not match, according to Blewett, the exact details of the narrative's description. Secondly, the image in the frontispiece adheres to

THE FRONTISPIECE 43

FIGURE 2.12
Frontispiece portrait from Daniel Defoe's *Robinson Crusoe* (1719).

FIGURE 2.13
Frontispiece portrait from Daniel Defoe's *Roxana* (1724).

FIGURE 2.14 Frontispiece portrait from an unidentified "early edition" of Daniel Defoe's *Moll Flanders*.

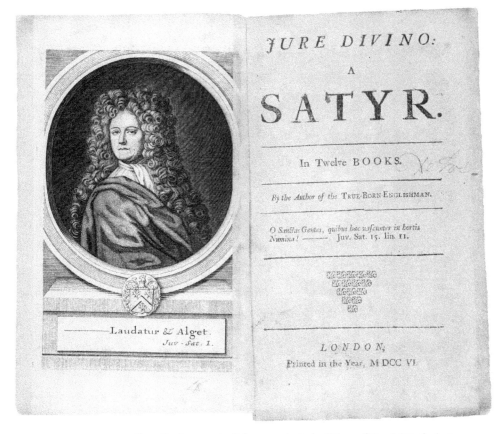

FIGURE 2.15 Frontispiece portrait from a pirated edition of Daniel Defoe's *Jure Divino* (1706).

a mode of illustration that Blewett describes as struggling with "the problem of time" (29). For exactly what moment in the author's life on the island does this image depict? The background ship rocking amidst heavy chop cannot depict the same ship as the one that stranded Crusoe, since it "is not wrecked but is under sail and headed out to sea" (*ibid.*, 27). Yet, if the vessel depicts the English rescue ship, why is Crusoe's gaze directed inland, towards the viewer, and away from the instrument of his rescue? The answer lies, suggests Blewett, in the fact that the frontispiece offers us a compression of various events in a single picture, in accordance with "a style of illustration still common in the eighteenth century" (29). The old-fashioned frontispiece offers us a "synoptic" illustration of the story in its entirety:

> The drama of the portrait is in the "theatre" of Crusoe's mind. He turns away from the ship, a convention indicating that he does not see it (since of course it is not actually there) but rather that he imagines it, remembering the ship that

brought him to the island and longing for the one that will arrive to take him away. His pensive expression and his undirected gaze indicate that his thoughts are turned inward to his lonely plight. (29)

Blewett concludes that the portrait "sums up the experiences of Crusoe – his strange costume, his solitude, his melancholy existence, his desire for rescue – ... with considerable sophistication" (29). Yet the "diachronic and synoptic" effects of the frontispiece pointed out by Blewett defy the temporal cohesion towards which Defoe's narrative, with its calendric details and tallies of days, constantly strives. And it is precisely this temporal cohesion that serves as the foundation for the fledgling novel's skeletal framework (more about this topic in Chapter 5). A summary frontispiece that renders Crusoe's wishes and memories as concrete objects open to the viewer's/reader's gaze has the effect of delivering Crusoe's story "under the Similitude of a Dream," aligning it with such stories as Bunyan's allegorical *The Pilgrim's Progress* (1678), which carried that subtitle. Thus the *Crusoe* frontispiece offers a mode of illustration that looks backwards to the text's literary heritage rather than forwards to a new print culture paradigm – as do the near-contemporary *Travels* and *Duncan Campbell* frontispieces.

The old-fashioned and allegorical summary "style of illustration" deployed by the portrait's design team of "Clark & Pine" thus proves irreconcilably out of step with the modernist realism and novelistic ambitions of Defoe's text.[69] It may be an example of interpretive multiplicity born out of a clash between designer and author of the sort Richardson tried to avoid by rejecting Hogarth's Pamelas. However, there is no evidence to suggest that this disjunction between image and text ever truly bothered Defoe. The few minor alterations made to the plate's background in a subsequent 1722 edition (a rougher sea, a darker sky, and a more troubled ship suffering from torn rigging and missing sails) do not "correct" the temporal incongruities posed by the earlier version, although they do identify the background vessel as the original ship that stranded Crusoe. As Blewett remarks, the alterations leave Crusoe looking "curiously unperturbed," adding a new interpretive problematic to the association between portrait and narrative – that of Crusoe's psychological detachment from his own story.

If a text's original presentation affects interpretation, does it matter whether that presentation is, in Genette's phrase, "more or less" sanctioned by the author? Does an image's long and iconographic association with a text override its dubious genesis? Is a novel's frontispiece any less a part of the accompanying narrative, any less an element of its complete "text," if it offers a visual interpretation that sits uneasily beside the verbal narrative? What if the author did not object to any resulting inconsistencies? The novelistic fictions surveyed thus far suggest that although marketing, generic authority, and shared concerns with identity and transparency drive the genre writ large to include frontispieces, decisions about the legitimacy of a portrait's local impact on interpretation must be made on a case-by-case basis. The interpretive problems posed by the Crusoe frontispiece, however, confront us with one final, frustrating irony. Of all the frontispiece portraits found in original editions of eighteenth-century novels discussed in this chapter, the Crusoe portrait is the only one repeatedly found in subsequent reprintings of the text. It is the only frontispiece to an eighteenth-century novel, in other words, that has attained anything close to literary or canonical status.

Although the early novel's generic use of the frontispiece portrait may not have established itself as canonical, by mid-century the material conventions of the novel as a printed book, particularly its use of the frontispiece portrait, had stabilized enough to be ridiculed. While Swift and Defoe manipulated the "old" readerly expectations of authority and veracity generated by the traditional author portrait found in other kinds of book, novelists of all sorts began to mock the "new" expectations generated by the novel's own literary use of the frontispiece portrait as a clue to interpretation. Take, for example, the frontispiece of Edward Kimber's minor novel *The Life and Adventures of Joe Thompson* (1750) (Figure 2.16).[70] The *Thompson* title page asserts the veracity of its narrative with a subtitle that proclaims it as "A Narrative founded on Fact" and the promise that it is "*Written by Himſelf*." Again, the frontispiece portrait depicts the image of the ostensible autobiographer with predictable visual fanfare. The name "*Joe Thompson*" is etched in elegant script into the masonry below his portrait, while various books, a quill in an inkstand, and musical and maritime paraphernalia tastefully clutter the scene. Yet this seemingly conventional frontispiece has bite. This image craftily adapts a custom within portrait engraving, namely that of acknowledging the provenance of a borrowed image. For, if an engraving was copied from a well-known painting, this provenance might not only be acknowledged in the engraved signature with an "after" attribution, but on occasion with a rendering of the famous canvas as part of the engraving, precisely in the manner that the *Joe Thompson* frontispiece does. For example, when Andrew Millar commissioned a likeness of Swift for an edition of the Dean's correspondence, the engraving so featured the famous Francis Bindon portrait of Jonathan Swift.[71] That the novel conveys Thompson's supposed portrait in this manner, implying that the text's fictional subject is so famous that the frontispiece must perform obeisance to an earlier oil, is, of course, part of the joke. No such visual touchstone exists of the imaginary protagonist, who, after all, is just a plain "Joe" (not even a Joseph) – this in spite of the frontispiece and title page's typographical efforts to lend his name distinction ("*Joe Thompson*" indeed). If this frontispiece pays homage to any prior image, it may very well be Hogarth's famous *Self-Portrait with Pug*,

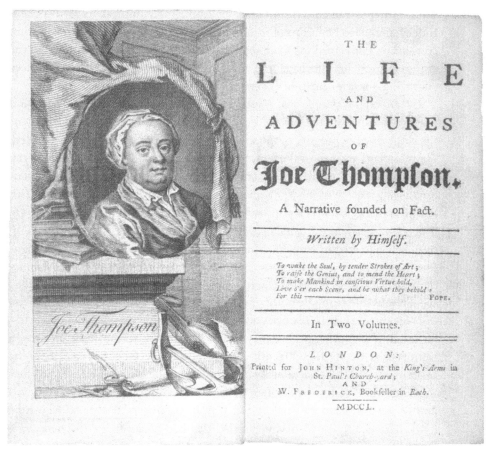

FIGURE 2.16 Frontispiece portrait and title to Edward Kimber's *The Life and Adventures of Joe Thompson* (1750).

painted in 1745 but published as an engraving the previous year in March of 1749. Hogarth used it as the frontispiece to bound sets of his prints.[72] Lacking only the dog to make the resemblance complete, the *Thompson* portrait aligns itself with Hogarth's comic self-presentation and satirical mode.

The jest mocks the now-familiar novelistic conceit of the supposed-author portrait. This is no longer an engraving that purports to depict a real person. This is a picture of a picture, a representation of a representation. The heavy drapery that encircles the bust of Joe Thompson deliberately fails to hide from view a section of the canvas portrait's telltale nail-studded edge, disclosing that the sitter for this frontispiece was already an artful illusion. Kimber's frontispiece is, like a Modernist gag, an image that playfully deconstructs visual conventions by fostering interpretive dissonance and flaunting the artifice of art. Only in the context of the novel genre's contemporary deployment of the author-portrait convention does the frontispiece unmask its own conceit. Indeed, in the later editions of *Joe Thompson*, when the counterfeit portraiture convention has waned (as I will demonstrate), the book asserts Kimber's true authorship on its title page and finds no further need for the frontispiece engraving – nor for the title's original typographical embellishment.[73]

Joe Thompson partakes of a growing mid-century self-consciousness and preoccupation with the novel's materiality, a self-consciousness that spawns the short-lived popularity of the so-called "it-narrator" during the 1750s. Here the material fetishism of the genre is apparent not only in its varied material construction as a printed book and its occasional, though always conspicuous, appropriation of the frontispiece, but also in its related narrative conceits. It was Francis Coventry's popular novel *The History of Pompey the Little; Or, The Life and Adventures of a Lap-Dog* (1751) that ignited the mid-century boom in novels narrated by non-human subjects and inanimate objects. The eighteenth century's fascination with material culture and the material permeability of social class (objects moved where people could not) fed the growing popularity of books told from the point of view of an "it-narrator."[74] Over the next few decades the numerous histories about, and ostensibly by, inanimate objects – narrated by a pin, atom, hackney-coach, flea, or banknote – would form a minor subgenre of the eighteenth-century novel.[75] Because the majority of the experimental fictions narrated by non-human subjects were inelegant productions, cheaply rendered and often devoid of illustration, Coventry's engraved author portrait is an unusual find in it-narrated novels: it depicts the canine hero majestically seated on his tasseled dog bed (Figure 2.17).[76] There are a few additional, though late, exceptions. Smollett's foray into the it-narrator genre with *The Adventures of an Atom* (London: Printed for Robinson and Roberts, 1769), for example, deserves brief mention as possibly sporting the most creative author portrait. Smollett's title page includes a curious printer's ornament graphically suggestive of a primitive atomic particle. Another notable exception is the politically evocative *Memoirs of an Old Wig* (London: Printed for Longman, 1815). Here an untenanted hairpiece prominently occupies the center of the *Old Wig*'s title page. Tweaking readerly curiosity, such bizarre pictorial fronts are emblematic of this subgenre's innovative materialism. Obviously, such images no longer serve the novel as signs of authority. Instead, as a parodic derivative of the author-portrait model, the mid-century portrait of *Pompey* unambiguously mocks (as it exploits) the novel's reliance upon graphic gimmickry to garner attention.

Perhaps the most outrageous example of the novel's self-conscious mid-century materiality is the "indecent romance" for which the rakish parson John Kidgell got into "trouble with his bishop," namely *The Card* (1755).[77] Here the title and hand-colored frontispiece jointly thwart a novel-reader's expectation by packaging a grand-tour romance with material artifacts of print

FIGURE 2.17
Frontispiece portrait from Francis Coventry's *The History of Pompey the Little* (1751).

culture which provide false clues to the novel's substance (Figure 2.18). Kidgell's epistolary novel is organized as a series of letters between the travelling young hero Archibald Evelyn and his family.[78] The brief title of Kidgell's book, however, offers the reader an enigma. The "*PREFACE TO THE READER*" promises that a reading of the work will explicate the cryptic title:

> The Apology which ought regularly to be first, is for the *Title* of the Work: But this it requires so little Pains to justify, or Eloquence to explain, that the Reader is only desired to proceed, and he will discover the Propriety of it himself. (ix)

Yet precisely when the reader proceeds, the title doggedly refuses to uphold its nominal function. None of the contemporary definitions listed in Samuel Johnson's *Dictionary* (1755) under the entry "card" (a playing card, a mariner's

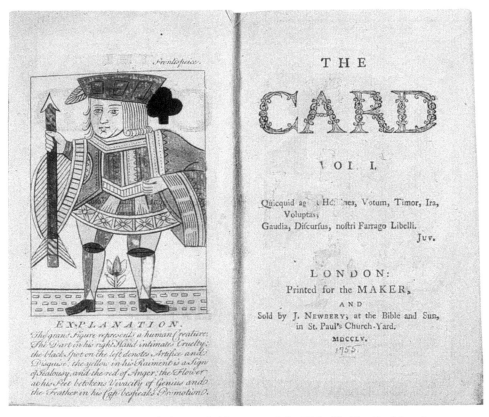

FIGURE 2.18 Frontispiece and title page to John Kidgell's *The Card* (1755).

chart, or a combing device for raw wool) presents an apt epithet for this epistolary tale about a young man's grand tour and romance – a novel in which these objects or meanings either do not appear paramount, or do not appear at all.[79]

Swift's project of building a new kind of reader by enlisting the physicality of the novel as a printed book (a project that Swift characteristically subverted even as he engaged in it) has – judging from Kidgell's critique – succeeded too well, producing a readership that is once again growing complacent in the new set of expectations about the relationship of form and content, image and text. Kidgell's project to thwart these expectations succeeded in confusing, at least, one contemporary reviewer. The reviewer initially attempts to dismiss the odd choice of title as salesmanship: "A title so novel, and to appearance, so inapplicable to any production from the press amounting to two volumes, has, no doubt, prevailed upon many to satisfy their curiosity by purchasing the performance."[80] The reviewer admits being confused by the printed apparatus prefacing the novel but expresses hope that the inscription of the frontispiece labeled "*EXPLANATION*" will compensate for the lack of explanatory subtitle. Yet even the anonymous reviewer acknowledges defeat in the face of the frontispiece:

> By this time the reader may have formed some idea of this work, with the *odd* title, the *Card*; the *frontispiece*, perhaps excepted: and here we acknowledge ourselves at a loss, as well as he. Why the *knave of clubs* should figure at the head of the *pack*, we cannot determine. It is true, as *Pam*, he rules the roast; but has no overbearing significance in other characters. That he stands *emblematical* is certain; let us see if the *explanation* at his feet may let us into the secret.
>
> '*The grand figure represents a human creature. The dart in his right hand intimates cruelty; the black spot on the left denotes artifice and disguise; the yellow in his raiment is a sign of jealousy, and the red of anger; the flower at his feet betokens vivacity of genius, and the feather in his cap bespeaks promotion.*'
>
> It would pose an *Oedipus* to unravel this.[81]

In the hope of establishing some meaningful connection between the frontispiece and the title, the reviewer draws upon the terminology of card playing, specifically the games of Loo and Ombre in which this knave is dubbed "Pam."[82] But, unlike Pope's Belinda, Kidgell's Archibald does not sublimate his erotic drive into card play.

Because image and text remain independent, the reviewer closes by surrendering to the tradition of the author portrait: "We must therefore beg leave to entreat the author . . . to let us know whether by the *knave*, he meant his own *arch self*, or, if not, where we may discover him from a *Non-entity*."[83] Yet, as a possible author portrait, the frontispiece to *The Card* also queries the related materialist fad of the "it-narrator." Kidgell, in fact, refers to Coventry's *Pompey the Little* by name in the course of his own satire.[84] Aware of this increasingly popular brand of fiction, a reader of Kidgell's title page and playing-card frontispiece might well have assumed that the non-human narrator of his novel would be a Jack of Clubs, whose adventures while passing through many hands would afford amusement. Yet, the ensuing story of gentleman Archibald Evelyn's grand tour, cast in a standard Richardsonian epistolary mode, deliberately violates the expectations generated by the verbal–visual text of its frontispiece and title.

Compounding the interpretive confusion fostered by the frontispiece are its political connotations. One reading that the anonymous reviewer does not consider (but that might very well be uppermost in the minds of other contemporary readers) is an interpretation of the card as a Jacobite emblem.[85] Playing cards, particularly face cards, appear as visual allegories of royal power and conflict in English books, broadsides, and visual arts throughout the handpress period – and have done so perhaps as long as playing cards have existed.[86]

FIGURE 2.19
George Bickham's pastiche of anti-Jacobite propaganda, *The Highlanders Medley, or the Duke Triumphant* (1746).

But by 1745, the Jack of Clubs had acquired emblematic status as a symbol of the Jacobite resistance movement; anti-Jacobite propaganda prints such as "The Highlanders Medley, or the Duke Triumphant" (1746), by George Bickham, include the Jack of Clubs as the mock coat of arms of the Stuart Pretender.[87] It is difficult to imagine that Kidgell intends his Jack as a genuine riposte to Richardson's politics. And even as a frontispiece to a story about an Englishman's marriage to a "popish" bride – a satirical inversion of the *Grandison* story-line – the Jacobite implications of the frontispiece fail to gloss

FIGURE 2.20
Frontispiece to Sarah Scott's *Millenium Hall* (1762).

meaningfully either Kidgell's plot or its Richardsonian origins. Again, the search *The Card* instigates for a definitive gloss of image, title, and text seems to come to a dead end. At every turn, Kidgell's *The Card* resists and derides the genre's rapidly coalescing structural and thematic speciation.

Just as the it-narrator genre, spawned in the 1750s, focussed attention on the novel's materialist fetishes, so the start of the next decade witnesses a new turn in the interests of the novel and, consequently, in the manner in which the frontispiece accommodates those new interests. Sarah Scott's novel *Millenium Hall* (1762), for example, appears during this transitional moment in the novel's evolution, a moment that witnesses the genre's dominant interest in "histories" of private persons giving way to histories of time and place.[88] *Millenium Hall*'s frontispiece creatively accommodates the burgeoning interest in place within the portrait genre (Figure 2.20). The plate depicts a thickly wooded vista fronted by two male figures. A large country estate is visible in the clearing just beyond the trees. Presumably one of the figures represents the novel's unnamed gentleman narrator and the other his coxcomb traveling companion Mr. Lamont, to whom we are introduced in the opening pages of the fiction. Yet, unlike some earlier prototypes of narrator portraits that depict the sitter(s) within an outdoor setting (*Crusoe*, for example), this narrator portrait is decidedly not the focus of the frontispiece. In fact, the picture marginalizes the men, dwarfing the back-facing figures with surrounding trees. Instead, the use of chiaroscuro in the engraving, as well as the lefthand figure's outstretched arm, direct the reader's gaze to the very center of the picture – to the sun-lit façade of the hall. The point of the image is the two males' separation from the mansion they gaze at through the cage-bars of the trees. Yet, despite its architectural focus, this frontispiece participates in the portrait genre after all. It is a portrait, not because it offers an ostensible image of the gentleman narrator of the piece, but because it depicts the title "character" of the novel, the residence of Millenium Hall.

In a sense, the novel's use of the author portrait comes full circle in *Millenium Hall*'s frontispiece. Compare, for example, the frontispiece in Delarivier Manley's *The Adventures of Rivella: Or, The History of the Author of the* Atalantis (1714) – one of the earliest narrator portraits in the novel's family tree (Figure 2.21). Published anonymously by Edmund Curll, *Rivella* is Manley's fictionalized autobiography.[89] Although acknowledged as a novelistic precursor, this narrative eludes generic definition and, like *Duncan Campbell* and Hannah Snell's fictionalized self-portrait, irrevocably hovers between fact and fiction – between pseudo-history and early-novel.[90] Its single illustration is a frontispiece signed "*P. LaVergne del*" and "*M. V.^{dr} Gucht Scul.*"[91] However, the frontispiece is not, as one might expect in this case, an image of the (in)famous novelist herself, or Rivella – as the title page styles her. Instead, the frontispiece assists this book's narrative conceit with a portrait of the fictional biographer and his original audience. Unlike its mid-century graphic descendants, the *Rivella* frontispiece portrait does not imitate the formal conventions of an engraved bust, blending as it does old-style attendant illustration with local portraiture (a blend also seen in some Defoe frontispieces). The frontispiece shows two fashionable men conversing beside a low wall that divides the manicured garden of a stately house from a calm stretch of the Thames, ornamented with a pair of obliging swans. Clouds in the evening sky emit the "rays of the setting sun" upon the river.[92] The text's title page and opening paragraph identify the setting as "Somerset-House Garden" and the two men as "the Young Chevalier D'Aumont" and "Sir Charles Lovemore." The moment depicted is that of the book's creation, for Lovemore supposedly narrates Manley's "Secret Memoirs" in this setting. Both men face the viewer so as to conspiratorially include him

 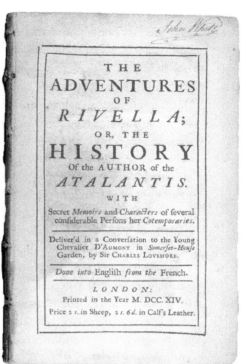

FIGURE 2.21 Frontispiece and title to Delarivier Manley's *The Adventures of Rivella* (1714).

or her in their conversation. Whether or not Manley specified the addition of this particular frontispiece portrait, the image of D'Aumont and Lovemore's evening conversation neatly introduces the narrative's bricolage of fantasy and fact. Manley's "history," writes Zelinsky, "is, in fact, a playful testimony to the uncertainty of origins and the unreliability of sources."[93] Its multiple layers of supposed translation and transcription suggest that Manley deliberately "problematizes conventional reductions of the self to a *bios*, a collection of life experiences that can be verified by means of authoritative sources."[94] As we saw, frontispieces in novelistic fictions by Swift, Defoe, and others will subsequently adopt and adapt the manner in which the *Rivella* frontispiece enhances that book's mystification of its own origins. By the 1720s, the novel has settled on a formal bust of the sitter as its preferred frontispiece design and, in so doing, makes the conceit of a formal author portrait a common feature of the early novel's self-presentation.

Millenium Hall literally and figuratively turns its back on the tradition of the "counterfeit" author portrait embodied (and possibly even initiated) by the frontispiece in Manley's fictional autobiography. What was "novel" about both Manley's fiction and its frontispiece in 1714 appears stale and conventional in contrast to the packaging of Scott's 1762 novel. As the novel genre enters a new evolutionary phase, the characteristics of the frontispiece portrait change. The *Millenium Hall* frontispiece offers a mirror image of the 1714 rococo prototype: not only do the faceless men in the Scott frontispiece turn their back upon the viewer, so as to blockade rather than facilitate access to the story's subject, but the setting for their encounter alters Manley's manicured garden into an untamed forest. Stepping from the world of Manley's frontispiece into that depicted by Scott's is to step off the raked path dissecting the early-century's velvet lawn and into the rough of the proto-Gothic wild field. Although she still shares many of Manley's narrative preoccupations (with, for example, gender, law, and amatory conventions), Scott's frontispiece signals a radical alteration in the intellectual landscape of the novel.

Although Scott, like Manley before her, challenges existing constructions of female identity, her text imagines a greatly expanded definition of female community and "self." Scott's novel narrates how specific social circumstances prompt six women to exchange their identities as wives, daughters, and widows for participation in an all-female society within the walls of Millenium Hall. It is the identity of the collective, rather than that of a specific occupant, that graces the novel's title page and frontispiece. The narrative structure of the book as an anthology of individual "Lives" also reflects this novel's increasing commitment to group identity (at the same time that it reveals the origins of the novel in the echoes to Manley's episodic habits in scandal fiction). Even the individual histories, or "Characters of the Inhabitants," are filtered through multiple layers of narration, as Mrs. Maynard's second-hand account of the members of the Hall is, in turn, communicated to the reader by the anonymous gentleman in his book-length epistle. Personal experience is thus related indirectly as part of a collective consciousness, rather than as a private history. Contrary to Manley's use of the likeable and romantic Lovemore as putative biographer, the final layer of anonymous male narration in *Millenium Hall* casts a patriarchal shadow over the whole of Scott's utopian vision. Not surprisingly, the publication of *Millenium Hall* coincides with the novel's generic embrace of expanding definitions of self that increasingly acknowledge the social construction of identity. Of course, the novel was, from its beginnings, interested in more than just private subjectivity or the inner self. "Its distinctive character," as Hunter writes, "involves the way it holds the individual will in tension with social and interactive values."[95] Yet, the novel's claim to history does appear to undergo a modest expansion at the end of the eighteenth century. The *Millenium Hall* frontispiece hints at this emerging late-century trend in the novel's growing interest in mapping, not private identity, but socially determined subjectivity. Scott's rejection of the counterfeit author-portrait model heralds a turn in the novel's intense interest in the single and singular individual.

The decline of the portrait frontispiece in late-eighteenth-century novels (except when produced as part of an author's collected works) is inversely proportional to this broadening in the novel's generic interests. In 1762, when *Millenium Hall* first appeared, the use of portrait frontispieces (of the fictional, not the real, author) to new novels was already growing less common. In fact, as we witnessed in the Fielding and Richardson portraits of the early 1760s, authentic portraits of novelists displace the counterfeit portrait phenomenon. When counterfeit portraits of supposed narrators do occasionally surface later on, as in the bizarre frontispiece to William Donaldson's *The Life and Adventures of Sir Bartholomew Sapskull, Baronet . . . BY SOMEBODY* (1768), which is labeled "The Reverse of Somebody" and profiles the back, rather than the front, of the supposed author's head, they are easily made to serve satirical functions – self-consciously upending the novel's aging conventions of graphic self-presentation. At the same time, English and continental book production saw a mid-century boom in attendant and elaborate illustration.[96] Thus the decline of the frontispiece portrait does not index the book industry's reluctance to invest in the visual dimension of the novel. The portrait frontispiece had been a convenient medium with which to signal the early novel's generic ambitions and augment its dominant interest in individual psychology, cult of celebrity, and private subjectivity. However, when the historical novel, the gothic novel, and the novel of manners address the broader socio-historical issues of national, generational, and civic identity, the frontispiece portrait of the individual narrative persona falls away. Titles and title pages to novels too, of course, reflect this generic trend towards presentations of communal identity. A loose catalogue of novel-titles, in fact, would sketch a shift from mid-eighteenth-century novels, however diverse, named primarily after individuals (Pamela, Clarissa, Tom Jones, Betsy Thoughtless, Tristram Shandy, even Fanny Hill) to early nineteenth-century novels named, instead, after places representing collections of people or the abstractions that motivate them. Such titles as *Sense and Sensibility* (1811), *Mansfield Park* (1814), *Wuthering Heights* (1847), and *Bleak House* (1853) signal the nineteenth-century novel's embrace of social consciousness, cultural history, and broader definitions of community.[97]

Exactly how titles and title pages evolved to reflect, like the frontispiece, the novel's changing project is, in fact, the subject of my next chapter.

CHAPTER 3

The title page

advertisement, identity, and deceit

> Hence springs each weekly Muse, the living boast
> Of Curl's chaste press, and Lintot's rubric post,
> Hence hymning Tyburn's elegiac lay,
> Hence the soft sing-song on Cecilia's day,
> Sepulchral lyes our holy walls to grace,
> And New-year Odes, and all the Grubstreet race.
> – Alexander Pope, *The Dunciad, Variorum* (1729), Book I, lines 37–42.

Pope's description of eighteenth-century publishing, satirized in the *Dunciad* as Dulness's "cave of Poverty and Poetry," ridicules a number of contemporary marketing strategies, including, in these lines from Book I, the posting of title pages as advertisements. Pope's own annotations gloss "Lintot's rubric post" as a reference to a bookseller who "adorn'd his shop with Titles in red letters." Edmund Curll's *Key* to Pope's poem adds that "Mr. LINTOT, in Fleet-street, is so fond of Red Letter Title-Pages to the Books he prints, that his Show-Boards and Posts before his Door are generally bedaubed with them."[1] A practice dating at least as far back as the sixteenth century, the posting of rubricated titles on "Show-Boards" around town remained in the early eighteenth century a routine way of advertising a bookseller's wares. Rodney Baine documents evidence that the novel, too, was subject to this practice: "The rubricated title pages for the editions of Defoe's *Col. Jack* in 1724 and 1738 would indicate that at least these titles were designed to be posted."[2] But it was not only title pages printed in red and black ink that served as advertisements. As Pope's singling out of Bernard Lintot's affectation suggests, rubrication primarily marked prestige books and thus only occasionally, as in Defoe's bold gesture, attached itself to fiction. Yet, whether rubricated or not, the early eighteenth-century title page remained "primarily the publisher's advertisement, or bill of fare, especially for popular literature like fiction and rogue biography."[3] Both Pope's lines and Curll's gloss give evidence that Lintot's fetish for crimson made his "bedaubed" "rubric post" stand out (as it was doubtless designed to) from the rest of such advertising space in Fleet Street, which continued to display a sea of modern titles in monochrome.

Because the early novel's title page shouldered the publisher's commercial burden, its composition fell largely outside of the author's domain. In fact, on the whole, bibliographers deny the title page authorial involvement. Some bibliographers dryly regard the eighteenth-century title page, as McKerrow does in seventeenth-century books, "not as part of the work to which it is prefixed, or as a production of its author, but rather as an explanatory label affixed to the book by the printer or publisher."[4] Others allow the author a minimal amount of input. For example, Philip Gaskell, in confirming that the graphic realization of a title page's constituent elements was typically left to the compositor, hints that the author might influence some elements of its construction: "Like the text, the title page was set from copy, which might indicate roughly how it was to be set out. Details of the layout, however, and choice of type were commonly left to the compositor."[5] Exactly just how "rough" the instructions to the compositor were presumably depended upon the author's fastidiousness and the printer's tolerance for such direction.

Thus, when we turn, as we do now, to the interpretive impact of title pages, we must largely leave authorial intent behind. Although occasional deviations from the trade's titular habits may prompt questions about the author's involvement, a study of the novel's title page is a study of publishing's practices and desires. This does not mean, however, that the constituent elements of a title page do not impact on the reader's experience with the book, influencing a literary interpretation. Indeed, they were intended to. And, Baine reminds us, "as every student of bibliography knows," a first edition's title page was "normally" set last; thus a title page offered (whether by the hand of the compositor or of the author) a summary "reading" or interpretation of a book, albeit a reading intended to titillate and promote.[6] Moreover, even bibliography's so-called accidentals can exert interpretive sway: as Genette warns, "no reader should be indifferent to the appropriateness of different typographical choices, even if modern publishing tends to neutralize these choices by a perhaps irreversible tendency toward standardization."[7] Finally, of all the paratexts possibly involved in the transition from manuscript to printed book, the title page is the sole required element in a text's packaging. Although the inclusion of frontispieces, illustrations or tables, and even the execution of punctuation were often subject to a printer's house style, a publisher's budget, or a compositor's whim, no novel entered the eighteenth century without a title page. Precisely because print culture both demands and constructs it, a title page – the printed book's vital organ – lies at the heart of the novel as a printed book.

In view of this centrality, it is surprising that so many of the early novel's title pages deliberately mislead. Virginia Woolf's remarks on *Robinson Crusoe* best capture the experience of being misled by the promises of exoticism and psychology made on that book's original title page.[8]

> Before we open the book we have perhaps vaguely sketched out the kind of pleasure we expect it to give us. We read; and we are rudely contradicted on every page. There are no sunsets; there is no solitude and no soul. There is, on the contrary, staring us full in the face nothing but a large earthenware pot. We are told, that is to say, that it was the 1st of September 1651; that the hero's name is Robinson Crusoe; and that his father has the gout. Obviously then, we must alter our attitude. Reality, fact, substance is going to dominate all that follows.[9]

Even though her father's scholarly library must have given her access to many eighteenth-century books, Woolf herself may not be responding here to *Crusoe*'s original labeling. She may have encountered Defoe in one of the many late-nineteenth- or early-twentieth-century reprintings which variously alter the novel's original title page (as well as its original illustrations, frontispiece, and organizational structure). In Woolf's case, the expectations she describes as flouted by the text are founded upon what she claims "we know" – in 1932 – of Defoe's "theme" and its "desert island" setting prior to our reading:

> It is, we know, the story of a man who is thrown, after many perils and adventures, alone upon a desert island. The mere suggestion – peril and solitude and a desert island – is enough to rouse in us the expectation of some far land on the limits of the world; of the sun rising and the sun setting; of man, isolated from his kind, brooding alone upon the nature of society and the strange ways of men.[10]

Interestingly, the original title page yielded this same information to the eighteenth-century reader. For even though that early reader would have been innocent of Romanticism's "brooding," the title page's promised shipwreck, years of remote isolation, and a pirate rescue undoubtedly evoked for the book's initial reader a picture that is similar, if not identical, to the one drawn by Woolf (see Figure 3.1). Before first-edition readers would "open the book," they too might glean from the title page the loose outlines of Crusoe's story – outlines that Woolf can simply claim "we know." When Woolf describes how the narrative's humdrum opening violates readerly expectation and forces, as early as in the first few pages, a conscious adjustment to the novel's style and intention, she describes precisely the experience set up by the novel's first

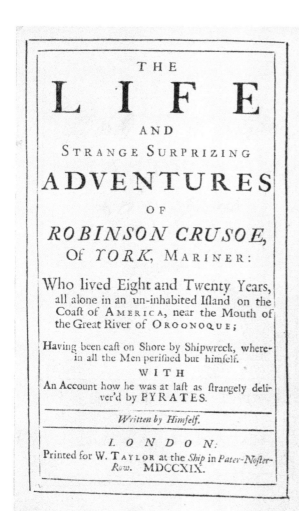

FIGURE 3.1
Title page to Daniel Defoe's *Robinson Crusoe* (1719).

titular descriptions. Two hundred years into the book's history, Woolf claims as a hallmark of Defoe's genius that he "thwarts us and flouts us at every turn."[11] For its original audience, an audience not yet schooled from infancy in the outlines of the *Crusoe* adventure, the book relied upon its title page to raise the romantic (small "r") expectations disappointed by the unassuming, middling matter-of-factness of Defoe's style. By means of that disappointment *Crusoe* tears down the wall of a reader's "old" preconceptions, building with its recycled stones a new house of fiction.

Although they sometimes raise stylistic expectations in order to flout them, other title pages of Defoe's are surprisingly continuous with the narratives they label. Take, for example, the 1722 title page to *Moll Flanders*. The cries of that title page are uttered in the mercantile lingua franca of Moll's story

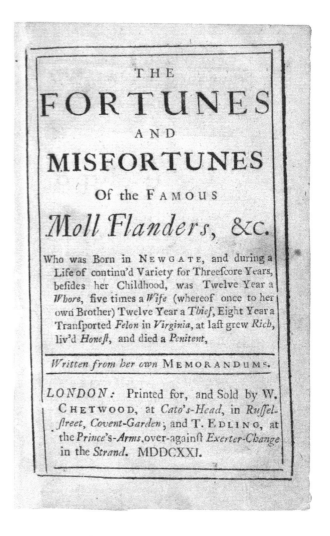

FIGURE 3.2
Title page to Daniel Defoe's *Moll Flanders* (1722).

(see Figure 3.2). Numerical accounting and calendric recitation dominate this summary title just as they dominate what Woolf claims is "the large earthenware pot" of Defoe's unadorned practicality. Both narrative and label are brimful of those tallies and mercantile computations that become the hallmark of Defoe's hyperrealism. Moll's avarice and the materialist sins for which she must make a penitent *account* are already evident in the language of the book's title page. It is, of course, a chicken-and-egg problem: does the title page imitate the language of Defoe's narrative or does Defoe's narrative imitate the lingua franca of commerce that is responsible for the book's label. Whether by Defoe's design or by (predictable) commercial accident, the language of the novel's paper label is implicated in the narrative's assessment of economic individualism.

Rather than debate whether or not such title pages reproduce a title suggested by the author, let us see what may be gained by awarding the title page modest interpretive status. Let us read the novel's titles as carefully as the eighteenth-century consumer, in the absence of true familiarity with the emerging genre, must have done. Such a consumer would have deployed a knowledge of contemporary print culture to decipher the clues to the text's nature, subject, and style embedded (for the moment, we shall ignore by whom) on the title page. Imagine the early novel's title pages as they first appeared on the "Show-boards" of booksellers. There the typography, arrangement, appearance, and verbal text of these fecund sheets could be mined for the graphic signifiers – from a book's name to its publisher's imprint and street address – that offered interpretive clues about the nature of the text.

Title pages to eighteenth-century novels accommodated much more information than the abbreviated title (nearly always the name of the hero or heroine) that is used to refer to a book in the vernacular. It is possible to dissect the early novel's title page into its constituent parts, labeling each feature before assessing its interpretive potential. To begin with, titles to early novels, as in eighteenth-century books of all sorts, did not just name; they summarized or explained. Many of the novel's early title pages are, in fact, uncomfortably crowded. A telltale sign of an experimental genre, a crowded title page usurps all available space as explanatory gloss.[12] Before the novel matures and is allowed to flaunt its confidence in a lavish extravagance of white space, it exploits every opportunity to identify and publicize itself. Because the title page of the eighteenth-century book inherited the commercial burden of its seventeenth-century forebears, a novel's full name often doubles as a précis. The full synopsis-title of *Robinson Crusoe* reads like the ad copy of its predecessors (see Figure 3.1):

> THE **LIFE** AND STRANGE SURPRIZING **ADVENTURES** OF ***ROBINSON CRUSOE***, Of *YORK*, MARINER: Who lived Eight and Twenty Years, all alone in an un-inhabited Iſland on the Coaſt of AMERICA, near the Mouth of the Great River of OROONOQUE; Having been caſt on Shore by Shipwreck, wherein all the Men periſhed but himſelf. WITH An Account how he was at laſt as ſtrangely deli-ver'd by PYRATES. *Written by Himſelf*.

The complete title to *Moll Flanders* repeats such prolix synopsizing, seizing upon that story's salacious content as energetically as any advertisement (see Figure 3.2):

> THE **FORTUNES** AND **MISFORTUNES** Of the FAMOUS ***Moll Flanders***, &c. Who was Born in NEWGATE, and during a Life of continu'd Variety for Threeſcore Years, beſides her Childhood, was Twelve Year a *Whore*, five times a *Wife* (whereof once to her own Brother) Twelve Year a *Thief*, Eight Year a Tranſported *Felon* in *Virginia*, at laſt grew *Rich*, liv'd *Honeſt*, and died a *Penitent*, *Written from her own* MEMORANDUMS.

Print culture must have anticipated the vernacular reduction of these titles.[13] Already the contemporary function of the half-title was, in part, to condense and reduce a book's name. Although these seldom grace early novels, half-titles commonly repeated an abbreviated nomenclature at the front of a book, ahead of the frontispiece and formal title page. Limitations of space might force further reductions at the bindery if, as was common, a leather binding identified the book with gilt lettering on its spine (since the wealthy frequently ordered their books bound in identical style, so as to create a matching library, spines needed to name). Genette argues that it is difficult to imagine some titles "ever being quoted *in extenso* in a conversation or even in an order placed at the bookstore, and their reduction was definitely expected, if not planned."[14] The typographical prominence of the hero and heroine's names on the early novel's title page seems calculated to aid such abbreviation.

The full titles of *Robinson Crusoe* and *Moll Flanders* offer typology as well as type. Aided and abetted by a host of faces and type sizes, they present themselves as biographical travel tales – as established genres that the book-buying public knew and for which the patterns of interaction between reader and text did not need to be reinvented. In a sense, borrowing preexisting genre identifiers allowed the novel to mitigate the experimentality of its projects, while also allowing it to leverage the authority of non-fiction to create a *frisson* that audiences, then and now, find compelling.

Within the double-ruled borders of their title pages, *Robinson Crusoe* and *Moll Flanders* also deploy those features of the title page that are constructed in strict adherence to the contemporary customs of print, namely the authorship declaration and publisher's imprint.[15] The claims that "**ROBINSON CRUSOE**" is "*Written by Himſelf*" and "**Moll Flanders**" is "*Written from her own* Memorandums" eventually prove false. But, like the fictional frontispiece portrait and the genre identifiers in the title, these formulaic tags mimic the conventional labeling of non-fiction in service of the emerging genre. The title pages, again in strict accordance with print convention, close with publishing information that allows the reader to locate the nearest vendor from whom a newly minted copy of, say, *Moll Flanders* might be purchased: "Printed for, and Sold by W. Chetwood, at *Cato's-Head*, in *Ruſſel-ſtreet, Covent-Garden*; and T. Edling, at the *Prince's-Arms*, over-againſt *Exerter-Change* in the *Strand*." In a London without street numbers, colorful imprints such as this one use local shop signs ("*Cato's-Head*" and "the *Prince's-Arms*") and neighborhood landmarks (spelled "*Exerter-Change*") to pinpoint a bookseller's location. The standard publishing information formula also fixes, for posterity, the book's birth date and location. Yet, the imprint on *Moll*'s 1722 title page reminds us that printer's errors can occur anywhere. Not only does the title page misspell Exeter and give the year falsely as '21 (possibly owing to a conventional slippage for January publications) but by substituting a "D" for a "C," the compositor places the book four centuries ahead of its time: "LONDON . . . MDDCXXI."[16]

Despite the prolixity of their wording, the title pages to Defoe's novels discussed here are in fact examples of titular minimalism: they contain merely the three basic elements of an eighteenth-century title page – a title at the head, an authorship declaration mid-page, and a publisher's imprint at the foot. Their double-ruled borders are these pages' only ornamentation, although compartments, *fleurons*, and wooden images in relief (such as could be set along with the rest of the page's type) feature elsewhere on contemporary titles. Defoe's pages are also bare of an evocative epigraphic quotation ("*To wake the Soul, by tender Strokes of Art* . . . POPE."). Similarly, bibliographical details ("𝕿𝔥𝔢 𝔖𝔢𝔠𝔬𝔫𝔡 𝔈𝔡𝔦𝔱𝔦𝔬𝔫 𝔠𝔬𝔯𝔯𝔢𝔠𝔱𝔢𝔡"); a device or printer's mark[17]; or retail price ("Price 2 *s.* in Sheep, 2 *s.* 6 *d.* in Calf's Leather") are absent here – although other titles to eighteenth-century fictions may contain such information.[18]

The hurly-burly of the title page's typographical pie does not require my augmentation. The cacophony of type speaks for itself. The interpretive effect of the conventional formulas for authorship and publication data are, however, less apparent. The novel was characteristically deceitful, or circuitous, in naming and housing itself, even when it came to identifying its author and publisher on its title page. Bibliographers and historians of the eighteenth-century book long ago ceased to rely wholly upon the attribution information offered by a title page, often deploying tortuous methods of detection to ascertain a printer's or author's association.[19] A lack of uniformity also complicates unreliability. While the layout of a title page's constituent elements is relatively fixed (the title-at-head and publisher-at-foot structure varies only in execution), the wording of these standard features varies greatly. And where there is multiplicity there is also interpretive possibility. Take the authorship declarations that are nearly always found mid-page, beneath the title and above the publisher's imprint. As a rule that admits few exceptions, the early novel adheres to conventions of anonymity and pseudonymity well past the century's mid-point. Yet the two articulations of authorship found on Defoe's title pages, one an autobiographical claim, the other a boast that the publication is based on the dead Moll's diary, give some indication that novels did not signal this conceit in the same manner. Anonymous attributions come in a variety of tags, creating different tones and authorial modes for the title page and its tale – from the elegantly gendered freshness of "By a Young Lady" to the comically affected "By an Adept."[20] Some front matter to books of the late seventeenth century had teased the reader with partial declarations of the author's identity ("*by* F K"); this convention of aposiopesis continues on the titles of scandal fictions penned during the early decades of the next

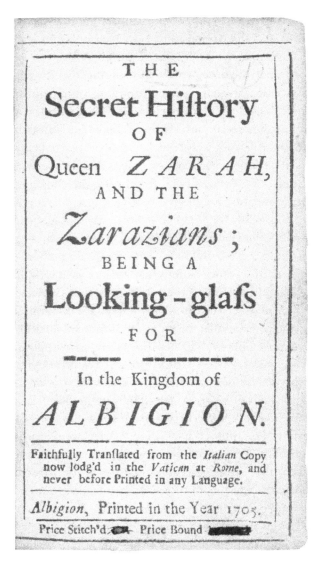

FIGURE 3.3
Title page to
Delarivier Manley's
*A Secret History of
Queen Zarah* (1705).

century.[21] Although anonymity masks their authors, the title pages of books by Manley and Haywood still highlight with line rule and dashes the coy refusal to name names that is central to their appeal (Figures 3.3 and 3.4). Pseudonymity also attaches itself to the novel in multiple guises. While Richardson's novels cloak themselves with the dignity of an "Editor," others dress up in satiric or self-conscious costume ("By the beſt WITS of the preſent Age" or "Printed for the MAKER").[22] The mask of paper anonymity is often semi-transparent. Richardson's identity as the supposed editor of *Clarissa*, for example, did not prevent Lady Bradshaigh's famous hate-mail from reaching its intended destination.[23] Nor did Sterne escape the notoriety for which he hungered when

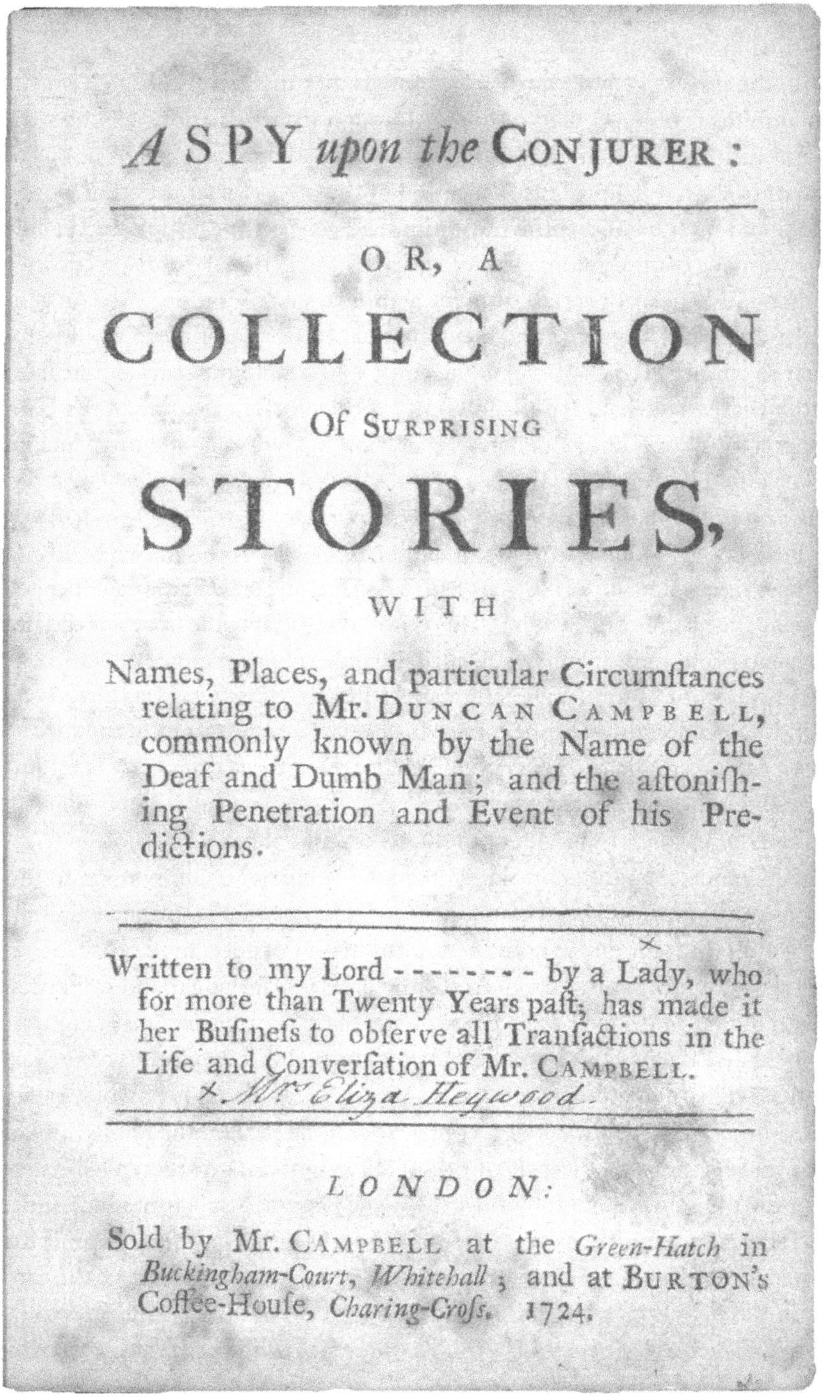

A SPY *upon the* CONJURER:

OR, A

COLLECTION

Of SURPRISING

STORIES,

WITH

Names, Places, and particular Circumstances relating to Mr. DUNCAN CAMPBELL, commonly known by the Name of the Deaf and Dumb Man; and the astonishing Penetration and Event of his Predictions.

Written to my Lord -------- by a Lady, who for more than Twenty Years past, has made it her Business to observe all Transactions in the Life and Conversation of Mr. CAMPBELL.
× Mrs Eliza Heywood

LONDON:

Sold by Mr. CAMPBELL at the *Green-Hatch* in *Buckingham-Court, Whitehall*; and at BURTON's Coffee-House, *Charing-Cross.* 1724.

FIGURE 3.4
Title page to Eliza Haywood's *A Spy Upon the Conjurer* (1724).

the first volumes of the *Life and Opinions of Tristram Shandy, Gentleman* were published in 1759.[24]

Still, the novel's generic fidelity to anonymity must have impacted on the local ambitions of particular authors. Although its articulations can be various and variously revealing, the novel's stubborn adherence to conventions of anonymity slowed the professionalization of the novel writer. In other words, while pseudonymity and anonymity stimulate generic innovation and enable the genre-wide counterfeiting of authority with the fictional frontispieces, they simultaneously delay the establishment of individual reputation based on genuine authorship. The genre's and the individual author's ambitions would thus appear to conflict. For example, in the context of a contemporary publication practice that tended to uphold anonymity with colorful pseudonyms or elaborate evasions, an author's defiant declaration of their true identity, such as in the plain "By Mrs. JANE BARKER" on *A Patch-Work Screen for the Ladies; Or, Love and Virtue Recommended: in a Collection of Instructive Novels* (1723) may have appeared false (surely the name "E. Curll" in the imprint did not instill confidence in the authority of such a claim) or smacked of a conceited independence from convention.[25] This is not to say that some novelists did not manage to build brand, either out of their success in genres not governed by anonymous publication (most famously Henry Fielding, who was already an established playwright when he turned his pen to fiction) or out of the success of prior fictions published anonymously ("By the Author of *DAVID SIMPLE*" or "By the Editor of PAMELA and CLARISSA").[26] Ironically it is from such circuitous branding of individual products that the novel as a whole eventually gains generic standing, breaking through the barrier of anonymity. In this circuitousness the novel is, of course, joined by most other eighteenth-century print genres. Indeed, throughout the century many writers "looked askance at their own activities as authors, deeming the press a trifle vulgar and somewhat beneath them."[27] As I have argued elsewhere, the early-century "print culture" that incubates the nascent novel has not yet internalized the notion of authorship that will come to be, by century's end, irrevocably tied to the published, printed book.[28] However, when it comes to graphic design, the anonymity of the novel succumbs to the cult of personality sometime in the 1760s. As we saw in the previous chapter, by then the novel begins to substitute individual brand (the genuine author portrait) for the novel's hitherto generic brand (the fictional frontispiece). So too with attribution. From the latter part of the century onwards, although the anonymous publication of novels continues to be regarded as genteel, novelists claim their presence with increasing authority and assurance on title pages.

The amount of variation found within imprints at the bottom of title pages to early eighteenth-century fictions is perhaps even more striking than that found in attributions – simply because less expected. Unless an imprint is blatantly satirical, such as that found on the 1643 political pamphlet mentioned in Chapter 2, *The Bloody Game at Cards* (the imprint reads "Shuffled at London, Cut at Weſtminſter, Dealt at Yorke, and Plaid in the open field. by the Citty-clubs, the country Spade-men, Rich-Diamond men and Loyall Hearted men"), we naturally assume that a publisher's name and address could not possibly qualify as a literary element of a text, since a po-faced imprint offers immutable facts only.²⁹ But does it? True, it is the absence of numerical designations to streets that forces the publisher's imprint to resort, as evidenced on *Moll Flander*'s title page, to colorful landmarks and quaint proximity indicators that guide a reader to so-and-so's printshop lying: "without *Temple-Bar*," "over-againſt *St. Clement's Church*, in the *Strand*" or "oppoſite *New Exchange Buildings* in the *Strand*."³⁰ Yet a glance at a map of eighteenth-century London reveals that most of these locations lie within a well-defined publishing district that offers little risk of a consumer getting lost. Accuracy in reporting only partially motivates the contortions of the addresses. It was not always necessary to know that the establishment of Andrew Millar was to be found "over-againſt *St. Clement's Church*, in the *Strand*" or five years later "opposite *Katharine Street*, in the *Strand*"; sometimes simply "A. MILLAR, in the *Strand*" sufficed.³¹ In other words, some elements of the imprint were optional embellishments – self-fashionings disguised as fact. Many such gratuitous exactitudes and descriptions of place allow imprints to avoid naming streets and neighborhoods notoriously associated with the phenomenon of Grubstreet and hack writing. Pope's choice of the route for his dunces in the *The Dunciad* most famously showed that the book industry of Grubstreet, although itself a myth, had specific concentrations along the city's most northerly bend of the Thames: publishers and booksellers spilled from the mercantile district of Cheapside west, via St. Paul's Churchyard, into Fleet Street and The Strand. This stretch of the city, crowded with bookstalls and print houses, lived (well before Pope's 1728 satire) in the imagination of eighteenth-century Londoners as Grubstreet. Even an imprint without euphemisms might distinguish an establishment along this route as a cut above the rest, as in "Printed for T. LOWNDS, at his Circulating Library in *Fleet-Street*."³² In other words, Grubstreet tended to gentrify its address whenever possible, usually with references to churches or other citadels of respectability. When an imprint offers a novel for sale "in *Threadneedle-ſtreet*" it pauses to mention the vendor's proximity to a church; when the address "in the Poultry" is unadorned, the imprint belongs to a prose oddity devoid of "high" literary claims.³³ Neither of these two imprints stress that Threadneedle Street and the Poultry reside in what Austen's characters still sneeringly whisper is "Cheapside."³⁴

Whereas it was not unusual for seventeenth-century imprints to advertise a vendor's nearness to a tavern ("Printed for *Henry Rhodes*, next door to the *Swan-Tavern*"), rarely is a novel offered for sale at (or opposite) a coffee house in the eighteenth century – although such establishments routinely doubled as both postal addresses and vendors for print.³⁵ When an imprint to a novel does direct the reader to a coffee house, the title page aims at a lowbrow popular audience. For example, the 1724 imprint on Eliza Haywood's *A Spy Upon the Conjurer*, a supposed biography of the "Deaf and Dumb Man" Mr. Duncan Campbell, flaunts its popular appeal. The *Spy*'s imprint, "Sold by Mr. CAMPBELL at the *Green-Hatch* in *Buckingham-Court, Whitehall*; and at BURTON's Coffee Houſe, *Charing Croſs*," titillates the potential consumer with the possibility of a personal encounter with the book's notorious subject at one of these watering holes. The same is true later in the century with the 1768 publication of William Donaldson's novel *Sapskull*, which, contrary to custom, boasts in the imprint that it can be purchased near a tavern: "Printed for J. Williams, No. 38, next the *Mitre* Tavern, *Fleet-Street*." Pseudononymously authored "BY SOMEBODY," and fronted by a cartoon of the back of the author's head, this comic novel makes no pretensions to high art and comfortably usurps the imprint as satirical space. The *Sapskull* imprint's self-consciousness is self-evident: London has, by midcentury, begun to adopt numerical addresses and Williams's establishment may now be found by its street number alone. The mention of a tavern is gratuitous – mere rhetorical flourish.

Of course, contorted formulations for proximity are also found in the imprints of non-fiction. Indeed, the variant "a little without *Temple Barr*" (a modification of the directive on Defoe's *A New Voyage* "without *Temple-Bar*") is found, for example, upon the title pages of science books, including Hooke's famous *Micrographia* (1667) (Figure 3.5). The *Micrographia* imprint reminds us of three things relevant to our exploration of imprints. First, these formulations had an extensive history, dating as far back as the sixteenth century. What strikes us as a vivid or deviant form of address, bursting with creative potential, might be dismissed by an eighteenth-century consumer as conventional and unworthy of close scrutiny. Secondly, although these addresses are evasive, they are not misleading. Neither printer nor publisher could afford to compromise an imprint's utility for long. Thirdly, and as Adrian Johns has demonstrated, the gentrification of publishing is neither confined to the novel nor indeed to the eighteenth century. As Johns argues for that category of science books represented by the *Micrographia*, rhetorical strategies that elevate, refine, and authorize are a routine element of the hand-press publishing business and served to create the modern-day notion of the book as a stable vehicle of authoritative information.³⁶ When the early novel participates in the routine self-fashioning that takes place on a book's title page, print culture extends it a hermeneutic space outside of its central text to fashion, not merely the trade writ large, but the individual book which that space labels. By extension, every novel's title page shapes the genre in its own image.

FIGURE 3.5
Title page to Robert Hooke's *Micrographia* (1667).

Bearing the *Micrographia*'s caveats in mind, let us return to the detail of the novel's imprints. Because of the iconography of the shop signs that also constitute, in the absence of street numbers, a legitimate feature of a publisher's address, inevitably interpretive inferences arise (even if these are utterly mistaken).

A novel published under the sign of "the *Bible* and *Crown*," "the *King's Arms*," "Plato's Head," or "the *Rofe*" may seem to describe itself by means of an iconic label.[37] Many such signs were, of course, like the fixed street numbers that subsequently replaced them, utterly unrelated to the quality and kind of literature sold under them – generically genteel. Yet they were by no means fixed. The shop signs of eighteenth-century booksellers already reflect the relatively recent affectations of the developing print culture: at the start of the previous century the shop signs displayed by printers and booksellers were less supercilious in their choice of iconography and might easily have been mistaken for the markings of an alehouse. For example, the works of Ben Jonson were purchased between 1609 and 1631 at legitimate print houses and bookshops displaying the animal signs of: "the Tigers head"; "the Spred Eagle", "the Beare"; and "the greene Dragon."[38] Peter W. M. Blayney has, in fact, used the signage of such imprints to map the bookshops clustered in one area of London from 1545 to 1675. If "Paul's Cross Churchyard" offers a representative cross-section of contemporary publishing practices, Blayney's unique cartography of this precinct suggests that the seventeenth-century bookshop was marked by flamboyance. In 1640, the row of adjoining bookshops located in St. Paul's Churchyard, between the establishments of the Marigold and the Three Pigeons, presented a consumer with a motley menagerie of painted signs: an image of a Brazen Serpent hung alongside the sign of the Parrot, followed by the Ship, Angel, Black Bear, Crane, White Greyhound, Rose, and Green Dragon. And whereas Blayney's initial map for 1545 shows that 25 percent of the booksellers along the yard were "not known to have used signs," trading under their own name, bookshops designated by eye-catching signage almost exclusively populate the yard after 1600.[39] At the turn of the next century, however, when the playful alehouse-like signs of seventeenth-century publishing eventually give way to a more refined iconography, new adjustments in signage reflect print culture's evolving sensibility.

Not only does this backward glance at the history of the printer's shop sign hint at the slow Augustan gentrification of the publisher's signage and accompanying imprint; some eighteenth-century printers made sudden and radical alterations to the iconography of their address. For example, in 1735, at the close of his infamous pamphlet war with Alexander Pope, Edmund Curll deliberately changed his sign from the respectable "The Dial and Bible" to the audacious "Pope's Head."[40] He even had wooden ornaments made to order, so that he could mark his publications, catalogues, and advertisements with an unflattering likeness of his enemy, trophy-like, at the head of his page (Figure 3.6).[41]

If, as the change in Curll's signage suggests, consumers (then as now) paid attention to shop signs, some authors and publishers may even have sought

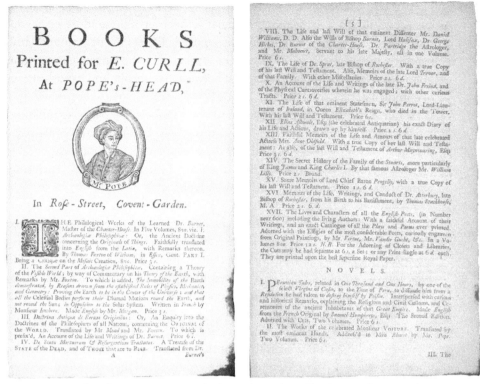

FIGURE 3.6 Advertisement pages attached to Edmund Curll's edition of *Love and Artifice* (1734), attributed to William Fitzmaurice Kelly.

collaborative bookseller arrangements that made for fitting combinations. The title page to the first edition of *Lasselia: Or, the Self-Abandon'd. A Novel. Written by Mrs. Eliza Haywood* (1724), for example, bears a relief image of a winged cupid, armed with bow and quiver, just above an imprint that lists one of the vendors as "S. CHAPMAN, at the *Angel* in *Pall-Mall*." Here the title's device (Chapman's shop sign adapted as an actual ornament) harbors a mnemonic function, since Haywood's growing reputation for amorous tales may have helped a consumer to remember her new book was sold at a location bearing the sign of a Cupid. Similarly, it may be more than mere coincidence that a first edition of *Robinson Crusoe* could be purchased "at the *Ship* in *Pater-Nofter-Row*." Defoe, usually so promiscuous in his professional associations, retains the proprietor of "*the Ship*" as the bookseller-publisher for both of *Crusoe*'s subsequent sequels.[42] Is it immaterial that his 1725 edition of *A New Voyage Round the World* bears the imprint "Printed for A. BETTESWORTH, at the *Red-Lyon*, in *Pater-Nofter-Row*; and W. MEARS, at the *Lamb*, without *Temple-Bar*"? Or does the familiar iconographic pairing of the *Lyon* and "seely"

Lamb reveal a religious agenda behind the façade of a mercantile voyage? Any answer would, I admit, be purely speculative. Yet even if these addresses do not resonate as religious iconography, the contrary figures of the lion and lamb neatly match the extremes of fortune encountered by the narrative's merchant sailors who find themselves cast about between the bucolic and brutish shores of commerce.

As hinted by the signage in Haywood's and Defoe's title pages, graphic signifiers may, to a limited extent, lurk almost anywhere on a novel's title page. The next section will explore further those elements of a novel's paper label that have proved the most resistant to editorial intervention and reprinting, namely the title, the subtitle, and the epigraph.

As they often resurface on subsequent editions, these are the longest-lived characteristics of the early novel's title page and exert the greatest impact upon interpretation. Like the frontispieces that many of them faced, the title and epigraph on a book's label also helped the genre to negotiate questions of authority, canonicity, and identity – in addition to (mis)guiding the reader's expectations.

Gérard Genette's work on titles can serve as a starting point. In *Paratexts*, Genette uses big brush strokes to paint the history of book titles from the late fifteenth century to the present day. In his treatment of the eighteenth-century novel, he suggests that title pages followed a long-at-the-beginning-of-the-century, short-at-the-end trajectory. Long titles, such as the original synopsis title of *Robinson Crusoe*, were, Genette concludes, a "fashion" that "seems to have died out early in the nineteenth century."[43] As well as the length of the titles themselves, Genette tracks two other title page features pertinent to the eighteenth-century novel's paratexts as signals of identity and authority: genre indications (what does the early novel call itself?) and epigraphic quotations. In respect of genre indications, Genette observes that novels "avoided flaunting a status Aristotle had never heard of, and contrived to suggest their genre status more indirectly by way of parageneric titles in which the words *history, life, memoirs, adventures, voyages,* and some others generally played a role."[44] As for epigraphs, Genette locates "scarcely any" in the "major novels" of the eighteenth century and points to the gothic novel as "the channel by which epigraphs in large numbers get into prose narrative."[45] These trajectories are broadly accurate, although individual novels from the 1750s frequently complicate Genette's brief history.

For not all early prose fictions participate directly, like *Robinson Crusoe* and *Moll Flanders*, in the tradition of the summary title, borrowing unreflectingly from the stylistic and titulary conventions of established genres to package and name themselves so as to avoid flaunting their own novelty. Some early fictions, in fact, used short titles to distinguish themselves from other genres and emphasise their innovation. Both William Congreve's *Incognita: or, Love and Duty Reconciled. A Novel* (1692) and Eliza Haywood's best-selling *Love in Excess; or, the Fatal Enquiry: A Novel* (1719–20) highlight their self-proclaimed modernity and originality by annexing the label "novel" to their (comparatively) pithy titles. Yet, despite the popularity and high-profile nature of these early uses of the term (*Love in Excess* can, along with its almost exact contemporary, *Robinson Crusoe*, lay claim to being one of the most popular works of eighteenth-century English fiction), the mainstream adoption of the label "novel" did not occur until the latter decades of the eighteenth century.[46] However, it is in the 1740s that what we now term novels begin to be acknowledged as the "new species of writing" (so-called by both Richardson and Fielding). The exact moment of the English novel's speciation continues to be energetically debated, but most major studies of the eighteenth-century novel share a guiding assumption that locates the synthesis of the mature genre arising out of the 1740s rivalry between Richardson and Fielding.[47] Hunter views the 1750s novel as the transitional period, locating there (slightly later than Watt and McKeon) the genre's defining moment of self-awareness: "By the 1750s . . . [t]he phenomenon [of the novel] was real, its characteristic features were (if not often articulated) abundantly clear, and its authors and readers knew they were participating in a cultural event of major proportions even if they didn't know what to call it."[48] Thus, although some late-seventeenth-century or early-eighteenth-century authors, such as Congreve and Haywood, labeled their stories "novels," theirs, demonstrates Hunter, are not the forms that best exemplify our use of that term. Derived from the French *roman* and the Italian *novelle*, the labels *romances* and *novels* "loosely" attached themselves in this period to any long prose fiction with doubtful claims to veracity.[49] Until quite late in the century, then, these terms were wielded by some critics as markers of triviality. Haywood's wide-ranging fame as "Mrs. Novel" (as Fielding dubbed her in 1730 in *The Author's Farce*) may actually have delayed the acceptance of the term "novel" to signify the genre that Fielding awkwardly insists, as late as 1742, upon defining in *Joseph Andrews* as "a comic Epic-Poem in Prose" and that he still worries about distinguishing from the "Swarm of Foolish Novels, and monstrous Romances" in *Tom Jones* in 1749.

With the label "novel" co-opted by amatory pens such as Haywood's, the title pages of subsequent fictions searched, as we saw in the Defoe titles, for other labels they could adopt or adapt. Eventually the novel, unsurprisingly, turns to the convention of the synopsis title for a space in which it can define itself without reference to traditional genre indications such as "life" and "adventures." For example, that hinge text between the fantastical stories of the pre-novel and the ever-increasing realism of the mature novel, *Pamela* (1740),

FIGURE 3.7
Title page to Richardson's first edition of *Pamela* (1740).

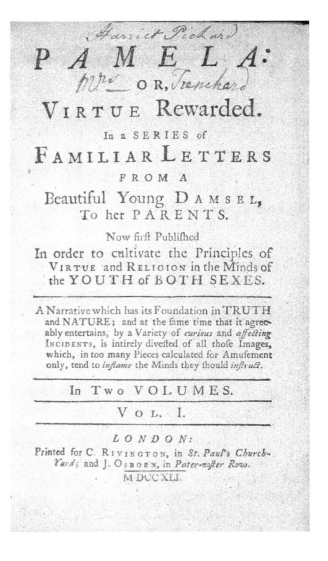

lacks a genre indication on its title page. Instead, printer-author Richardson seizes upon the conventional glossing function of summary titles to provide a preliminary, pre-narrative, interpretation and definition of his book. While *Pamela*'s title is, like that of *Robinson Crusoe* and other predecessors, long, it is not "simple in status" – as Genette judges the fashion.[50] To begin with, the full title of *Pamela* interprets the story in addition to describing it (Figure 3.7). The phrase "OR, VIRTUE Rewarded" already explicates "*PAMELA*" and by promising a morally just ending guides a reader into an interpretation of the work. The title does more than name and summarize, a task essentially completed by the first full stop: the remainder of the title demarcates the audience and literary rules of the new "Narrative." Richardson's title page directs itself to an audience of young men and women (and, implicitly, their parents) and aided by typographical emphasis stakes out the territory of realism for the accompanying fiction ("A Narrative which has its Foundation in TRUTH and NATURE"). It also defines the novel's didactic goal, "to cultivate the Principles of VIRTUE and RELIGION in the Minds of the YOUTH of BOTH SEXES," thus promising a high moral utility. Yet, although the phrase "In a SERIES of FAMILIAR LETTERS" conveys the book's epistolary mode, Richardson's title page lacks a traditional genre indication. Only the words "FROM A Beautiful Young DAMSEL" indubitably mark the text as a fiction in the tradition of Romance. Rather than borrow the labels of existing genres, as others did before him, Richardson – who evidently also wishes to distinguish his work from contemporary pulp and amatory fiction ("is intirely diveſted of all thoſe Images, which, in too many Pieces calculated for Amuſement only, tend to *inflame* the Minds they ſhould *inſtruct*") – removes conventional genre indications from his title page and uses the space to define the boundaries, audience, and aims of his nameless mode. In 1742 *Joseph Andrews* offers a slightly less prolix demarcation of the genre with a title that defines through association: "THE HISTORY OF THE ADVENTURES OF *JOSEPH ANDREWS*, And of his FRIEND Mr. *ABRAHAM ADAMS*. Written in Imitation of The *Manner* of CERVANTES, Author of *Don Quixote*." If it were not for the fact that readers were meant to recognize "Andrews" as Pamela's maiden name (another naming device with which Fielding defines his project by association) the title of Fielding's fiction could hardly be more distinct from Richardson's. The "species" desperately needed a classification.

In the wake of *Joseph Andrews*, the novel temporarily resolves its identity crisis by settling on the label "history" as the preferred genre indication. Shorter titles result, as authors and publishers move toward an agreed-upon cultural shorthand.[51] In naming his subsequent novels Richardson (forever the "poor pruner") abridges his titles somewhat by reverting to a traditional indication of genre: "**CLARISSA.** OR THE HISTORY OF A YOUNG LADY: Comprehending *The moſt* Important Concerns *of* Private LIFE. And particularly ſhewing, The DISTRESSES that may attend the Miſconduct Both of PARENTS and CHILDREN, In Relation to MARRIAGE" (1748) and "THE **HISTORY** OF SIR CHARLES GRANDISON. IN A SERIES of LETTERS Published from the ORIGINALS, By the Editor of PAMELA and CLARISSA" (1754). In an early modulation towards the titulary brevity Genette locates in the novels of Austen and Sir Walter Scott, mid-century novel titles shorten significantly, once "history" becomes the novel's dominant genre indicator. Even Eliza Haywood, who between 1720 and 1748 promiscuously borrows the terms *novel*, *memoirs*, *adventures*, *life*, and *progress*, for some of her fictions, follows suit with three consecutive "histories" crisply named: *The History of Cornelia* (1750), *The History* *of Miss Betsy Thoughtless* (1751), and *The History of Jemmy and Jenny Jessamy* (1752).⁵² And while Henry Fielding seems relatively indecisive about labels in the multi-tagged *Joseph Andrews*, he seems much more certain in "THE HIS-TORY OF TOM JONES, A FOUNDLING" (1749). With *Tom Jones* Fielding breaks the novel's conventions of anonymity and, in essence, becomes one of the genre's earliest claims of brand. In 1751, the prominently placed phrase "BY *Henry Fielding*, Efq;" seems to render any further genre indication for plain "AMELIA" superfluous.

There is a corollary to this neat and tidy titular trajectory. Just as the 1750s witness the stabilization of the novel's titular conventions, the decade also, paradoxically, witnesses the re-explosion of genre categories on title pages. This, I believe, is due to the decade's awareness of having now witnessed the birth of the novel, of living through what Hunter styles a "cultural event of major proportions." For, whereas Genette sees a consistent pattern of genre indications and a slow diminution across the century's title pages to novels, I see a deliberate reversal of these trends in the 1750s- a self-conscious and mocking mid-century return to the early-century's titulary conventions. Francis Coventry with *The History of Pompey the Little: Or, The Life and Adventures of a Lap-Dog* (1751); Tobias Smollett with *The Adventures of Peregrine Pickle. In Which are included, Memoirs of a Lady of Quality* (1751)⁵³; Charlotte Lennox with *The Life of Harriot Stuart. Written by Herself* (1751) and *The Female Quixote; Or the Adventures of Arabella* (1752)⁵⁴; Sarah Fielding and Jane Collier with *The Cry: A New Dramatic Fable* (1754); Samuel Johnson with *The Prince of Abissinia. A Tale* (1759); and Laurence Sterne with *The Life and Opinions of Tristram Shandy, Gentleman* (first installment, 1759) – these 1750s novelists wink at the newly established conventions by returning to outdated and widely diverging genre indicators in their titles.

In addition to returning to the Defoe-esque genre indication of "Surprifing LIFE *and* ADVENTURES," Hannah Snell's *The Female Soldier* (1750) also cooks up a spoof with the traditional recipe of the synoptic title (Figure 3.8). Once the novel seizes upon a dominant titular convention, it almost immediately challenges this accepted way of packaging itself. As anyone searching a database of eighteenth-century books will have noticed, it remains very difficult, long after 1750, to determine by its original title whether a text is or is not a novel. This difficulty remains not merely because the genre's titular claims to historicity risk confusion with other types of book, but because many novels so freely and promiscuously continue to deploy a variety of traditional genre indications well past the century's midway point. Many of the 1750s titles name stories that are self-mocking or offer satirical commentaries on the by-then-established conventions of the genre-not-yet-called-the-novel. The common denominator on the title pages of mid-century novels is, therefore, not the specific genre

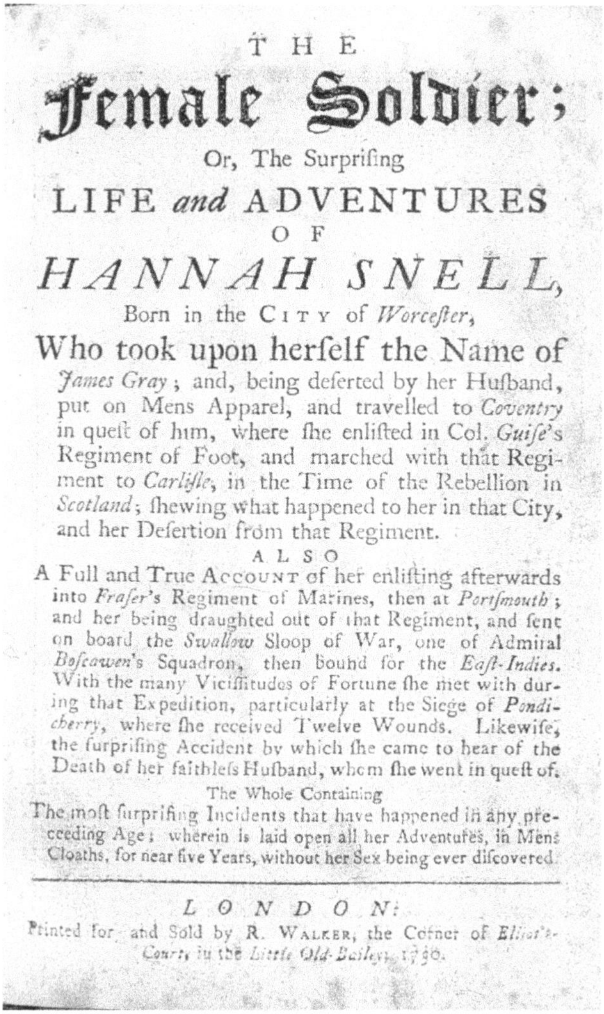

FIGURE 3.8 Title page to Hannah Snell's *The Female Soldier* (1750).

> THE
> **Female Soldier;**
> Or, The Surprising
> LIFE *and* ADVENTURES
> OF
> *HANNAH SNELL,*
> Born in the CITY of *Worcester*,
> Who took upon herself the Name of *James Gray*; and, being deserted by her Husband, put on Mens Apparel, and travelled to *Coventry* in quest of him, where she enlisted in Col. *Guise's* Regiment of Foot, and marched with that Regiment to *Carlisle*, in the Time of the Rebellion in *Scotland*; shewing what happened to her in that City, and her Desertion from that Regiment.
> ALSO
> A Full and True ACCOUNT of her enlisting afterwards into *Fraser's* Regiment of Marines, then at *Portsmouth*; and her being draughted out of that Regiment, and sent on board the *Swallow* Sloop of War, one of Admiral *Boscawen's* Squadron, then bound for the *East-Indies*. With the many Vicissitudes of Fortune she met with during that Expedition, particularly at the Siege of *Pondicherry*, where she received Twelve Wounds. Likewise, the surprising Accident by which she came to hear of the Death of her faithless Husband, whom she went in quest of.
> The Whole Containing
> The most surprising Incidents that have happened in any preceeding Age; wherein is laid open all her Adventures, in Mens Cloaths, for near five Years, without her Sex being ever discovered.
>
> LONDON:
> Printed for and Sold by R. WALKER, the Corner of *Elliot's*-Court, in the *Little Old-Bailey*, 1750.

indications themselves (although "HISTORY" dominates), but the shared self-consciousness about a rapidly coalescing set of conventions attached to the packaging of a now autonomous genre.

One can see the self-conscious return to traditional titular convention in, for example, the complete title of the anonymously published *Ephraim Tristram Bates* (1756), which like *The Female Soldier* exploits the tendency of early novelists to use titles as plot summaries.[55] The *Bates* title takes this tendency to its extreme with an abstract that approaches an independent narrative (Figure 3.9). The *Bates* title ridicules through caricature one early characteristic of popular novelistic title pages, namely their tendency towards excess, and perhaps also the conceit of authorial control behind their construction. This

FIGURE 3.9
Title page to *The Life and Memoirs of Ephraim Tristram Bates* (1756).

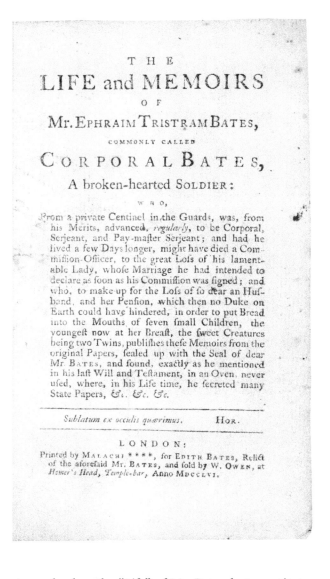

protracted title does not merely gloss the "Life" of <u>Mr</u>. Bates, but constitutes the whole of the independent autobiography of his common-law wife. The introductory note "To the Reader" explains that owing to the specifications of her husband's will, Edith Bates has been "forbid joining the least Little to these memoirs . . . only in the Title Page, which he had, some how or other unwarily omitted" (iii). Thus, although this title appears to cohere to explanatory convention, it actually represents a narrative, that of the self-styled Mrs. Bates, that is wholly distinct from the voice of the central text. We glean from the constituent components of the title page that Edith Bates is utterly overwhelmed by financial distresses and hopes that the proceeds of this self-financed text will alleviate her fiscal grief. The text of the prolix title elides death and debt: "his lamentable Lady . . . who, to make up for the Loſs of ſo dear an Huſband, and her Penſion." The ironical epigraphic selection lifts a phrase about mournful loss from Horace's reflections on the false god of Mammon, a particularly inappropriate source text on this occasion. Even the imprint at the foot of the page asserts financial hardship: here the unusual aposiopesis of the imprint underscores Edith's debts by mysteriously hiding the printer-publisher's identity behind the faint suggestion of a Jewish moneylender: "Printed by MALACHI ****, for EDITH BATES, Relict of the aforeſaid Mr. BATES, and ſold by W. OWEN, at *Homer's Head, Temple-bar*, Anno MDCCLVI". Various doubled genres – two lives, two memoirs, two wills (Mr. Bates's legal document and Mrs. Bates's autonomous desires), and two autobiographies – compete in the novel's text and paratext.

The satirical titulary habits of the 1750s did not always, of course, express themselves through prolixity. For example, the title page of Kidgell's 1755 novel *The Card* refuses, as we saw earlier with the frontispiece, to explicate the text it precedes (Figure 3.10). Here the title page holds the print conventions of titular nomenclature up for scrutiny and ridicule. The full title of *The Card* is just that, *The Card*. In violation of the titular practices of the day, there is no subtitle, no summary, no genre indication – no hint of explanation. The imprint, too, shrouds the text in palpable mystery: "Printed for the MAKER." Aside from the accompanying colored frontispiece, whose indeterminacy has already been discussed, the only element of excess accompanying the title is the baroque typography of the word "**CARD**" The ornate typography of the title satirizes conventional summary and explicatory titles by turning the name of Kidgell's novel into an illustration of itself. Usually reserved for alphabet letters in picture books or poster-sized advertisements, woodblock characters such as these rarely appear on title pages of contemporary books. The only genre in which the title's ornamental letters might appear of a piece with print convention is that of eighteenth-century juvenile literature. The link between juvenile literature and the novel is reinforced on Kidgell's title page with the name of the bookseller, J[ohn] NEWBERY, a publisher of early children's books.[56] Hence, while Richardson's titular claim in *Pamela* to be addressing the "YOUTH" was intended to assert the novel's moral authority at a time when the demarcation between literature for adults and literature for children remained vague, the graphic gesture on this "illustrated" title page uses the implied link to a juvenile audience to query the genre's status as well as its by-then conventional packaging and self-presentation. In light of the fact that the narrative of Kidgell's epistolary satire targets the Richardsonian novel, the anonymous contemporary reviewer attributes the "author's choice of his title" to a critique of epistolary prolixity:

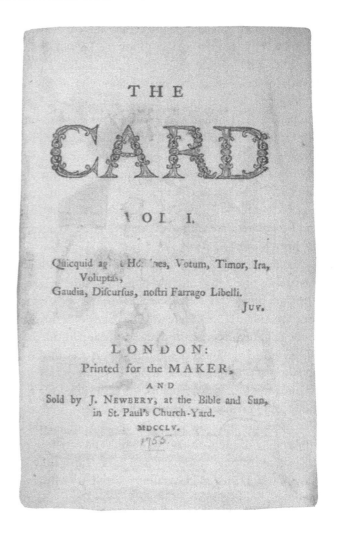

FIGURE 3.10
Title page to John Kidgell's *The Card* (1755).

His design, in our opinion, is to expose the spun-out superfluity of female chit-chat, which we meet with in some late productions of the epistolary kind: if so, what title more proper than the *Card*, which is now become the *common* vehicle of correspondence among the *ladies*?[57]

The Card's paratextual puzzle would not be ill at ease in an exhibit of Modernist art, perhaps as an eighteenth-century companion piece to Magritte's *Ceci n'est pas une pipe* – with the added twist that the frontispiece, if torn out, is exactly what the title purports it to be.

The novel's titles grow quieter and more sedate in the wake of the intensely experimental 1750s. Although titles, of course, continue to serve as paratextual glosses on the texts they name, the novel no longer needs to announce itself so boisterously, nor gloss its literary identity or moral authority with quite the same force. When the lengthy summary title occasionally reemerges it is as a pastiche, used, as Genette judges, "ironically or affectionately" by "authors imbued with a sense of tradition and inclined to wink" – English authors such as Dickens and Thackeray.[58]

The self-consciousness of the title page of the 1750s novel is also apparent in its deployment of the epigraph. When considering epigraphs, Genette finds that "in the major novels of the eighteenth-century" there are

> scarcely any epigraphs except at the head of *Tom Jones* ("Mores hominum multorum vidit" [he saw the customs of many men], with no indication of the source [*Ars poetica* 141–42]) and *Tristram Shandy* ("It is not things themselves that disturb men, but their judgements about these things," from Epictetus' *Encheiridion*).[59]

While Genette may have missed a few, including the previously discussed mottoes on the frontispieces to Swift's *Travels* and the epigraphs at the head of each of the three volumes of Haywood's *Love in Excess* (both best-sellers must qualify as "major" works even if not full-fledged "novels") his generalization seems largely true.[60] Canon-revisionism and semantics aside, few of the best-known eighteenth-century fictions have epigraphs. This absence of epigraphs is in itself noteworthy. As Genette demonstrates, the epigraph is decidedly a mark of eighteenth-century print culture. Genette finds "no trace" of epigraphs used on title pages to books "before the seventeenth century" and suggests that it is only in the eighteenth century that "the custom of using epigraphs becomes more widespread."[61] As the lines from Horace on the *Micrographia*'s title page imply, and Johns's larger claims contextualize, the epigraph partakes of the book industry's rhetorical strategies to authorize and gentrify print – even in the area of science. Genette's assessment that this practice is "widespread" is, in fact, an understatement. From the panoply of epigraphs printed at the tops of periodicals, such as each original sheet of the *Tatler* and *Spectator*, to the epigraphs fronting such diverse literary projects as Pope's *Rape of the Lock* (1714) and Johnson's *Dictionary* (1755), eighteenth-century print culture abounds with epigraphs. Figure 1.1 in the first chapter, for example, shows how that issue of *The Tatler* which contained Swift's *Shower* bore an apt selection from Juvenal. Epigraph usage in literary works was, indeed, so ubiquitous that Fielding in *The Author's Farce* (1730) can poke fun at a lively Grubstreet trade in the adaptation of Latin and Greek mottoes.[62] Why does the novel, otherwise eager to plunder contemporary print of its authoritative icons, largely avoid this conventional gesture of literary authority? The novel's motivation to shun

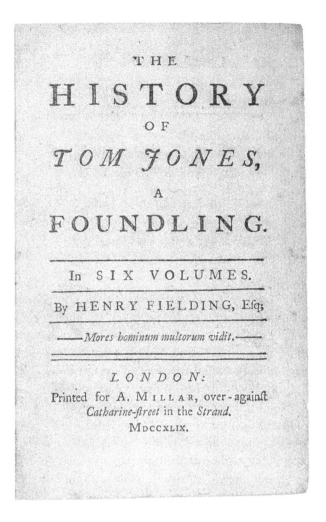

FIGURE 3.11 Title page to Henry Fielding's *Tom Jones* (1749).

the epigraph comes better into focus when we look at the century's middle decade, a time when the genre briefly trials this convention.

It cannot be insignificant that the "major" exceptions to the absence of epigraphs noted by Genette bookend the 1750s, with Fielding's 1749 *Tom Jones* at the front and Sterne's initial 1759 installment to *Tristram Shandy* at the close.[63] Although not all of the epigraph-adorned fictions published between these literary milestones qualify as major works, something happens in the self-conscious 1750s to complicate Genette's observations about this paratextual locus of authority and tradition. Actually it is probably not Fielding, but Smollett who, with *Roderick Random* in 1748, launched the mid-century's epigraphic fad (Figures 3.11 and 3.12).[64] In the wake of *Roderick Random* and *Tom Jones*, a number of fictions adorn their title pages with epigraphs borrowed from ancient writers of satire and epic, including:

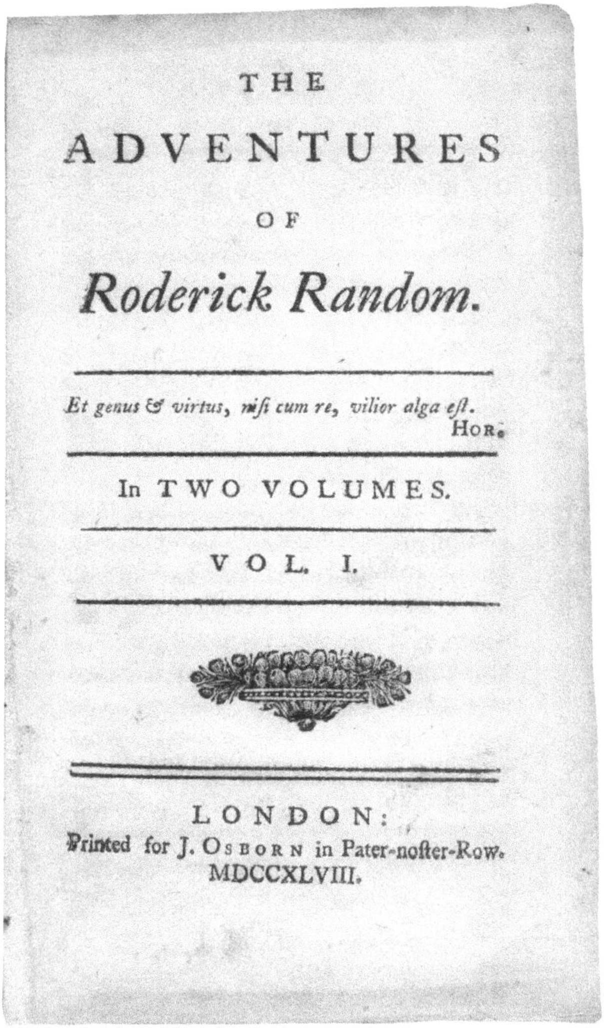
THE
ADVENTURES
OF
Roderick Random.

Et genus & virtus, niſi cum re, vilior alga eſt.
HOR.

In TWO VOLUMES.

VOL. I.

LONDON:
Printed for J. OSBORN in Pater-noſter-Row.
MDCCXLVIII.

FIGURE 3.12 Title page to second edition of Tobias Smollett's *Roderick Random* (1748).

Tobias Smollett's *Peregrine Pickle* (1751)[65]
Francis Coventry's *Pompey the Little* (1751)[66]
Henry Fielding's *Amelia* (1752)[67]
Sarah Fielding's and Jane Collier's *The Cry* (1754)[68] (see Figure 3.13)
John Kidgell's *The Card* (1755)[69] (See Figure 3.10)
The unattributed *Bates* (1756)[70] (See Figure 3.9).

Sterne's initial installment of *Tristram Shandy* in 1759 concludes this line of epigraph-users with – following Fielding's early lead in *Amelia* – another epigraph in elite Greek lettering: Ταράσσει τους 'Ανθρώπους ὀυ τὰ Πράγματα, ἀλλὰ τὰ περὶ τῶν Πραγμάτων, Δόγματα (Genette translates it above: see

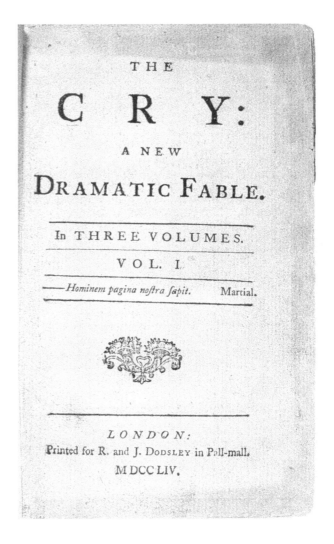

FIGURE 3.13
Title page to Sarah Fielding and Jane Collier's *The Cry* (1754).

page 85).[71] With Smollett and Fielding both twice affirming their epigraphic intent to stamp the novel as learned, the list of participants in this type of packaging is formidable. Unlike the circuitous and deceptive use of other front matter, the epigraphs chosen by these writers seem, on the whole, calculated as straightforward caste labels – signaling with borrowed authority the *gravitas* of the novel's literary heritage. Fewer writers from this decade appear content to use English epigraphs and, by extension, mark their novelistic projects as having a nationalist and populist appeal. A survey of all the mid-century fictions previously mentioned produces the following list of novels bearing epigraphs from English sources, a list which is as unimpressive as it is short:[72]

Sarah Fielding's *The Governess* (1749)[73]
Edward Kimber's *The Life and Adventures of Joe Thompson* (1750)[74]
William Goodall's *The Adventures of Capt. Greenland* (1752).[75]

It is from drama, particularly tragedy, that these B-grade novels select their epigraph of choice. Whether quoting Shakespeare, Pope, Dryden, or Congreve, the English epigraph links the novel to the theatre (interestingly, Henry Fielding avoids this titular link to the stage in spite of the many references to drama within his narratives). After the mid-1750s, the novel's short-lived penchant for epigraphs on titles becomes the target of some self-conscious ridicule. For example, in *The Anti-Gallican* (1757) Edward Long ridicules both the novel's continental borrowings as well as its Englishness with this epigraph: "*No* Smuggled, Pilfer'd *Scenes from* France *we ſhow*, / *He's* Engliſh, Engliſh, *Sirs, from Top to Toe.*"[76] A few years later, Charles Johnstone muddles "low" and "high" with a Shakespearean and Latin combination on the title page of *Chrysal; Or, the Adventures of a Guinea* (1760).[77]

The epigraph, briefly *de rigueur* during the 1750s, disappears from the mature novel's title page. Although the epigraph surfaces on the title pages of some late-century fiction, it moves, as Genette suggests, predominantly into the central text of the gothic and historical novel, as chapter headers in, for example, Anne Radcliffe's *Mysteries of Udolpho* (1794), Matthew Lewis's *The Monk* (1795), and the many novels of Sir Walter Scott. Although short-lived, in light of the paucity of epigraphs elsewhere in the early novel's history, the title pages of the 1750s novel constitute a veritable explosion of this paratextual gesture. Yet the 1750s come too late in the novel's genesis to be satisfactory as a late-acquired signal of literary authority (such may have been the effect achieved with Swift's and Haywood's early use of literary quotations in their front matter). While there exists a residual desire in some 1750s novelists to shore up their authority with ancient references, the epigraphic trend seems to come up against the decade's escalating self-consciousness about the way the emerging novel presents itself in printed form.[78] Unsurprisingly, when Smollett, the instigator of the novel's epigraph, publishes *The Adventures of Sir Launcelot Greaves* (1762), his title page is bare of epigraphic trimming.

Kidgell's *The Card* may exhibit in miniature the 1750s novel's larger interrogation of the epigraphic dynamic between paratext and central text, presentation and interpretation. Kidgell's novel contains a scene in which the literal meaning conveyed by a classical quotation is distinct from its visual significance within a text. During one of her garden walks, young Miss Evelyn discovers a poem pencilled on the walls of a gazebo. This amorous wall-sonnet concludes with a short quotation in Greek from Homer. While the anonymous sonnet is written in an unfamiliar hand and signed in a language Miss Evelyn cannot read, the very presence of what she terms "the Greek and Hebrew at the Bottom" reveals to her the identity of its author, her brother's tutor Mr. Molesworth:

> Miss *Evelyn* did not know the *Hand-writing* well enough to distinguish whose it was, but the under-written *Motto* she could discover to be no *modern* Language, and with the Help of a very little consideration, concluded from what Point of the Compass it came there. (1, 104)

Just as the mere presence of the foreign characters on the gazebo wall identifies for Miss Evelyn the author of the poem, the presence of the Latin quotation from Juvenal on Kidgell's title page attributes specific expectations to *The Card* – even for the non-classically educated reader. To even those readers who, like Miss Evelyn, cannot decipher its literal meaning, the mere presence of mottoes on title pages announces (arrogantly and often deceptively) the novel's scholarly qualifications. Miss Evelyn represents, like Isabel Archer after her, an unschooled and naïve reader who allows herself to be chiefly guided by the novel's architecture. As Genette concludes about the nineteenth-century epigraphs that appear at the heads of individual chapters, the "choices of author are more significant than the texts of the epigraphs themselves."[79] One does not need to read either Greek or Latin to gloss the presence of an epigraph in either tongue as an elitist caste label. But while the label is recognized by all, the meaning is accessible to only a few. For even if a smidgen of Latin or Greek unlocks the literal meaning of an epigraph (for example, a little Latin may discover the *Bates*'s epigraph as a mournful lament), only a familiarity with the fuller context of the passage from which the line is lifted (in the case of *Bates*, Horace's ode on the curse of Mammon) reveals to a very few the hidden joke or irony behind its selection. In other words, on every level (from naïve to elite) the novel's use of the epigraph is all about context, rather than text. Sterne's esoteric inclusion of the Greek characters on the first installment of *Tristram Shandy* smiles, along with Kidgell, upon the novel's many adolescent experiments with dressing itself "up" in the hand-me-downs of other print genres to appear more authoritative and serious. Now that the novel has reached young-adulthood, by mid-century, it can acknowledge those experiments as gimmickry and ridicule its own visual history and early graphic affectations.

In fact, many experiments with the novel's paratextual design lost their efficacy after the 1750s. Yet these early experiments with form are worth reconstructing – as the remaining chapters will show. In fact, the remaining chapters focus on specific experiments with the novel's design, rather than offer, as my initial chapters have done, a panorama of generic form. In particular, the various graphic designs authored and printed by Samuel Richardson deserve close scrutiny, both for their creative use of type and their impact upon contemporaries. After Richardson's two failed experiments with the illustration of *Pamela* – the Hogarth commission and the slowly selling sixth-edition engravings by Hayman and Gravelot – he abandons pictorial engraving, opting instead to apply the design tools available to him as master printer to the production of his subsequent fictions. Thus we turn in the next two chapters to a few neglected graphics moments in what is arguably the century's most important fiction, *Clarissa* (1748).

First, in all of the editions of *Clarissa* printed on Richardson's press an eighteenth-century reader would have encountered an engraved musical score. How their encounter with that single and singular page may have shaped a reading of the novel's story is my next subject.

CHAPTER 4

Clarissa's musical score

a novel's politics engraved on copper plate

> Of music! Then pray speak aloud. It is of all subjects my delight. I must have my share in the conversation, if you are speaking of music. There are few people in England, I suppose, who have more true enjoyment of music than myself, or a better natural taste. If I had ever learnt, I should have been a great proficient.
> – Lady Catherine De Bourgh in *Pride and Prejudice* (1813)[1]

> I am doatingly fond of music – passionately fond; – and my friends say I am not entirely devoid of taste;... I absolutely cannot do without music. It is a necessary of life to me;... Certainly I had been accustomed to every luxury at Maple Grove; but I did assure him that two carriages were not necessary to my happiness, nor were spacious apartments. "But," said I, "to be quite honest, I do not think I can live without something of a musical society. I condition for nothing else; but without music, life would be a blank to me."
> – Mrs. Elton in *Emma* (1816)[2]

Jane Austen places her greatest praise of music in the mouths of some of her most perverse caricatures of the female poseur. Yet Austen by no means dismisses the importance of music as a female accomplishment. She is careful to note, though never to dwell on, the musical proficiencies of all of her heroines. Indeed modest musical skills, skills that carefully avoid the self-indulgencies of the "great proficient," refract a heroine's personality and moral potential. In *Pride and Prejudice* Elizabeth Bennet's performance at the pianoforte is characteristically agreeable though lacking in maturity and dexterity: "But then I have always supposed it to be my own fault – because I would not take the trouble of practising."[3] Similarly, Anne Elliot's introverted playing in *Persuasion*, "although better than either of the Miss Musgroves," is so quietly unassuming as to go unnoticed, "giving pleasure only to herself."[4] Only when Anne undertakes the "office of musician" so that others can dance is she praised (perhaps too fulsomely) by Mr. and Mrs. Musgrove: "Well done, Miss Anne! very well done indeed! Lord bless me! how those little fingers of yours fly about!"[5] Lest such a remark be taken as a sign of Anne's musical abandon, Austen takes great pains to mitigate such a compliment to her heroine, carefully pointing out that it is Anne's kindness, rather than a showy style of playing, which solicits these warm acknowledgments.

When it comes to musical entertainments, Austen's women must know how to "perform with credit."[6] Although more than one man bestows the gift of a pianoforte upon his beloved songbird, men themselves are rarely seen to play or sing in Austen's world. If they do, it is immediate cause for suspicion, as in Frank Churchill's "surprise" performance at the Coles's dinner party, where his self-indulgence prompts Mr. Knightly's accusation "that fellow thinks of nothing but shewing off his own voice."[7] Musical performers must achieve a golden mean between feast and famine in order to receive the reader's approbation: in her heroines Austen carefully avoids either a connoisseurship that risks immodestly eliding talent and self-indulgence (as in Marianne Dashwood or Miss Fairfax) or a lack of skill that betrays mediocrity (as in the unfortunate Mary Bennet). Musical performance remains a female prerequisite in Austen's world, serving as an important calibration of a woman's ability to improve herself and triumph despite scant educational opportunities.

Austen's heroines, and the nineteenth-century ideals they embody, inherit their musical genes, at least in part, from their eighteenth-century forebears, many of whom betray and display their musical talents in novels.[8] Unsurprisingly, Samuel Richardson – of whom Austen was particularly fond – similarly made musical performance and appreciation a heroine's prerequisite. As a component of eighteenth-century daily life, music makes predictable appearances in all of Richardson's epistolary novels, though Richardson is perhaps slightly more fulsome than Austen in singing his heroines' praises when they perform. In *Pamela* Richardson's heroine entertains company with her "Singing and Dancing" and spinet playing[9]; in the sequel Richardson devotes a lengthy letter to the sensational spectacle of opera[10]; in *Clarissa* he gives the heroine's musical accomplishments prominent expression, even in the Will in which she bequeaths "my harpsichord, my chamber-organ, and all my music-books" to her cousin, Dolly Hervey[11]; and, in *Sir Charles Grandison*, Richardson insists that his heroine, Harriet Byron, can "play and sing" Mr. Handel's "fine air" with "ease," though she had "never but once before played it over."[12] In effect, Richardson consistently portrays musical education as an essential part of a young woman's aesthetic, spiritual, and cultural development. All of his heroines are schooled, albeit to differing degrees, in musical appreciation, reading and performance. Music in Richardson's novels is, as it continues to be for Austen, a traditional index of a woman's class and upbringing.[13] It is to be expected, therefore, that Richardson, who assumes a certain level of musical literacy across his readership, occasionally relies in his narratives on metaphors and terminology borrowed from the discourse of music. What is surprising is that on one occasion Richardson "borrows" the music itself, inserting it as an engraved folding plate into every edition of *Clarissa* over which he had control as printer-author (Figure 4.1). With the insertion of this engraved score into *Clarissa*, a graphic design which involved significant planning and expense, Richardson fuses the printed code of a piece of music with his own verbal text, calling particular attention to the performative aspects of his fiction, the book-making process, and the significant role music plays in the world of the novel.

Like so many of the early novel's graphic elements, the engraved score has receded from view in modern editions of *Clarissa*, which significantly transform, delete, or reposition this page of text.[14] Modern critical consideration of *Clarissa* has, probably as a result of this silent textual reshuffling, largely lost sight of the novel's musical score.[15] But, as Steven R. Price concurs, Richardson's engraved page of music constitutes an important experiment in graphic design.[16] Using his visual acumen as master printer, Richardson here places a scene's verbal text within a unique visual context in order to augment a particular interpretation of his fiction. Indeed, in its unusual combination of word and design, Richardson's musical page resembles, or anticipates, the work of Sterne. Like Sterne, Richardson violates a novel-reader's expectations by incorporating a familiar cultural artifact into the novel. And like Sterne's unconventional marbled page, Richardson's musical page calls attention to itself because it is visually and generically inconsistent with the rest of the novel's format; in Richardson's own words, "it was not expected."[17] The engraved musical score is, of course, unique precisely because it is music. The notes constitute a visual code for an auditory performance, bestowing upon this single page a hermeneutic three-dimensionality which the rest of Richardson's pages do not possess. Here Richardson overlaps three kinds of text: the visual text, or graphic design, of the oversized engraving; the verbal text of the fiction and the accompanying poem; and the auditory text of the musical score.

How are we to interpret this unique three-dimensional moment in *Clarissa*? And how did Richardson expect his contemporary readership to "read" this sheet of music as part of the novel's text? I will explore this strangely synesthetic moment by reconstructing the different facets of the page within the material context of eighteenth-century print. This cultural context is crucial to an understanding of the interpretive function of the singular "illustration." For like

FIGURE 4.1 Musical score folded closed (a) and opened out (b) from the first edition of Samuel Richardson's *Clarissa*, 7 vols. (1748), II, 50.

the marbled page in *Tristram Shandy*, Richardson's musical page alludes to the materiality of book-making. Just as Sterne's first readers would have recognized the marbled page as a misplaced feature of contemporary book production (the endpapers of a book inserted into the middle of the text), so Richardson's reader recognizes in the interpolated engraving features borrowed from a wide variety of printed musical scores. Building upon this readerly familiarity, Richardson uses the musical page to highlight Clarissa's attempts to define a feminine politics and to implicate the reader of the novel in that project.

The appearance of the score within the world of the fiction – the synesthetic moment's full narrative context – must be established first. The musical engraving appears when Clarissa, dreading her sacrifice to the despicable Roger Solmes on the altar of her family's ambition, retreats to her room to "compose [her] angry passions at [her] Harpsichord" (II, 50). In this scene she plays an original composition in which she sets to music a poem "not unsuitable to my unhappy situation" (II, 50). In the final paragraphs of a letter to Anna Howe, enclosing her music, Clarissa explains what prompted this musical exercise:

> *Eleven o'Clock at Night.*
> I HAVE been forced to try to compose my angry passions at my Harpsichord; having first shut close my doors and windows, that I might not be heard below. As I was closing the shutters of the windows, the distant whooting of the Bird of Minerva, as from the often-visited Woodhouse, gave the subject in that charming ODE to WISDOM, which does honour to our Sex, as it was written by one of it. I made an essay, a week ago, to set the three last Stanza's of it, as not unsuitable to my unhappy situation; and after I had re-perused the Ode, those were my Lesson: And, I am sure, in the solemn address they contain to the All-wise and All-powerful Deity, my heart went with my fingers.
> I inclose the Ode, and my effort with it. The subject is solemn: My circumstances are affecting; and I flatter myself, that I have not been quite unhappy in the performance. If it obtain your approbation, I shall be out of doubt: And should be still more assured, could I hear it tried by *your* voice and finger.
>
> (II, 50)

Clarissa then transcribes for Anna all but the last three stanzas of the poem *Ode to Wisdom*, which Richardson identifies as having been written "*By a LADY.*" This transcription is followed by a large copper-plate engraving containing the remaining stanzas of the *Ode*'s verbal text and Clarissa's musical setting.

Richardson printed four editions of *Clarissa* on his own press (in 1748, 1749, 1751 [in two formats], and 1759). In each of these editions he inserts the engraved music into this scene of the novel, almost as if the musical score substituted for an attendant illustration.[18] This striking non-pictorial engraving is unusual, even for the visually experimental printer-author Richardson. The elaborate sixth edition of *Pamela* (1742) with its twenty-nine engraved illustrations of rococo designs by Hayman and Gravelot, offers nothing akin to this musical engraving. Indeed, in the *Pamela* plates, the heroine's musical talents are not given any pictorial expression. Although in these plates we "see" Pamela engaged in many different rooms and domestic activities, no musical instrument or performance features in any of the pictured scenes. And although Richardson describes, in each of his novels, the musical "accomplishments" of his characters, nowhere else does he provide his readers with an actual score, a tangible record of compositional prowess. Thus the unique and emphatic depiction of the music in *Clarissa* suggests that music, although it features modestly in every one of his books, plays a different and more significant function there. The page is also unusual in its estimated production cost. If, as Angus Ross reports, Richardson "commissioned the music and had it engraved at considerable cost," he must have judged it an essential part of his text.[19] Richardson had likely lost money on the lavishly illustrated sixth edition of *Pamela*. Unsurprisingly, after 1742 Richardson abandoned the conventional illustrated book for a more economically prudent means of production. Indeed, bibliographer William Sale documents the printer-author's laborious efforts to reduce cost by minimizing the waste of paper (paper being the most expensive aspect of book production at this time) during the printing of *Clarissa*.[20] Given this drive to economize, the oversized musical engraving, the reverse of which is left wholly blank, seems decidedly lavish – a book-making decision which sacrifices economic criteria to artistic ones.

Unfortunately, previous critical consideration of this moment in the novel has dwelt, not on the artistic function of the musical score, but on the embarrassing story of Richardson's appropriation of *Ode to Wisdom*, a poem by the celebrated Bluestocking, Elizabeth Carter.[21] Richardson, it appears, lifted the ode from a circulating manuscript copy without Carter's knowledge or permission. Upon discovering her poem transposed into the pages of Richardson's new novel, Carter complained of "a proceeding so very ungenerous and unworthy of a man of reputation."[22] Richardson apologized, replying that he did not mean to offend "a lady, . . . the intention of my work being to do honor to the sex, to the best of my poor abilities."[23] Richardson's "faithful relation of the occasion of the trespass" appeased the irate Carter, with whom he eventually became friends.[24] But in addition to offering an uncharacteristically abashed image of their author, Richardson's letters to Carter evidence, above all, his obsessive involvement with the minutiae of his work's visual design. In one of the letters, he justifies his plagiarism by reference to the unique way in which he has inserted Carter's ode into his novel:

> I presumed not to make my character, though the principal one, claim it, only doing intentional honour to it, by setting it to music, which is done in a masterly manner. I caused it to be engraved and wrought singly, the more to distinguish it. And all this trouble I might have spared, and the expense with it, as, though the Ode would have been an ornament to any work, and an honour to any character, it was not expected.
>
> Upon the whole, give me leave to say that I was not, in this re-acknowledged trespass, governed by any low or selfish views.[25]

Richardson's primary aim in this letter is, of course, to absolve himself of unethical behavior. Thus Richardson claims that the act of doing "intentional honour to [the ode], by setting it to music" came at considerable personal "expense." The addition of the musical engraving must indeed have been troublesome and costly. Yet the setting does not merely, as Richardson claims, pay magnanimous "honour" to Carter's appropriated ode. Rather, it partakes of a visual strategy furthering Richardson's own interpretive intentions in his novel.

In the text of *Clarissa* Richardson reiterates the claim that the musical setting honors the poem; Clarissa insists that her music highlights the ode's denouement. And the musical page does indeed "distinguish" the ode's last three stanzas by rendering them in italic script as part of the engraved musical score. While it would have been far more conventional to provide a reader with the music at the beginning of the ode, thereby setting all its stanzas to music, Richardson chooses to engrave the final stanzas with musical accompaniment. In this manner, his "ornamentation" of the ode has built a visible as well as audible crescendo, emphasizing those passages Clarissa says she deems the most important moral "Lesson" of the poem. Yet the engraved score does not simply emphasize the moral philosophy of Carter's ode or even the poetic lyricism of the ode-turned-lyric. Rather, the music's presence in the novel underscores the performative qualities of the book of which the musical page is now a part. Even if a reader of the novel does not pause to actually play or sing Clarissa's composition, the elaborate presentation of this scene in the novel as a piece of sheet music underscores the dramatic possibilities inherent in the new genre. The musical page argues that, like an actual score, the novel may be (literally or figuratively) performed, read aloud, or – in this instance – even sung. Richardson's musical page reminds the reader that, although the new "species" of writing stimulates private reading and fosters an increasingly sequestered, even passive, audience, it nonetheless remains the kind of text which can be communally shared and enacted. The musical score thus calls attention to the act of reading itself.

As a page of text which highlights the activity of reading, the score also functions as a self-conscious interruption of the reading process. In the first three editions of *Clarissa*, the leaf of the musical score unfolds to more than twice the size of any other page in the novel. Thus, the music sheet disrupts established textual boundaries, physically extending the textual space of the novel outward past the established margins of the text. It is precisely the unexpected oversized format of the ode's graphic presentation that directs the reader's gaze to this moment in the novel. Like the protruding feather of Clarissa's concealed pen – which reveals to those searching her rooms "such of her hidden Stores [of writing implements] which," Clarissa predicts, "I intend they shall find" – the musical setting's protruding page flags this moment in the novel for Richardson's own audience (II, 307). By "distinguish[ing]" the ode with the engraved musical accompaniment, Richardson emphasizes a moment in his own text.

Richardson did not, of course, invent the folding illustration. Oversized, folding pictorial engravings and diagrams are not uncommon in eighteenth-century publications, particularly illustrated periodicals and reference books. Some contemporary prose fictions, histories, and travel books also sport folding maps, illustrations conventionally placed at the front of a work or volume. For example, both of Defoe's own 1719 sequels to *Robinson Crusoe*, known as the *Farther Adventures* and the *Serious Reflections*, originally included elaborate folding maps of the island at the front of each book. Although only the map of Laputa in the 1735 Faulkner edition is large enough to demand a fold, the five well-known maps in Swift's *Travels* similarly preface each of Gulliver's journeys. In fiction and non-fiction alike, folding pages supplement the verbal text with either an attendant illustration or, in the case of maps, a point of reference. The fact that eighteenth-century readers were familiar with folding engravings in other types of book does not diminish the element of surprise in *Clarissa*'s. Nor does the fact that the genre of the novel itself remained in some flux during the mid-century production of *Clarissa* complicate claims about the "unconventionality" of Richardson's musical illustration. The appearance of such a score in an Austen novel would, admittedly, have far less of a chance of disappearing into the ether of editorial intervention; the folding illustration is, after all, a frequent feature of the eighteenth-century book. What makes the appearance of the score in *Clarissa* noteworthy is not its ostensible violation of print convention, but its self-conscious adaptation of existing printing techniques. With this page Richardson imports an eclectic combination of oversized format, *in medias res* insertion, and musical content in an otherwise uniform piece of prose fiction. And, unlike the familiar folding map or pictorial illustration, the function of the musical score as part of the novel's text is not immediately apparent. The folding musical page in *Clarissa* thus asserts itself as a textual curiosity – a singular page which, despite its mimetic conceit and musical conventionality, aligns the novel not with the private epistle or even the epistolary novel but with the protean variety of contemporary print culture.

In calling attention to the novel as a physical artifact, the design of the musical page links it with other categories of mid-eighteenth-century books. Specifically, when Clarissa glosses her musical "essay" as a "Lesson," the visual rendering of her music in an engraved format invokes a contemporary reader's familiarity with the pedagogical genre of the musical "lesson book." A wide variety of so-called "suites of lessons" for the harpsichord was available to a mid-eighteenth-century consumer. These collections of (often engraved) musical exercises bear titles such as: *Six Suites of Easy Lessons for the Harpsichord or Spinet*; *[T]he Most Celebrated Lessons Collected and Fitted to the Harpsichord*; *A Collection of Lessons for the Harpsichord*; and *Six Sonatas or Lessons for the Harpsichord*.[26] Richardson's verbal–visual allusion to the musical "lesson book" helps to underscore the didactic function he assigns musical education. By explicitly locating in Clarissa's musical exercise a moral "lesson," while simultaneously rendering this moral in a published format reminiscent of musical textbooks and pedagogical miscellanies, Richardson equates musical instruction with instruction in moral conduct. In the engraved plate of music, Clarissa's moral "essay" and her musical composition become indistinguishable "lessons."

The music's moral pedagogy is augmented by its value as self-expression. In addition to evoking the pedagogical "lesson book," the engraved format of the musical score visually aligns Clarissa's composition with genteel songs of the Vauxhall tradition, reinforcing a particular characterization of the heroine. Clarissa's musical composition is, like her letters, an act of self-authorship. Literally born out of an attempt to compose her*self* ("I HAVE been forced to try to compose my angry passions at my Harpsichord"), Clarissa's musical exercise yields a form of textual self-expression which supplements her epistolary autobiography. In a sense, the musical page offers the reader a companion-piece to Clarissa's tenth "Mad Paper," that other uncommonly printed page in the novel.[27] While Richardson graphically presents his heroine at her most "composed" in the musical score, he later conveys her post-rape fragmentation and psychological decomposition in the layout of this "mad" page. Richardson is careful to present Clarissa's initial moment of graphic self-authoring in the most favorable light. Hiding his didactic visual strategy behind the convenient conceit of mimetic transcription, Richardson uses the social class that the professionally engraved score of Clarissa's music evokes to augment his heroine's respectability and noble character. Vauxhall songs and fashionable ballads would often – like Clarissa's score – be engraved "singly" and sold in "loose half sheet" format for "a penny a-page" (Figures 4.2 and 4.3).[28] Thus a contemporary reader's prior familiarity with music in this popular format explains the singularity of the musical score in the novel. In the fiction, as in the real world, the reader encounters genteel songs "singly," engraved upon individual half-sheets. The quality of Richardson's engraving nearly approaches that of what is arguably the most elaborately embellished collection of fashionable music in the century: George Bickham's *Musical Entertainer* of 1740, a lavishly illustrated folio reminiscent of a modern coffee-table book (Figure 4.4).[29]

Conversely, Richardson's large, engraved page, precisely because it is engraved, would never be mistaken for a selection from the letterpress music found in contemporary periodicals or the less-expensive duodecimo collections of popular songs (Figures 4.5 and 4.6).[30] Already dissimilar in appearance, these letterpress collections of "merry" tunes also do not resemble Clarissa's composition in musical style, complexity, or subject-matter; instead, they are filled with robust music of the type favored by Squire Western in *Tom Jones*.[31] Similarly, Clarissa's music visually disassociates itself even from the middle-class genre of pastoral song books, collections of popular lyrics with titles such as *The Hive*, *The Robin*, *The Linnet*, and *The Thrush*.[32] Such pastoral collections of "the most celebrated songs" lack scores like *Clarissa*'s, for they offer only the verbal text of lyrics meant to be sung to well-known tunes. Situated within this visual spectrum of contemporary music, the graphic design of the novel's score distinguishes it from provincial or popular music, reinforcing instead Clarissa's genteel and ambitious self-presentation.

Musically, Clarissa's song also augments the characterization of the heroine, evoking an educated, almost aristocratic, milieu. The march-like opening; the stately *Andante* tempo; the complexity of the harmonies; the movements in quarter notes; the dotted rhythms; the aspiring ascent of the vocal line (in measures two and four); the professional "short-hand" of the independently melodic bass line meant to be expanded into two hands by the harpsichordist; even the value-laden, "grand" key of E major – all these aspects of Clarissa's music mark its professionally majestic style.[33] Richardson appears to want to impress his readers with Clarissa's musical talents in addition to her other accomplishments. Yet the capacity of these lofty musical features to reinforce Clarissa's learning relies, of course, on the ability of Richardson's own audience to read the musical score and recognize its participation in a school of bourgeois musical discourse. In this sense, the musical score functions as a device for differentiating between readers.[34] The education of exactly that group of "accomplished" young women which was part of the undisputed *Clarissa* audience – despite arguments about who else read Richardson – would have included at least rudimentary training in the reading, singing, and playing

FIGURE 4.2
From *A Collection of the Choicest Songs and Dialogues* (London, 174?).

FIGURE 4.3
From *A Collection of the Choicest Songs and Dialogues* (London, 174?).

FIGURE 4.4
From a 1965 facsimile reprint (New York: Broude Bros.) of *The Musical Entertainer... Engraved by George Bickham, Junr.*, 2 vols. (London: Printed for and sold by Charles Corbett Bookseller, 1740), II, 11.

of music.[35] Richardson's readership thus overlaps precisely with the group of eighteenth-century women who, trained in music, would be able to read the score as part of the novel's "text." Richardson's use of engraved music to distinguish between different kinds of novel reader thus parallels the epigraphs and classical allusions discussed in the previous chapter. Just as classical references encouraged a cultural literacy requirement for readers of the "new species"

FIGURE 4.5
From *An Antidote against Melancholy. Being a Collection of Fourscore Merry Songs, Wherein Those of the Same Subject and Key Are Placed in Agreeable Succession in Relation to the Different Measures of Time, After the Manner of Suits of Lessons* (London: Printed for Daniel Brown, 1749), 32–33.

of writing, the use of musical notation in *Clarissa* suggests that Richardson also imagined the ideal novel reader to have a specific, though distinct, level of cultural sophistication. In the complete narrative context of the fiction, the music, in addition to displaying the heroine's scholarship, also asserts Clarissa's participation in a particular community, one defined primarily by gender. The discourse of music is, in fact, decidedly gendered throughout the novel and exchanged as a sign of fellowship between close female friends. To engage the discourse of music in this novel is to participate in a community of like-minded women. The Bluestocking philosophy of Carter's *Ode to Wisdom*, the poem which both inspires and becomes Clarissa's song, hails a maiden community reinforced through the arts.[36] The ode is addressed to Pallas Athena who, while acknowledged as a war-goddess, is primarily invoked as a patron of the arts, one who "inspires" the "poet's song" (II, 54). Athena, autonomous from birth, is saluted as a stock icon of independent "intellectual life" and of "retirement's" maiden community to which Clarissa pledges allegiance throughout the novel (II, 54). The ode, writes Clarissa, "does honour to our Sex." Thus Clarissa's request that her music be tried by Anna's "voice and finger" reinforces not only their harmonious friendship and intellectual affinity, but also their mutual attraction to what Clarissa elsewhere terms "the Single Life."[37]

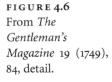

FIGURE 4.6 From *The Gentleman's Magazine* 19 (1749), 84, detail.

Tho' all the pow'rs around us join
To shake thy love, or alter mine,
Tho' nature change her wonted course,
And filial tears should lose their force,
Tho' tend'rest parents tyrants prove,
Yet still my Myra still I'd love.

Tho' avarice (curs'd bane of peace)
Should keep me from my happiness,
Yet still my love should follow thee,
From ev'ry base suspicion free:
My heart should adverse fate defy,
And triumph in my constancy.

Tho' all the num'rous train of woes,
That love inflicts, or absence knows,
Should be my lot, and made compleat

By this the last but heaviest weight;
Bar each avenue, and deny
The poor indulgence of a sigh.

Should tyrants dare the hand of heav'n
To force you where no vows are giv'n,
Yet still I'd keep my prize in view,
Would still my leading star pursue;
In artless numbers make my moan,
And thus pursue thee tho' unknown.

Oh! love instruct her willing eyes
To trace me thro' this dark disguise,
To view my passion void of art,
And all the meltings of my heart.
Then her own suff'rings will incline,
By sympathy, to think on mine.

This maiden community, however, demands qualities of soul, rather than specific behaviors, musical skill, or gender narrowly defined. Not all women in the novel may participate in the community, even when they engage in the discourse of music. Music is an outward expression of an affinity of mind and spirit. When women who lack these qualities affect musical behavior, they are rejected from the community as impostors, much like Austen's Lady Catherine and Mrs. Elton. For example, only a few pages prior to this scene, Bella nonchalantly strikes the keys of Clarissa's harpsichord. Bella's assumption of the air of female friendship and intimacy which this musical gesture would ordinarily denote is met with indignation by Clarissa: "And how do you think Bella employed herself while I was writing? – Why, playing gently upon my harpsichord: And *humming* to it, to shew her unconcernedness" (I, 299).[38] Clarissa's indignation at Bella's musical intrusion stems from her assessment of her sister as spiritually and emotionally "masculine":

> O my dear! what a hard-hearted Sex is the other! . . . Yet my Sister, too, is as hard-hearted as any of them. But this may be no exception neither: For she has been thought to be masculine in her air, and in her spirit. She has then perhaps, a soul of the *other* Sex in a body of *ours*. (II, 201)

While Bella engages in an outward sign of female friendship through the playing of music, she does not possess the disposition required for membership in the maiden community. Instead she betrays her incapacity for genuine female intimacy. Interestingly, Clarissa does not comment on Bella's musical skill or lack thereof. Thus Richardson avoids the all-too-easy connection between the singing of false notes and Bella's falsity of character.

The idea of a "maiden" community invoked through music persists throughout the novel. When we finally see Anna at her harpsichord it is during a visit from Mr. Hickman. Anna plays and sings not to impress her gentleman caller, as does Harriet Byron in *Grandison*, but to assert her independence. "I am so much accustomed," writes Anna,

> to Hickman's whining, creeping, submissive courtship, that I now expect nothing but whine and cringe from him; and am so little moved with his nonsense, that I am frequently forced to go to my harpsichord, to keep me awake, and to silence his humdrum. (III, 170–71)[39]

Anna's defiant playing manifests her allegiance to the all-female community segregated from marriage and men called forth by Clarissa's earlier song – a "STILL, DOMESTIC Life" (II, 54). At the novel's close, Richardson again resituates Clarissa within this context when Anna recalls how her friend preferred musical "diversion" to a game of cards when in the company of "her intimates": "four or five friends of like years and inclinations" who would often "engage her to read, to talk, to touch the keys, or to sing, when any new book, or new piece of music, came down" (VIII, 211–12). Within such small, domestic gatherings of like-minded women (for so I read the terms "intimates" and "friends" above), musical performance augments established female friendships and reinforces communal intellectual pursuits.

In the third edition Richardson greatly enhances Anna's closing reminiscences about Clarissa's leadership in these musical gatherings and, by extension, again reinforces the importance of music in the novel's politics. Highlighting his additions with marginal bullets, Richardson not only further praises Clarissa's "melodious" voice in the third edition ("But if her voice was melodious when she *re'd*, it was all harmony when she *sung*"), he also adds an extensive list of Clarissa's advice to Anna about singing before company (VIII, 207). The stilted inventory of Clarissa's many corrections of Anna's improper musical conduct reads as if cribbed directly from a conduct-book illustrating the same golden mean philosophy of musical performance upheld by Austen. Richardson's conduct-book-esque appendage to the third edition of *Clarissa*, namely the *Collection of Sentiments* (1751), in fact directs a reader browsing under the sister-arts heading of "Comedies. Tragedies. Music. Dancing." to this newly inserted inventory of musical directives (more about this and other such indexing appendages in Chapter 7):

- When *very young*, I was guilty of the fault of those who want to be courted to
- sing. She cured me of it, at the first of our happy intimacy, by her own *example*;
- and by the following correctives, occasionally, yet privately enforced.
    - 'Well, my dear, shall we take you at your word? Shall we suppose, that you
- sing but indifferently? Is not, however, the *act of obliging* (the company so worthy!)
- preferable to the *talent of singing*? And shall not young Ladies endeavour to
- make up for their defects in *one part* of education, by their excellence in
- *another*?'
    - Again, 'You must convince us, by attempting to sing, that you *cannot* sing;
- and then we will rid you, not only of *present*, but of *future* importunity.'—An
- indulgence, however, let me add, that but *tolerable* singers do not always wish
- to meet with.
    - Again, 'I know you will favour us by-and-by; and what do you by your
- excuses, but raise our expectations, and enhance your own difficulties?'
    - At another time, 'Has not this accomplishment been a part of your *education*,
- my Nancy? How then, for *your own* honour, can we allow of your excuses?'
    - And I once pleading a cold, the usual pretence of those who love to be
- entreated—'Sing, however, my dear, *as well as you can*. The greater the
- difficulty to you, the higher the compliment to the company. Do you think
- you are among those who know not how to make allowances? You *should*
- sing, my Love, lest there should be any-body present who may think your
- excuses owing to affectation.'
    - At another time, when I had *truly* observed, that a young Lady present sung
- better than I; and that therefore I chose not to sing before that Lady—'Fie!'
- said she (drawing me on one side) 'is not this pride, my Nancy? Does it not
- look as if your principal motive to oblige, was to obtain applause? A generous
- mind will not scruple to give advantage to a *person of merit*, tho' not always
- to *her own* advantage. And yet she will have a high merit *in doing that*.
- Supposing this excelling person absent, who, my dear, if your example spread,
- shall sing after *you*?' (VIII, 207–208)

Above all, Clarissa's detailed instructions insist upon communal participation: "You *should* sing." False modesty matters less to her than the continuation of musical performance: "Who," asks Clarissa, if Anna's prideful refusal to be outsung lays down a pattern of silence, "shall sing after *you*?" Earlier, Belford's description of Clarissa's coffin as resembling a harpsichord elided the death of the heroine with the death of music: "It [the coffin] is placed near the window, like a harpsichord, tho' covered over to the ground" (VII, 331). Towards the close of the novel, music has assumed such a symbolic importance in the shaping of female community and education that, along with the heroine's death, its cessation threatens to snuff out all female lights. Thus it is vitally important that, upon Clarissa's death, the heroine's leadership role in this colony of female artists and intellectuals be symbolically transferred to her cousin Dolly Hervey – the recipient of her harpsichord, chamber organ, and music books.

If by playing music a woman aligns herself with "the Single Life" and an all-female community, then by abandoning her music she disavows her female friendships and associations. When Lovelace expresses his disdain for female *friendship* as merely "a fashionable word," "nothing but chaff and stubble, liable to be blown away by the very wind that raises them," he, too, refers to music as the emblem of female solidarity. He asserts that "when a *man* comes in between the pretended *inseperables*, [such friendship] is given up, like their Music, and other maidenly amusements" (V, 254).[40] In the *Collection of Sentiments*, Richardson glosses Lovelace's remark as a caution that "Music, and other maidenly amusements, are too generally given up by women, when married, v. 254" (VIII, 320).[41] In his other fictions, too, Richardson advocates the maintenance of a female community – sustained, in part, by music – even after marriage.[42] *Pamela* had already listed the playing of music among the most desirable employments of a wife.[43] And in *Grandison* Richardson again makes a woman's music the barometer of domestic felicity by marking the crisis of the marital difficulties between Lady and Lord G with Lord G's destruction of his wife's harpsichord.

Precisely because Richardson presents Clarissa's music as a gesture of female friendship and solidarity, it might be assumed that Lovelace threatens to silence, through marriage or violence, what he himself describes as "her musical voice" (IV, 51). However, Lovelace poses a threat to music in the novel, not because he stifles song, but precisely because he endorses and promotes its performance. Lovelace is, first of all, not devoid of musical accomplishments, but a rather skilled musician:

> the danceing, the singing, the musical Ladies were all fond of my company: For who [I am in a humour to be vain, I think!—for who] danced, who sung, who touched the string, whatever the instrument, with a better grace than thy friend? (I, 198)

Lovelace boasts to Belford of his musical virtuosity as if this confirmed his sexual prowess with the "musical Ladies." And, indeed, music for Lovelace (in the tradition of Watteau and Hogarth) is always in the service of seduction. Lovelace's appearances at the musical theatre, for example, are a fundamental part of his reputation as a rake: "he used to be often at plays, and at the Opera, with women; and every time with a different one" (II, 154). Similarly, when Anna fears for a "sweet pretty girl, . . . just turned of Seventeen!" (II, 154) whom Lovelace has dubbed "his Rosebud," she incriminates him with an anecdote that equates sexual overtures with musical performance:

> He puts her upon singing. He praises her wild note.—O my dear, the girl's undone!—must be undone!—The man, you know, is LOVELACE. (II, 155)

Lady Bradshaigh, who responds to this scene in her copy of *Clarissa* with the marginal annotation "*No great harm or imodesty in singing*," might be deemed representative of a readership whom Richardson aimed to instruct in music's social and symbolic significance.[44] Lovelace's plot to capture and seduce Clarissa is also a plot to "put her upon singing." He desires to make her his caged songbird, a wild creature slowly conditioned to sing for its "keeper":

> How, at first, refusing all sustenance, it beats and bruises itself against its wires, till it makes its gay plumage fly about, and overspread its well-secured cage . . . And after a few days its struggles to escape still diminishing as it finds it to no purpose to attempt it, its new habitation becomes familiar; and it hops about from perch to perch, resumes its wonted chearfulness, and every day sings a song to amuse itself, and reward its keeper. (IV, 14)

In the third edition, Richardson adds extensively to this passage, making Lovelace's analogy between Clarissa and the caged songster painfully (and perhaps unnecessarily) explicit:

> • To let her fly now, what a pretty jest would that be!—How do I know,
> • except I try, whether she may not be brought to sing me a fine song, and
> • to be as well contented as I have brought other birds to be, and very shy
> • ones too? (IV, 15)[45]

Again and again, the threat Lovelace poses to Clarissa is enacted as a threat to her music; he aims to supplant the community of like-minded women which comprised Clarissa's original musical company and to become her audience-of-one. Lovelace corrupts the intellectual and communal function behind music, yoking it to erotic power. His desire to master music in the novel, a music which functions as the symbolic bond between educated women, recapitulates his violent attempts to isolate and direct Clarissa's "harmonious voice" throughout the book (IV, 55).

Presenting Clarissa's music as a tangible sheet of engraved musical text, as opposed to a mere narrative description, Richardson invites the musically literate reader to participate in Clarissa's musical community and to thwart Lovelace's desire to co-opt her music. The score, by soliciting reader participation, aims to build a community in which music remains an expression of intellectual achievement, solidarity, and friendship. It invites the reader to act the part of Clarissa and try her music with "voice and finger." For while Clarissa's invitation to do so is directed at Anna, it is never explicitly accepted in the fiction. Anna acknowledges receipt of the musical setting in a postscript, remarking that Clarissa "has given new beauties to the charming Ode," but never recounts having performed it (II, 66). Possibly Anna's failure to perform the musical score echoes her refusal to sing when "*very young*." Perhaps her example again risks silencing the musical community nurtured by Clarissa, urging the reader to step in. Certainly Clarissa's invitation to join her in song, to perform an act of the utmost sympathy and intimacy, seems deliberately open-ended. The absence of the music sheet in certain copies of the original editions might even suggest that some readers interpreted the musical engraving as an invitation to tear the music out of the novel and place it, as they would any similar sheet of music, upon their harpsichord stand for playing.[46] In this manner the musical engraving encourages an extraordinary kind of reader-response. It invites the reader to sing along with Clarissa.

In some respects Richardson's engraved invitation to his readers fully extends only to the musically proficient female readers of the novel. While the printed text of the letters cannot encode the gender of the writer, musical notation in this instance can. For a musically literate reader the piece's range (of one and a quarter octaves up to high A) is decidedly gender-specific: it is a soprano voice which leaps off the page of the engraved score. In order for a male singer to perform Clarissa's song, it would have to be transposed. By extension, the musical page might be interpreted to signal that only a female reader is granted direct access to the "maiden" community of friendship portrayed in the text of the song and in the novel as a whole. Admittedly, such a reading has to acknowledge that the piece's vocal range is indeed typical of genteel songs of the period; eighteenth-century tenors were expected to sing from the treble clef with (often unmarked) octave transposition. Nonetheless, it is likely that Richardson uses the print conventions of musical notation to mark the boundaries of the community shaped by music in the novel.

While Clarissa's music identifies her as part of a community, it also locates her as isolated from the larger social universe depicted in the text. Martha Bowden argues that music in this novel is ultimately private, not public, music.[47] After all, Clarissa plays her harpsichord in seclusion, and only after "closing" her "doors and windows" so that she "might not be heard below." Unlike the enthusiastically applauded musical performances of Pamela and Harriet Byron, Clarissa's song does not solidify her place in a larger social community. Clarissa's solitary "performance," in fact, signals her isolation from any society other than an idealized one open only to a select group of women. Yet if the musical score offers the reader, as it were, an engraved invitation to sing, then Richardson's graphic design constructs a maiden colony outside the novel. In this manner music extends rather than restricts Clarissa's community.

Richardson's musical page may have exerted a modest influence on a few minor eighteenth-century novelists, prompting a string of contemporaries to insert music, literally, into their books. Yet none of these imitations embrace the manner in which music becomes an integral part of a novel's politics. Richard Griffith, for example, follows Richardson's lead in his novel *Something New* (1772), closing each of its two volumes with the printed score of a song. Griffith's closing chapter, entitled "A Dirge," offers a "sort of a funeral anthem" on the occasion of the book's end (Figure 4.7).[48] The score offers, like *Tristram Shandy*'s black page, a mockery of ritual mourning, for "by measuring the song part of it with the lines in the last chapter," the text "may be chanted" in tune with the funereal accompaniment.[49] However, not all contemporary reaction to Richardson's graphic score was this playfully approving; some vehemently opposed the master printer's literal-minded approach to the sister arts. For example, John Kidgell's satire of the Richardsonian novel, *The Card*, alludes to *Clarissa*'s folded musical score by means of two unusual illustrations in his own text: a folded playing card and a musical minuet entitled "*LO CARTA*" (Figures 4.8 and 4.9). Both "cards" continue the game of interpretive tomfoolery initiated by the frontispiece and title of the book and both obliquely mock *Clarissa*'s musical "illustration." Upon the reverse of Kidgell's folded playing card, possibly a card from the same deck as the frontispiece, someone has written a message, thereby making it serve the added function of a calling card. A nearby passage situates the object within the fiction:

> They were sure the Doctor would be so obliging as to come with Pleasure, and for Sir *James* to go, would be but Fatigue and Inconvenience. In Consequence of this Decision, Miss *Evelyn* obtained the Favour of *the ten of Clubs*, to wait upon Doctor *Elwes*, on the fairer Side of which, (etched in beautiful Manuscript) was this important Commission. (1, 12)

Just as Richardson's musical engraving offered a mimetic reproduction of a character's original holograph, Kidgell too inserts into his book a cameo of

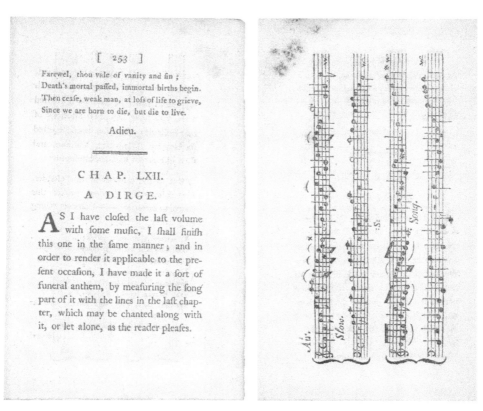

FIGURE 4.7 From Richard Griffith's *Something New*, 2 vols. (1772), II, 253–[255].

the "Manuscript" itself in the form of a pseudo-facsimile of one of the book's original mini-epistles. However, Kidgell's folded text cannot be opened like Richardson's musical page; moreover, the pictured fold permanently obscures a large part of its contents. While Richardson's illustrations purport to make additional information available to the reader, Kidgell's images deliberately thwart a secure knowledge of the text. In so doing Kidgell may argue for the futility of Richardson's use of pictures as graphic enforcers of interpretation. In the "Short Digression" which follows the engraving of the folded card in Kidgell's text, the author explicitly comments on the artificiality of his own illustration:

> [T]his elaborate Representation of a *Message* is devoted to the Perusal of the *Curious*. By this Artifice doth the *Author* ingeniously project a Method to preserve himself from total *Oblivion*; humbly conceiving, that when this *neglected Treatise* under the Character of Waste-Paper, shall be doomed to share the Fate of it, some little *Master* or *Miss* may be kindly advertised of the Picture of that harmless *Card* which adorns one happy Leaf of it, and which began about the

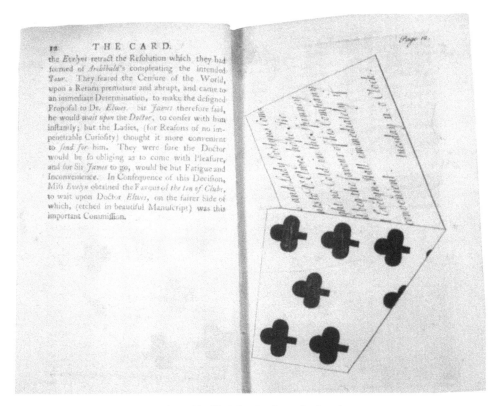

FIGURE 4.8 From John Kidgell's *The Card*, 2 vols. (1755), I, 12.

Year One thousand Seven hundred and Fifty, to be universally respected as an high *Messenger of Honour*. (1, 13)

If this moment satirizes the folding illustration in *Clarissa*, Kidgell's text claims that Richardson's visual gimmickry is not integral to his literary project and quaintly serves only to document outdated cultural practices.[50] Echoing some early criticisms leveled at Richardson's work, Kidgell suggests that the appeal of his epistolary fictions lies merely in their short-lived novelty.[51]

Kidgell continues his graphic derision of the music in *Clarissa* in the song entitled "*LO CARTA*" (see Figure 4.9). Unlike the elaborately engraved musical score in *Clarissa*, Kidgell's musical illustration of relief notes is visually (and cheaply) integrated into the printed page of type. While obviously integral to Kidgell's satirical project, the music exhibits no thematic relationship to *The Card*'s plot; it simply appears. To deliberately compound superfluity with ludicrous redundance, Kidgell provides a supposed translation of the Italian notes into an English musical composition, as if the universality of musical notation was in this case hampered by distinctions similar to those in linguistics:

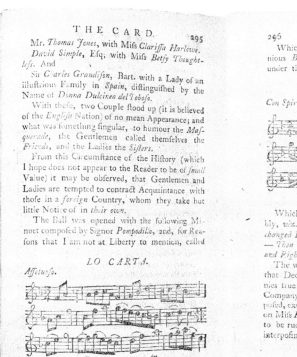

FIGURE 4.9 From John Kidgell's *The Card*, 2 vols. (1755), II, 295–96.

The Ball was opened with the following Minuet composed by Signor *Pompodillo*, and for Reasons that I am not at Liberty to mention, called
LO CARTA.
Affetuoso.

Which was immediately *translated* by an ingenious *British* Gentleman into a Country Dance, under the Name, Style and Title of,

THE CARD.

Con Spirito.

(II, 295–96)

The Italian "Minuet" and English "Country Dance" are presented as "ingenious" translations from one musical idiom to another. Yet, while the minuet and dance are culturally distinct, musically speaking these two pieces are merely variations on a simple theme. The redundancy of this cultural translation, of course, burlesques the romantic problematic of Richardson's final novel (the plot of *Grandison* is satirized throughout Kidgell's text), in which the English hero's infatuation with an Italian beauty rocks the foundations of national identity. Apparently Kidgell found Richardson's musical setting of Elizabeth Carter's *Ode* in *Clarissa* similarly redundant and jejune – a vapid act of cultural posturing.

By ignoring the engraved score in *Clarissa*, editorial tradition has endorsed Kidgell's view. As a result, literary interpretations of *Clarissa* have overlooked more than the role of music in the novel's female politics. By failing to acknowledge an interpretive purpose behind Richardson's decision to print Carter's *Ode* as part of a musical score, critics have neglected Richardson's instincts to encode meaning in the material production of his fiction. Although we faithfully reproduce and debate the playful physical features of *Tristram Shandy*, written only a decade later, we have not devoted equal attention to Richardson's radical experiments with graphic design.[52] Perhaps Richardson's *Clarissa* does not, at least at first, project the same kind of preoccupation with the materiality of the printed book that Sterne's work does.[53] Yet the graphic design of this single page of text in *Clarissa* offers the reader a vital clue to interpreting the novel. Like Sterne's textual anomalies, Richardson's specially designed page of music is a highly self-conscious feature of his book. Richardson's documented involvement with the minutest details of his fiction's visual production should likewise instruct us to respect the printing techniques deployed in his books as an integral part of the literary "text." Within the context of eighteenth-century print culture Richardson's neglected musical score, in particular, asserts itself as an important page in *Clarissa*, a page deserving of reproduction, reconsideration, and – for a select group of readers – even performance.

Although no other graphic feature of *Clarissa* exerts the musical score's profound thematic sway, the manner in which the small printer's ornaments augment the novel's temporal dimension deserves a closer look. Whereas the engraved score involved a commissioned setting and the costly addition of an intaglio engraving to a relief text, the small rosettes, or *fleurons*, found throughout all editions of *Clarissa* exhibit Richardson's innovative application of those design tools that were already part of his stock in the printing trade. Thus, in the printer's ornaments of *Clarissa* we see the printer-novelist apply hermeneutic pressure to existing pieces of type rather than forge new shapes.

CHAPTER 5

The space of time

graphic design and temporal distortion

> All the letters are written while the hearts of the writers must be supposed to be wholly engaged in their subjects (The events at the time generally dubious): So that they abound not only with critical Situations, but with what may be called *instantaneous* Descriptions and Reflections (proper to be brought home to the breast of the youthful Reader); as also with affecting Conversations; many of them written in the dialogue or dramatic way.
> – Samuel Richardson, Preface to the first edition of *Clarissa* (1, viii)

Richardson's well-known claim that his epistolary technique offers an "*instantaneous*" record of experience is, of course, a lie – a fiction about a fiction that hinges upon a series of temporal distortions. The lie enables the argument that the epistolary novel's "to-the-moment" style is the source of its intrinsic appeal and "affecting" intensity. However, unlike omniscient narration or interior monologue and despite Richardson's emphatic claim (the italics are his) that it is "*instantaneous*," the epistolary form must accommodate a temporal interval between action and narration. At the very least the epistolary novel must allow for the time it takes a character to reach a writing desk and record physical activity. The actions narrated in the letters are, therefore, not related instantaneously, but from the perspective of what Gérard Genette terms "the immediate *post-event* future."[1] With this narrative technique, according to Genette, "the eighteenth-century novel, from *Pamela* to *Obermann*, exploited that narrative situation propitious to the most subtle and the most 'irritating' counterpoints: the situation of the tiniest temporal interval."[2] This "interval" admits of a difference between an initial point of view and a second perspective which Genette describes as "displaced just enough to create dissonance."[3] Of course, such generic epistolary "dissonance" is subject to interpretive unease. For if a character has had time to reflect upon an experience, the spontaneity of the narrative and, by extension, its veracity are compromised. As Richardson struggles with the interpretive uncertainty of his form and the subjectivity of his characters, he must also struggle with "epistolary time" – those tiny temporal intervals that must occur between action in the world and reaction on the page. The greater the temporal gap between event and letter, the greater the potential narrative dissonance and interpretive risk.

In a letter to Aaron Hill written during the composition of *Clarissa*, Richardson acknowledges a related temporal problem posed by the epistolary form, namely that of plausibility. In this letter, Richardson describes the struggle to reconcile his own prolixity with the novel's commitment to realism:

> Length is my principal Disgust, at present . . . The fixing of Dates has been a Task to me. I am afraid I make the Writers do too much in the Time. If Lazy Ladies that is to say, Ladies, who love not Writing, were to be Judges, they would think so: especially if not Early Risers.[4]

Despite Richardson's self-conscious "fixing of Dates," the temporal plausibility of *Clarissa* remains a significant problem for many readers. George Sherburn, for example, notes that "during the period from 6 A.M. to midnight of June 10, Lovelace along with normal activities of the day is supposed to write something like 14,000 words."[5] Mark Kinkead-Weekes responds to such observations in a manner reminiscent of Henry Fielding's comical fixing of dates in the *Joseph Andrews* errata: "it is silly to calculate how many hours a day characters must have had to spend scribbling."[6] Terry Castle, in turn, disagrees with Kinkead-Weekes, countering that "[T]he fact that we invariably do [calculate] (even if secretly or intermittently) points to the unresolved difficulty in the form itself – one that ultimately undermines the mimetic contract with the reader."[7] Though they differ in their assessments of the relative importance of accurate time-keeping in *Clarissa*, all these critics acknowledge the interpretive fissures created by the distortions of temporal realism in the epistolary novel.

While modern literary criticism has noted the temporal incongruities in the plotting of Richardson's fictions, it has overlooked Richardson's articulation of temporal structure through the ornamentation of his books.[8] These elements of graphic design in eighteenth-century texts (indeed any text from the hand-press period) are ordinarily dismissed under the rubric of bibliographical "accidentals" and – like the more prominent graphic innovation of the musical score – silently eliminated from modern reprintings of his novels as a matter of editorial routine. Yet, I will argue, Richardson assigns these pieces of graphic type a significant role in the management of time, particularly in *Clarissa*. Richardson enlists the generic non-pictorial ornaments termed "printer's flowers," or *fleurons*, as signifiers of temporal duration, interruption, and division. These typographical markers (each of which is ultimately, in the third edition, linked to a specific fictional character) have a significant impact on the temporal organization of *Clarissa* and, by extension, its interpretation. This is not to say that Richardson resolves the problems of time-management cited in his own correspondence and deliberated by the above critics, who – incidentally – discuss Richardson with reference solely to modern reprints. But he does render "real" time more concretely in the pages of *Clarissa* than previously acknowledged.

Supplementing the temporal office of Richardson's punctuation (discussed in the next chapter), the *fleurons* in *Clarissa* narrow the temporal fissures attendant upon the epistolary form and exert greater control over the novel's nagging moments of narrative dissonance. In those original editions of *Clarissa* over which Richardson had control as printer, he used graphic design to articulate within the *visual space* of the printed page the *temporal space* of the fiction.

In a much-quoted passage from his correspondence with Sophia Westcomb, Richardson hails the familiar letter as an intimate conversation free from domestic interruption:

> Who then shall decline the converse of the pen? The pen that makes distance, presence; and brings back to sweet remembrance all the delights of presence; which makes even presence but body, while absence becomes the soul; and leaves no room for the intrusion of breakfast-calls, or dinner or supper direction, which often broke in upon us.[9]

The ideal setting for the writing of familiar letters is therefore, according to Richardson, an utterly secluded place:

> Retired, the modest Lady, happy in herself, happy in the Choice she makes of the Correspondent of her own Sex...; uninterrupted, her Closet her Paradise, her Company, herself, and ideally the beloved Absent.[10]

Richardson's view of the letter-writer seems akin to Wagner's view of the ideal listener – both are to be placed in hermetically sealed closets, free from outside influence. Yet Romanticism's tension between the idealized self and the messy facts of social living would appear to clash early. For in *Clarissa* Richardson allocates "room" for precisely those mundane "intrusion of breakfast-calls" which he urges letter-writers to avoid:

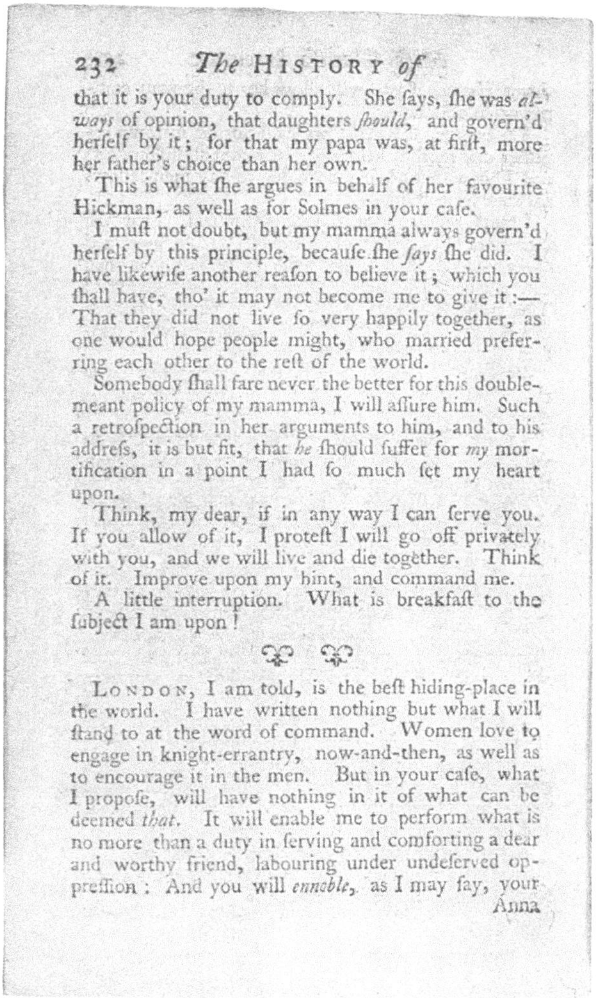

232 *The* HISTORY *of*

that it is your duty to comply. She ſays, ſhe was *always* of opinion, that daughters *ſhould*, and govern'd herſelf by it; for that my papa was, at firſt, more her father's choice than her own.

This is what ſhe argues in behalf of her favourite Hickman, as well as for Solmes in your caſe.

I muſt not doubt, but my mamma always govern'd herſelf by this principle, becauſe ſhe *ſays* ſhe did. I have likewiſe another reaſon to believe it; which you ſhall have, tho' it may not become me to give it:—That they did not live ſo very happily together, as one would hope people might, who married preferring each other to the reſt of the world.

Somebody ſhall fare never the better for this double-meant policy of my mamma, I will aſſure him. Such a retroſpection in her arguments to him, and to his addreſs, it is but fit, that *he* ſhould ſuffer for *my* mortification in a point I had ſo much ſet my heart upon.

Think, my dear, if in any way I can ſerve you. If you allow of it, I proteſt I will go off privately with you, and we will live and die together. Think of it. Improve upon my hint, and command me.

A little interruption. What is breakfaſt to the ſubject I am upon!

LONDON, I am told, is the beſt hiding-place in the world. I have written nothing but what I will ſtand to at the word of command. Women love to engage in knight-errantry, now-and-then, as well as to encourage it in the men. But in your caſe, what I propoſe, will have nothing in it of what can be deemed *that*. It will enable me to perform what is no more than a duty in ſerving and comforting a dear and worthy friend, labouring under undeſerved oppreſſion: And you will *ennoble*, as I may ſay, your

Anna

FIGURE 5.1 From the first edition of Samuel Richardson's *Clarissa*, 7 vols. (1748), II, 232.

A little interruption. What is breakfast to the subject I am upon!

LONDON, I am told, is the best hiding-place in the world.

(1st edn., II, 232; see Figure 5.1)[11]

In passages such as this one the realism of the novel contends with the intimacy of the private letter. The epistolary novel's commitment to recording the minutiae of daily life means that letter-writing takes place amidst the cacophony of ordinary household activity – activity which breaks in upon the "delicious intimacy" of the letters.[12] *Clarissa* upholds, as Castle terms it, its "mimetic contract" with the reader by finding ways of accommodating the mundane necessities of eating and sleeping. The heroine is allowed to eat:

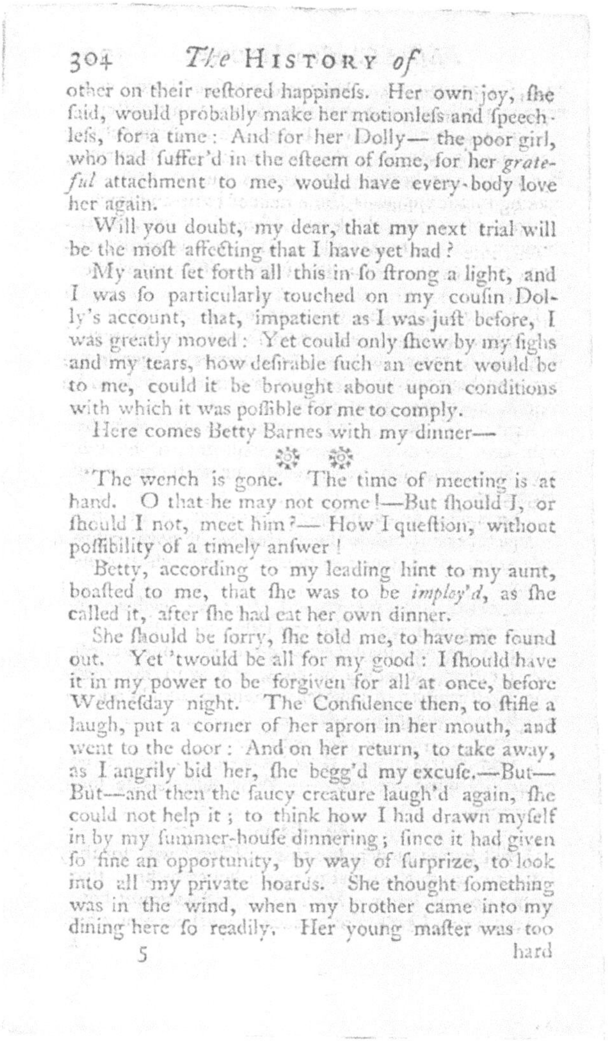

304 *The* HISTORY *of*

other on their reſtored happineſs. Her own joy, ſhe ſaid, would probably make her motionleſs and ſpeechleſs, for a time: And for her Dolly— the poor girl, who had ſuffer'd in the eſteem of ſome, for her *grateful* attachment to me, would have every-body love her again.

Will you doubt, my dear, that my next trial will be the moſt affecting that I have yet had?

My aunt ſet forth all this in ſo ſtrong a light, and I was ſo particularly touched on my couſin Dolly's account, that, impatient as I was juſt before, I was greatly moved: Yet could only ſhew by my ſighs and my tears, how deſirable ſuch an event would be to me, could it be brought about upon conditions with which it was poſſible for me to comply.

Here comes Betty Barnes with my dinner—

The wench is gone. The time of meeting is at hand. O that he may not come!—But ſhould I, or ſhould I not, meet him?— How I queſtion, without poſſibility of a timely anſwer!

Betty, according to my leading hint to my aunt, boaſted to me, that ſhe was to be *imploy'd*, as ſhe called it, after ſhe had eat her own dinner.

She ſhould be ſorry, ſhe told me, to have me found out. Yet 'twould be all for my good: I ſhould have it in my power to be forgiven for all at once, before Wedneſday night. The Confidence then, to ſtifle a laugh, put a corner of her apron in her mouth, and went to the door: And on her return, to take away, as I angrily bid her, ſhe begg'd my excuſe.—But—But—and then the ſaucy creature laugh'd again, ſhe could not help it; to think how I had drawn myſelf in by my ſummer-houſe dinnering; ſince it had given ſo fine an opportunity, by way of ſurprize, to look into all my private hoards. She thought ſomething was in the wind, when my brother came into my dining here ſo readily. Her young maſter was too

5 hard

FIGURE 5.2
From the first edition of *Clarissa*, 7 vols. (1748), II, 304.

Here comes Betty Barnes with my dinner—

The wench is gone. The time of meeting is at hand. O that he may not come!—

(1st edn., II, 304; see Figure 5.2)

The villain, in turn, interrupts his own correspondence in order to plague Clarissa with countless invitations to "dine" with him. Such requests often interrupt highly charged moments and thus have the secondary effect of emphasizing a passage by virtue of its curtailment. This brief cliff-hanger effect is achieved in the passage where Lovelace first articulates the possibility of a rape:

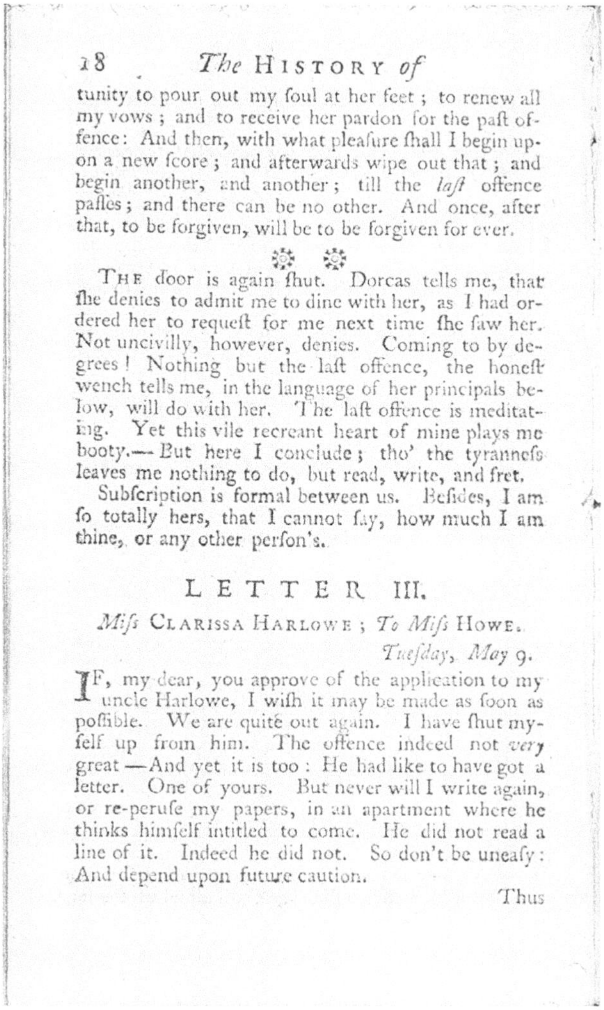

FIGURE 5.3 From the first edition of *Clarissa*, 7 vols. (1748), IV, 18.

> And then, with what pleasure shall I begin upon a new score; and afterwards wipe out that; and begin another, and another; till the *last* offence passes; and there can be no other. And once, after that, to be forgiven, will be to be forgiven for ever.
>
> ❁ ❁
>
> THE door is again shut. Dorcas tells me, that she denies to admit me to dine with her. (1st edn., IV, 18; see Figure 5.3)

During Clarissa's London captivity, meals gain increasing significance in the story as they become charged arenas of conflict and negotiation for the central protagonists. Donnalee Frega in her book *Speaking in Hunger* has helped to focus critical attention on Clarissa's ritualized fasting and her refusals to partake

FIGURE 5.4
From the first edition of *Clarissa*, 7 vols. (1748), IV, 124.

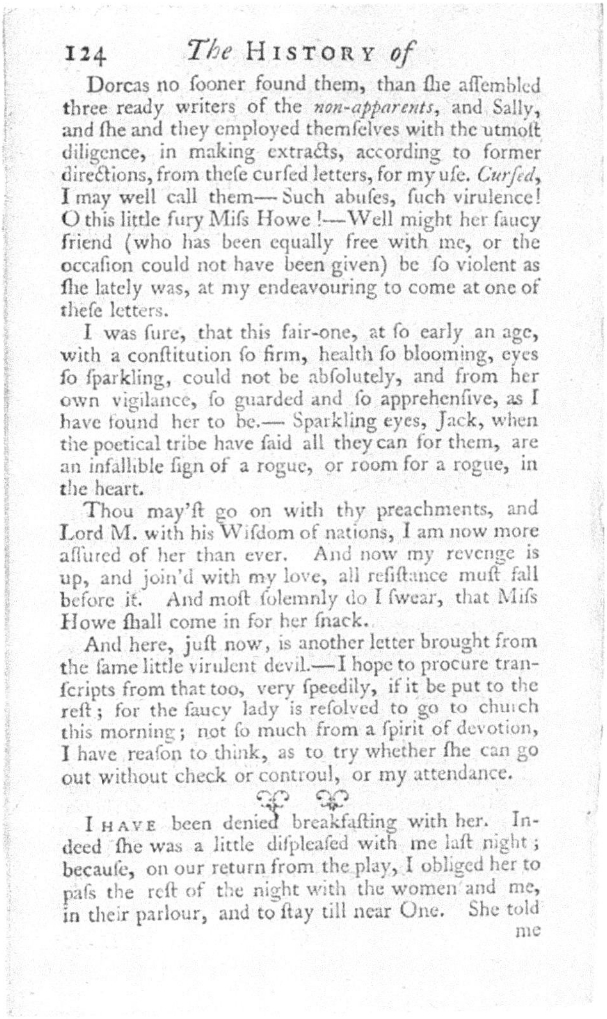

> 124   *The* HISTORY *of*
>
> Dorcas no sooner found them, than she assembled three ready writers of the *non-apparents*, and Sally, and she and they employed themselves with the utmost diligence, in making extracts, according to former directions, from these cursed letters, for my use. *Cursed*, I may well call them—Such abuses, such virulence! O this little fury Miss Howe!—Well might her saucy friend (who has been equally free with me, or the occasion could not have been given) be so violent as she lately was, at my endeavouring to come at one of these letters.
>
> I was sure, that this fair-one, at so early an age, with a constitution so firm, health so blooming, eyes so sparkling, could not be absolutely, and from her own vigilance, so guarded and so apprehensive, as I have found her to be.—Sparkling eyes, Jack, when the poetical tribe have said all they can for them, are an infallible sign of a rogue, or room for a rogue, in the heart.
>
> Thou may'st go on with thy preachments, and Lord M. with his Wisdom of nations, I am now more assured of her than ever. And now my revenge is up, and join'd with my love, all resistance must fall before it. And most solemnly do I swear, that Miss Howe shall come in for her snack.
>
> And here, just now, is another letter brought from the same little virulent devil.—I hope to procure transcripts from that too, very speedily, if it be put to the rest; for the saucy lady is resolved to go to church this morning; not so much from a spirit of devotion, I have reason to think, as to try whether she can go out without check or controul, or my attendance.
>
> ❧ ❧
>
> I HAVE been denied breakfasting with her. Indeed she was a little displeased with me last night; because, on our return from the play, I obliged her to pass the rest of the night with the women and me, in their parlour, and to stay till near One. She told
> me

of meals.¹³ These refusals become, as in the following passage where Lovelace pleads to share "breakfast," interruptions in the novel's text, marking, as it were, absence with presence:

> the saucy lady is resolved to go to church this morning; not so much from a spirit of devotion, I have reason to think, as to try whether she can go out without check or controul, or my attendance.
>
> ❧ ❧
>
> I HAVE been denied breakfasting with her.
>
> (1st edn., IV, 124; see Figure 5.4)

Such interruptions convey not only the text's generic mimetic fidelity, they can also reveal the symbolic dimensions of a passage. In the quoted passage, the placement of the *fleurons* highlights the implied link between religious ritual (Clarissa's resolution to attend morning services) and morning meals. To breakfast with Lovelace would entail, literally, to "break" her "fast" by breaking bread with her enemy. By breaking in on the text at the moment it glosses the activity of "breaking," Richardson graphically activates an intended pun. As Frega's study of fasting in *Clarissa* attests, the etymology of the word "breakfast" resounds throughout the novel.

These small ornaments represent a significant step in the visual evolution of Richardson's fiction and its notation of interruption and temporal realism. To go back to *Pamela* and the articulation of that novel's temporal dimension: there Richardson employed not ornaments but a combination of prose headlines, printed rule, and white space to demarcate time visually. In the eighteenth-century epistolary novel, a genre routinely set in contemporary society, time is generally rendered as an approximation of the "present."[14] In keeping with the epistolary form's generic immediacy, Pamela's letters and diary entries are left undated; only (occasionally) do they note the days of the week. As a result, these verbal temporal notations mark not the passage of "real" time (clock-time or calendar-time) in this novel but of universal time. Time-keeping in *Pamela* records, by extension, the universality of the heroine's experience. Pamela's narrative opens with an undated letter, a letter whose only recognition of temporal sequence is the roman numeral ("LETTER I") which the editor has presumably assigned it. As the story unfolds, Pamela's entries (particularly those during her forty-day captivity at the Lincolnshire estate) evidence her heightened awareness of time passing. Indeed, in her diary Pamela develops a detailed personal calendar of events: "Friday, the 36th day of my imprisonment . . . Five o'Clock is come . . . Seven o'clock . . . Saturday morning."[15] Yet despite these increasingly accurate temporal announcements, time in *Pamela* remains, owing to the lack of specific calendar dates, relatively abstract. The temporal increments measure not a historical day, but a hypothetical present suffused with biblical echoes. Pamela's "forty days of spiritual suffering" become a contemporary allegory of temptation.[16] Time in *Pamela*, although rooted in subjective experience, is universal. In addition to including these verbal increments, Richardson also organizes Pamela's letters with plain rule, separating them visually if they end mid-page (Figure 5.5). Like the protractedness of the dash to signal temporal pauses in speech, these dividing lines visually denote an unspecified measure of time passing between the letters.

Time's universality in *Pamela* becomes increasingly complicated, however, when interruptions occur in the writing process, and the hypothetical "present" must be postponed momentarily. As a consequence of the relative brevity of Pamela's individual letters and diary entries, the novel's domestic or dramatic activities rarely need to impinge upon the moment of composition. When

FIGURE 5.5
From the first edition of *Pamela*, 2 vols. (1740), I, 17.

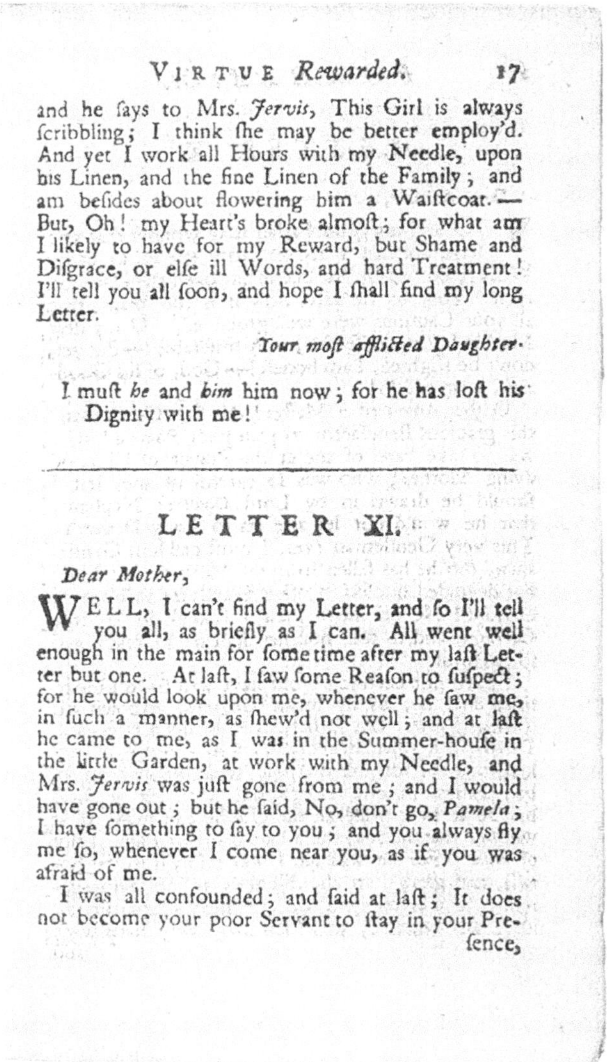

the occasional interruption takes place, Richardson separates the temporally distinct parts of Pamela's narrative with white space, distinguishing between passages written prior- and post-interruption:

> This was very good in Mrs. *Jervis*; but it intimated, that she thought as ill of his Designs as I; and as she knew his Mind more than I, it convinc'd me, that I ought to get away as fast as I could.
>
> My Master came in, just now, to speak to Mrs. *Jervis* about Houshold Matters. (I, 55; see Figure 5.6)

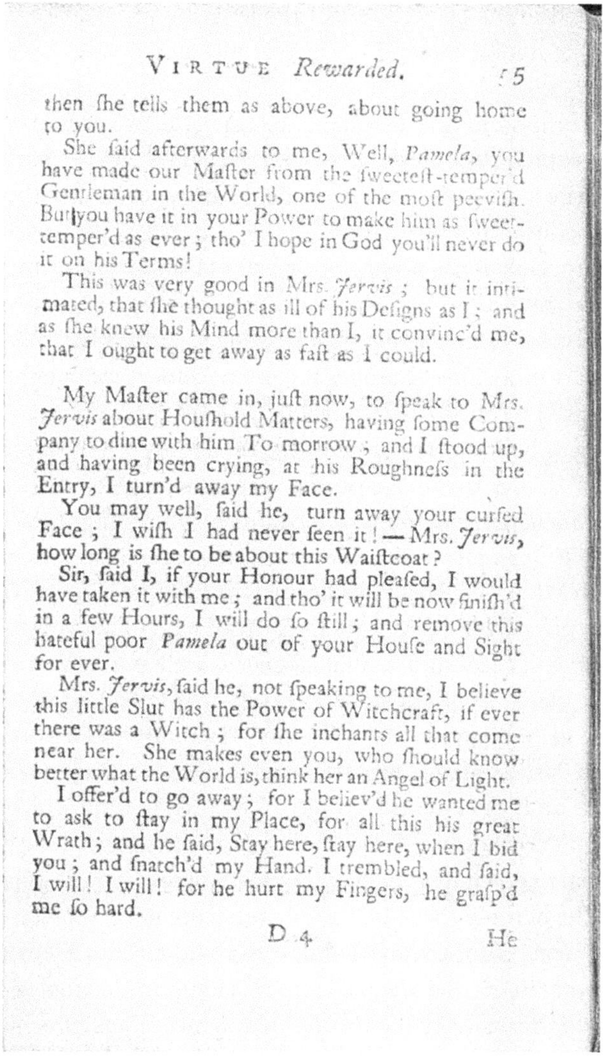

VIRTUE *Rewarded.* 55

then ſhe tells them as above, about going home to you.

She ſaid afterwards to me, Well, *Pamela*, you have made our Maſter from the ſweeteſt-temper'd Gentleman in the World, one of the moſt peeviſh. But you have it in your Power to make him as ſweet-temper'd as ever; tho' I hope in God you'll never do it on his Terms!

This was very good in Mrs. *Jervis*; but it intimated, that ſhe thought as ill of his Deſigns as I; and as ſhe knew his Mind more than I, it convinc'd me, that I ought to get away as faſt as I could.

My Maſter came in, juſt now, to ſpeak to Mrs. *Jervis* about Houſhold Matters, having ſome Company to dine with him To morrow; and I ſtood up, and having been crying, at his Roughneſs in the Entry, I turn'd away my Face.

You may well, ſaid he, turn away your curſed Face; I wiſh I had never ſeen it!—Mrs. *Jervis*, how long is ſhe to be about this Waiſtcoat?

Sir, ſaid I, if your Honour had pleaſed, I would have taken it with me; and tho' it will be now finiſh'd in a few Hours, I will do ſo ſtill; and remove this hateful poor *Pamela* out of your Houſe and Sight for ever.

Mrs. *Jervis*, ſaid he, not ſpeaking to me, I believe this little Slut has the Power of Witchcraft, if ever there was a Witch; for ſhe inchants all that come near her. She makes even you, who ſhould know better what the World is, think her an Angel of Light.

I offer'd to go away; for I believ'd he wanted me to ask to ſtay in my Place, for all this his great Wrath; and he ſaid, Stay here, ſtay here, when I bid you; and ſnatch'd my Hand. I trembled, and ſaid, I will! I will! for he hurt my Fingers, he graſp'd me ſo hard.

D 4 He

FIGURE 5.6
From the first edition of *Pamela*, 2 vols. (1740), I, 55.

Pamela is presumably writing this letter in the servants' quarters or kitchen when Mr. B's entrance momentarily disrupts her writing. He was, in other words, present during precisely that temporal interval represented by a deliberate physical absence – the white, empty space – in Pamela's printed letter.[17] On this page of "to-the-moment" text we do not receive Pamela's initial reaction to Mr. B's entrance through her unmediated voice, but must view it later through the eyes of a Pamela who is an unspecified measure of time older than the Pamela whose initial narrative is thus interrupted. Admittedly, both paragraphs are retrospective accounts and narrated in the past tense. Yet these narratives are separated by a brief, though indeterminate, interval of time – an interval visually represented in the printed text of the letter by white space.[18] Gérard Genette's "tiniest temporal interval" is in this instance figured by a marked absence of text.[19]

The use of white space compounds the dissonance between the two narrative halves that Pamela's interrupted page contains and thereby enhances the ambiguity that shrouds her true feelings for Mr. B. For the white space, unlike the artificial utterances of the editor's numerical headers, appears as a natural part of Pamela's letter: she, it appears, is the author of this empty space. Following the visual break, Pamela narrates a dramatic scene distinct from her preceding and decidedly more introspective narrative (see Figure 5.6). Indeed her self-avowed resolution to depart in the first section ("it convinc'd me, that I ought to get away as fast as I could") is sharply contradicted by her immediate agreement, in the continuation of her narrative, to do Mr. B's bidding ("Stay here, stay here, when I bid you"). After the break, on the very same page of text in which she vowed immediate departure, she now recounts how she "trembled" and agreed "I will! I will!" (1, 55). Her verbal account of the scene blames her sudden change of heart on Mr. B's violence: "for he hurt my Fingers, he grasp'd me so hard" (1, 55). Yet the physical separation on the printed page of her vow to leave and her pledge to remain suggests a textual lacuna, as well as a temporal interval. Like the smaller blank space Richardson prints in a letter by Anna Howe which asks Clarissa to "[f]ill up the blank I leave.—I cannot find a word bad enough," the blank in Pamela's letter suggests an aposiopesis, a character's deliberate refusal to name an idea or phrase (II, 153). The information which we read into the blank on Pamela's page might mitigate the inconceivability of the novel's "happy" marriage-ending by allowing for a range of emotions verbally unexpressed by the heroine (because socially unacceptable), yet visually accounted for in her text. On the other hand, one could also, as Henry Fielding does, read the motivations of a *Shamela* into this temporal/textual lacuna. The final result of this visual–verbal narrative dissonance is interpretive multiplicity. In his next novel, Richardson alters his graphic organization of time, introducing *fleurons* as a series of increasingly artificial temporal markers. With these new markers Richardson attempts to exert greater control over the moments of narrative dissonance in *Clarissa*, over those nagging temporal intervals between action and narration which remain integral to the epistolary form.

In *Clarissa*, where letters are significantly longer than they were in *Pamela* and where they continue to lengthen with each passing volume, the interruption of composition is inevitable – as is interpretive dissonance. Most interruptions are a necessary mechanism for the furtherance of a dramatic plot, forcing characters to halt their correspondence abruptly, to "break off!", when their attendance is required elsewhere (1, 259). Rather than suspend the action of the fictional world completely during the writing of all the letters by the characters, Richardson introduces a series of new marks into his text as cues to the reader that the act of writing has been momentarily halted. In more than 200 instances of interruption, time in *Clarissa* is thus marked, not by an absence of text as in *Pamela*, but by a presence of text – a new visual link between the different temporal moments on the page:

> *Friday, Three o'Clock.*
> As soon as I had transcribed it, I sent it down to my Brother by Mrs. Betty.
> The wench came up soon after, all aghast, with a *Laud, Miss*! What *have* you done?—What *have* you written? For you have set them all in a *joyful* uproar!
> ❈ ❈
> MY Sister is but this moment gone from me: She came up all in a flame; which obliged me abruptly to lay down my pen: ... (II, 44–45)

The printer's ornaments augment the temporal urgency of the fiction's verbal accounts: "My Sister is but this moment gone from me." Such interruptions graphically assure the reader that time is not as seamless as that experienced in *Pamela*. There the main letter-writer is kidnapped and secluded from the outside world for a large part of the story, a fate that provides her with ample leisure to write. The ornaments in *Clarissa* extenuate the luxury implied by the quantities of free time necessary for the writing of the characters' prolix epistles. Unlike *Pamela*, *Clarissa* is a novel with multiple actors and letter-writers, plots and counter-plots; the action increasingly takes place, indeed must take place, while some of the letter-writers sit at their respective writing desks.

With the aid of the printer's ornament, news in *Clarissa* dramatically breaks, not simply between letters, but during their composition. These interruptions animate the act of writing. When Clarissa writes while waiting at the Ivy Summer House for Lovelace, the ornaments breaking up her page provide (in addition to the wealth of dashes discussed in the next chapter) visual markers of suspense as well as temporal suspension:

> It would be hard, if I, who have held it out so sturdily to my Father and Uncles, should not—But he is at the garden-door—
> ❈ ❈
> I WAS mistaken !—How many noises *un-like*, be made *like* to what one fears!—Why flutters the fool so!—
> ❈ ❈
> I WILL hasten to deposit this. (II, 315)

Like the dash which operates on the sentence level, the ornament animates the unit of the letter. The ornaments visually enliven the text, offering the reader a visible substitute for the auditory sounds which cause Clarissa to halt her

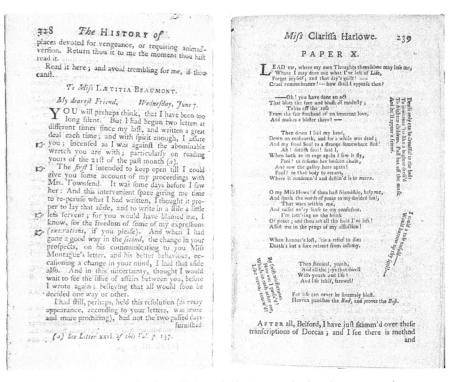

FIGURE 5.7 (a) From the first edition of *Clarissa*, 7 vols. (1748), IV, 328 and V, 239.

writing. Here the ornaments do not merely represent temporal interruptions but record on the printed page the "noises" heard by Clarissa. The second interruption need not, indeed, be explained verbally in Clarissa's letter; the recurrence of the ornament documents a second "noise" on her page.

Sometimes the printed ornaments substitute for "authentic" visual evidence of interruption or haste which the published text of the original letter cannot render into print. Anna Howe reflects, "I have written thro' many interruptions: And you will see the first sheet creased and rumpled, occasioned by putting it into my bosom, on my Mother's sudden coming upon me" (III, 174). While the reader of the novel cannot "see" those creases and rumples, as Clarissa presumably can, the reader is able to recognize the printed ornaments as marking the repeated suspension of writing owing to Mrs. Howe's intrusion:

> I am not surprised, now I have read your narrative, that so bold, and so contriving a man—I am forced to break off—
>
> You stood it out much better and longer—Here again comes my bustling, jealous Mother!

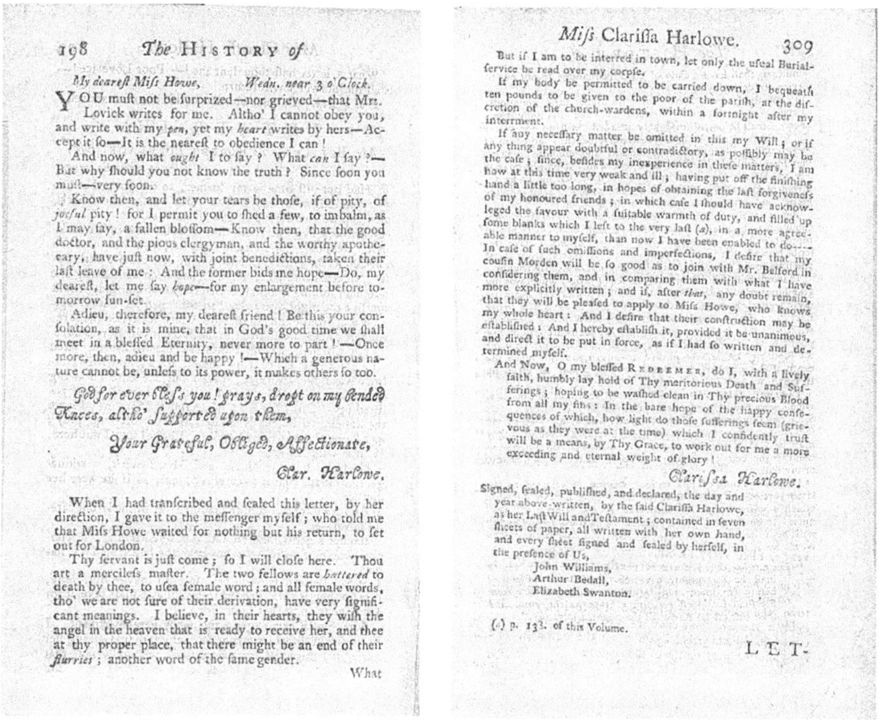

FIGURE 5.7 (b) From the first edition of *Clarissa*, 7 vols. (1748), VII, 198 and 309.

🙶 🙶

DON'T be so angry at yourself. Did you not do for the best at the time?

(III, 34)

In this particular instance, the ornaments substitute for an authentic visual characteristic of Anna's letters which, though described by the verbal text, the printing press cannot imitate.

The *fleurons* are, in fact, not the only graphic instance of printerly mimicry in the novel. *Clarissa* periodically strays from its visual uniformity as a printed book in order to approximate graphically the look of original letters. Lovelace's marginal pointing hands in an intercepted letter by Anna; the arrangement of the heroine's disjointed thoughts in the "mad" PAPER X; and the cursive script of Clarissa's signatures found in her last letter to Anna and upon her "Last Will and Testament;" – in each of these moments the novel breaks the printed forme of its typographical regularity in the service of mimesis (Figure 5.7). By occasionally breaking away from the pica roman font, Richardson, argues Steven R. Price, exploits the "manuscript motif."[20] The engraved script font of the two signatures, for example, "accentuates the potential reality of Clarissa's hand."[21] The musical score already discussed offers the reader another printed object as a pseudo-facsimile of Clarissa's original manuscript (see Figure 4.1). In each of these textual moments the printed page adds to its role as published transcription that of physical substitute for the unavailable holograph of the letters.

Yet, as we saw in the musical page, such moments of attempted mimesis ironically highlight the printing press's artifice, alerting the reader to *Clarissa*'s status as a printed book. As Terry Castle has noted, the effect of PAPER X, in which Clarissa's "mutilation of her own discourse" is rendered upon the printed page as a series of hysterically disjointed fragments of type, is "peculiar" and may raise "suspicions about the epistemological status of the text of *Clarissa* itself."[22] The overwhelming physicality of these moments may counteract, rather than further, the novel's mimetic conceits and draw attention to themselves not as innocent approximations but as telltale evidence of the habits of a master printer. At least one of Richardson's contemporary readers shared Castle's "suspicions" about Richardson's fetishizing his novel through its typographical affectations. Seizing upon several graphic moments in *Clarissa*, the Swiss critic Albrecht von Haller complained in a lengthy review of 1749 (rapidly translated and published in two parts in *The Gentleman's Magazine*): "Is there not something trifling in the incoherences, which *Clarissa* writes in her delirium? In the counterfeit signing of her name by letters cut in wood, in which (by the way) there appears to be some degree of affectation?"[23] On the other hand, Jane Collier defended Richardson against Haller's charges of printerly "affectation" in her letter of response, dated 19 September 1749, to the magazine's publisher, Edmund Cave:

> Indignation prompts me to say, That to those who are not affected with the Pathetic Incoherence of those Scatter'd Pieces of Paper, they *may perhaps* appear Trifling; nor can any other Answer be given to any Objections that might be raised to those Passages which are addressed intirely to the Heart, and not to the Head. Of the same Kind is Clarissa's signing her Hand in that particular Manner to the Will, and her last Letter to Miss Howe. And if the Author understood Human Nature well enough to know that there were some Hearts capable of being touched by such uncommon and surprisingly pathetic Passages, is it not hard that by the UNFEELING He shou'd be accused of Affectation?[24]

Collier's claim that these "uncommon and surprisingly pathetic Passages" in *Clarissa* communicate the pathos of the heroine by means of graphic design can be applied to the novel genre's graphic enthusiasm writ large. Her comments reinforce the prevalent experimentation with graphic design throughout the new species of writing as a graphic means of intensifying a reader's emotional response. For some readers the "affect" of print was emotionally affecting – and effective.

Of course, the small *fleuron* is not strictly a mimetic device. It makes no pretense of being a visual mark embedded in the original holographs of the letters. Readers of the fiction are not asked to imagine that, at every interruption or pause in their writing, Clarissa and Anna draw fancy ornamental flowers or curlicues upon their pages to document a temporal interval. Lovelace may admit to having "marked" the margins of one of Anna Howe's letters with "indices"; consequently the letter's curious pointing hands, ordinarily a conventional mark of print, could claim a mimetic purpose there. However, nowhere in *Clarissa* do the fictional characters say that they have recorded interruptions in their writing with visual markers. The printer's ornament remains an articulation of the printing press, a conventional feature of book production which designates the text in which it appears as a public novel, not a private letter. Yet by contributing to the novel's temporal authenticity, the ornaments do perform mimetic work. The temporal dimensions of the ornament transcend, as it were, the appearance of the "original letters," chronicling a temporal feature of their construction which the letters themselves record solely with words (and, occasionally, with no words at all).

In *Clarissa*, as in *Pamela*, Richardson uses the verbal text of datelines to partially articulate the novel's temporal dimensions. Indeed, as the plot progresses and the intervals between significant actions shorten, the datelines in *Clarissa* become increasingly precise in their recording of time. While the lack of calendar dates in *Pamela* attests to the universality of the protagonist's experience, the precise dates in *Clarissa*, which span roughly a calendar year (from 10 January to 18 December), build a comparable universality in this novel, but one grounded in temporal specifics.[25] What begins as an epistolary record of single or multiple calendar days, announced as:

LETTER I.
Miss ANNA HOWE, *To Miss* CLARISSA HARLOWE.
Jan. 10.

and

LETTER III.
Miss CLARISSA HARLOWE, *To Miss* HOWE.
Jan. 13, 14.

soon unfolds into a more precise diurnal ledger that is increasingly divided into parts of days:

LETTER IX.
Miss CLARISSA HARLOWE, *To Miss* HOWE.
Feb. 26. *in the Morning.*

By the second volume the letters are, as Clarissa notes, "written down to the last hour" (II, 319). In Letter XLV, for example, Richardson adds multiple datelines to a single letter to tell accurately the passing of hours between its sections. This letter by Clarissa commences on "*Sunday Morning (April 9.)*" and announces the time on six additional occasions before concluding: "*Sunday, Four in the Afternoon . . . Sunday Evening, Seven o'Clock . . . Sunday Night, Nine o'Clock . . . Monday Morn. April 10. Seven o'Clock . . . Nine-o'Clock*" (II, 301–304). Clarissa, who has agreed to meet Lovelace on that very Monday morning, is understandably obsessed with time passing. Readers, equally, are not allowed to take their eyes off the clock.

These datelines, modified from those in *Pamela*'s journal entries, are admittedly more chronometrically accurate than the printer's ornaments in their demarcation of "real" time. The printer's ornaments, after all, do not represent a clock face and only record undifferentiated and unmeasured temporal intervals.[26] Yet the majority of letters in *Clarissa* do not contain multiple datelines (Letter XLV is, indeed, an unusual case), and Richardson seems to prefer the use of ornaments for localized interruptions to the cumbersome addition of multiple datelines. The datelines in *Clarissa* tell time only by the whole hour, despite the fact that early eighteenth-century clock technology was capable of tracking time reliably in minutes, even seconds.[27] It is the ornaments (although imprecise in the exact increments of time they record) with which Richardson signals short pauses, those brief interludes in composition which do not warrant a look at the clock. Perhaps most significantly, because the ornaments are not, unlike the datelines which are presumably written by the characters, part of the original holographs but an artificial articulation of the printing press, their non-mimetic relationship to the "original letters" allows the ornaments to influence the process of reading the novel as a printed book.

The ornament's function is, therefore, not simply to document interruption but to interrupt. As a signal rather than a recording of pause, the *fleurons* govern not just the fiction but the reader's experience. A few years before the publication of *Clarissa*, Henry Fielding claimed in a chapter in *Joseph Andrews*, entitled "Of Divisions in Authors," to have adapted chapter divisions to the "new species" of writing.[28] He asks that the reader look upon "those little Spaces between our Chapters . . . as an Inn or Resting-Place, where he may stop and take a Glass, or any other Refreshment, as it pleases him."[29] Fielding thus offers the empty "Spaces" between chapters as an "Advantage for our Reader" – convenient places in the text for a reader to "repose" and "consider what he hath seen in the Parts he hath already past through."[30] J. Paul Hunter, in a discussion of Sterne's playful use of chapter divisions, describes how Fielding's metaphor for the device of the chapter "provide[s] the rationale and define[s] its uses" in the early novel.[31] One of the early novel's distinguishing characteristics was, after all, its length. Hunter reminds us that the fictions of Manley, Defoe, and the early Haywood "tended to be without chapter divisions" (though earlier writers had used them), and speculates that "the popularity of the epistolary form may be partly due to its clean divisions, unit by unit or day by day – divisions which allowed readers the convenience of stopping and not losing their places."[32] Indeed, the closest analogue to Fielding's chapter divisions in Richardson's fictions are the numbered headers which conveniently organize and separate individual letters. Richardson's use of the printer's ornaments as additional subdivisions of the letters in *Clarissa*, however, suggests that he saw a need to supplement what Hunter calls the epistolary novel's "formal advantage" with additional breaks for pause and reflection. In those letters in *Clarissa* that surpass the length of an ordinary "chapter" and defy a reader's staying power, the ornaments – in addition to mitigating the persistent dilemma of narrative probability – offer the reader not only additional places to "rest" in the text but ask for special consideration.

The fictional characters themselves often ask each other to pause for consideration at precisely those moments in the text which Richardson, reinforcing their verbal invitation with his own graphic design, has marked with a printer's ornament as a "resting place." For example, Clarissa writes to Anna in Fieldingesque fashion:

> I lay down my pen here, that you may consider of it a little, if you please.
>
> I RESUME, to give you my opinion . . .   (I, 277)

The pause in her letter, marked for emphasis by an ornament in the published text, is both a pause in Clarissa's writing ("I lay down my pen here") and a meditative pause in reading requested of her fictional reader ("that you may consider of it a little"). This same reflective pause is invited of Richardson's real-world reader by the presence of the ornament in the printed book. Similarly, fatigue on the part of the letter-writer may be projected upon the reader: "But here," writes Clarissa, "having tired myself, and I dare say you, I will lay down my pen. ❀ ❀ Mr. SOLMES is almost continually here" (II, 73). In such an instance the ornaments provide both a record of a temporal rest on the part of the writer, and a visual "resting place" for the eye of the novel reader. Thus, in addition to dramatizing interruption and articulating the temporal dimensions of the fictional world, the ornaments synchronize the pace of the real-world readers with their fictional counterparts.

By prompting his reader to internalize the temporal information conveyed by the printed *fleurons*, Richardson attempts to use the novel's characteristic moments of "narrative dissonance" for his own interpretive ends. In *Pamela*, the white spaces in the text essentially record interruptions as lacunae, allowing the reader to interpret these blanks as symbolic representations of missing text. In *Clarissa,* Richardson fills the white spaces with markers which he teaches his readers how to interpret. In all editions, the reader's familiarity with the *fleuron* builds over the first few volumes. In the third edition text, for example, the first *fleuron* appears on page 34, where Clarissa duly recounts having just been interrupted ("Just now, my Mother has rejoiced me with the news that my requested permission [to visit Anna] is granted"). Lest the reader dismiss the mark as an anomaly, Richardson repeats it, along with a similar gloss, on the next and opposite page where Clarissa's sudden change in tense and relation of new events explains the new break as owing to her having briefly gone downstairs to speak with her family: "I will acquaint you with what passed at the general leave given me to be your guest." A measured distance, hence another declared interruption, warrants a *fleuron*: "I have been just now to look at the place, and find it will answer."³³ Of the seventeen *fleurons* scattered throughout the first volume, all are accounted for by the verbal text as corresponding to acknowledged pauses in composition owing to breaking news, visits from other characters, or changes in activity. Once the interruptive function of the ornaments has been established in the text, their visual presence need no longer always be "explained" or glossed by a verbal acknowledgment of a pause in writing. It is then that the ornaments cease to signal an interruption of the character by someone else, or an acknowledged break in composition, and instead can stand in for brief contemplative hiatuses between ideas as they are expressed by the character on the page.

In the following passage from a letter by Clarissa, for example, the letter-writer gives no verbal explanation for the pause visually documented by an ornament in the published text:

> But while you give me the charming hope, that, in order to avoid one man, I shall not be under the necessity of throwing myself upon the Friends of the other; I think my case not absolutely desperate.
>
>
>
> I see not any of my family, nor hear from them in any way of kindness. This looks as if they themselves expected no great matters from that Tuesday's conference which makes my heart flutter every time I think of it.   (II, 166)

In such letters (and the number of similarly unglossed stops in the novel grows as the text proceeds) the presence of the ornament signals a verbally unverified hesitation or pause in writing – an interior monologue to which the reader has no verbal access, nor any record other than this printed mark. These *fleurons* attest to an interruption of indefinite length which the character herself does not admit to having experienced. In the passage above, the implied hesitation after Clarissa's hopeful "I think my case not absolutely desperate" betrays her; the temporal distortion in her letter substitutes for a verbal transition (a transition she appears incapable of generating) between her professed hopefulness about a reconciliation on the one hand and the incompatible reality that "makes [her] heart flutter" on the other. In this manner Richardson marks for special consideration a moment in the fiction where a reader may expect to find a character's true feelings buried in the text.[34] The ornaments unearth the letter-writer's anxieties for the reader who, like Anna, closely scrutinizes Clarissa's letters for those emotions (the "throb, throb, throb" of the heart), which she may even be hiding from herself (I, 62). These marks highlight a subtle "contradiction" within Clarissa's letter and locate a guarded moment that the reader must ponder and decipher. The temporal function attributable to the printer's ornament thus evolves into a symbol of emotional realism; the mark now signals temporal pauses which are themselves indicative of psychological authenticity, not mimetic veracity.

Like the novel's didactic footnotes, these artificial markers are part of an editorial machinery which attempts to restore interpretive cohesion. William Beatty Warner's reading of how Richardson's editorial "addenda work to replace one kind of time with another" may be applied to the ornaments as well.[35] The temporal present of the letters is, as characterized by Warner, "discontinuous from one moment to the next."[36] While the epistolary form's temporal uncertainty and multiplicity heightens suspense, it is not hermeneutically stable: "But as Richardson begins to (try to) close down the struggles of interpretation, and as he offers his own interpretation of this text, we find him advocating a very different notion of time."[37] Warner focusses on the verbal "addenda" to the text in his brief discussion of the hermeneutics of time in *Clarissa*. Yet, like the editorial footnotes, the ornaments are artificial interruptions of the fiction and exist in this same temporal dimension which Warner describes as "belong[ing] to a single authoritative act of retrospective interpretation."[38] With these small ornaments, as with the footnotes, Richardson supplants his characters' volatile moment-to-moment perspective with the retrospective and cohesive time of the editor.

Building upon his reader's familiarity with these signs, Richardson continues to exploit the temporal and interpretive dimensions of the *fleuron* in his next novel, *The History of Sir Charles Grandison* (1753–54), where even the intimacy of the breastfeeding of Lady G.'s "voracious" little "marmouset" is marked as a graphic interruption of the novel's printed page (Figure 5.8).

But before he continues with this sign in *Grandison*, Richardson adds to the temporal dimensions of the printer's ornaments in the third edition of *Clarissa* (1751) another, seemingly unrelated, interpretive characteristic – that of identification. In this edition Richardson assigns a particular ornament to each principal character in the fiction. This graphic consistency is absent from

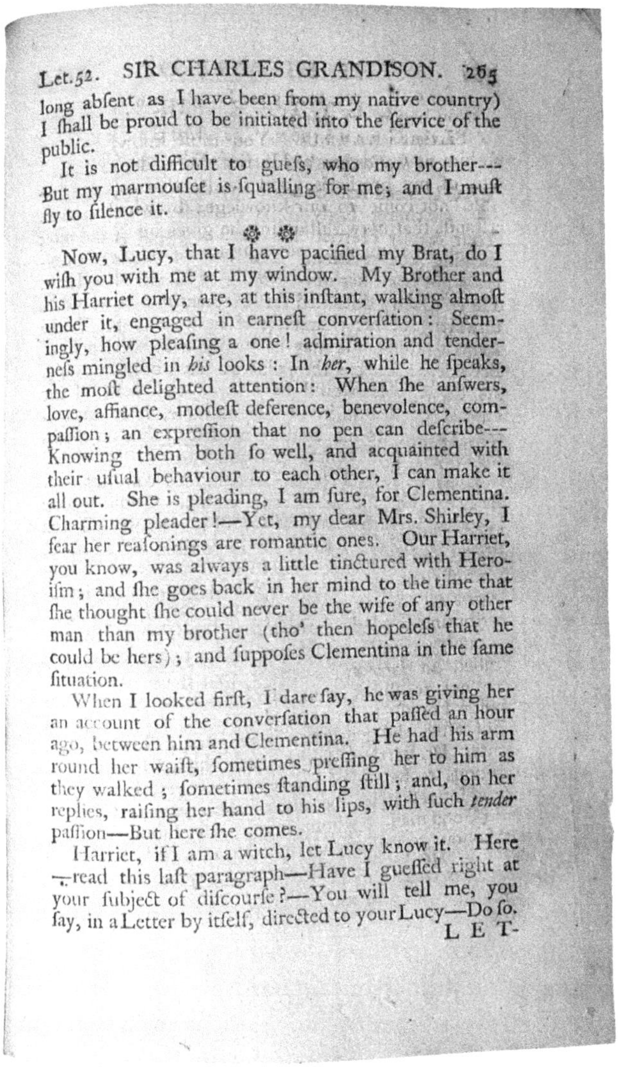

FIGURE 5.8
From the second edition of Samuel Richardson's *Sir Charles Grandison*, 6 vols. (1754), IV, 265.

> Let. 52.   SIR CHARLES GRANDISON.   265
>
> long absent as I have been from my native country) I shall be proud to be initiated into the service of the public.
> It is not difficult to guess, who my brother––– But my marmouset is squalling for me; and I must fly to silence it.
>
> ❊ ❊
>
> Now, Lucy, that I have pacified my Brat, do I wish you with me at my window. My Brother and his Harriet only, are, at this instant, walking almost under it, engaged in earnest conversation: Seemingly, how pleasing a one! admiration and tenderness mingled in *his* looks : In *her*, while he speaks, the most delighted attention: When she answers, love, affiance, modest deference, benevolence, compassion; an expression that no pen can describe––– Knowing them both so well, and acquainted with their usual behaviour to each other, I can make it all out. She is pleading, I am sure, for Clementina. Charming pleader!—Yet, my dear Mrs. Shirley, I fear her reasonings are romantic ones. Our Harriet, you know, was always a little tinctured with Heroism; and she goes back in her mind to the time that she thought she could never be the wife of any other man than my brother (tho' then hopeless that he could be hers); and supposes Clementina in the same situation.
> When I looked first, I dare say, he was giving her an account of the conversation that passed an hour ago, between him and Clementina. He had his arm round her waist, sometimes pressing her to him as they walked ; sometimes standing still; and, on her replies, raising her hand to his lips, with such *tender* passion—But here she comes.
> Harriet, if I am a witch, let Lucy know it. Here ––read this last paragraph—Have I guessed right at your subject of discourse?—You will tell me, you say, in a Letter by itself, directed to your Lucy—Do so.
> L E T-

earlier editions of *Clarissa*. In the first and second editions the same *fleurons* interrupt almost indiscriminately letters penned by Anna, Clarissa, Lovelace, and others. In those same editions, visually distinct sets of ornaments even mark time in the same letter (Figure 5.9). Yet the visual pattern set by the *fleurons* in these earlier editions may not be wholly random either – and may even harbor interpretive intent. In the opening volumes of the first edition, the assigning of a particular *fleuron* to a specific character is relatively consistent. Only in the novel's second installment, just as Clarissa leaves her family's estate, do the novel's graphic markings begin to reflect the collapse of a sign system that proffered a direct relationship between symbol and name. Indeed, it may be

FIGURE 5.9
From the first edition of *Clarissa*, 7 vols. (1748), IV, 316.

that Lovelace's strategies of mimicry and appropriation extend to the printed text of his letters, letters which usurp those little printed emblems found in the early letters of Anna and Clarissa. In her unique survey of ellipsis marks in literary texts, Anne C. Henry concurs, noting that Lovelace "appropriates" Clarissa's ornament "for his own script."[39] Other characters, in turn, may be said to exhibit Clarissa's influence when they "borrow" her printed symbol in the printed text of their letter; the printed "sign" associated with Clarissa becomes, in fact, the most ubiquitous *fleuron* in the printed text of the first edition. Clarissa's own letters throughout the first edition are exempt from graphic sway and, although her mark is frequently appropriated by others, her letters remain free of a visual indicator betraying external influences. The static nature of Clarissa's mark evidences graphically her purity and spiritual autonomy.[40]

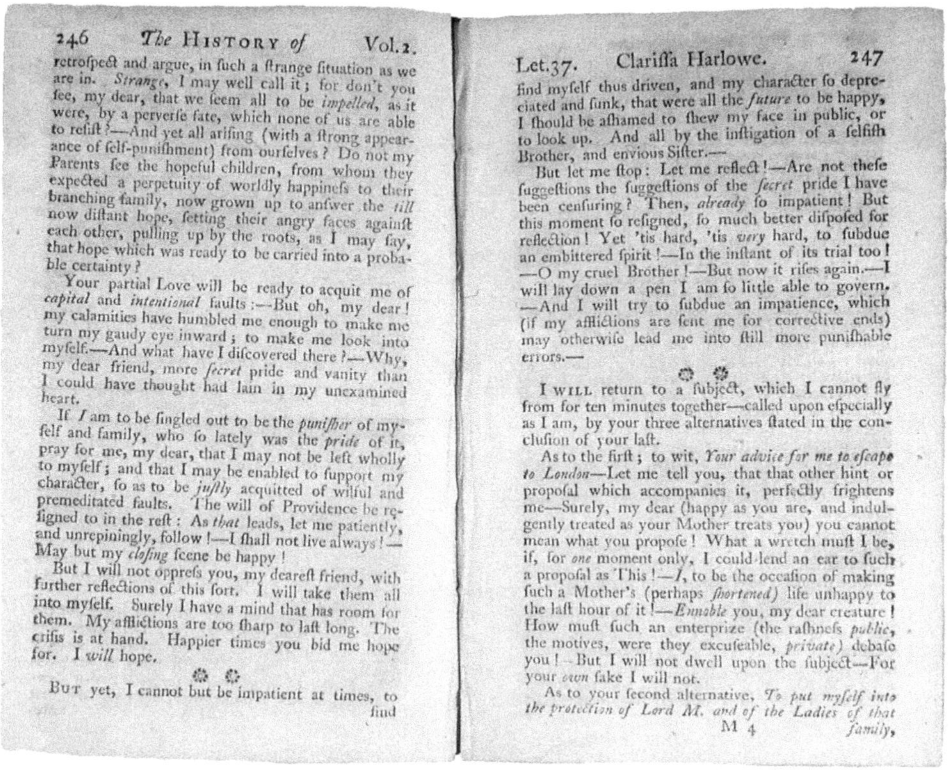

FIGURE 5.10 From the third edition of *Clarissa*, 8 vols. (1751), II, 246–47.

But the overall effect of these graphic borrowings between characters in the first edition is chaotic, especially in the later volumes. Only if a reader recalls the graphic pattern set by the novel's first installment – its opening distribution of specific signs to specific characters – are they able to note, for example, the many graphic pilferings that enact the dissolution of Lovelace's integrity.

In the third edition of 1751, the assigning of specific *fleurons* to individual characters is stable throughout that text's eight volumes, allowing for a more sustained association between graphic symbol and letter-writer. In this edition, unique pairs of ornaments interrupt each character's letters and, like Wagnerian motifs, proffer themselves as recurrent hallmarks of the protagonist. Whenever Clarissa pauses briefly in her writing in the third edition, her letters are interrupted only by the now-familiar pair of rosettes that marked so many of her letters in earlier editions (Figure 5.10).[41] So, too, when a two-hour visit by Mr. Hickman suspends Anna's letter to Clarissa, her writing bears a set of temporal markers which in this edition appears only in her letters and is first introduced mid-way through the initial volume (Figure 5.11).[42] And although Belford's mark enters the novel at a late date, namely at the end of the sixth

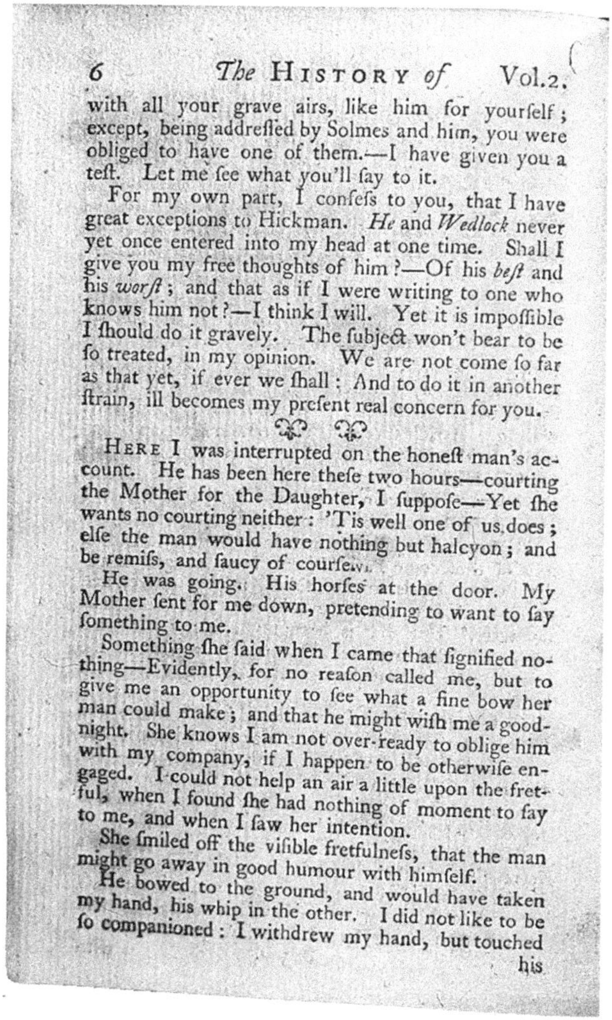

FIGURE 5.11
From the third edition of *Clarissa*, 8 vols. (1751), II, 6.

volume, his temporal interruptions are also recorded with unique printer's ornaments in his third-edition letters; his ornaments may, in this case, appear in one of two visual arrangements on the page (Figure 5.12).[43] In the last two volumes, when Judith Norton and Colonel Morden each pause once in their writing, these minor characters, too, are assigned a particular, and distinct, *fleuron* found nowhere else in the text.[44]

The villain is outfitted with an entirely new "sign" of temporal interruption not found in previous printings of the novel. This new sign graphically belies Lovelace's claims to veracity by evoking the print tradition of textual lacunae. In the 1751 edition, when Lovelace takes a break from writing to indulge, for example, in a fiendish fit of laughter, his letter records this interruption with a constellation of asterisks:

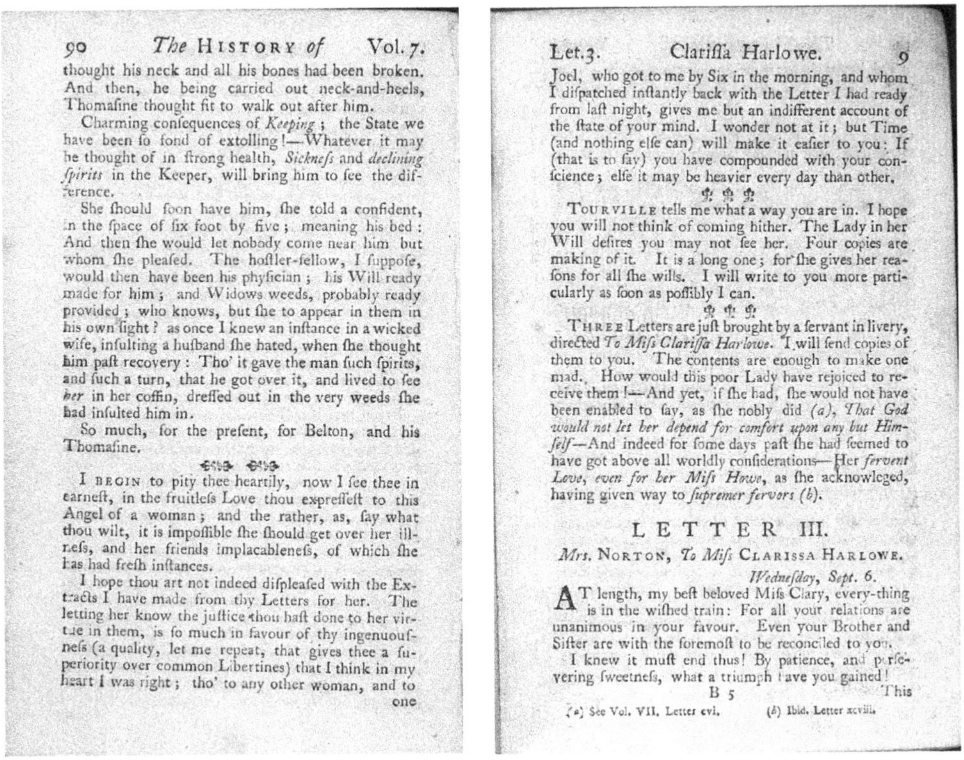

FIGURE 5.12 From the third edition of *Clarissa*, 8 vols. (1751), VII, 90 and VIII, 9.

The Sex! The Sex, all over!—Charming contradiction!—Hah, hah, hah, hah!—I must here—I must here, lay down my pen, to hold my sides; for I must have my laugh out now the fit is upon me.

* * * *
 *   *

I BELIEVE—I believe—Hah, hah, hah!—I believe, Jack, my dogs conclude me mad. (III, 30; see Figure 5.13)

In this same passage in the first edition, where characters usurp the printed signs of others, this temporal interruption was marked by an utterly different set of ornaments – ornaments also found in that edition in letters authored by other characters (Figure 5.14). The introduction, in the third edition, of an entirely new mark of temporal interruption, one that substitutes a constellation of asterisks for the familiar rosettes and *fleurons* deployed in Lovelace's text in prior editions, brings to mind the lacunae found in contemporary editions of ancient texts. In late-seventeenth and early eighteenth-century scholarly editions, a gap, flaw, or missing element from an old manuscript was commonly acknowledged by the insertion of asterisks in the printed page of text. For

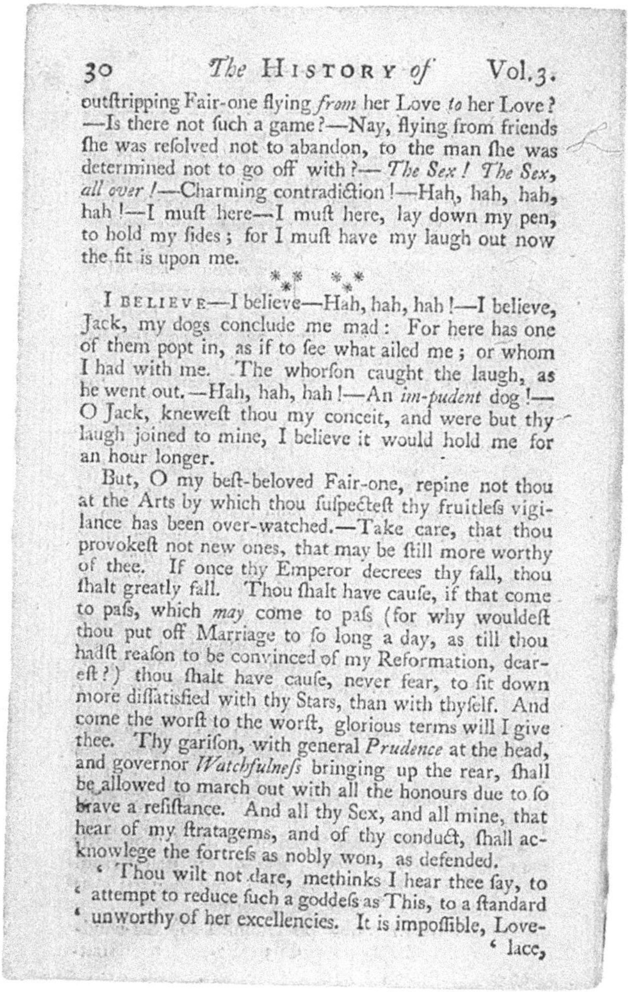

30 *The* HISTORY *of* Vol. 3.

outſtripping Fair-one flying *from* her Love *to* her Love? —Is there not ſuch a game?—Nay, flying from friends ſhe was reſolved not to abandon, to the man ſhe was determined not to go off with?—*The Sex! The Sex, all over!*—Charming contradiction!—Hah, hah, hah, hah!—I muſt here—I muſt here, lay down my pen, to hold my ſides; for I muſt have my laugh out now the fit is upon me.

⁂ ⁂

I BELIEVE—I believe—Hah, hah, hah!—I believe, Jack, my dogs conclude me mad: For here has one of them popt in, as if to ſee what ailed me; or whom I had with me. The whorſon caught the laugh, as he went out.—Hah, hah, hah!—An *im-pudent* dog!—O Jack, kneweſt thou my conceit, and were but thy laugh joined to mine, I believe it would hold me for an hour longer.

But, O my beſt-beloved Fair-one, repine not thou at the Arts by which thou ſuſpecteſt thy fruitleſs vigilance has been over-watched.—Take care, that thou provokeſt not new ones, that may be ſtill more worthy of thee. If once thy Emperor decrees thy fall, thou ſhalt greatly fall. Thou ſhalt have cauſe, if that come to paſs, which *may* come to paſs (for why wouldeſt thou put off Marriage to ſo long a day, as till thou hadſt reaſon to be convinced of my Reformation, deareſt?) thou ſhalt have cauſe, never fear, to ſit down more diſſatisfied with thy Stars, than with thyſelf. And come the worſt to the worſt, glorious terms will I give thee. Thy gariſon, with general *Prudence* at the head, and governor *Watchfulneſs* bringing up the rear, ſhall be allowed to march out with all the honours due to ſo brave a reſiſtance. And all thy Sex, and all mine, that hear of my ſtratagems, and of thy conduct, ſhall acknowlege the fortreſs as nobly won, as defended.

'Thou wilt not dare, methinks I hear thee ſay, to 'attempt to reduce ſuch a goddeſs as This, to a ſtandard 'unworthy of her excellencies. It is impoſſible, Love-

'lace,

FIGURE 5.13 From the third edition of *Clarissa*, 8 vols. (1751), III, 30.

example, in the graphic design of his *A Tale of a Tub* (1704) Jonathan Swift can poke fun at this common visual practice in academic tomes, confident that his readers will recognize the satire's graphic flourishes as a mockery of scholarly discourse. Just in case, Swift adds shoulder notes (that other telltale feature of seventeenth-century scholasticism) to gloss the rows of asterisks in his text as "*Desunt nonnulla*" and "*Ingens hiatus hic in MS*" (Figure 5.15). In 1751, Richardson's arrangement of asterisks in Lovelace's letters resembles this practice, perhaps casting doubt with reference to print tradition on the authenticity of Lovelace's discourse. That is, he alludes by means of this graphic mark of textual "imperfection" to the villain's moral deficiencies and dubious talent for convenient omission. Interestingly, Richardson's text nowhere adopts the asterisk as an authentic sign of a lacuna in the supposed manuscript of the

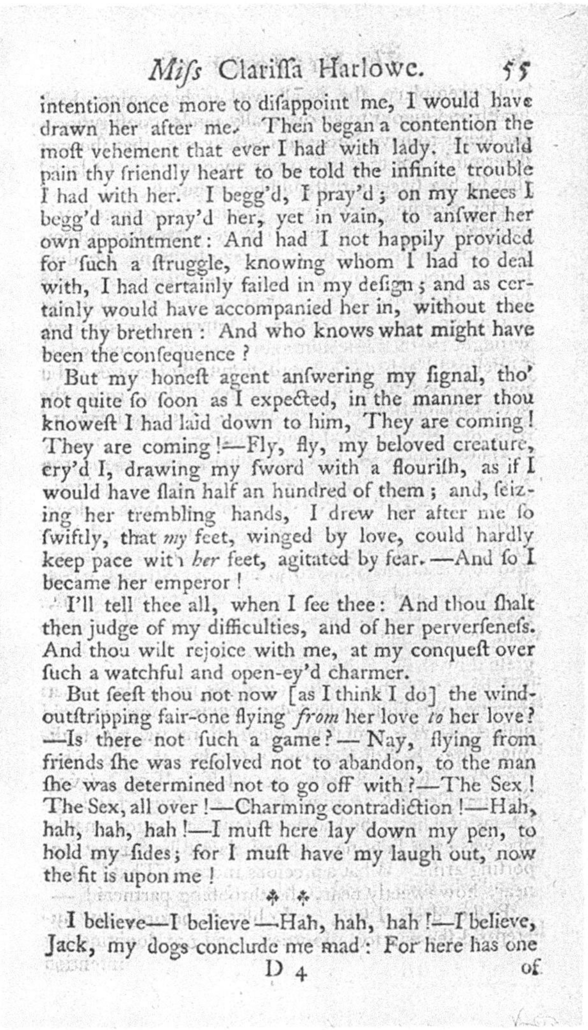

FIGURE 5.14
From the first edition of *Clarissa*, 7 vols. (1748), III, 55.

> *Miss* Clarissa Harlowe.   55
>
> intention once more to disappoint me, I would have drawn her after me. Then began a contention the most vehement that ever I had with lady. It would pain thy friendly heart to be told the infinite trouble I had with her. I begg'd, I pray'd; on my knees I begg'd and pray'd her, yet in vain, to answer her own appointment: And had I not happily provided for such a struggle, knowing whom I had to deal with, I had certainly failed in my design; and as certainly would have accompanied her in, without thee and thy brethren: And who knows what might have been the consequence?
>
> But my honest agent answering my signal, tho' not quite so soon as I expected, in the manner thou knowest I had laid down to him, They are coming! They are coming!—Fly, fly, my beloved creature, cry'd I, drawing my sword with a flourish, as if I would have slain half an hundred of them; and, seizing her trembling hands, I drew her after me so swiftly, that *my* feet, winged by love, could hardly keep pace with *her* feet, agitated by fear.—And so I became her emperor!
>
> I'll tell thee all, when I see thee: And thou shalt then judge of my difficulties, and of her perverseness. And thou wilt rejoice with me, at my conquest over such a watchful and open-ey'd charmer.
>
> But seest thou not now [as I think I do] the wind-outstripping fair-one flying *from* her love *to* her love?—Is there not such a game?—Nay, flying from friends she was resolved not to abandon, to the man she was determined not to go off with?—The Sex! The Sex, all over!—Charming contradiction!—Hah, hah, hah, hah!—I must here lay down my pen, to hold my sides; for I must have my laugh out, now the fit is upon me!
>
> ❊ ❊
>
> I believe—I believe—Hah, hah, hah!—I believe, Jack, my dogs conclude me mad: For here has one
>   D 4   of

original letters, whereas in *Tristram Shandy* and one of its precursors it does. There asterisks mark comic moments where the text fails to capture the low whisperings of the novel's characters (Figures 5.16 and 5.17). As the figures attest, the anonymous *Tristram Bates* (1756) and Laurance Sterne's *Tristram Shandy* (1759–67) are prominent examples of the use of asterisks as lacunae in line with Swift's intentions in the *Tale*. Later novelists continued to deploy the asterisk as a traditional symbol of textual omission: possibly the singular row of asterisks found, inexplicably, in the middle of *Jane Eyre* (1847) may meaningfully be glossed in reference to this same tradition. There, reminiscent of Pamela, Jane narrates her painful departure from her "dear master" after the thwarted marriage ceremony and the discovery of his mad wife:

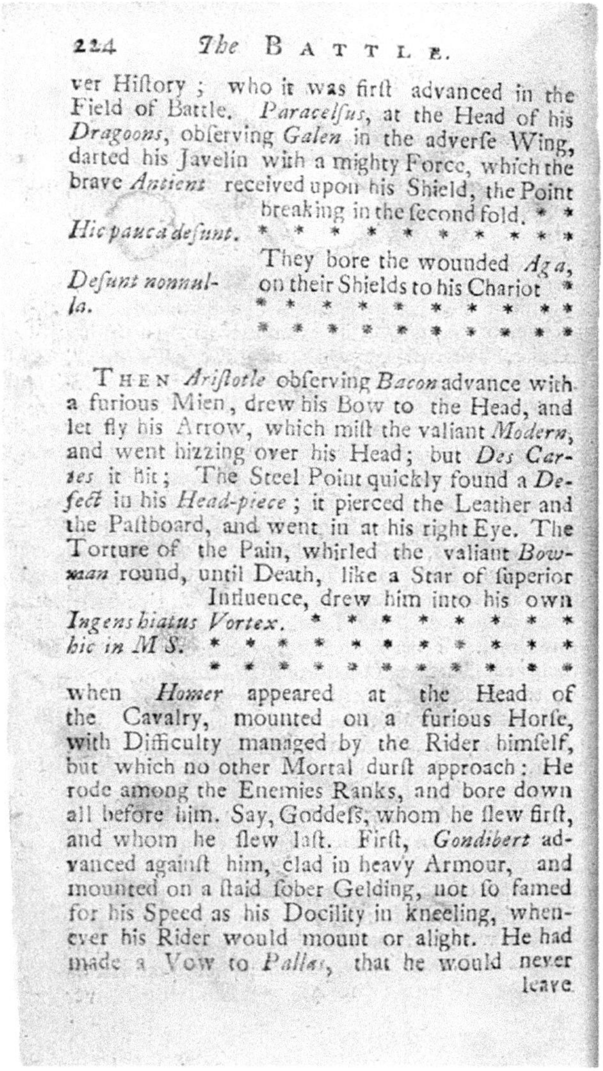

224 *The* BATTLE.

ver Hiſtory ; who it was firſt advanced in the Field of Battle. *Paracelſus*, at the Head of his *Dragoons*, obſerving *Galen* in the adverſe Wing, darted his Javelin with a mighty Force, which the brave *Antient* received upon his Shield, the Point breaking in the ſecond fold. * *

Hic pauca deſunt. * * * * * * * * *

They bore the wounded *Aga*, on their Shields to his Chariot *

Deſunt nonnulla. * * * * * * * * *

* * * * * * * * * *

THEN *Ariſtotle* obſerving *Bacon* advance with a furious Mien, drew his Bow to the Head, and let fly his Arrow, which miſt the valiant *Modern*, and went hizzing over his Head; but *Des Cartes* it hit; The Steel Point quickly found a *Defect* in his *Head-piece* ; it pierced the Leather and the Paſtboard, and went in at his right Eye. The Torture of the Pain, whirled the valiant *Bowman* round, until Death, like a Star of ſuperior Influence, drew him into his own *Vortex.* * * * * * * * *

Ingens hiatus hic in MS. * * * * * * * * * * *

* * * * * * * * * * * *

when *Homer* appeared at the Head of the Cavalry, mounted on a furious Horſe, with Difficulty managed by the Rider himſelf, but which no other Mortal durſt approach: He rode among the Enemies Ranks, and bore down all before him. Say, Goddeſs, whom he ſlew firſt, and whom he ſlew laſt. Firſt, *Gondibert* advanced againſt him, clad in heavy Armour, and mounted on a ſtaid ſober Gelding, not ſo famed for his Speed as his Docility in kneeling, whenever his Rider would mount or alight. He had made a Vow to *Pallas*, that he would never leave

FIGURE 5.15 From a 1741 edition of Jonathan Swift's *A Tale of a Tub* (1704), 224.

"Farewell!" Was the cry of my heart, as I left him. Despair added,—"Farewell, for ever!"

* * * * * *

That night I never thought to sleep: but a slumber fell on me as soon as I lay down in bed.

Thus the lacuna in *Jane Eyre* offers the missing transition between Jane's waking and dreaming nightmares (she dreams of "the red-room at Gateshead") and marks the wordless emotional void that follows the destruction of the heroine's romantic hopes.[45]

FIGURE 5.16 From the second edition of Sterne's *Tristram Shandy* (1761), III, 73.

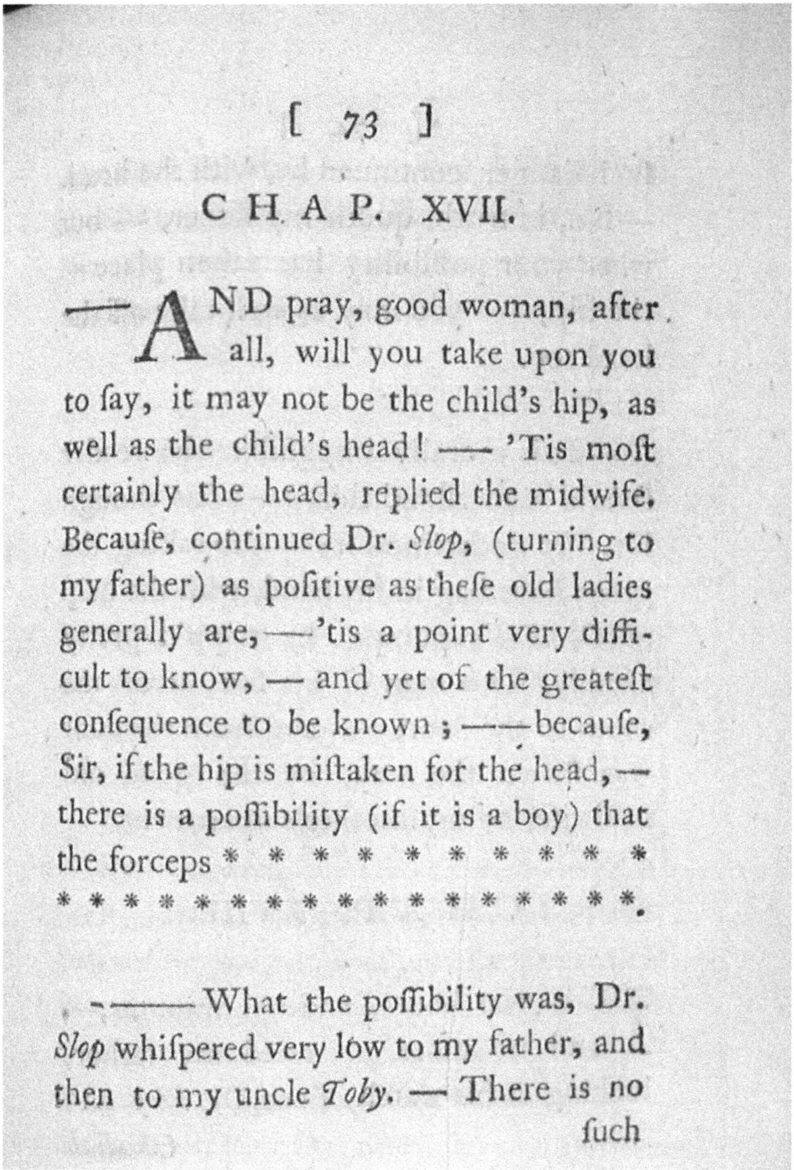

[73]

CHAP. XVII.

——AND pray, good woman, after all, will you take upon you to say, it may not be the child's hip, as well as the child's head!——'Tis most certainly the head, replied the midwife. Because, continued Dr. *Slop*, (turning to my father) as positive as these old ladies generally are,——'tis a point very difficult to know,—— and yet of the greatest consequence to be known;——because, Sir, if the hip is mistaken for the head,—— there is a possibility (if it is a boy) that the forceps *.

·———— What the possibility was, Dr. *Slop* whispered very low to my father, and then to my uncle *Toby*.—— There is no
such

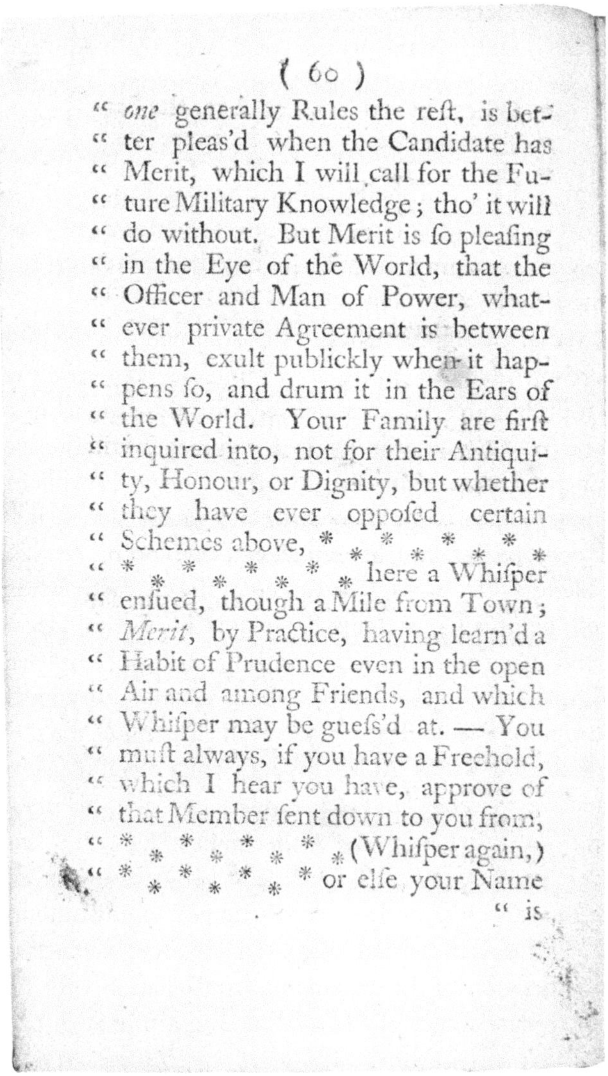
(60)
" *one* generally Rules the reſt, is bet-
" ter pleas'd when the Candidate has
" Merit, which I will call for the Fu-
" ture Military Knowledge; tho' it will
" do without. But Merit is ſo pleaſing
" in the Eye of the World, that the
" Officer and Man of Power, what-
" ever private Agreement is between
" them, exult publickly when it hap-
" pens ſo, and drum it in the Ears of
" the World. Your Family are firſt
" inquired into, not for their Antiqui-
" ty, Honour, or Dignity, but whether
" they have ever oppoſed certain
" Schemes above, * * * * * * * *
" * * * * * * * * * here a Whiſper
" enſued, though a Mile from Town;
" *Merit*, by Practice, having learn'd a
" Habit of Prudence even in the open
" Air and among Friends, and which
" Whiſper may be gueſs'd at. — You
" muſt always, if you have a Freehold,
" which I hear you have, approve of
" that Member ſent down to you from,
" * * * * * * * * * (Whiſper again,)
" * * * * * * * * * * or elſe your Name
" is

FIGURE 5.17 From the anonymous *The Life and Memoirs of Ephraim Tristram Bates* (1756), 60.

Irrespective of the asterisk's evocation of scholarly print traditions, Richardson controlled the printing of his third-edition text to such an extent that even a casual reader of the novel can discern the identity of the letter-writer in any epistle that bears an ornament without looking at its header or printed signature.[46] Not every letter, of course, includes a printer's ornament; their primary function remains the demarcation of interruption and the evidencing of psychology. But to the extent that the letters do include *fleurons*, or printer's flowers, they can be reliably traced to a specific letter-writer. Richardson, who was presumably unable to mimic the distinct hand of each character with a cumbersome variety of fonts (as he does twice with Clarissa's signatures in the early editions), seems to have devised an alternative (and less costly) way of visually reconciling the individuality of the private epistle with the medium of print. In this edition his careful selection of printer's ornaments may substitute for the wax seals of the "original letters," visual marks which similarly identify a sender and attest to a letter's authenticity: Clarissa warns Anna "to look carefully to the Seals of my Letters, as I shall to those of yours" (III, 297). The printed texts of her letters cannot, of course, be scrutinized or authenticated in this manner. Yet through his ornamentation Richardson provides his reader with an alternative printed "seal" of authenticity.

Precisely because the remarkable consistency of the ornaments in the third edition evidences Richardson's detailed control over minutiae of *Clarissa*'s visual production, it is tempting to read these small signs as miniature icons of the characters in whose letters they appear. Up to a point, the verbal text of the fiction invites this kind of iconographic interpretation. The novel explicitly hails Clarissa as "the flower and ornament" of the Harlowe family (II, 199). And the heroine's mark does, in fact, look like small, petaled blooms. As such, the rosettes in Clarissa's letters offer a symbolic cameo of the character whom Lovelace (a self-described "painful Bee" ranging "from flower to flower") terms his "Tender Blossom!" and "Charming Flower!" (III, 281 and 280).[47] Similarly, the text allows for a reading of the star-like asterisks which repeatedly ornament Lovelace's letters as an ominous astrological constellation influencing the plot. Just before celebrating at Sinclair's that "At last my lucky Star has directed us into the desired Port, and we are safely landed," Lovelace describes his intention to prevent Clarissa from "soaring upward to her native Skies" and keep her with "us Subluniaries" (III, 283 and 276). On at least two occasions, these same asterisks, or stars, in letters by Lovelace are rearranged to illustrate the villain's protean nature. This didactic visual lesson depends for its effectiveness upon the reader's association of the ornamental constellation with this character. For example, Lovelace writes of Clarissa's arrival at the St. Albans Inn:

> She cast a conscious glance, as she alighted, upon her habit, which was *no habit*; and repulsively, as I may say, quitting my assisting hand, hurried into the house. ✶ ✶ ✶
>
> Ovid was not a greater master of metamorphoses than thy friend. To the mistress of the house I instantly changed her into a Sister.   (III, 50)

Here Richardson reinforces Lovelace's protean talent for "metamorphoses" with a visual gimmick: a new arrangement of the pieces of type, the asterisks, that comprise the villain's hallmark. Similarly, in a later and newly added passage in the third edition, Lovelace experiences a contrite moment: "She was born, I told her, to make me happy, and to save a soul. ✶ ✶ ✶ ✶ " (III, 164).

This second visual alteration of Lovelace's characteristic icon (the same asterisks appear twice on the facing page of text in their usual constellation) casts this moral metamorphoses in a skeptical light, stressing Lovelace's protean nature rather than his capacity for lasting moral growth.

The dominant marks of interruption in Lovelace's writing are stars that, like Clarissa herself, have been "brushed down" by his ego:

> How it swells my pride, to have been able to outwit such a vigilant Charmer! I am taller by half a yard in my imagination than I was. I look *down* upon everybody now. Last night I was still more extravagant. I took off my hat, as I walked, to see if the Lace were not scorched, supposing it had brushed down a star; and, before I put it on again, in mere wantonness, and heart's-ease, I was for buffeting the moon. (III, 32)

Such passages, brimming with symbols paired with the iconography of the printer's ornaments, reinforce the significance of these visual marks in the fiction. Like "the primitive symbolic alphabet of the coffin emblems" which critics such as Terry Castle and Margaret Anne Doody have read "graphemically," Richardson's printer's ornaments interlineate the text of the novel with emblematic signs and symbols.[48]

Admittedly, a similar reading of the more abstractly shaped "acorns" and "stylized plants" found in the letters by Belford and Anna is impossible to sustain.[49] Richardson can only go so far in incorporating the generic features of the printed book into the literary "text" of his novel. Yet the symbolic relationship of the ornamental stars and flowers to the two main characters in whose letters they appear implies that Richardson selected these so-called accidentals for their relative visual appropriateness. In this sense the selection criteria for the small printer's ornaments in the third edition may also apply to those used for the larger ornamental woodblocks that frame each volume of *Clarissa*. To some degree, the pictorial images of flower-filled urns, angels, and cupids found in the head- and tailpieces to each volume shape interpretation.[50] As a general print feature of the third edition, these larger ornaments stand, like the "vases, flower-pots, and figures, without number" in the "little garden" in Dover Street's "inner house," as pathetic monuments to a ravaged Eden (III, 179; see Figure 5.18).[51] Specific ornaments may also resonate with the volumes in which they are embedded. For example, and as earlier critics have noted, the fifth volume of the third edition, the volume that includes the rape, ends with a tailpiece of Europa and the bull (Figure 5.19).[52] As Jocelyn Harris comments, "the visual allusion underlines the fact that sexual pursuit, cruelty, rivalry and change dominate this book with the same ruthlessness as they do Ovid's."[53] Although none of the woodcuts featured in *Clarissa* are unique to that book (all ornament other books printed on Richardson's press), their

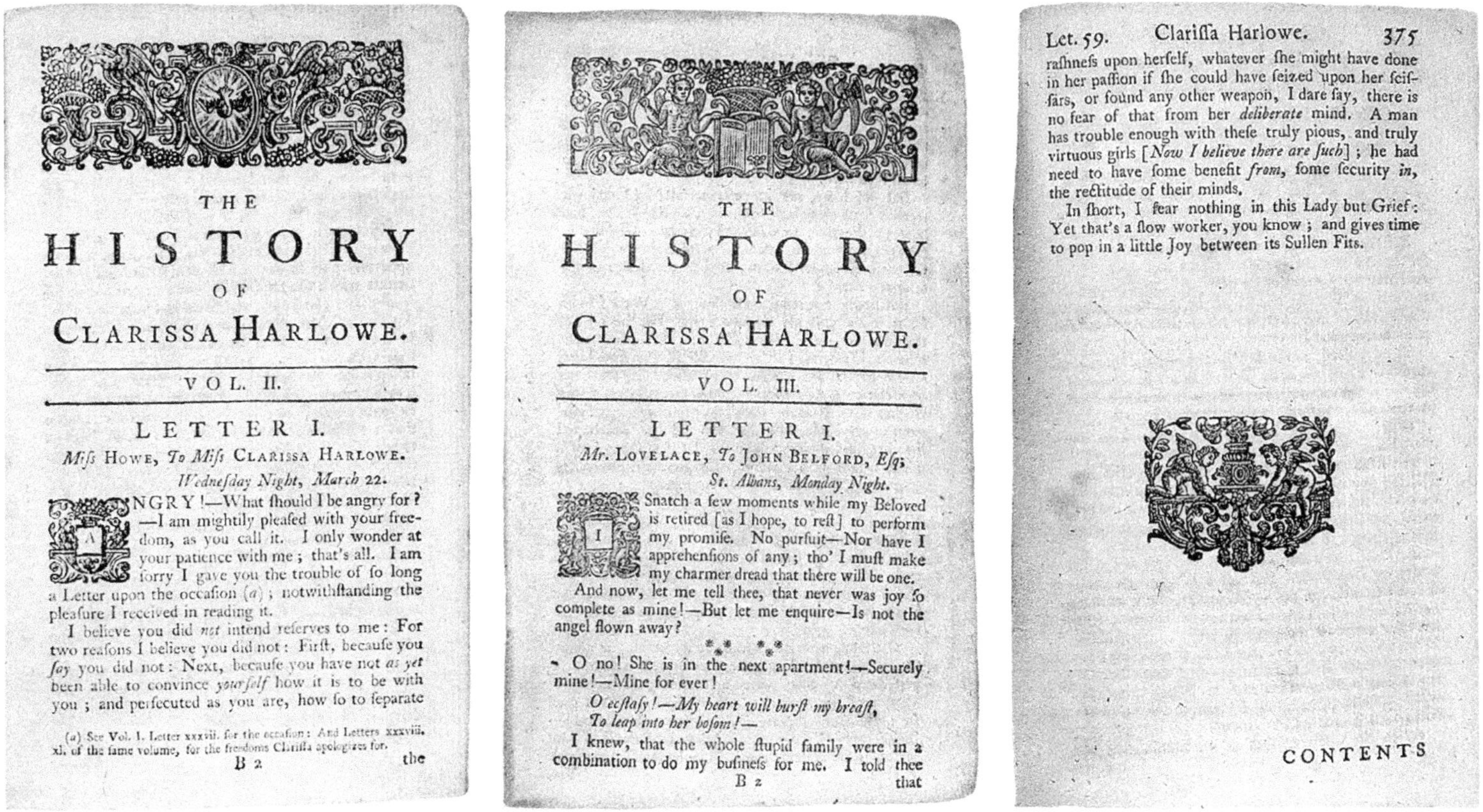

Lct. 59. *Clarissa Harlowe.* 375

rashness upon herself, whatever she might have done in her passion if she could have seized upon her scissars, or found any other weapon, I dare say, there is no fear of that from her *deliberate* mind. A man has trouble enough with these truly pious, and truly virtuous girls [*Now I believe there are such*]; he had need to have some benefit *from*, some security *in*, the rectitude of their minds.

In short, I fear nothing, in this Lady but Grief: Yet that's a slow worker, you know; and gives time to pop in a little joy between its Sullen Fits.

CONTENTS

THE HISTORY OF CLARISSA HARLOWE.

VOL. III.

LETTER I.

Mr. LOVELACE, *To* JOHN BELFORD, *Esq*;

St. Albans, Monday Night.

Snatch a few moments while my Beloved is retired (as I hope, to rest) to perform my promise. No pursuit—Nor have I apprehensions of any; tho' I must make my charmer dread that there will be one. And now, let me tell thee, that never was joy so complete as mine!—But let me enquire—Is not the angel flown away?

*· O no! She is in the next apartment!—Securely mine!—Mine for ever!

*O ecstasy!—My heart will burst my breast,
To leap into her bosom!—

I knew, that the whole stupid family were in a combination to do my business for me. I told thee that

THE HISTORY OF CLARISSA HARLOWE.

VOL. II.

LETTER I.

Miss HOWE, *To Miss* CLARISSA HARLOWE.

Wednesday Night, March 22.

ANGRY!—What should I be angry for?—I am mightily pleased with your freedom, as you call it. I only wonder at your patience with me; that's all. I am sorry I gave you the trouble of so long a Letter upon the occasion (*a*); notwithstanding the pleasure I received in reading it.

I believe you did *not* intend reserves to me: For two reasons I believe you did not: First, because you *say* you did not: Next, because you have not *as yet* been able to convince *yourself* how it is to be with you; and persecuted as you are, how so to separate

(*a*) See Vol. I. Letter xxxiii. for the occasion: And Letters xxxviii. xl. of the same volume, for the freedoms Clarissa spoke given for the

FIGURE 5.18 From the third edition of *Clarissa*, 8 vols. (1751), II, [3]; III, [3]; and IV, 375.

FIGURE 5.19
Tailpiece to Volume v in the third edition of *Clarissa*, 8 vols. (1751).

visual appropriateness evidences Richardson's desire to endow the physical features of his novel with as suggestive a graphic design as his stock of materials allowed.

Ornamentation, it appears, is a graphic cousin of punctuation. M. B. Parkes recounts how the *hedera* (or ivy-leaf symbol ❦), the symbol that is "probably the oldest punctuation mark in the West, appearing in inscriptions of the second century B.C.," evolved into a printer's ornament. Even before the advent of print, manuscripts exploited "its decorative potential." Parkes describes how, in the seventh and eighth centuries, the mark appears at the beginnings and ends of sections in manuscripts; by the twelfth century "there is evidence to suggest that its function as a mark of punctuation was no longer understood." Cast nonetheless in type during the sixteenth century, the *hedera* enters the printed book, where it appears "most frequently . . . as an ornament, usually on title-pages" (although at times in "circumstances which stimulate speculation that its original function had been rediscovered").[54] I have argued that Richardson's use of existing, generic printer's ornaments as temporal markers works in reverse. Richardson seems to recognize in these ornamental *fleurons* (graphic descendants of the *hedera*) a potential for division and organization. Particularly in *Clarissa*, where he uses such small ornaments to indicate temporal interruption in the letters, Richardson revives the non-ornamental qualities of the printer's ornament. He activates, as it were, the ancient function of the *hedera* as a mark of punctuation. When Richardson awakens this ability of the ornaments to punctuate, organize, and mark emphasis, he gains greater control over the fiction's temporal dimensions. He then exploits this control to give the reader an indication of the psychology of his characters.

It need be no surprise then that Richardson seizes with equal enthusiasm upon the interpretive function of punctuation marks – particularly the use of the dash. Richardson's innovations in the printing of direct dialogue and recounted speech and the influence of these innovations upon contemporaries such as Sarah Fielding and Laurence Sterne form the subject of the next chapter.

CHAPTER 6

Sarah Fielding's *David Simple*

a case study in the interpretive significance of punctuation

> In modern Wit all printed Trash, is
> Set off with num'rous *Breaks*—and *Dashes*—
>
> > – Jonathan Swift, "On Poetry: A Rapsody" (1733)[1]

Soon after the initial publication of Sarah Fielding's first novel *The Adventures of David Simple* (1744), her brother Henry assumes editorial control over a second edition, making hundreds of changes to the original text.[2] The title page of the new edition of *David Simple* flaunts Henry Fielding's involvement: "The Second Edition, Revised and Corrected by Henry Fielding, Esq." Sarah had published the first edition anonymously ("By a LADY") and, as a result, Henry is the only Fielding whose name appears on the title page of the second edition. A casual reader might easily suspect that Henry Fielding himself had authored the novel, that his assumption of the identity of a reviser and corrector was analogous to Richardson's "editing" of *Pamela*. At least one nineteenth-century edition of the novel, in fact, falsely attributes authorship to Henry Fielding.[3] Given Henry Fielding's fame and his sister's relative obscurity, any misattributing presumptions almost certainly further improved the book's swift sales.[4] Yet, if Henry Fielding's advertised involvement in *David Simple* was born of such generosity, it seems suspiciously like the kind of magnanimity that is actually the expression of ego, as though Henry Fielding's goal was to displace his anonymous sister as the controlling force behind the novel's production. If the history of scholarship on *David Simple* is any guide, Henry Fielding succeeded in eclipsing his sister's authorship – until quite recently, when she was rescued in the campaign to expand the canon along gender lines.

But even when her novel was rescued from historical obscurity, what was resurrected was not Sarah Fielding's first edition, but the second edition, a text heavily edited by her brother, Henry. Because the second edition of

David Simple contained Henry Fielding's preface, "a major contribution to eighteenth-century theoretical discussions of the novel," it inevitably was the revised edition that became, as Peter Sabor reports, "part of literary history."[5] For example, Malcolm Kelsall's 1969 edition chose the heavily edited second edition as his copy text, conceding that while Henry's alterations were perhaps not "entirely for the good" they were "usually for the best."[6] In some ways such modern editions did not improve much upon the earlier set of twentieth-century critics who had compared the two editions of *David Simple* not to recover Sarah Fielding's original project but rather to identify Henry Fielding's contributions.[7] In contrast, I wish to take another look at Henry Fielding's corrections in order to better understand Sarah Fielding's original intentions. Peter Sabor's return to the first-edition text in his 1998 Kentucky Press edition of *David Simple* has recently seen to it that there is no further need to call for a new edition of the novel.[8] However, the case of Sarah Fielding's *David Simple* impacts upon textual studies in a wider sense. Because many of Sarah Fielding's supposed "errors" bear upon editorial concerns, particularly the literary significance of punctuation, I wish to examine them in light of the novel genre's graphic experimentality.

The most interesting of Sarah Fielding's alleged "Grammatical and other Errors in Style," is her punctuation, above all her unconventional use of the dash.[9] What might, at first glance, appear an eccentric or sloppy application of a vague marker, serves a vital interpretive function – indicating the depth of Sarah Fielding's control over the details of her writing and its visual production. Her original punctuation conveys information through graphic rather than verbal means. Specifically, Sarah Fielding's use of print allows her to echo the non-verbal world which the women of her novel increasingly come to inhabit. Moreover, her punctuation deliberately aligns her novel with a Richardsonian literary tradition resisted by her brother. Understood in this narrative and historical context, Henry Fielding's many "corrections," though seemingly minor, reveal the so-called "accidentals" of *David Simple* to be of critical importance in a reading of the novel. By extension, the accidentals of punctuation – that dense nebula of printed signs that occupies neglected space in the better-charted galaxies of grammar and graphic – may potentially impact on our interpretation of any eighteenth-century book. Even more so than does Richardson's orchestration of the accidentals of ornamentation in *Clarissa*, the "case" of Sarah Fielding's punctuation flies in the face of bibliography's fundamental distinctions between authoritative and "accidental" elements of a book's production. Richardson's status as printer easily explains his desire and ability to maximize the interpretive function of his work's graphic potential. If, on the other hand, a woman with limited means, almost no reputational clout, and only modest access to printers and printing could exert control over those needling marks that punctuate her prose, then perhaps any writer who cared to might control similar aspects of their text. The fact that Sarah Fielding's brother Henry painstakingly removes the hundreds of dashes from her prose in the second edition already hints that there was something more at stake in the novel genre's deployment of this graphic mark than appears at first glance.

In his *Preface* to the second edition, Henry Fielding justified his many revisions:

> *There were some Grammatical and other Errors in Style in the first Impression, which my Absence from Town prevented my correcting, as I have endeavoured, tho' in great Haste, in this Edition: By comparing the one with the other, the Reader may see, if he thinks it worth his while, the Share I have in this Book, as it now stands, and which amounts to little more than the Correction of some small Errors, which Want of Habit in Writing chiefly occasioned, and which no Man of Learning would think worth his Censure in a Romance; nor any Gentleman, in the Writings of a young Woman.* (vii)[10]

In this criticism of his sister's work, Henry Fielding measures his sister's text against decidedly masculine standards of "correctness." Although the preface faintly praises the author as naturally gifted, it also notes her "*Want of Habit in Writing.*" The result of this "*Want of Habit*" is an unsophisticated text marred by errors commonly found in "*a Romance*" or in "*the Writings of a young Woman.*" In turn, these errors mark its author as unschooled in the developing discourse of the novel. Henry Fielding "excuses" Sarah Fielding's "*Errors in Style*" as the results of her gender and education. He thus displaces the responsibility for the "*Errors*" from the personal to the social. In the next paragraph, for example, Henry Fielding recounts how the author's mistakes arose "*not from want of Genius, but of Learning*" (viii). He announces that it is the "*first Performance of one, whose Sex and Age entitle her to the gentlest Criticisms*" (viii). In each locus, the preface points to gender as the fundamental cause of Sarah Fielding's literary immaturity. Her sex traps her native "*Genius*" within a prose style whose deviations from convention reflect unsurprising feminine errors. Henry Fielding's preface, in fact, recapitulates various mechanisms of mid-eighteenth-century social control, establishing the dominance of his discourse and the subservience of his sister's. His patronizing rhetoric even raises the specter of class when he identifies himself as a "*Gentleman*" judging the "*Writings of a young Woman,*" as opposed to the editor of the slightly more genteel "LADY" prominently mentioned on the title page. Yet, he speaks here of his own sister, someone most definitely from the same social class. Why construct such artificial social distinctions between himself and his sister? What are the specific "*Errors in Style*" that warrant this charged rhetoric and forceful correction?

Taking up Henry Fielding's invitation to compare the two editions yields, on the surface, surprisingly meager results. Although his interventions are numerous, taken individually they are minute and rarely involve substantial changes to the narrative.[11] Malcolm Kelsall, editor of the Oxford edition of *David Simple* (1987), judges the most important of the changes to be those that introduce the subject of Don Quixote into the narrative's discussion of friendship, changes which "remind the reader of the roots in tradition of the kind of fiction he and his sister are writing."[12] In addition, Peter Sabor sees "Henry Fielding the lawyer giving a more solid legal foundation to such issues as bequeathing an estate and witnessing the signing of a will."[13] Such local corrections usually only involve the substitution of a word or the insertion of a brief phrase. As a result, page numbers for most passages in the second edition text correspond neatly to those in the first, because Henry's corrections rarely upset more than a single line of the original.[14] For example, on page 38 in Volume I (of both editions), Henry Fielding prefers "which" over "that," "consider" over "think," and "examined" over "consider"; he also changes "convinced, to" to "convinced that to" and inserts an unequivocal "absolutely." Numerically, the greatest portion of Henry Fielding's minor changes are stylistic, concerning what Kelsall dismisses as "matters of punctuation, spelling or grammar only."[15] Specifically, notes Kelsall, "Henry Fielding particularly disliked his sister's characteristic form of punctuation – the dash."[16] In fact, this "dislike" prompts Henry Fielding to alter his sister's punctuation throughout the novel, consistently deleting or replacing hundreds of her dashes. This seems odd, given the quality of the rhetoric in the preface, because it means that Henry Fielding deploys the heavy guns of patriarchy against, of all things, the dash.

It is impossible to gloss Henry Fielding's criticisms without considering the context of syntactical and stylistic practice in mid-eighteenth-century England. The fact is that there were no set rules governing punctuation. M. B. Parkes's study of the evolution of punctuation demonstrates that many graphic syntactical markers, including the dash, remained in flux throughout the century.[17] As a result of the continued instability of certain printed symbols, punctuation in the eighteenth-century novel was "approximate at best."[18] Without the precision of codified rules, punctuation in eighteenth-century print reflected the habits of individual printers, compositors, and authors, serving as a visual guide for readers rather than as an exact map to syntax. Of course, the general instability of printed symbols robs Henry Fielding's objections to his sister's punctuation of their self-proclaimed authority. He is not measuring her "*Errors*" against a rigid, objective grammatical standard, but rather is imposing his own subjective stylistic preferences as though they were themselves that standard. Yet, if punctuation is merely a matter of preference, his vehement objections to her dashes seem problematic, even unjustified.

Before tackling this problem, it is necessary to be as certain as possible that the dashes in Sarah Fielding's edition are actually her own and not those of a compositor. As mentioned previously, bibliographers term dashes, along with italics, punctuation, ornamentation, and capitalization, "accidentals," a term which captures the common eighteenth-century practice of leaving these details of a text to the discretion of the compositor. From a bibliographical standpoint, the appearance of the page (including the placement of dashes) was often an "accident" of the physical production of the book rather than an intended part of the author's text. However, bibliography's technical vocabulary can be misleading, as accidentals are not always accidents of the printing process. In some cases, there is clear evidence that authors controlled the accidentals of their texts. "Accidental alterations" from edition to edition, writes bibliographer Philip Gaskell, "have no authority, but are merely the result of carelessness, or zealousness, of the compositor . . . *unless* there is reason to believe that the author himself ordered them."[19] Sometimes it is easy to find such a reason. Samuel Richardson, for example, printed his own novels; as a result, we can assume that his pages look the way he wanted them to look.

In Sarah Fielding's case, deciding who controlled her accidentals presents more of a challenge. Because her holograph for *David Simple* (or indeed for any of her fictions) has not been recovered, we may never know with complete certainty that the punctuation of the printer's copy was not systematically altered by the compositor. Such alterations have been known to occur in book production throughout the hand-press period. In addition, it is not inconceivable that the distribution of work among different compositors may account for variations in a work's punctuation from one volume, or section of text, to another.[20] Yet, in the case of *David Simple*, the distribution of dashes exhibits such internal textual coherence, as will become clear, that it is difficult to think that they could have been placed there by a compositor or compositors. Moreover, it is now known that Henry Fielding controlled his own accidentals in Andrew Millar's printshop, which also printed Sarah Fielding's novel. Martin C. Battestin, one of the editors of the Wesleyan Edition of Henry Fielding, locates patterns of interpretive emphasis in the accidentals in *Tom Jones* which indicate that, at least in Henry Fielding's books, italics and capitals were not left to the preference or whim of the compositor in Millar's shop but were deliberately placed there by the author.[21] The fact that Millar allowed the famous author Henry Fielding to dictate accidentals is, of course, no guarantee that the relatively obscure Sarah Fielding enjoyed the same privilege. It does prove, however, that Millar's shop was amenable to such requests from authors. Ultimately, it is Henry Fielding himself who authorizes my claim that Sarah

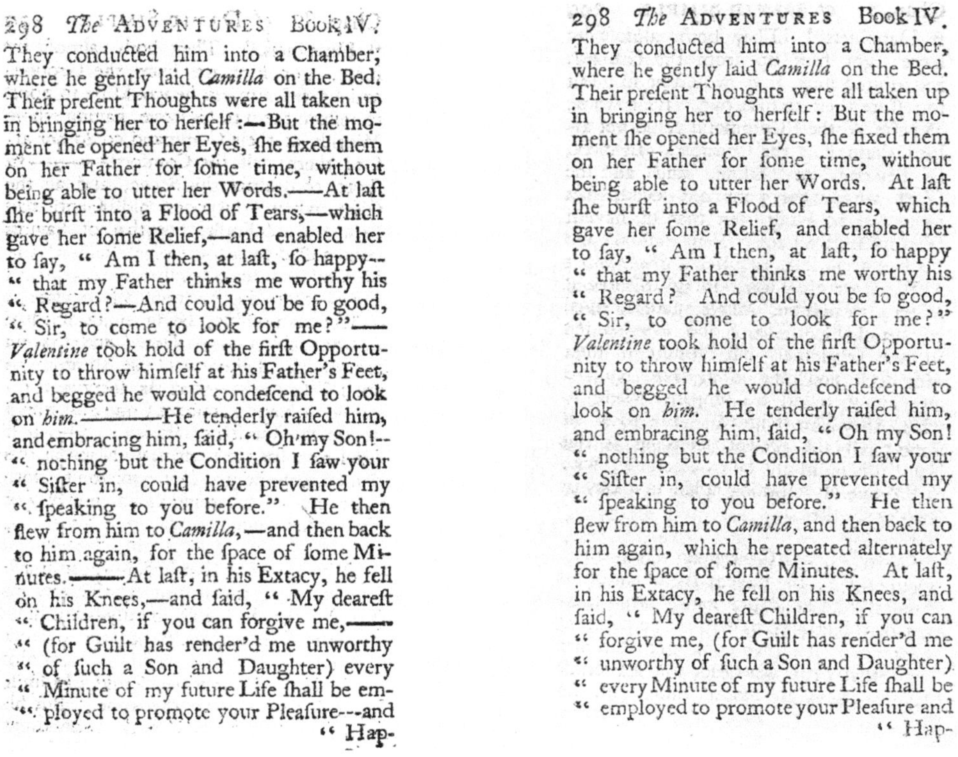

298 *The* ADVENTURES BOOK IV.
They conducted him into a Chamber, where he gently laid *Camilla* on the Bed. Their present Thoughts were all taken up in bringing her to herself:—But the moment she opened her Eyes, she fixed them on her Father for some time, without being able to utter her Words.—At last she burst into a Flood of Tears,—which gave her some Relief,—and enabled her to say, " Am I then, at last, so happy— " that my Father thinks me worthy his " Regard?—And could you be so good, " Sir, to come to look for me?"— *Valentine* took hold of the first Opportunity to throw himself at his Father's Feet, and begged he would condescend to look on *him*.————He tenderly raised him, and embracing him, said, " Oh my Son!— " nothing but the Condition I saw your " Sister in, could have prevented my " speaking to you before." He then flew from him to *Camilla*,—and then back to him again, for the space of some Minutes.————At last, in his Extacy, he fell on his Knees,—and said, " My dearest " Children, if you can forgive me,—— " (for Guilt has render'd me unworthy " of such a Son and Daughter) every " Minute of my future Life shall be em- " ployed to promote your Pleasure---and " Hap-

298 *The* ADVENTURES Book IV.
They conducted him into a Chamber, where he gently laid *Camilla* on the Bed. Their present Thoughts were all taken up in bringing her to herself: But the moment she opened her Eyes, she fixed them on her Father for some time, without being able to utter her Words. At last she burst into a Flood of Tears, which gave her some Relief, and enabled her to say, " Am I then, at last, so happy " that my Father thinks me worthy his " Regard? And could you be so good, " Sir, to come to look for me?" *Valentine* took hold of the first Opportunity to throw himself at his Father's Feet, and begged he would condescend to look on *him*. He tenderly raised him, and embracing him, said, " Oh my Son! " nothing but the Condition I saw your " Sister in, could have prevented my " speaking to you before." He then flew from him to *Camilla*, and then back to him again, which he repeated alternately for the space of some Minutes. At last, in his Extacy, he fell on his Knees, and said, " My dearest Children, if you can " forgive me, (for Guilt has render'd me " unworthy of such a Son and Daughter) " every Minute of my future Life shall be " employed to promote your Pleasure and " Hap-

FIGURE 6.1 Page 298, Volume II, as it appears in the first (left) and second (right) editions of Sarah Fielding's *The Adventures of David Simple*, 2 vols. (London: Printed by A. Millar, 1744).

Fielding controlled her first edition's punctuation. Above all, Henry Fielding's editorial emendations and prefatory account of a feminine style assert that the unconventional punctuation found in the first edition must be attributed to its original author, Sarah Fielding.

In the context of eighteenth-century convention, Sarah Fielding's application of the dash gives little cause for objection. Although she wields it with uncommon frequency, she does not violate the syntactical, organizing function for which many other eighteenth-century writers employ the dash. On the level of the sentence, the dash paces Sarah Fielding's narrative in familiar ways. It marks pauses, rhetorical transitions, approximate syntax, and moments of aposiopesis – the intentional refusals to complete an idea, name or phrase so common in eighteenth-century literature. She also frequently uses the dash in combination with other marks of punctuation, even placing dashes between sentences already syntactically distinguished by full stops. On page 298 in Volume II of the first edition, neither grammar nor syntax requires any of the dashes seen on this page (Figure 6.1, left). Here, in all fourteen occurrences of the dash, it is either syntactically unnecessary or accompanied by another, self-sufficient punctuation mark. Indeed when Henry Fielding removes all the dashes on this page, he does not have to substitute any other marks of punctuation in their place (Figure 6.1, right). However, such a redundant application of the dash (often to signal greater and smaller pauses) is also not altogether unprecedented in eighteenth-century texts. The ubiquity and distribution of Sarah Fielding's dashes in *David Simple*, however, is unusual. Something other than the ignorance ascribed by her brother must explain this distinctive use of a graphic device that was itself in flux at this time.

In Sarah Fielding's original edition the dash appears with increasing frequency as the story develops, slowly emerging as a highly visible and self-conscious element of her printed page. The first instance of a dash deployed as a mark of punctuation (as opposed to hyphens or omission of names in, say, "my Lady —") occurs on page 122 of this 600-page novel. Almost all of the final 108 pages of Sarah Fielding's original text (there are 5 exceptions) contain multiple uses of the punctuating dash. Roughly the first 20 percent of *David Simple*, that is, lacks any use of the dash as a form of punctuation, while the final 20 percent of the text contains multiple dashes on almost every page. In the intervening 60 percent of the novel's central text, the dash occurs with increasing frequency. Once Sarah Fielding gives the dash an organizing function in her prose, it slowly assumes an expanding role as a visual feature of her printed text. Any interpretive evaluation of Sarah Fielding's dashes, or her brother's objections to them, must account for this uneven numerical distribution.

Sarah Fielding divides her two-volume text into four "Books" of roughly equal length. I have charted the number of occurrences of the dash in each of her four books alongside a tally of those removed by her brother in the second edition, in order to locate more exactly the trends in punctuation marked by the dash in the different editions:

David Simple divisions	No. of dashes in first edition	No. of dashes removed by HF	Approximate % of dashes removed
Volume I, Book 1 pp. 1–137	11	3	27
Volume I, Book 2 pp. 138–278	108	82	76
Volume II, Book 3 pp. 1–146	86	72	84
Volume II, Book 4 pp. 147–322	603	570	95

These numbers indicate two patterns: one regarding Sarah Fielding's use of the dash; the other regarding Henry Fielding's excision of it. It can be shown that Sarah Fielding uses the dash to express the different modes of communication between her characters, including the increasingly non-verbal communication that is a characteristic of the sentimental novel. The data also suggests that Henry Fielding's efforts to remove the dash from his sister's printed pages grow at a rate in excess of Sarah Fielding's increased production of dashes. Henry Fielding, one could say, appears to become disproportionately concerned with the presence of the dash in the first-edition text.[22] The dash's rhetorical status within the context of eighteenth-century print culture may account for Henry Fielding's agitations, revealing literary concerns entirely unrelated to considerations of syntactical clarity.

To start with the first edition, Sarah Fielding manipulates the dash to enhance the meaning of her text in two, seemingly contradictory, ways: as a visual sign both of conversation and silence. As visual markers of spoken speech, the dashes promote the sense of conversational immediacy and psychological affect. And, as graphic markers of silence, the dashes allow Sarah Fielding to emphasize the important role non-verbal communication plays in the novel.

The dashes create a conversational effect by signaling the transitions, interruptions, and momentary hesitations of direct speech. Conversations and exclamations in the first edition are peppered with dashes of differing lengths. When, for example, Isabelle relates her tragic family history of jealousy and betrayal, the dashes convey her conversationally fractured grammar and spontaneous changes in thought:

> WHAT a Condition was I in—what could I think!---My Brother--*Dorimene*--*Dumont*---all seemed involved in one common Madness.[23]

Visually augmenting the verbal text, Sarah Fielding's dashes substitute for connectives ordinarily elided from spoken language, helping to relate the "---Hum—and Ha—" of ordinary spoken speech (II, 228). In combination with italics and quotation marks, the liveliness and immediacy of a conversation are conveyed in printed form. This is true even when an exclamation is narrated indirectly, without quotation marks:

> The Words *Horrid Stuff*——*Was ever such Nonsense!*——*Bad Plot! &c.*——were re-echoed throughout the House.   (I, 123)

And when snippets of conversation are overheard from a great distance, the dash's conversational "immediacy" codes not for a spontaneity of accretions, but for the muddled, fragmented perception of the listener:

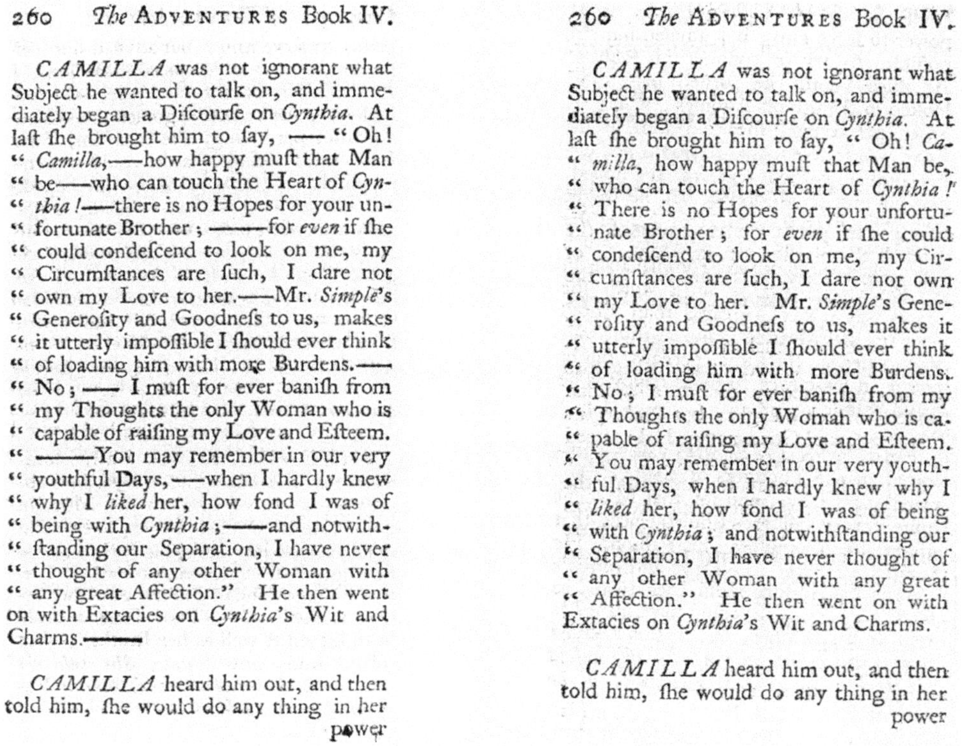

> | 260 *The* ADVENTURES Book IV. | 260 *The* ADVENTURES Book IV. |
> |---|---|
> | CAMILLA was not ignorant what Subject he wanted to talk on, and immediately began a Discourse on *Cynthia*. At last she brought him to say, —— "Oh! " *Camilla*,——how happy must that Man " be——who can touch the Heart of *Cyn-* " *thia !*——there is no Hopes for your un- " fortunate Brother ; ——for *even* if she " could condescend to look on me, my " Circumstances are such, I dare not " own my Love to her.——Mr. *Simple*'s " Generosity and Goodness to us, makes " it utterly impossible I should ever think " of loading him with more Burdens.—— " No ; —— I must for ever banish from " my Thoughts the only Woman who is " capable of raising my Love and Esteem. " ——You may remember in our very " youthful Days,——when I hardly knew " why I *liked* her, how fond I was of " being with *Cynthia* ;——and notwith- " standing our Separation, I have never " thought of any other Woman with " any great Affection." He then went on with Extacies on *Cynthia*'s Wit and Charms.—— | CAMILLA was not ignorant what Subject he wanted to talk on, and immediately began a Discourse on *Cynthia*. At last she brought him to say, " Oh! *Ca-* " *milla,* how happy must that Man be, " who can touch the Heart of *Cynthia !* " There is no Hopes for your unfortu- " nate Brother ; for *even* if she could " condescend to look on me, my Cir- " cumstances are such, I dare not own " my Love to her. Mr. *Simple*'s Gene- " rosity and Goodness to us, makes it " utterly impossible I should ever think " of loading him with more Burdens. " No ; I must for ever banish from my " Thoughts the only Woman who is ca- " pable of raising my Love and Esteem. " You may remember in our very youth- " ful Days, when I hardly knew why I " *liked* her, how fond I was of being " with *Cynthia* ; and notwithstanding our " Separation, I have never thought of " any other Woman with any great " Affection." He then went on with Extacies on *Cynthia*'s Wit and Charms. |
> | CAMILLA heard him out, and then told him, she would do any thing in her power | CAMILLA heard him out, and then told him, she would do any thing in her power |

FIGURE 6.2 Page 260, Volume II, as it appears in the first (left) and second (right) editions of Sarah Fielding's *The Adventures of David Simple*, 2 vols. (London: Printed by A. Millar, 1744).

> he could not make much of what they said; only he confusedly heard the words Love—Passion—the Marquis *de Stainville*—*Isabelle*—and by what he could gather, he fancied he had very convincing Proofs that there was an Intrigue carrying on between them. (II, 185)

In each of these passages, Sarah Fielding uses the dash to heighten the realism of the novel: it visually documents auditory and temporal aspects of "real" speech which cannot be adequately captured by verbal transcription alone.[24]

As markers of spoken speech, Sarah Fielding's dashes also convey the speaker's emotional state. Like visual signposts of a character's genuine sentiment, the dashes appear in the text whenever characters relate events of emotional importance. Dashes heighten the novel's emotional realism in, for example, Valentine's passionate declaration of love for Cynthia (Figure 6.2, left). Here, by means of the dashes, Sarah Fielding's page conveys the authenticity of Valentine's passion visually as well as verbally. The narrator tells us that "*Valentine* followed his Sister into her Room, and seemed almost choked for want of Power to utter his Thoughts" (II, 259). Sarah Fielding communicates to the reader the hesitations and awkward transitions of Valentine's "choked" emotionalism, his rambling, passionate outbursts, by means of the dash. While the verbal text of this scene in the second edition remains identical, Henry Fielding's dash-less version of Valentine's speech lacks the intensity and sought-after sincerity of the verbal–visual original (Figure 6.2, right).

By enabling her to convey the conversational and emotional nuances that underlie printed speech, Sarah Fielding's dashes also mediate the narrative distance created by the multiple layers of narration in *David Simple*. While the novel opens with an omniscient narrator, this authorial persona is slowly supplanted by the voices of the characters themselves as they offer to tell David, and by extension the reader, their life stories. Indeed, as the novel progresses, the omniscient narrator fades away. Ironically, the telling of tales from the perspectives of different characters, a process which often involves the recounting of whole conversations in the third person, enlarges the narrative distance between the reader and these doubly, sometimes triply, narrated events. When, for example, Cynthia tells of a rivalry between two sisters, Corinna and Sacharissa, the dialogue, itself an odd mixture of quotation and third-person narration, regains some of its lost immediacy with the visual insertion of dashes:

> *Sacharissa*, with whom I con-
> versed as often as I could get liberty,
> told me, that *Corinna* often asked her,
> "How long she thought she should
> "reign thus *absolute*—in her Husband's
> "House,—if she made an *humble fond*
> "*Wife*,---and did not continually shew
> "him how much he was *obliged to her*---
> "for *chusing him?*" I will relate to you
> one Scene that passed between them,
> Word for Word, as *Sacharissa* told it me.
> (II, 253–54)

In this instance, the running quotation marks and italics assist the dashes in the graphic animation of indirect speech by visually imposing "original" speech patterns, stress, and tone upon the printed verbal narrative. Interestingly enough, while Henry Fielding eliminates the dashes from this passage, he does not alter the first edition's italics. Nor does he remove the unnecessary quotation marks from this third-person narration. Henry Fielding's alterations in this passage are, in fact, representative of his editorial method: he singles out the dash for criticism in places where other accidentals appear equally (or more) deserving of correction.

Perhaps the most intriguing aspect of Sarah Fielding's dashes is the manner in which they embody the wide spectrum of silent communication in the world of *David Simple*. Towards the end of the novel, precisely at that juncture in the text where the ubiquity of the dash becomes increasingly apparent, the four main characters fall in love. Here, as in many sentimental fictions of the period, romantic feelings begin to impede speech. Valentine's "choaked" expression of love for Cynthia is a good example of this. Similarly, David is described as "lov[ing] *Camilla* so sincerely, that whatever Resolutions he made to declare it to her, the great Awe with which he was seized whenever he approached her, took from him the Power of speaking" (II, 262). Because of their specific circumstances, debts, and loyalties, each character also feels honor-bound not to put his or her affections into words: "And [David] was afraid to mention it to her Brother first, lest she should be offended, and think he was *mean* enough to expect a Compliance from them both, on account of the Obligations they owed him" (II, 262). When this emotional and socially induced paralysis takes hold, the characters are described as being "deprived . . . of the Power of Speech" or speaking only with "faultering Voice" (II, 300; 296). It is then that silent signals such as looks, blushes, and glances are exchanged as alternative, even if often inadvertent, means of spontaneous communication. In asking the body's speechlessness to code for emotional authenticity, Sarah Fielding is not breaking new ground. Observable physical manifestations of feeling are a defining feature of sentimental fiction in this period. In a stock sentimental narrative tears, sighs, and glances offer reliable evidence of emotion and virtue.[25] *David Simple* participates in this sentimental tradition. The final book of this novel, especially, is filled with non-verbal communiqués. David, for example, "fix'd his Eyes stedfastly on *Camilla*, till he saw her blush, and seem out of countenance" (II, 259). In accordance with the prevailing model of sensibility, the narrator claims that such silent exchanges rival the eloquence of speech: "[T]he Wanness of their Looks, . . . and the faultring of their Voices, more strongly pointed out their Thoughts than the most laboured Eloquence could possibly have done" (II, 273–74). While reading the physical body as a text is characteristic of sentimental fiction, Sarah Fielding's creative use of the dash offers her readers a new way of observing these signs. The dash literalizes the metaphor of the body as a text by reenacting these non-verbal signs in the textual body of the printed page.

This use of the dash gives Sarah Fielding a unique way of communicating most particularly the emotional states of her female characters. Although all the characters, male as well as female, suffer from these awkward, emotionally induced silences, the women find it especially difficult to voice their feelings. While Valentine can express his love for Cynthia (no matter how "choaked"), his sister finds herself incapable of privately confessing her similar passion for David:

> ——Poor *Camilla* could have sighed as well as her Brother; ---but I don't know how it was; *She could not so easily unfold Griefs of that Kind to* Valentine, *as he could to her.* (II, 261)

Although the narrator claims ignorance of the cause of Camilla's silence, the novel implicitly asserts that while declaring one's affections may be problematic for anyone, it is particularly difficult for women. Punctilio forbids the women in *David Simple* from expressing feelings for the opposite sex. Silenced on matters of love by social convention, women turn to visual cues in order to communicate the unspoken: when "[Camilla] alternately blushed,——turned pale,——and seemed to be in the greatest Agitation of Spirits imaginable," her body silently and visually acknowledges emotions she may not (as well as cannot) put into words (II, 265–66). Sarah Fielding's dashes must be read, not only as evidence of sentimentalism but as textual manifestations of a woman's coerced emotional silence. She means for the dash to represent the gendered non-verbal world inhabited by women.

Working within a medium that privileges the word, Sarah Fielding finds in the dash a way for print to acknowledge the double-edged role of silence in contemporary life. When Henry Fielding takes the dashes out of his sister's text, he undermines the privileged position of silence in her sentimental novel. The dashes give Sarah Fielding a way to express silent sentiment concretely on the page; when Henry Fielding takes them out, what is left of this silent internal world is, literally, nothing. He eradicates moments in which silence, as in Valentine's broken speech or Camilla's be-dashed blushes, is evidence of profound sentiment and virtue. The second-edition text essentially amputates a whole range of emotional expression from the novel, including the hesitations, glances, and intonations associated with the dash throughout the text. Indeed, by removing the graphic, non-verbal representations of such silent gestures, he also eliminates precisely the visual mode of expression upon which the novel's women in particular depend for their emotional "voice." So, in this sense at least, Henry Fielding's editorial emendations reflect an eradication of a "feminine" style after all. This is not to say that Henry Fielding was correct in designating the dash as a telltale mark of female authorship. Indeed, as will become clear below, the popularizers of the dash in contemporary prose fiction were men such as Dunton, Richardson, and Sterne. But, by eliminating the printed equivalent of silences from Sarah Fielding's writing, her brother eliminates a form of expression from her pages which, in part, symbolizes a socially dictated silence imposed upon the women of this novel.

Finally, any account of the interpretive impact of Sarah Fielding's dashes must acknowledge their cumulative effect upon the reading experience as they build towards a visual crescendo in the novel's final book. The distribution of the dashes indeed suggests a self-conscious effort on the part of Sarah Fielding to enliven her text with a graphic dynamism. The dashes animate her book, not merely within isolated passages and dialogue, but as a whole, for they convey a growing sense of immediacy, even urgency, as one gets closer to the end of the novel. Thus the dashes lend a progressive visual evolution to Sarah Fielding's pages. Because of the dash, the canvas of the page upon which the novel's events are drawn increasingly asserts itself as a "picture" in its own right – a visual context animating the verbal text of the novel. When Henry Fielding eliminates the dashes from the two volumes of *David Simple*, he also eradicates this overarching visual dynamism. His corrections subdue the vitality of Sarah Fielding's fiction by conventionalizing its appearance. The second edition reads more uniformly than the first, not because Henry Fielding's corrections provide an uneven work with a needed regularity, but because they deliberately eliminate the forward thrust and unorthodox animation produced by Sarah Fielding's visual design.

Whether because she ultimately acquiesced to her brother's preferences regarding punctuation, or because her subsequent projects did not demand the same graphic exegesis of female silence, Sarah Fielding does not reinstate *David Simple*'s particular experiments with the dash in her subsequent fictions. This, in spite of the fact that she will continue to play about with the novel's graphic vitality (as in *The Cry*'s deployment of the layout of printed plays).

That Sarah Fielding's dashes aim to convey realism, sentimentalism, and the silent world of the women in the novel does not fully explain Henry Fielding's increasingly vehement objections. Indeed, he frequently replaces her dashes with commas, even in those instances where they serve an essential syntactical function, such as separating phrases or clauses. The trading of a dash for a comma suggests that the former mark occupied a rhetorical position within print culture not shared by the latter. Samuel Johnson's *Dictionary* (1755), indeed, confirms the existence of a long-standing rhetorical prejudice against the dash in mid-eighteenth-century print culture. Johnson defines a punctuating "dash" as:

> A DASH n. f. [from the verb.]
> 3. A mark in writing; a line—, to note a pause, or omission.

Johnson then cites two illustrative quotations:

> He is afraid of letters and characters, of notes and *dashes*,
> which, set together, do signify nothing. *Brown's Vulgar Err.*
> In modern wit all printed trash is
> set off with num'rous breaks and *dashes*.   *Swift*[26]

As is the case with many of the *Dictionary*'s entries, Johnson's own inclinations and opinions emerge through his selection of textual illustrations. These excerpts from Sir Thomas Browne's *Vulgar Errors* (1645) and Jonathan Swift's "On Poetry: A Rapsody" (1733) show that Johnson endorsed Browne and Swift in their disapproval of the visual gimmickry of popular printed works.[27] The selection from Swift, written more than a decade before *David Simple*, designates the dash as a telltale mark of the lowly Grubstreet hack. This must already have been Henry Fielding's conviction when, in *The Author's Farce* (1730), he names his play's down-and-out cast of "scribblers" Mr. Scarecrow, Mr. Quibble, Mr. Blotpage, and Mr. Dash. Henry Fielding's resistance to his sister's dashes should then be seen in this larger context and within this long-standing, widespread objection to a device labeled as lower-class and ephemeral by prominent voices.

The work of printer-author John Dunton epitomizes the kind of Grubstreet application of the dash to which Browne, Swift, Johnson, and, apparently, Henry Fielding unanimously objected. In the late seventeenth century, long before the emergence of Henry Fielding's new "species" of writing, Dunton's eclectic combinations of travel literature, spiritual autobiography, and journalism combined a penchant for gimmickry and novelty with visual artistry. Dunton's creative use of punctuation and typography in his *A Voyage Round the World; or a Pocket-Library* (1691) resembles Sarah Fielding's visual experimentation with the dash in *David Simple* (Figure 6.3). With Dunton as one of the most infamous examples of an inveterate dash user, the dash (particularly when applied in large numbers) connoted informality, formlessness, and an attempt at popular appeal – the visual equivalent of easy listening. In light of the dash's associations with Grubstreet writers, Henry Fielding's objections to his sister's punctuation imply concern regarding the reading level and audience to which she was implicitly appealing.[28] Henry Fielding found in his sister's manipulation of print convention a threat to the status of that species of writing of which he considered himself the founder.

Although Dunton's work may have been "technically way ahead of its time," the visually innovative *Voyage* was "not a commercial success."[29] Dunton's visual novelty was only appreciated after 1762 when, upon the success of Laurence Sterne's *Tristram Shandy*, a clever publisher reprinted Dunton's narrative as *The Life, Travels, and Adventures of Christopher Wagstaff, Gentleman, Grandfather to Tristram Shandy*.[30] As this re-titling of the digressive *Voyage* implies, Dunton's work, in both its verbal ramblings and its visual experimentality, pre-figures Sterne. Similarly, Sarah Fielding's "characteristic" use of the dash foreshadows a well-known Shandean feature (Figure 6.4). Ian Watt writes that "the most obvious indication of [Sterne's] conversational style is the punctuation, and especially the use of the dash."[31] Sterne himself identifies his overall narrative

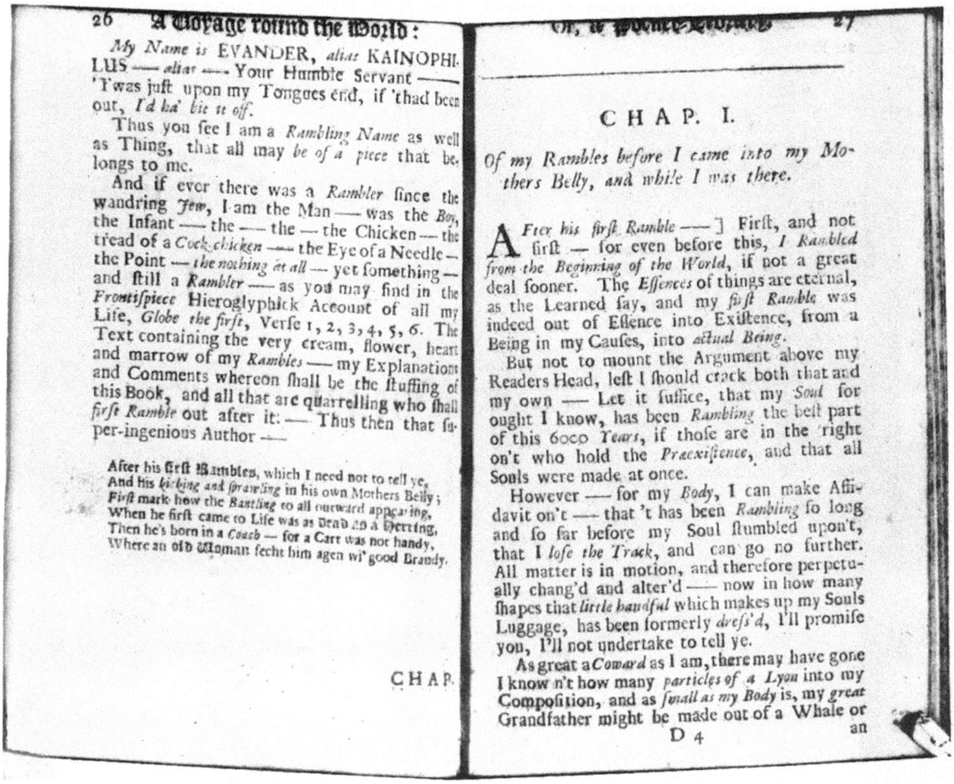

26 A Voyage round the World:

My Name is EVANDER, *alias* KAINOPHILUS — *alias* — Your Humble Servant — 'Twas juſt upon my Tongues end, if 'thad been out, *I'd ha' bit it off.*

Thus you ſee I am a *Rambling Name* as well as Thing, that all may *be of a piece* that belongs to me.

And if ever there was a *Rambler* ſince the wandring *Jew*, I am the Man — was the *Boy*, the Infant — the — the — the Chicken — the tread of a *Cock-chicken* — the Eye of a Needle — the Point — *the nothing at all* — yet ſomething — and ſtill a *Rambler* — as you may find in the *Frontiſpiece* Hieroglyphick Account of all my Life, *Globe the firſt*, Verſe 1, 2, 3, 4, 5, 6. The Text containing the very cream, flower, heart and marrow of my *Rambles* — my Explanations and Comments whereon ſhall be the ſtuffing of this Book, and all that are quarrelling who ſhall *firſt Ramble* out after it: — Thus then that ſuper-ingenious Author —

After his firſt Rambles, which I need not to tell ye,
And his *kicking and ſprawling* in his own Mothers Belly;
Firſt mark how the *Bantling* to all outward appearing,
When he firſt came to Life was as Dead as a Herring,
Then he's born in a *Coach* — for a Cart was not handy,
Where an old Woman fecht him agen wi' good Brandy.

CHAP.

Or, a Pocket-Library. 27

CHAP. I.

Of my Rambles before I came into my Mothers Belly, and while I was there.

AFter his firſt Ramble —] Firſt, and not firſt — for even before this, *I Rambled from the Beginning of the World*, if not a great deal ſooner. The *Eſſences* of things are eternal, as the Learned ſay, and my *firſt Ramble* was indeed out of Eſſence into Exiſtence, from a Being in my Cauſes, into *actual Being.*

But not to mount the Argument above my Readers Head, leſt I ſhould crack both that and my own — Let it ſuffice, that my *Soul* for ought I know, has been *Rambling* the beſt part of this 6000 *Years*, if thoſe are in the right on't who hold the *Praexiſtence*, and that all Souls were made at once.

However — for my *Body*, I can make Affidavit on't — that 't has been *Rambling* ſo long and ſo far before my Soul ſtumbled upon't, that I *loſe the Track*, and can go no further. All matter is in motion, and therefore perpetually chang'd and alter'd — now in how many ſhapes that *little handful* which makes up my Souls Luggage, has been formerly *dreſs'd*, I'll promiſe you, I'll not undertake to tell ye.

As great a *Coward* as I am, there may have gone I know n't how many *particles of a Lyon* into my Compoſition, and as *ſmall as my Body* is, my *great* Grandfather might be made out of a Whale or an

D 4

FIGURE 6.3 From a microfilm reproduction of John Dunton's *A Voyage Round the World: or, a Pocket-Library, Divided into several Volumes. The First of which contains the Rare Adventures of Don Kainophilus . . .* (London: Printed for Richard Newcome, [1691]), I, 26–27.

technique as conversational when Tristram announces: "Writing, when properly managed, (as you may be sure I think mine is) is but a different name for conversation" (II, xi). Printed devices such as the dash play an important role in Sterne's stylistic "manage[ment]" of his "conversation" with the reader. Sarah Fielding's manipulation of print to enhance her novel anticipates the type of visual experimentation to which Sterne ultimately gave prominent expression during the 1760s.[32] "[T]here must be very few pages of *Tristram Shandy*," asserts Watt, "which do not have many more dashes than is usual in any but the most amateurish writing."[33] Given the Grubstreet association with the dash and a prevailing contemporary prejudice against its use, Watt's assertion that the prolix use of the dash was, in the mid-eighteenth century, a mark of "amateurish writing" is in line with Henry Fielding's assessment of his sister's writing as unschooled. Henry Fielding's death in 1754 preempted any criticisms he might have had of Sterne's prolix use of the dash. However, his

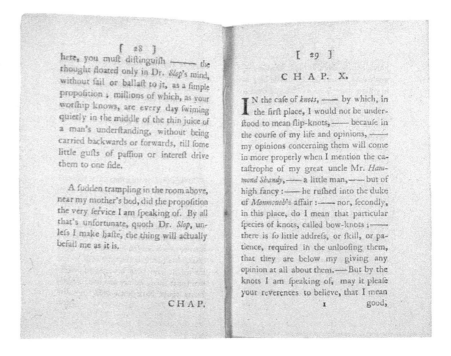

FIGURE 6.4 From Laurence Sterne's *Tristram Shandy*, second edition (1761), III, 28–29.

editorship of *David Simple* in 1744 confirms that, at that time, he objected to importing such typographical gimmickry into the novel.[34]

If Henry Fielding objects to his sister's dashes because of their long-standing associations with Grubstreet gimmickry, he also, perhaps, resists her creative use of typography because it smacks of the influence of his most formidable literary rival, Richardson.[35] Like Dunton, Richardson's printings of his works are, observes Vivienne Mylne, particularly "rich in dashes."[36] Extending Mylne's observation, Steven R. Price argues that "Lovelace's extensive use of the em dash," in particular, sets the villain's letters apart and proposes that Richardson applies accidentals such as the dash – along with italics and small capitals in letters by Brand and Belford, respectively – to "define each letter writer" and offer the reader "idiosyncrasies" akin to those in a collection of actual holographs.[37] But unlike Dunton's failed experiments, Richardson's application of innovative punctuation techniques in the printing of his fictions proves eminently successful and influential. In fact, Parkes credits Richardson with popularizing the dash in prose fiction dialogue:

> During the course of the eighteenth century novelists had introduced other graphic devices intended to recall particular features of spoken language. Samuel Richardson – a master printer as well as a novelist – drew upon his taste for the drama, and his experience of printing plays, to introduce marks like the em-rule, or dash, and a series of points to indicate those hesitations and

sudden changes in the direction of thought associated with spoken discourse. Richardson's *Clarissa* (1748) was especially influential on the practice of later authors.[38]

But Henry Fielding's vehement objections to his sister's prominent use of the dash argue that Richardson's *Pamela* (1740), not just his later *Clarissa*, might already have begun to influence the appearance of the novel as early as 1744.

To a limited extent, the text of *Pamela* does exhibit Richardson's characteristic use of the dash.[39] The expressive dashes of variant lengths found in even the first edition of *Pamela* are similar to Sarah Fielding's in *David Simple*.[40] Vivienne Mylne characterizes Richardson's dashes in *Pamela* as visual markers of "drama and tension":

> In the first twenty letters of *Pamela*, we find sixty-three dashes. Ten of these occur at the point where there is a change of speaker, and the remaining fifty-three indicate interruption, agitation, etc. Later on in the book, where there are longer scenes of drama and tension, dashes become even more frequent on the page. In *Clarissa* and *Sir Charles Grandison* the extensive use of this sign is continued.[41]

Richardson, claims Mylne, uses the dash throughout his writings to augment visually the text's sense of high emotion: "[T]he mere look of a page of talk in Richardson often suggests tension and excitement by its wealth of dashes."[42] Sarah Fielding's use of the dash in *David Simple* aims at precisely these same effects. And, as Joe Bray has demonstrated with the revisions of italics in *Pamela*, Richardson's attention to dashes are part of that author-printer's larger concerns with minute variations in bibliographical accidentals from edition to edition.[43] Thus, according to Richardson's formal paradigm, Sarah Fielding's "errors in style" are not errors at all; her use of the dash resembles a literary manipulation of print exhibited by the Richardsonian novel.[44]

The translation of one of Richardson's novels into French by "A. F. Prévost d'Exiles," better known as the French novelist Abbé Prévost, offers an unusual parallel to Henry Fielding's editorship of his sister's text. With the production of Prévost's translation of *Clarissa* by a French printer in 1751, Richardson's use of the dash was eliminated and supplanted with the printing conventions commonly applied to indicate direct speech in French texts.[45] Mylne describes how the French printings of Richardson's text "do not give the same visual impression" as the original, and suggests that, as a result, they alter the intended "overall effect" experienced by English readers.[46] By extension, when the Prévost translation eliminates the original punctuation, it "compresses and tones down the liveliness of Richardson's dialogue."[47] Thus both the edited text of Sarah Fielding's *David Simple* and the translated text of Richardson's *Clarissa* undergo similar visual transformations – transformations which yield diminished narratives that suffer from a curtailed textual dynamism and a loss of immediacy.

Sarah Fielding's correspondence testifies to collaboration with Richardson on matters regarding the visual production of her novels. Such collaboration improves the possibility that Sarah Fielding's punctuation is a conscious imitation of Richardson's style. For, although no known correspondence of Sarah Fielding's directly addresses the printing of *David Simple*, at least one of her letters to Richardson expresses detailed concerns about punctuation. On 14 December 1758, Sarah Fielding writes to Richardson, worried about Millar's printing of her then-latest novel, *The Countess of Dellwyn*:

> Dear Sir,
> ... I have ... sent Mr. Millar a manuscript of two volumes ...
> ... Shall I beg that you will be so very kind to cast an Eye on the printing of it if your Health will permit without injury and pray be not scrupulous to alter any Expressions you deslike, ...
> I am very apt when I write to be too careless about great and small Letters and Stops, but I suppose that will naturally be set right in the printing.
> S Fielding[48]

At first glance, this letter supports Henry Fielding's removal of his sister's dashes from her earlier work: perhaps they, too, were but "careless" errors on her part and not deliberate violations of convention.[49] But Sarah Fielding's letter refers only to her being "careless about great and small Letters and Stops." In other words, she voices uncertainty about her placement of capitals and periods, not dashes. And whatever her polite, self-professed inadequacies, the letter indicates that Sarah Fielding was keenly aware of her use of typographical "accidentals." More importantly, she seeks Richardson's, not Millar's, assistance on matters relating to the visual production of her writing. The fact that she sought his printerly advice on the minutest details of the printing process, combined with the distinct similarity between the punctuation in *David Simple* and the dash's visual role in the Richardsonian novel, improves the possibility that Sarah Fielding deliberately modeled her experimental punctuation after Richardson.

When placed within the visual and historical context of print culture, Henry Fielding's elimination of a seemingly insignificant punctuation mark thus unearths larger concerns about printerly influences, possibly including Richardson's, on the novel's physical form. Perhaps, by criticizing his sister's use of the dash, Henry Fielding implicitly attacks the Richardsonian style that depends more heavily than his own does on printerly strategies and visual impact. He is able to say things about his sister's writing that he could not about Richardson's: that it is unlearned, non-aristocratic, immature, and feminine.

Henry Fielding's "corrections" of his sister's text allow him indirectly to strike at his literary rival.

Yet, in the light of his own experiments with the graphic packaging of the emerging novel, Henry Fielding's critique of his sister's dashes erects a false opposition between the visual gimmickry of the Richardsonian style and the crisp, uncluttered wordiness of his own literary model. Henry Fielding is, in fact, far more printerly minded than the revisions of his sister's text – and his related rivalry with Richardson – imply. The mock errata at the head of *Joseph Andrews* (1742), for example, display Henry Fielding's marked willingness to play about with the emerging novel's printed parts and, by means of that play, to acknowledge the young novel's ambiguous authority as a printed book. Later, epigraphic adornments, discussed previously in Chapter 3, allow Henry Fielding to use yet another feature of print to proclaim the novel's authority instead. Similarly, the panoply of lists and tables embedded in his fictions (these are considered in my next chapter) give evidence of an author who was attuned to, and eagerly put to use, the flexibility of the novel's graphic form. Moreover and more to the point, the first edition of *Joseph Andrews* (also printed by Millar), although perhaps not as be-dashed as the first edition of *David Simple*, contains plenty of eyebrow-raising uses of the dash as a redundant punctuation mark. While Henry slightly reduces his own dashes in subsequent editions of *Joseph Andrews*, he does not excise this mark from his own writings/printings to the extent that he does from his sister's text.[50] In fact, the third edition of *Joseph Andrews*, printed by Millar in 1743, a year before *David Simple*, not only abounds with numerous dashes (especially in dialogue) but explicitly markets Henry Fielding's text through graphic means: "The THIRD EDITION, illustrated with CUTS" boasts the title page. Martin Battestin considers this edition, along with the first, second, and fourth, as authoritative and notes the text's significance as "the first illustrated edition of *Joseph Andrews*" as well as "the first edition to bear Fielding's name on the title-page."[51] Although they may appear in an "authoritative" edition, the graphics of the third seem oddly out of keeping with Henry Fielding's literary project. The twelve designs by J. Hulett that attend various scenes in the third edition seize upon the text's most lascivious and titillating moments for illustration: the first plate pictures Mistress Booby, preposterously unappareled in her bed during her conversation with Joseph, who sits primly by as she attempts to seduce him by flaunting her bosom, nipples exposed, to his view.[52] What is comedic about Joseph's predicament in the allusive text is made dimly pornographic through the presence of the engraving. Indeed, some of the illustrations in the third edition are faintly suggestive of that continental tradition of indecent, or *galant*, engravings that occasionally surfaces in parallel with polite commercial versions of the same plates.[53] Although there is no further evidence to suggest that Millar marketed the third edition, with its dozen curious "Cuts," to a prurient clientele, the Hulett illustrations certainly do not promote the serious literary ambitions or epic dimensions of Henry Fielding's species of writing. If Henry Fielding disapproved of the titillating graphics of the 1743 edition, his objections had little impact, for Millar reused all the engravings in the fourth (1748) and fifth (1751) editions of the novel; the fourth, at least, was again emended by the author. It is possible that Henry Fielding's 1744 reaction to his sister's punctuation was partly in response to his own heightened sensitivity to print culture's graphic packaging of the novel genre after his first foray into illustration with *Joseph Andrews* a year earlier. Whatever the reason, Henry Fielding's growing suspicions of matters typographical and graphic are reflected in the novel's maturing generic sensibilities. For, as the century wears on, the novel reflects an increasing disquiet about its own graphic dress.

But before this disquiet takes hold, the early novel trials one other graphic accessory, namely the catalogue, or taxonomic list, that is such a prominent feature of Enlightenment thought.

CHAPTER 7

The list and index

a culture of collecting imprints upon the novel

> In those cases where animal signals really are of mutual benefit, they will tend to sink to the level of a conspiratorial whisper . . . If signal strength increases over the generations this suggests, on the other hand, that there has been increasing sales resistance on the side of the receiver.
> – George C. Williams, *Adaptation and Natural Selection* (1966)[1]

Metaphors from evolutionary biology are frequent, even if largely unacknowledged, in discussions of the novel – its evolution, niche, cross-pollination, and speciation. Williams's description of the evolution of animal signals, itself a mixture of Smith and Darwin, can be applied to the changing shape of the novel as a printed book after the close of the eighteenth century. The visible "signals" or packaging around a modern novel have sunk to a conspiratorial whisper, at least within the printed body of the book, because novelistic form is so generally accepted (for the "mutual benefit" of readers and writers, as it were). Although today's novels may shout their wares on the jacket or cover of the book, the elaborate paratexts and graphic design of the eighteenth-century novel are largely absent from its nineteenth- and twentieth-century descendants. Early in the genre's emergence as a mass mode, "louder" signals in the architectural margins of the work itself served to overcome the wary consumer's "sales resistance" by exciting curiosity or feigning authority. Over time these signals assumed quiet conspiratorial status as the genre's survival proved secure. Previous chapters have documented the manner in which, in the wake of the cacophony of the 1750s novel, the signal strength of the genre's most prominent paratexts, namely the frontispiece portraits and exuberant title pages, diminished. After the 1759 edition of *Clarissa*, the last over which Richardson had control, his specially designed musical page faded from the novel – as do the temporal and psychological dimensions embedded in the fiction's original ornamentation. As a result of Henry Fielding's editorial interventions, the dash's special role in *David Simple*, too, disappeared almost as soon as it had appeared in 1744.

Although these local experiments with graphic design exerted influence on both immediate contemporaries and the next generation of writers, their materiality was relatively short-lived. This would appear to be also the fate of the interrelated packaging discussed in this chapter: the list and index.

Although the project of indexing a novel may seem antithetical to the novelist's art, the index is not uncommon in the modern novel. A surprisingly long list of recent writers have experimented with indexing their narratives, including – in addition to a fair number of lesser-knowns – Lewis Carroll (*Sylvie and Bruno*, 1889); Virginia Woolf (*Orlando*, 1928); Vladimir Nabokov (*Pale Fire*, 1962); and John Updike (*The Centaur*, 1963).[2] Indexes serve different authors in different ways. In *Orlando*, Woolf uses the index to dress her novel in the guise of non-fiction, while the lesser-known Lucy Ellman in *Sweet Desserts* (1988) "uses the index to advertise the fictive status of her novel" and highlight the artificiality of the printed text.[3] Even in books that are roughly contemporary with each other, such as *Pale Fire* and *The Centaur*, indexes can serve contrary functions: Updike's index, which enumerates for the reader the epic parallels in a story seemingly about small-town Pennsylvania, smacks of the academic hubris mocked by Nabokov's pseudo-scholarly appendage. The thing that unites these disparate uses of indexes by modern authors is that they are signals of transgression and the avant-garde. Thus, the characteristic that defines the twentieth-century novelistic index is precisely what separates it from its eighteenth-century original. Whereas the modern index has become a conspiratorial, transgressive whisper exchanged with a knowing wink between novelist and reader, the eighteenth-century index, especially as pioneered in fiction by Samuel Richardson, signalled the genre's literary *gravitas*.

This chapter focusses primarily on the groundbreaking catalogues and compendiums attached to Richardson's novels. Richardson's lists have their roots in his training as a printer. As a young apprentice Richardson was reared in the growing print trade in lists, charts, and tables: John Wilde, whom he served for seven years, cultivated almanacs as "one of his specialties."[4] In later years, much of Richardson's experimentation with the novel's printed shape was again facilitated by his overlapping roles as author, printer, and publisher. In fact, in an age when publishers and printers added advertisements and commercial lists of their own to books as a matter of routine and even purchasers reshaped texts through bookbinding decisions, it is Richardson's close management of the physical production of his novels that makes his work a controlled example of the literary dimension of graphic design.

In the physical production of his final novel, *The History of Sir Charles Grandison* (1753–54), Richardson appends addenda of all kinds, increasing the bulk of his already mammoth epistolary narrative with an extensive machinery of framing puffs and catalogues.[5] At the start of the work he includes a self-congratulatory Preface, a laudatory sonnet by T[homas] E[dwards], and a one-page catalogue labeled "Names of the Principal Persons." At the end of the final volume he supplies his reader with: "A Concluding Note by the Editor"; an "Address to the Public" complaining of the novel's Dublin piracy; an awkward compilation of the book's "Similes and Allusions"; and a 100-page "Historical and Characteristical Index." The complementary pair of framing catalogues, namely the list of characters at the front of *Grandison* and the lengthy index at the back, constitute the twin focus of this chapter.

The *Grandison* inventories demonstrate an affinity with other types of lists found in the eighteenth-century novel and reflect the culture of collecting and taxonomic endeavor that, in part, incubated the new species of writing. As interpretive tools attached to a particular book, these flanking catalogues guide the reader of *Grandison* by exerting influence over both the anticipation and the recollection of the novel. The design of the prefatory list predisposes a reader to navigate the text and its characters along a specific set of moral and social axes. Conversely, the index exerts control over a reader's recollection, or revisitation, of specific moments in the narrative. To shape his paratextual packaging, Richardson borrows from other genres in eighteenth-century print culture – particularly drama and science. In so doing, he self-consciously positions the novel within established print tradition and consequently stakes a claim for the cultural permanence and moral utility of his new genre.

To adopt a slightly different evolutionary metaphor, when a new niche is colonized in biological evolution, an explosive proliferation of experimental forms is usually followed by a drastic reduction as a handful of lineages become the dominant generators of novelty. Historical scholarship of the novel has identified the dialectically opposed fictions of Richardson and Fielding as the two strains of fiction that emerged as dominant progenitors. Indexes as such did not endure as a feature of the mature novel in either lineage, although prefatory lists, tables of contents, and internal catalogues did survive in both sets of descendants. Yet in order to understand the evolution of the genre and to identify its genomics, we need to study the full range of early experiments with accessorizing – the shapes shed by the novel as it evolved, as well as those it retained.

Lists crowd the early English novel. Long before they embrace the early novel materially, as do the indexing appendages to *Grandison* or tables of contents found in other fictions, they elbow their way into the central narratives of eighteenth-century fictions thinly disguised as verbal narrative. Textual collections, itemizations, and enumerations constantly interrupt the central narratives. Indeed, the eighteenth-century novel seems as much preoccupied with lists and catalogues as the epic towards which it occasionally gestures, perhaps more so. Here, for example, is Gulliver's inventory of Yahoo culture, a Swiftian satire of Homer's catalogue of ships:

> I wanted no Fence against Fraud or Oppression: Here was neither Physician to destroy my Body, nor Lawyer to ruin my Fortune: No Informer to watch my Words and Actions, or forge Accusations against me for Hire: Here were no Gibers, Censurers, Backbiters, Pick-pockets, Highwaymen, House-breakers, Attorneys, Bawds, Buffoons, Gamesters, Politicians, Wits, Splenetics, tedious Talkers, Controvertists, Ravishers, Murderers, Robbers, Virtuosos; no Leaders of Followers of Party and Faction; no Encouragers to Vice, by Seduction or Examples: No Dungeon, Axes, Gibbets, Whipping posts, or Pillories; no cheating Shop-keepers or Mechanicks: No Pride, Vanity or Affectations: No Fops, Bullies, Drunkards, strolling Whores, or Poxes: No ranting, lewd, expensive Wives: No stupid, proud, Pedants: No importunate, over-bearing, quarrelsome, noisy, roaring, empty, conceited, swearing Companions: No Scoundrels raised from the Dust upon the Merit of their Vices; or Nobility thrown into it on account of their Virtues: No Lords, Fiddlers, Judges or Dancing-Masters.[6]

As Claude Rawson has argued, such rants are derived from Rabelais's explosive semantics and generate in Swift's satire a "combination of exuberance and astringency" that permits "hideous energies" to accumulate in strange pairings and juxtapositions.[7] Amplifying its rhetorical force is the list's thin graphic dimension. Its crowd of capital letters has the effect of turning behavior and activities into abstractions, lending them almost allegorical force. True, Gulliver's list is not embodied in print in a manner that wholly distinguishes it from the rest of the text, which itself abounds with the capitalization of nouns still common in early eighteenth-century texts.[8] Instead, the list forms part of both Gulliver's printed text and his rhetorical habit of mind. And yet, even though the paragraph is continuous with the rest of the narrative and its satirical project, it does evoke its autonomous cousin, the reference book. The passage's satirical bite is derived from the resemblance to a reference text: as a catalogue of professions and character types, the list strives towards epistemological and moral, rather than historical, comprehensiveness. Yet Gulliver's comprehensiveness fails to comprehend, lumping together with equal vehemence the petty and the principal – larceny and rape, "tedious Talkers" and "Murderers." Throughout the *Travels* Swift rebukes the attempt at technological inclusiveness of the New Science and ridicules Gulliver's own pseudo-scientific observations and naïve empiricism, partly through the occasional ranting list.

More problematically, Richardson, too, deploys encyclopedic language and the act of listing, skeptically scrutinizing the New Science and its penchant for empiricist collecting. Yet, Richardson's use of lists is more complicated than Swift's because his lists appear in so many (and contradicting) guises. Kevin Cope's inventory of inventories demonstrates the ubiquity of this device in Richardson's books:

> Pamela numbers the days before and after her wedding; she counts her blessings; she gives Mrs. Jervis a collection of trinkets accumulated during the three major phases of her life (*Pamela*, I: 66–8); she opens the second volume of her story with a mesh of household inventories, cataloguing everything down to the "woodbines, jessamines, and vines" (II:1). Clarissa and her colleagues never stop indexing and enumerating. There is a list of poets' opinions on love (*Clarissa*, 146); an inventory of Lovelace's character (182); a catalogue of Clarissa's books (many of them anthologized collections) (525); a comparison of Lovelace's character to characters in anthologies of witchcraft anecdotes by Glanvill, Baxter, and King James; a topic index of Clarissa's symptoms and sufferings (1012); a gothicized inventory of Clarissa's last bedchamber (1126); a miscellany bequeathed to Mrs. Lovick (1417); and, finally, a series of eulogistic letters arriving after Clarissa's demise (1367) . . . *Sir Charles Grandison* . . . is likewise overrun with collections, from Lord G.'s shells and butterflies (one thinks of a Royal Society virtuoso like Robert Hooke) to the specially designed three-section servant's library.[9]

To Cope's list we can add what is possibly the most perverse example of the Richardsonian novel's dissection of the world into collections, namely Lovelace's fantasy of the "mincing of . . . matter." In a mad fit of pseudo-scientific scrupulousness, Lovelace demands that Clarissa's dead body be "opened and embalmed" and its parts dissected, dispersed, and preserved in a manner evocative of contemporary antiquarian collections of biological specimens: her heart kept "in spirits," her bowels returned to her family, and locks of her hair sent to various admirers.[10] Richardson uses Lovelace's "mincing" fantasy to shock the reader with an epistemology-gone-awry and lay bare the inanity and inhumanity of a contemporary pseudo-science that sent flocks of curious London tourists to view collections of bones and so-called monstrosities at St. James's Palace and other early museums.[11] Through Lovelace's mental autopsy of Clarissa's body into its constituent parts, Richardson, like Swift in the *Travels*, indicts not only his villain but also the larger cultural preoccupation with enumeration and dissection that Lovelace displays.[12] The problem arises when Richardson's own penchant for lists risks aligning itself with Lovelace's pseudo-scientific preoccupations. That is, whenever Richardson lends his lists a certain autonomy by endowing them with graphic distinction in the layout

(199)

I presently understood w'at she meant, and told her, Madam, I believe I understand you; I thank God, tho' I want Friends in this Part of the World, I do not want Money, so far as way be Necessary, tho' I do not abound in that neither: This I added, because I would not make her expect great things, well Madam, *says she*, that is the thing indeed, without which nothing can be done in these Cases; and yet, *says she*, you shall see that I will not impose upon you, or offer any thing that is unkind to you, and if you desire it, you shall know every thing before hand, that you may suit your self to the Occasion, and be either costly or sparing as you see fit.

I told her, she seem'd to be so perfectly sensible of my Condition, that I had nothing to ask of her but this, that as I had told her that I had Money sufficient, but not a great Quantity, she would order it so, that I might be at as little superfluous Charge as possible.

SHE *replyed*, that she would bring in an Account of the Expences of it, in two or three Shapes, and like a *Bill of Fare*, I should chuse as I pleas'd, and I desir'd her to do so.

The next Day she brought it, and the Copy of her three Bills was as Follow.

		l.	s.	d.
1.	For Three Months Lodging in her House, including my Dyet at 10s. a Week	06	00	0
2.	For a Nurse for the Month, and Use of Child-bed Linnen	01	10	0
3.	For a Minister to Christen the Child, and to the Godfathers and Clark	01	10	0

4. For

(200)

		l.	s.	d.
4.	For a Supper at the Christening if I had five Friends at it	01	00	0
	For her Fees as a Midwife, and the taking off the Trouble of the Parish	03	03	0
	To her Maid-Servant attending	00	10	0
		13	13	0

THIS was the first Bill, the second was in the same Terms.

		l.	s.	d.
1.	For Three Months Lodging and Diet, &c. at 20s. per Week	13	00	0
2.	For a Nurse for the Month, and the Use of Linnen and Lace	02	10	0
3.	For the Minister to Christen the Child, &c. as above	02	00	0
4.	For a Supper, and for Sweetmeats	03	03	0
	For her Fees, as above	05	05	0
	For a Servant-Maid	01	00	0
		26	18	0

THIS was the second rate Bill, the third, *she said*, was for a degree Higher, and when the Father, or Friends appeared.

		l.	s.	d.
1.	For Three Months Lodging and Diet, having two Rooms and a Garret for a Servant	30	00	0
2.	For a Nurse for the Month, and the finest Suit of Child-bed Linnen	04	04	0

3. For

(201)

		l.	s.	d.
3.	For the Minister to Christen the Child, &c.	02	10	0
4.	For a Supper, the Gentlemen to send in the Wine	06	00	0
	For my Fees, &c.	10	10	0
	The Maid, besides their own Maid only	00	10	0
		53	14	0

I LOOK'D upon all the three Bills, and smil'd, *and told her*, I did not see but that she was very reasonable in her Demands, all things Consider'd, and for that I did not doubt but her Accommodations were good.

SHE *told me*, I should be judge of that, when I saw them: *I told her*, I was sorry to tell her that I fear'd I must be her lowest rated Customer, *and perhaps, Madam, said I, you will make me the less Welcome upon that Account*. No not at all, *said she,* for where I have One of the third Sort, I have Two of the Second, and Four to One of the First, and I get as much by them in Proportion, as by any; but if you doubt my Care of you, I will allow any Friend you have to overlook, and see if you are well waited on, or no.

THEN she explain'd the particulars of her Bill; in the first Place, Madam, *said she*, I would have you Observe, that here is three Months Keeping, you are but 10s. a Week, I undertake to say, you will not complain of my Table: I suppose, *says she*, you do not live Cheaper where you are now; no indeed, *said I*, nor so Cheap, for I give six Shillings *per* Week for my Chamber, and find my own Diet as well as I can, which costs me a great deal more.

THEN

FIGURE 7.1 From Defoe's *Moll Flanders* (1722), 199–201.

of a book's design, he calls upon the very authority of scientific discourse that Lovelace's fantasy indicts.

To reveal the genesis of Richardson's graphic elevation of the fictional list which leads eventually to the *Grandison* index, it is necessary to turn to Defoe. This is because master printer Richardson is not the first to give graphic form to the novel's tendency to list-making. Internal lists in *Robinson Crusoe* (1719) reflect contemporary culture with apparent approval and are, occasionally, awarded graphic distinction. Hailed as "the primary textbook of capitalism," *Robinson Crusoe* reinforces the inventory-keeping that is the hallmark not merely of the contemporary scientific observation deconstructed by Gulliver's rants but of private enterprise. "Every page is a merchant's catalogue of hardware, woollens, leather goods and crockery," as Nigel Dennis notes.[13] However, in Defoe, such lists often appear as materially separate entities, interrupting the narrative not merely as verbal enumerations or compendia (although they do that too, as in *Moll Flander*'s title page) but also as graphic oddities in the layout of a page. Take, for example, these pages of printed text from *Moll Flanders* (1722), where three lists appear during Moll's consultation with a midwife about the cost of her lying-in (Figure 7.1).

Unlike Gulliver's integrated adaptation of the language of compendia, Moll's lists and numerical "accounts" graphically disrupt and interrupt the narrative. Moll's printed narrative mimetically reproduces the three different tariffs, each representing different levels of service, offered her. Moll activates a pun on "account" when she opts for the cheapest accommodation: "I was sorry to tell her that I fear'd I must be her lowest rated Customer, and *perhaps Madam*, said I, *you will make me the less Welcome upon that Account*." An additional pun mediates the printed text to the reader, as these numerical bills are tendered as physical evidence of Moll's veracity: with them she literally and figuratively offers the reader an exacting "account." Thus the graphic realization of these numerical lists in Defoe becomes part of the novel's argument and contributes to its striking mimetic fidelity – what Woolf terms Defoe's "earthenware pot." Inversely, verbal argument is re-styled as a graphic list when Crusoe, the true *Homo economicus*, constructs an account of the "Evil" and "Good" suffered on the island, inventorying his experiences and feelings in double columns evocative of contemporary bookkeeping. His emotional experience appears on the printed page as a graphically distinct inventory akin to a bill of sale. Contrary to Gulliver's and Lovelace's lists, the inventories in Defoe do not falsely atomize the universe into chaotic and sinister elements. Instead, through their objective ability to sort and distinguish, they offer transparency, shape, and the promise of meaning and order in a Hobbesian universe.

Other writers, including Henry Fielding, Sarah Fielding, and Tobias Smollett, occasionally follow Defoe's example, fashioning sections of their verbal

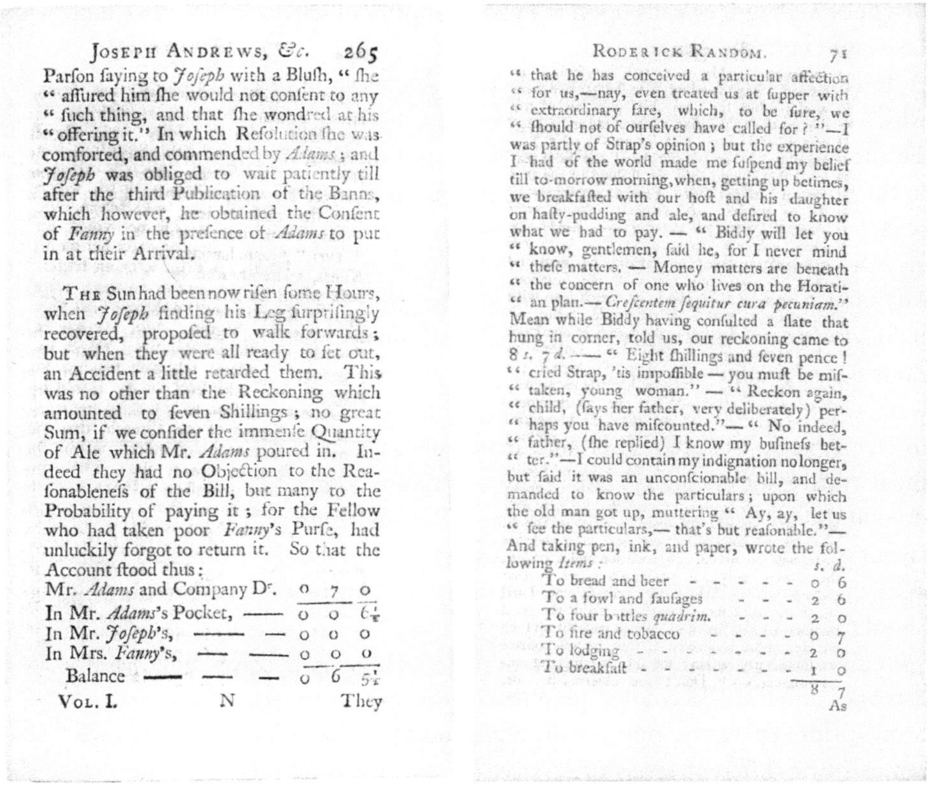

JOSEPH ANDREWS, &c. 265

Parſon ſaying to *Joſeph* with a Bluſh, "ſhe "aſſured him ſhe would not conſent to any "ſuch thing, and that ſhe wondred at his "offering it." In which Reſolution ſhe was comforted, and commended by *Adams*; and *Joſeph* was obliged to wait patiently till after the third Publication of the Banns, which however, he obtained the Conſent of *Fanny* in the preſence of *Adams* to put in at their Arrival.

THE Sun had been now riſen ſome Hours, when *Joſeph* finding his Leg ſurpriſingly recovered, propoſed to walk forwards; but when they were all ready to ſet out, an Accident a little retarded them. This was no other than the Reckoning which amounted to ſeven Shillings; no great Sum, if we conſider the immenſe Quantity of Ale which Mr. *Adams* poured in. Indeed they had no Objection to the Reaſonableneſs of the Bill, but many to the Probability of paying it; for the Fellow who had taken poor *Fanny*'s Purſe, had unluckily forgot to return it. So that the Account ſtood thus:

Mr. *Adams* and Company Dr.	0	7	0
In Mr. *Adams*'s Pocket, ——	0	0	6½
In Mr. *Joſeph*'s, —— —	0	0	0
In Mrs. *Fanny*'s, — ——	0	0	0
Balance —— — —	0	6	5½

VOL. I. N They

RODERICK RANDOM. 71

"that he has conceived a particular affection "for us,—nay, even treated us at ſupper with "extraordinary fare, which, to be ſure, we "ſhould not of ourſelves have called for?"—I was partly of Strap's opinion; but the experience I had of the world made me ſuſpend my belief till to-morrow morning, when, getting up betimes, we breakfaſted with our hoſt and his daughter on haſty-pudding and ale, and deſired to know what we had to pay. — "Biddy will let you "know, gentlemen, ſaid he, for I never mind "theſe matters. — Money matters are beneath "the concern of one who lives on the Horati-"an plan.—*Creſcentem ſequitur cura pecuniam.*" Mean while Biddy having conſulted a ſlate that hung in corner, told us, our reckoning came to 8 *s.* 7 *d.* —— "Eight ſhillings and ſeven pence! "cried Strap, 'tis impoſſible — you muſt be miſ-"taken, young woman." — "Reckon again, "child, (ſays her father, very deliberately) per-"haps you have miſcounted."— "No indeed, "father, (ſhe replied) I know my buſineſs bet-"ter."—I could contain my indignation no longer, but ſaid it was an unconſcionable bill, and demanded to know the particulars; upon which the old man got up, muttering "Ay, ay, let us "ſee the particulars,— that's but reaſonable."— And taking pen, ink, and paper, wrote the following *Items*:

	s.	*d.*
To bread and beer - - - - - -	0	6
To a fowl and ſauſages - - -	2	6
To four bottles *quadrim.* - - -	2	0
To fire and tobacco - - - - -	0	7
To lodging - - - - - - - - -	2	0
To breakfaſt - - - - - - - -	1	0
	8	7

As

FIGURE 7.2 From Henry Fielding's *Joseph Andrews*, 2 vols. (1742), I, 265 and from the second edition of Tobias Smollett's *Roderick Random*, 2 vols. (1748), I, 71.

narratives into the graphic dress of the printed list. Thus monetary bills and accounts appear intact in mainstream novels of the eighteenth century, set off ever so slightly from the rest of the verbal text by means of their graphic composition as a bill of sale (Figures 7.2 and 7.3). In their numerical recitation of economic concerns and their recordings of the minute details of ordinary life, these lists, which graphically resemble Defoe's, are concomitant with the novel's generic commitment to realism and contemporaneity. However, not all such enumerative interruptions insipidly reinforce the ubiquity of commercial transaction. For example, with the second instance of a narrator turned list-maker in *Joseph Andrews*, namely in the chapter where "*the Gentleman relates the History of his Life*," Henry Fielding aligns form and content to indict his character's youthful folly. Here the transition from verbal story to exacting list is not sudden but measured. The page's rhetoric slowly and insidiously enacts the increasing vapidity and moral decline of, to borrow Hogarth's phrase, the rake's progress. In the two paragraphs prior to the list's appearance, the now-reformed rake describes his once-typical morning activities with language that

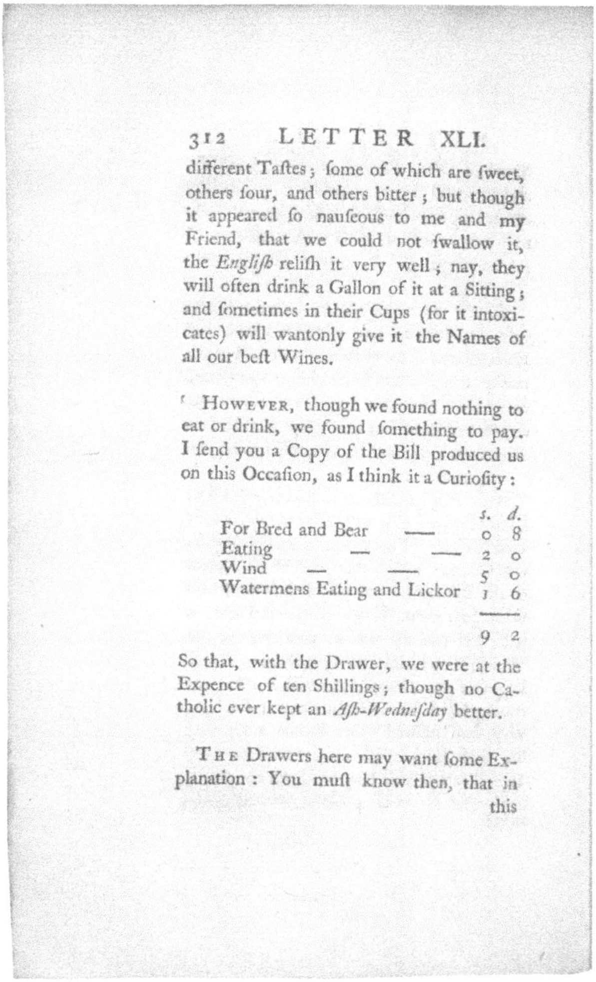

FIGURE 7.3
From Sarah Fielding's *Familiar Letters*, 2 vols. (1747), II, 312.

> 312   LETTER XLI.
>
> different Tastes; some of which are sweet, others sour, and others bitter; but though it appeared so nauseous to me and my Friend, that we could not swallow it, the *English* relish it very well; nay, they will often drink a Gallon of it at a Sitting; and sometimes in their Cups (for it intoxicates) will wantonly give it the Names of all our best Wines.
>
> ' However, though we found nothing to eat or drink, we found something to pay. I send you a Copy of the Bill produced us on this Occasion, as I think it a Curiosity:
>
> | | s. | d. |
> |---|---|---|
> | For Bred and Bear | 0 | 8 |
> | Eating | 2 | 0 |
> | Wind | 5 | 0 |
> | Watermens Eating and Lickor | 1 | 6 |
> | | 9 | 2 |
>
> So that, with the Drawer, we were at the Expence of ten Shillings; though no Catholic ever kept an *Ash-Wednesday* better.
>
> The Drawers here may want some Explanation: You must know then, that in this

exhibits an increasing syntactical movement towards list-making and a marked diminution of descriptive detail from a story already riddled with erasures:

> In the Morning I arose, took my great Stick, and walked out in my green Frock with my Hairs in Papers, (*a Groan from* Adams) and sauntered about till ten.
> Went to the Auction; told the Lady — she had a dirty Face; laughed heartily at something Captain — said; I can't remember what, for I did not very well hear it; whispered Lord —; bowed to the Duke of —; and was going to bid for a Snuff-box; but did not, for fear I should have had it.[14]

Next, the bare graphic record of the day's remaining hours abbreviates the rake's other activities to mere phrases ("drest myself" and "dined") and locations ("Coffee-house" and "*Lincoln's-Inn-Fields*") and reduces Adams's accompanying moral exasperations to mere grunts ("A Groan" twice)

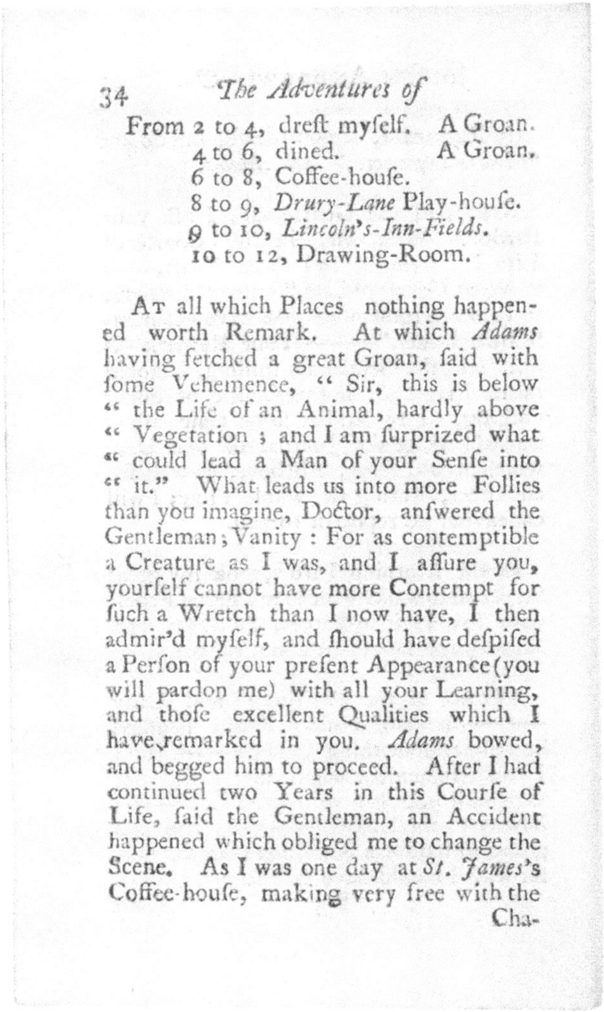

FIGURE 7.4
From Henry
Fielding's *Joseph
Andrews*, 2 vols.
(1742), II, 34.

> 34   *The Adventures of*
> From 2 to 4, dreft myfelf.   A Groan.
>   4 to 6, dined.   A Groan.
>   6 to 8, Coffee-houfe.
>   8 to 9, *Drury-Lane* Play-houfe.
>   9 to 10, *Lincoln's-Inn-Fields*.
>   10 to 12, Drawing-Room.
>
> AT all which Places nothing happen-
> ed worth Remark. At which *Adams*
> having fetched a great Groan, faid with
> fome Vehemence, " Sir, this is below
> " the Life of an Animal, hardly above
> " Vegetation ; and I am furprized what
> " could lead a Man of your Senfe into
> " it." What leads us into more Follies
> than you imagine, Doctor, anfwered the
> Gentleman ; Vanity : For as contemptible
> a Creature as I was, and I affure you,
> yourfelf cannot have more Contempt for
> fuch a Wretch than I now have, I then
> admir'd myfelf, and fhould have defpifed
> a Perfon of your prefent Appearance (you
> will pardon me) with all your Learning,
> and thofe excellent Qualities which I
> have remarked in you. *Adams* bowed,
> and begged him to proceed. After I had
> continued two Years in this Courfe of
> Life, faid the Gentleman, an Accident
> happened which obliged me to change the
> Scene. As I was one day at *St. James's*
> Coffee-houfe, making very free with the
>   Cha-

(Figure 7.4). Here the text's descent into the flat Defoe-esque list embodies, while it records, the rake's vapid expenditure of youth, time, and money.

One significant section of *Pamela*'s narrative is similarly printed in double columns in all the editions issued from Richardson's press (Figure 7.5). But this graphic distinction invokes legal rather than economic discourse and concerns, for it is here that Pamela enumerates Mr. B's indecent proposals "to make me a vile kept mistress" and simultaneously offers her point-by-point rejection of the seven "articles" of his original offer. In contrast to Defoe and Fielding, Richardson's double columns of text style themselves graphically not as a "bill" of complaint, but as a legal reference text. Although double columns were common features of both eighteenth-century bookkeeping and periodical

250 *PAMELA*: Or,

commodated to what I should have most lov'd, could I have honestly promoted it, your Welfare and Happiness. I have answer'd them, as you'll, I'm sure, approve; and I am prepared for the worst: For tho' I fear there will be nothing omitted to ruin me, and tho' my poor Strength will not be able to defend me, yet I will be innocent of Crime in my Intention, and in the Sight of God; and to him have the avenging of all my Wrongs, in his own good Time and Manner. I shall write to you my Answer as to his Articles; and hope the best, tho' I fear the worst. But if I should come home to you ruin'd and undone, and may not be able to look you in the Face; yet Pity and inspirit the poor Pamela, to make her little Remnant of Life easy; for long I shall not survive my Disgrace. And you may be assured it shall not be my Fault, if it be my Misfortune.

'To Mrs. PAMELA ANDREWS.

'The following ARTI-
'CLES are propos'd
'to your serious Con-
'sideration; and let me
'have an Answer, in
'Writing, to them;
'that I may take my
'Reflexions accordingly.
'Only remember,
'that I will make tri-
'fled with, and which-
'you leave for Answer,
'will absolutely decide
'your Fate, without
'Expostulation or fur-
'ther Trouble.

'LIF

VIRTUE Rewarded. 251

'therefore return the
'ANSWER following,
'to what shall be the
'Consequence.

'I. AS to the first Arti-
'cle, Sir, it may be-
'bore me, that I may not
'deserve, in your Opinion,
'the opprobrious Terms of
'forward and artful, and
'the like, to declare so-
'lemnly, that Mr. *Willi-
'ams* never had the least
'Encouragement from me,
'as to what you hint; and
'I believe his principal
'Motive was the appre-
'hended Day of his Fa-
'tion, quite contrary to
'his apparent Interest, to
'affist a Person he thought
'in Distress. You may,
'Sir, the better believe me,
'when I declare, that I
'know not the Man breath-
'ing I would wish to mar-
'ry; and that the only one
'I could honour more
'than another, is the Gen-
'tleman, who, of all others,
'seeks my everlasting Dis-
'honour.

'II. I will directly
'make you a Present of
'500 Guineas, for your
'own

252 *PAMELA*: Or,

'own Use, which you
'may dispose of to any
'Purpose you please:
'And will give it abso-
'lutely into the Hands
'of any Person you shall
'appoint to receive it;
'and expect no Favour
'in Return, till you are
'satisfy'd in the Posses-
'sion of it.

'III. I will likewise
'directly make over to
'you a Purchase I lately
'made in *Kent*, which
'brings in 250*l. per An-
'num*, clear of all De-
'ductions. This shall be
'made over to you in full
'Property for your Life,
'and for the Lives of any
'Children, to Perpetuity;
'(that you may happen to
'have: And your Fa-
'ther shall be immedi-
'ately put into Possession
'of it in Trust for these
'Purposes. And the
'Management of it, will
'yield a comfortable Sub-
'sistence to him and your
'Mother, for Life; and
'I will make up any De-
'ficien-

reject it with all my Soul.
'Money, Sir, is not my
'chief Good: May God
'Almighty desert me,
'whenever it is; and when-
'ever, for the Sake of that,
'I can give up my Title
'to that blessed Hope,
'which will stand me in
'stead, at a Time when
'Millions of Gold will not
'purchase one happy Mo-
'ment of Reflection on a
'past misspent Life!

'III. Your third Propo-
'sal, Sir, I reject, for the
'same Reason; and am
'sorry you could think
'my poor honest Parents
'would enter into their
'Part of it, and be con-
'cerned for the Manage-
'ment of an Estate, which
'would be owing to the
'Prostitution of their poor
'Daughter. Forgive, Sir,
'my Warmth on this Oc-
'casion; but you know
'not the poor Man, and
'the poor Woman, my
'ever dear Father and Mo-
'ther, if you think that
'they would not much ra-
'ther chuse to starve in a
'Ditch, or rot in a noi-
'some Dunghill, than ac-
'cept

FIGURE 7.5 From the first edition of Samuel Richardson's *Pamela*, 2 vols. (1740), I, 250–52.

printing (see Figures 1.1 and 1.2 of the *Tatler*), they were equally typical of legal texts. Since the context of law is already suggested by Pamela's treatment of Mr. B's proposals as contractually binding "articles," her pages' distinctive layout recalls the manner in which legal documents were drawn up into two parallel columns of text. As part of a printed book, Pamela's articles evoke the most widely used legal reference text, the form book. As the name implies, the form book was to lawyers what Richardson intended *Familiar Letters* (1741) to be to letter-writers.[15] Legal form books were structured into dual columns so as to reflect the different applications of a point of law in the two courts, the King's Bench and the Court of Common Pleas (Figure 7.6).

With the initials of *K. B.* (King's Bench) or *B. R.* (Bancus Regis) on one side and *C. B.* (Common Bench) or *C. P.* (Common Pleas) on the other, this legal text closely resembles Pamela's dual-columned page. In a similar fashion, Richardson's layout succinctly reflects the separate moral jurisdiction of the two characters. Prior to Mr. B's conversion, the graphic design insists that the characters appear utterly incompatible in both their personal action and their spheres of influence. What the design's affinity with a legal form book does not do, however (and what such legalese does when found in Sterne), is call into question the pomposities of legalistic discourse. Richardson borrows the rhetorical status of the list along with the appearance of a legal reference text to endow his character's predicament with legal solemnity and reinforce the real-world consequences of her moral choice. And yet, as we saw in the deployment of the frontispiece, the authority of printed signs can degrade, especially if mimicked too often. Stories about law and lawyers abounded in contemporary magazines and the pseudo-legal discourse that pervaded popular print.[16] As a result, *Pamela*'s graphic legal posturing risks aligning the novel with Grubstreet and its mastication of all things legalistic. In contrast, when *Tristram Shandy* sprinkles 𝔟𝔩𝔞𝔠𝔨 𝔩𝔢𝔱𝔱𝔢𝔯 𝔱𝔶𝔭𝔢 throughout the marriage settlements of Walter and Elizabeth, these deviations from the text's standard Roman typeface do not give visual testimony to that document's legitimacy but comically acknowledge a typographical "look" long-associated in print with "the lawyer's hand".

Although various authors, from Defoe to Smollett, may distinguish their narrative lists from the rest of a novel's text through typeface or layout, their resulting graphic designs are still not in the same category as the paratextual frame of lists that encases *Grandison*, a fiction sandwiched between reference texts. Yet these earlier narrative intrusions of lists do indicate where that novel's prefatory inventory of characters and its extensive index came from, that is, the eighteenth century's conviction of the authority and veracity of the list that is matched by an equally strong skepticism about the scientific, economic, or legal discourse that such a list can embody.

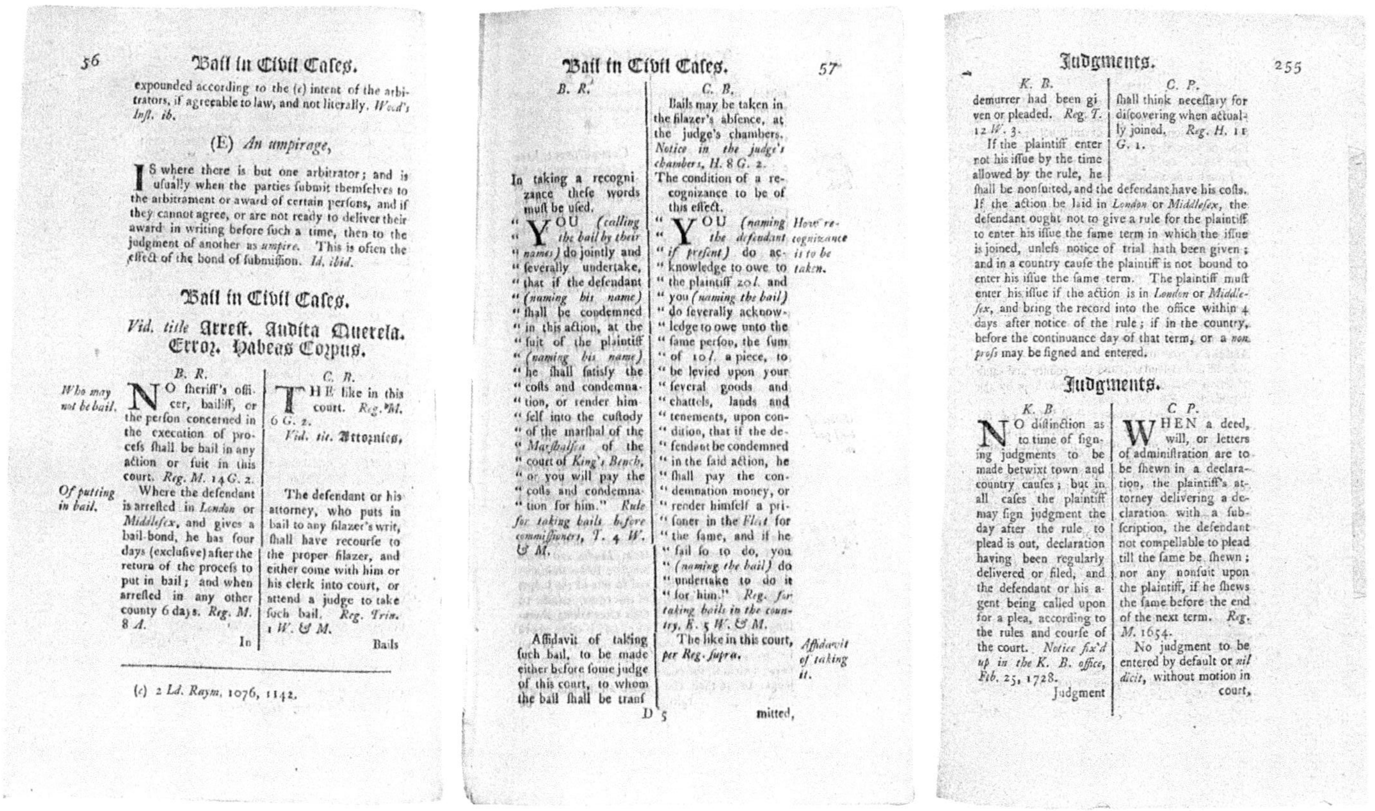
56 Bail in Civil Caſes.

expounded according to the (c) intent of the arbitrators, if agreeable to law, and not literally. *Wood's Inſt. ib.*

(E) *An umpirage,*

IS where there is but one arbitrator; and is uſually when the parties ſubmit themſelves to the arbitrament or award of certain perſons, and if they cannot agree, or are not ready to deliver their award in writing before ſuch a time, then to the judgment of another as *umpire.* This is often the effect of the bond of ſubmiſſion. *Id. ibid.*

Bail in Civil Caſes.

Vid. title Arreſt. Audita Querela. Error. Habeas Corpus.

B. R.	C. B.
Who may not be bail. NO ſheriff's officer, bailiff, or the perſon concerned in the execution of proceſs ſhall be bail in any action or ſuit in this court. *Reg. M.* 14 *G.* 2.	THE like in this court. *Reg. M.* 6 *G.* 2. *Vid. tit.* Attornies.
Of putting in bail. Where the defendant is arreſted in *London* or *Middleſex*, and gives a bail-bond, he has four days (excluſive) after the return of the proceſs to put in bail; and when arreſted in any other county 6 days. *Reg. M.* 8 *A.*	The defendant or his attorney, who puts in bail to any filazer's writ, ſhall have recourſe to the proper filazer, and either come with him or his clerk into court, or attend a judge to take ſuch bail. *Reg. Trin.* 1 *W. & M.*

In ... Bails

(c) 2 *Ld. Raym.* 1076, 1142.

Bail in Civil Caſes. 57

B. R.	C. B.
In taking a recognizance theſe words muſt be uſed. "YOU (*calling the bail by their names*) do jointly and "ſeverally undertake, "that if the defendant "(*naming his name*) "ſhall be condemned "in this action, at the "ſuit of the plaintiff "(*naming his name*) "he ſhall ſatisfy the "coſts and condemnation, or render him"ſelf into the cuſtody "of the marſhal of the "*Marſhalſea* of the "court of *King's Bench*, "or you will pay the "coſts and condemnation for him." *Rule for taking bails before commiſſioners, T.* 4 *W. & M.*	Bails may be taken in the filazer's abſence, at the judge's chambers. *Notice in the judge's chambers, H.* 8 *G.* 2. The condition of a recognizance to be of this effect. "YOU (*naming the defendant if preſent*) do ac"knowledge to owe to "the plaintiff 20*l.* and "you (*naming the bail*) "do ſeverally acknow"ledge to owe unto the "ſame perſon, the ſum "of 10*l.* a piece, to "be levied upon your "ſeveral goods and "chattels, lands and "tenements, upon con"dition, that if the de"fendant be condemned "in the ſaid action, he "ſhall pay the con"demnation money, or "render himſelf a pri"ſoner in the *Fleet* for "the ſame, and if he "fail ſo to do, you "(*naming the bail*) do "undertake to do it "for him." *Reg. for taking bails in the country, E.* 5 *W. & M.* *How recognizance is to be taken.*
Affidavit of taking ſuch bail, to be made either before ſome judge of this court, to whom the bail ſhall be tranſ-	The like in this court, *per Reg. ſupra.* *Affidavit of taking it.*

D 5 ... mitted,

Judgments. 255

K. B.	C. P.
demurrer had been given or pleaded. *Reg. T.* 12 *W.* 3. If the plaintiff enter not his iſſue by the time allowed by the rule, he	ſhall think neceſſary for diſcovering when actually joined. *Reg. H.* 11 *G.* 1.

ſhall be nonſuited, and the defendant have his coſts. If the action be laid in *London* or *Middleſex*, the defendant ought not to give a rule for the plaintiff to enter his iſſue the ſame term in which the iſſue is joined, unleſs notice of trial hath been given; and in a country cauſe the plaintiff is not bound to enter his iſſue the ſame term. The plaintiff muſt enter his iſſue if the action is in *London* or *Middleſex*, and bring the record into the office within 4 days after notice of the rule; if in the country, before the continuance day of that term, or a *non proſ* may be ſigned and entered.

Judgments.

K. B.	C. P.
NO diſtinction as to time of ſigning judgments to be made betwixt town and country cauſes; but in all caſes the plaintiff may ſign judgment the day after the rule to plead is out, declaration having been regularly delivered or filed, and the defendant or his agent being called upon for a plea, according to the rules and courſe of the court. *Notice fix'd up in the K. B. office, Feb.* 25, 1728.	WHEN a deed, will, or letters of adminiſtration are to be ſhewn in a declaration, the plaintiff's attorney delivering a declaration with a ſubſcription, the defendant not compellable to plead till the ſame be ſhewn; nor any nonſuit upon the plaintiff, if he ſhews the ſame before the end of the next term. *Reg. M.* 1654. No judgment to be entered by default or *nil dicit*, without motion in

Judgment ... court,

FIGURE 7.6 From the fifth edition of *The Attorney's Compleat Pocket-Book*, 2 vols. (1764), II, 56–57 (left) and II, 255 (right).

Such an accommodation of lists is not, of course, exclusive to eighteenth-century fiction: a list of literary list-makers would stretch back from Rabelais and Chaucer to Virgil and Homer and forwards from Flaubert and Melville to Joyce and Nabokov. But the abundance of lists in the eighteenth-century novel interacts with and reflects the cultural preoccupations of the age. Most of the age's major projects in science, history, and literature are essentially taxonomic collections, united to each other and to the novel in a desire to parse, categorise, and preserve. Famous listing activities include: the foundation of the Royal Society in London (1660) and the Academy of Sciences in Paris (1666), which placed a new emphasis on empirical observation and record-keeping; Ephraim Chambers's groundbreaking *Cyclopaedia* (1728), followed by Denis Diderot's gigantic *Encyclopédie* (1751–65) and its English cousin the *Encyclopaedia Britannica* (1768–71); the founding of the Society of Antiquaries of London (1707) and the establishment of the British Museum (1753), which arose out of the mania for collecting and collections[17]; Carolus Linnaeus' *System Naturae* (1758), which provided a classification system for the creatures on earth, while Charles Messier's *Catalogue* of fixed nebulae (1774 and 1780) mapped the objects in the heavens; and, of course, Samuel Johnson's catalogue of the English language in the *Dictionary* (1755) as well as his canon-building *Lives of the Poets* (1781), both of which are also inventories that reflect taxonomic presuppositions. Unsurprisingly, these high-profile examples of list-making projects imprint themselves upon the novel.[18]

Taxonomic systems, definitive lists, and collections promised the eighteenth century order but did not guarantee it. The most remarkable and best-preserved example of chaotic systems of classification in the Enlightenment is Sir John Soane's collection, begun in the later decades of the eighteenth century and formally established as a museum in 1833. The architect's museum, once his home, retains the collection's authentic eighteenth-century "arrangement" of objects in its original location in Lincoln's Inn Fields.[19] The collection juxtaposes a jumble of classical fragments and Egyptian artifacts with contemporary eighteenth-century objects, shelving rows of popular eighteenth-century books alongside Renaissance bric-à-brac and statuettes. The Soane museum, with its Shandean mix of objects, double-hinged panels, mirrors, and *trompe l'œil*, is, to borrow Woolf's description of eighteenth-century discourse, arranged "higgledy-piggledy."[20] The collection embodies a discordant, if endearing, universe in keeping with the lack of hierarchy displayed by the objects on Belinda's dressing table – the "Puffs, Powders, Patches, Bibles, Billet-doux."[21] Indeed, Michael McKeon argues that the novel emerges during a time of "categorical instability" so severe that the moment registers as an "epistemological crisis."[22] Only the novel, he says, could accommodate competing epistemological systems of value. Its long narrative form and its choice of young, socially mobile

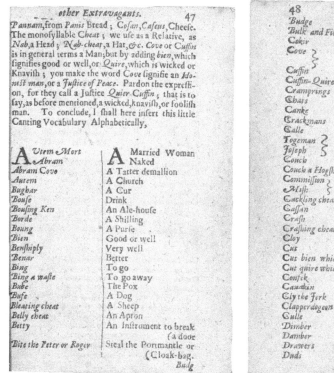

FIGURE 7.7 From Richardson Head's *The English Rogue Described in the Life of Meriton Latroon* (1672).

characters as subject allowed the novel to mediate conflicting determinations, both traditional and progressive, of virtue and value. In the novel's lists and catalogues we can see the narrative form interacting with the formal structures common to alternative epistemologies – those taxonomic projects so popular in the eighteenth century.

In a sense, listing, parsing and enumerating are embedded in the novel's genetic code. The novel has inherited its propensity to list, like many of its other qualities, from precursors that include the conduct-book, journalistic accounts, travel narratives, and histories.[23] For example, Richardson Head's clumsy but comical fiction of mercantile practices, *The English Rogue Described* (1672), includes a "little Canting Vocabulary" list that alphabetically enumerates some of the colloquialisms in this story about urban commerce (Figure 7.7). Head's list resembles Defoe's and Smollett's, in that it adds local colloquial color and emphasizes a book's comic economics. The novel's rise also coincides with the emergence of the literary miscellany – bundles of contemporary, fashionable print materials that prefigure the historically panoramic anthology of the

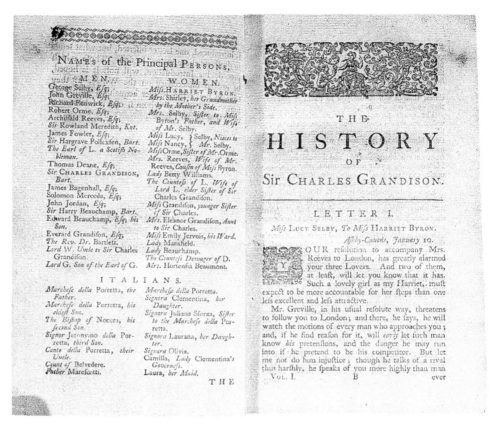

FIGURE 7.8 From the second octavo edition (published simultaneously with the first in duodecimo) of Samuel Richardson's *The History of Sir Charles Grandison*, 6 vols. (1754), 1, [viii] and [1].

nineteenth century.[24] The miscellany, like so many of the century's collecting projects, "prompts the formation of a canon."[25] Thus the miscellany, too, offers a sort of literary taxonomy that resembles the listing, collecting, and bundling activities found in the novel. Lists may also, like the it-narrator genre, reflect the novel's endemic materialism. Although eighteenth-century novelists rarely supply the richly upholstered descriptions found in nineteenth-century fiction, their taste for cataloguing and documenting through the use of lists may represent both the genre's descriptive potential and its materialist obsession in embryonic form.[26]

In turning to the "Names of the *Principal* Persons" at the front of Richardson's *Grandison*, we step away from lists that are modestly embedded within the novel's mimetic conceit to consider those that defiantly front, frame, and package the genre as a printed book (Figure 7.8). Richardson's primary print

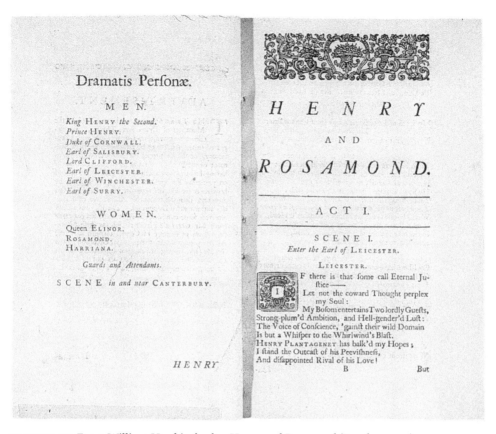

FIGURE 7.9 From William Hawkins's play *Henry and Rosamond* (London, 1749).

model for his catalogue of characters is, of course, the list of *dramatis personae* at the front of a printed play, such as we find in the numerous plays produced in his workshop.[27] As in *Grandison*'s single-page catalogue, such lists conventionally provide information about rank and affiliation and often divide characters and actors by gender. The historical tragedy *Henry and Rosamond*, written by William Hawkins and printed on Richardson's press in 1749, exemplifies the standard segregation by gender (Figure 7.9). Sometimes, as in the list of "PERSONS" in Edward Young's *The Brothers*, printed by Richardson the year before *Grandison*'s publication, the layout also separates characters of different nationalities (Figure 7.10). *The Brothers* applied brackets, in addition to verbal headers, to segregate physically the play's Roman minority from its Greek majority. The obvious similarities in graphic design between such lists of *dramatis personae* and the list of characters found in *Grandison* suggest that Richardson expected his reader to recognize the theatrical nature of the list, despite its new narrative context.[28] Like the folding score in *Clarissa*, which invites performance, the dramatic packaging of *Grandison* modifies the reader's relationship

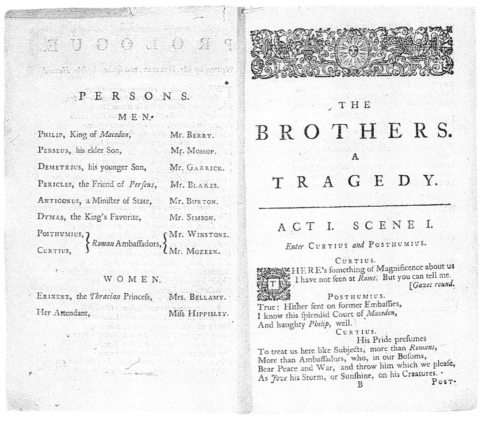

FIGURE 7.10 From Edward Young's play *The Brothers. A Tragedy*. (London, 1753).

to its epistolary genre. The list's theatrical design forces the reader to shed the role of a secret voyeur of private correspondence, because its resemblance to a visual feature of a printed play assigns the reader a seat among the imaginary audience of a theatrical, public performance. It reflects the epistolary novel's larger theatricality: what Mark Kinkead-Weekes calls Richardson's "dramatic art."[29] Thus, the printed cast list externalizes what is already an integral part of the Richardsonian novel as printed book. Every one of Richardson's fictions is cluttered with graphic props borrowed from printed plays, particularly in the layout and punctuation of dialogue (Figure 7.11).[30] Jocelyn Harris observes that "the techniques of the stage are used freely and with no sense of impropriety" throughout the novel.[31] Of course, Richardson is not alone in indulging in the amateur theatrics of the novel's graphic self-presentation: Sarah Fielding and Jane Collier's experimental novel *The Cry* (1754), which enacts the whole of its three-volume narrative as a dramatic dialogue between the heroic Portia and a collective entity reminiscent of a Greek chorus, most remarkably expresses

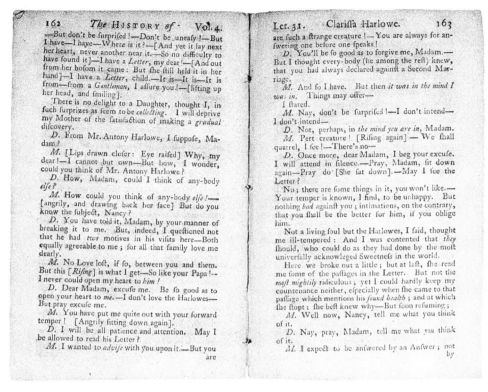

FIGURE 7.11 From the third edition of *Clarissa*, 8 vols. (1751), IV, 162–63.

the way that the eighteenth-century novel usurps the printed conventions of drama (Figure 7.12). In this larger context of the novel's dramatic pilferings, the prefatory list of principal actors thus flaunts, rather than fabricates, *Grandison*'s dramatic dress.

While none of Richardson's editions of *Pamela* contains a cast list, all his various editions of *Clarissa* include a prefatory list of the fiction's characters. The *Grandison* list, however, marks an important change in graphic presentation for Richardson, because it differs in significant ways from its predecessors. In the first edition of *Clarissa*, the four-page description of the major characters headed "*A brief Account of the principal Characters throughout the Whole*" serves a blunt, didactic function, for each name in this list is followed by a judgment of the character's ethical integrity (Figure 7.13). In these characterizations Richardson praises Clarissa, for example, as "Mistress of all the accomplishments, natural and acquired, that adorn the sex" and vilifies Lovelace as "haughty, vindictive, and humorously vain." Combining character sketches with information about familial relationships, some of the entries even foreshadow the plot with pedagogical bluntness:

FIGURE 7.12 From the first volume of Sarah Fielding and Jane Collier's *The Cry*, 3 vols. (London: Printed for R. and J. Dodsley, 1754).

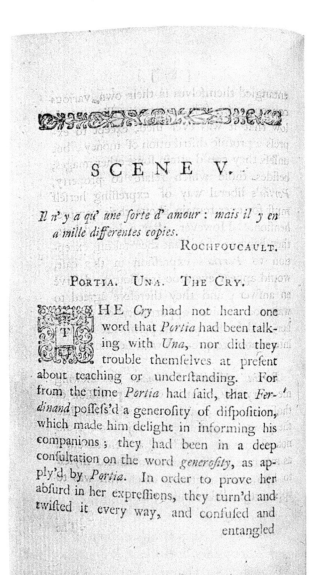

JAMES HARLOWE, *Esq*; *the Father of Miss* Clarissa, *Miss* Arabella, *and Mr*. James Harlowe: *Despotic, absolute; and, when offended, not easily forgiving.*
Lady CHARLOTTE HARLOWE, *his Wife, Mistress of fine Qualities; but greatly under the Influence not only of her arbitrary Husband, but of her Son.*
JAMES HARLOWE, *jun. proud, fierce, uncontroulable, and ambitious; jealous of the Favour his Sister* Clarissa *stood in with the Principals of the Family; and a bitter and irreconcileable Enemy to Mr.* Lovelace.

This coarse instrument was ineffective in influencing the reader in the way that Richardson desired. Richardson's struggle with his readers' "misinterpretations" is well known and his exasperation with interpretive multiplicity well documented: "*O Madam: that Clarissa's Character, and Lovelace's too, were better understood!*"[32] Richardson enlists here the hermeneutic power of Enlightenment empiricism, with its fondness for lists, in his battle with the epistolary novel's indeterminacy.

The character lists fronting the second (1749) and third (1751) editions of *Clarissa* more closely approach the model eventually deployed in *Grandison* (Figures 7.14 and 7.15). In these editions, both the length and the pedantry of the prefatory catalogue are reduced from four pages of text to one. Protracted descriptions of moral integrity are distilled into: familial relationships ("Father of Clarissa"); short phrases that lend the protagonist pseudo-aristocratic authority ("A young Lady of great Beauty and Merit"); or a judicious epithet awarding individual value ("A worthy Divine"). Although the 1751 list alters little of the text of its immediate 1749 precursor, it refashions the cramped and shabby look of a list that sat awkwardly atop a section of the table of contents by distinguishing it with the rhetorical grandeur of white space and repositioning it opposite the opening of the novel's central narrative. Both the scaled-down, single-page versions of the list in the 1749 and 1751 editions not only resemble more closely a printed list of *dramatis personae*, giving greater graphic expression to the novel's theatricality, but also feign greater scientific objectivity than their verbose predecessor of 1748. For example, the bland description of Lovelace ("an Admirer of her" in 1749 and "Her Admirer" in 1751) puts him, at first, upon equal footing with Solmes ("An Admirer of Clarissa" in 1749, to which the 1751 edition adds the phrase "favoured by her friends"). However, a clue in the description of Captain Tomlinson towards the bottom of the list ("The assumed Name of a vile Pander to the Debaucheries of Mr. Lovelace") continues to instruct the attentive reader as to the villainies of Lovelace.

In *Grandison*, Richardson's alterations again affect the potency and graphic elegance of his prefatory list of characters. This time he mixes the design of a play with the formal qualities of a printed subscription list, encoding in the typography and layout of his list the moral and social categories through which he wants his readers to view the story. Despite the fact that the list of principal characters in *Grandison* names a dozen more characters than did the final *Clarissa* list, it fits similarly on a single page (see Figure 7.8). It even has room for the extravagance of an ornamental header. What makes this possible is the absence of all adjectives and moral descriptions: the list confines itself solely to names, official titles, and relationships (Esq., Nobleman, Aunt, Maid, and so forth). It is precisely this formal minimalism which gives the streamlined list its appearance of objectivity, for rather than placing the reader on the defensive through didactic appeals, it purports to offer unbiased data. But the list's apparent objectivity is illusory, on account of its selectivity. In fact, the catalogue relies upon a reader's familiarity with contemporary print

> [ix]
>
> A brief Account of the principal Characters throughout the Whole.
>
> M^{ISS} CLARISSA HARLOWE, *a young Lady of great Delicacy; Mistress of all the Accomplishments, natural and acquired, that adorn the Sex; having the strictest Notions of filial Duty.*
>
> ROBERT LOVELACE, *Esq; a Man of Birth and Fortune: Haughty, vindictive, humourously vain; equally intrepid and indefatigable in the Pursuit of his Pleasures— Making his Addresses to Miss* Clarissa Harlowe.
>
> JAMES HARLOWE, *Esq; the Father of Miss* Clarissa, *Miss* Arabella, *and Mr.* James Harlowe: *Despotic, absolute; and, when offended, not easily forgiving.*
>
> Lady CHARLOTTE HARLOWE, *his Wife, Mistress of fine Qualities; but greatly under the Influence not only of her arbitrary Husband, but of her Son.*
>
> JAMES HARLOWE, jun. *proud, fierce, uncontroulable, and ambitious; jealous of the Favour his Sister* Clarissa *stood in with the Principals of the Family; and a bitter and irreconcileable Enemy to Mr.* Lovelace.
>
> Miss ARABELLA HARLOWE, *elder Sister of Miss* Clarissa; *ill-natured, overbearing, and petulant; envying her Sister; and the more, as* Mr.

> [x]
>
> *Mr.* Lovelace *was first brought to make his Addresses to herself.*
>
> JOHN HARLOWE, *Esq; elder Brother of Mr.* James Harlowe, *sen. an unmarried Gentleman; good-natured, and humane; but easily carried away by more boisterous Spirits.*
>
> ANTONY HARLOWE, *Third Brother, who had acquired a great Fortune in the Indies; positive, rough, opinionated.*
>
> Mr. ROGER SOLMES, *a Man of sordid Manners; disagreeable in his Person and Address: Immensely rich: Proposed with an high hand for an Husband to Miss* Clarissa Harlowe.
>
> Mrs. HERVEY, *Half-Sister of Lady* Charlotte Harlowe; *a Lady of good Sense, and Virtue: In her Heart against the Measures taken to drive her Niece to Extremities; but not having Courage to oppose herself to so strong a Stream, sailing with it.*
>
> Miss DOLLY HERVEY, *her Daughter; good-natured, gentle, sincere; and a great Admirer of her Cousin* Clarissa.
>
> Mrs. NORTON, *a Gentlewoman of Piety, and good Understanding; the Daughter of an unpreferred Clergyman of great Merit, whose Amanuensis she was:—Married unhappily (and left a Widow), engaged to nurse Miss* Clarissa Harlowe: *In whose Education likewise she had a principal Share.*
>
> Colonel MORDEN, *a Man of Fortune, Gentrosity, and Courage, nearly related to the* Harlowe-

FIGURE 7.13 (a) From Samuel Richardson's first edition of *Clarissa*, 7 vols. (1748), 1, ix–x.

culture to assert the supremacy of moral virtue over social rank, proclaim the sovereignty of the author, establish the plot's inevitability, and highlight the novel's theatricality and expanded mandate.

First, the *Grandison* list deliberately accommodates competing ideologies of virtue, calling into question, by means of its graphic organization of the novel's cast, the dominant caste system of social rank. Placed at the fiction's threshold, *Grandison*'s prefatory list mixes the titles of aristocratic ideology with new categories of non-aristocratic value: what McKeon terms "progressive ideology."[33] At first glance, this list, which prominently divides the characters under the headings "MEN," "WOMEN," and "ITALIANS," appears to avoid class-based categories by grouping characters according to distinctions central to the action of *Grandison*: gender and nationality, sex and culture are the plot's main catalysts. The page layout relegates "ITALIANS" to a position literally subsequent to and figuratively beneath the English, just as Richardson portrays

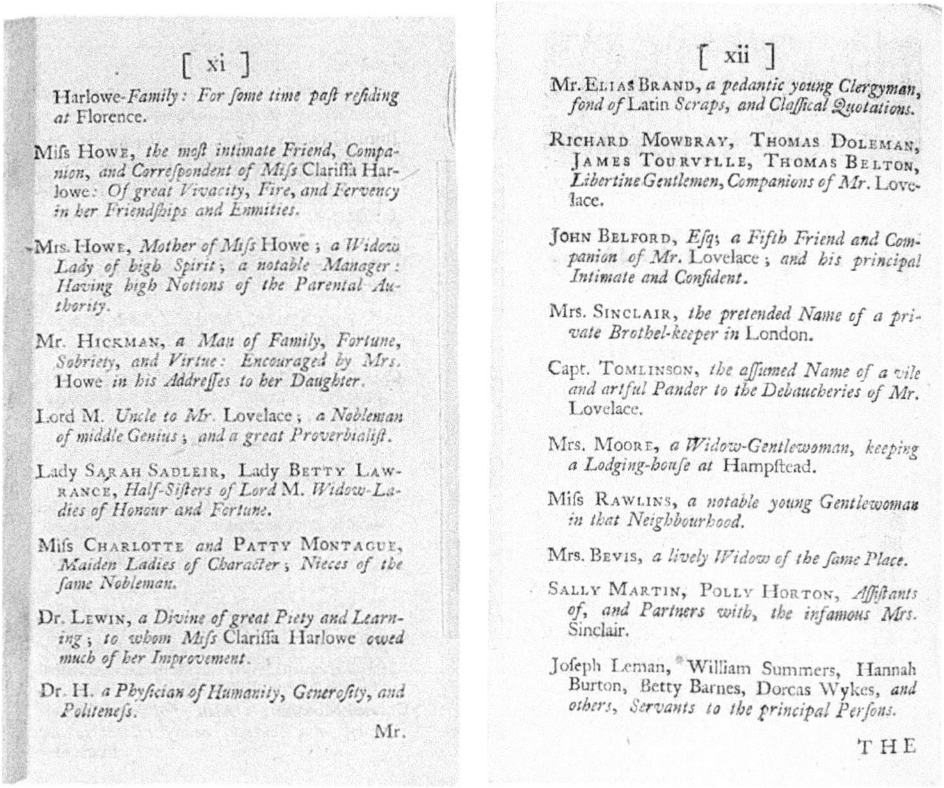

FIGURE 7.13 (b) From Samuel Richardson's first edition of *Clarissa*, 7 vols. (1748), I, xi–xii.

them in this nationalistic novel. The comic and mildly xenophobic suggestion implied by this grouping, namely that "ITALIANS" represent the novel's third sex, is not entirely without force in a novel about the incompatibility of an English–Italian romance.[34]

While the list links the power dynamics of gender to those of nationality, it also simultaneously reinforces and challenges the ideological elision of moral value and social rank embodied in the peerage, as is true of Richardson's stories. This is because Richardson deploys a reader's familiarity with yet another graphic feature of books in contemporary print culture: the subscription list. The *Grandison* list's graphic affinity with a list of subscribers commonly found prefacing many eighteenth-century works illustrates how Richardson's prefatory catalogue concurrently asserts and erodes traditional aristocratic ideology. A reader's undoubted familiarity with subscription lists means that specific expectations hover about this page of the novel's text. Richardson inevitably printed many editions by subscription over the course of his career as a London

FIGURE 7.14
From Samuel Richardson's second edition of *Clarissa*, 7 vols. (1749), I, v.

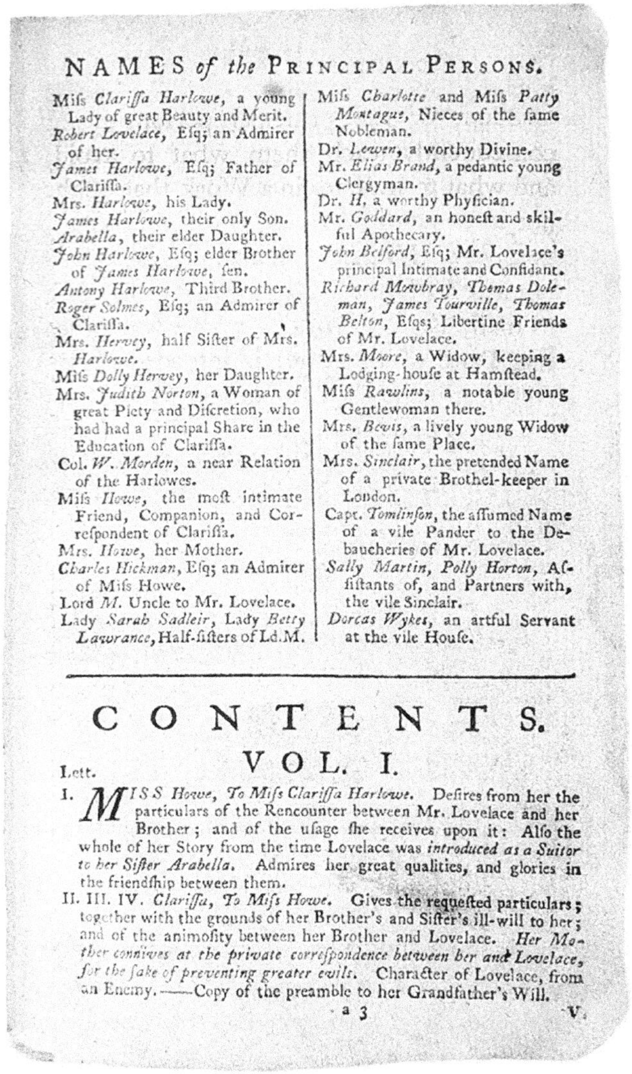

NAMES of the PRINCIPAL PERSONS.

Miss *Clarissa* Harlowe, a young Lady of great Beauty and Merit.
Robert Lovelace, Esq; an Admirer of her.
James Harlowe, Esq; Father of Clarissa.
Mrs. *Harlowe*, his Lady.
James Harlowe, their only Son.
Arabella, their elder Daughter.
John Harlowe, Esq; elder Brother of *James Harlowe*, sen.
Antony Harlowe, Third Brother.
Roger Solmes, Esq; an Admirer of Clarissa.
Mrs. *Hervey*, half Sister of Mrs. Harlowe.
Miss *Dolly Hervey*, her Daughter.
Mrs. *Judith Norton*, a Woman of great Piety and Discretion, who had had a principal Share in the Education of Clarissa.
Col. *W. Morden*, a near Relation of the Harlowes.
Miss *Howe*, the most intimate Friend, Companion, and Correspondent of Clarissa.
Mrs. *Howe*, her Mother.
Charles Hickman, Esq; an Admirer of Miss Howe.
Lord *M*. Uncle to Mr. Lovelace.
Lady *Sarah Sadleir*, Lady *Betty Lawrance*, Half-sisters of Ld. M.

Miss *Charlotte* and Miss *Patty Montague*, Nieces of the same Nobleman.
Dr. *Lewen*, a worthy Divine.
Mr. *Elias Brand*, a pedantic young Clergyman.
Dr. *H*, a worthy Physician.
Mr. *Goddard*, an honest and skilful Apothecary.
John Belford, Esq; Mr. Lovelace's principal Intimate and Confidant.
Richard Mowbray, *Thomas Doleman*, *James Tourville*, *Thomas Belton*, Esqs; Libertine Friends of Mr. Lovelace.
Mrs. *Moore*, a Widow, keeping a Lodging-house at Hamstead.
Miss *Rawlins*, a notable young Gentlewoman there.
Mrs. *Bevis*, a lively young Widow of the same Place.
Mrs. *Sinclair*, the pretended Name of a private Brothel-keeper in London.
Capt. *Tomlinson*, the assumed Name of a vile Pander to the Debaucheries of Mr. Lovelace.
Sally Martin, *Polly Horton*, Assistants of, and Partners with, the vile Sinclair.
Dorcas Wykes, an artful Servant at the vile House.

C O N T E N T S.
VOL. I.

Lett.
1. *MISS Howe*, To *Miss Clarissa Harlowe*. Desires from her the particulars of the Rencounter between Mr. Lovelace and her Brother; and of the usage she receives upon it: Also the whole of her Story from the time Lovelace was *introduced as a Suitor to her Sister Arabella*. Admires her great qualities, and glories in the friendship between them.
II. III. IV. *Clarissa*, To *Miss Howe*. Gives the requested particulars; together with the grounds of her Brother's and Sister's ill-will to her; and of the animosity between her Brother and Lovelace. Her Mother *connives at the private correspondence between her and Lovelace, for the sake of preventing greater evils*. Character of Lovelace, from an Enemy.——Copy of the preamble to her Grandfather's Will.

a 3
v.

---

printer.[35] Subscription lists were usually inserted between a book's prefatory puffs and the first page of central text, which means that mid-eighteenth-century readers would have been accustomed to finding them precisely where they found the list of "*Principal* PERSONS" in *Grandison*. Moreover, such readers would have anticipated a specific layout from such a prefatory catalogue of names: subscribers were usually grouped alphabetically, with the names under each alphabetical grouping listed in accordance with social status in the peerage.

Richardson subverts this standard model. His "new order" is not simply a satirical inversion of the peerage, but rather a complete abandonment of

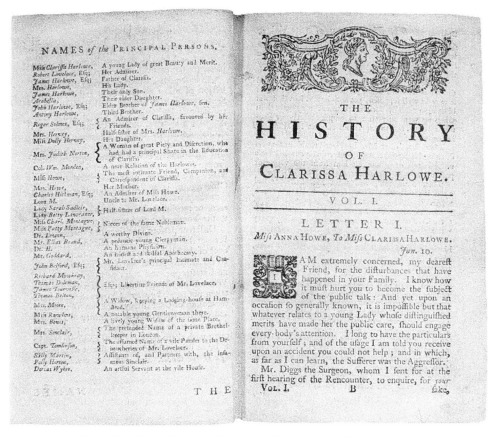

FIGURE 7.15 From the third edition of *Clarissa*, 8 vols. (1751), I, [xii] and [1].

such titular placement on the page. By so conspicuously defying the social and political hierarchy of his time, Richardson encourages his readers to form classless opinions of his characters. A character's moral stature and catalytic role in the plot, not his or her social title, determine the nature of the reader's response. As Richardson declares in his own correspondence: "The great are not great to me, unless they are good."[36] He returns to the traditional ranking of the peerage when listing the "ITALIANS" at the bottom of the page. The reader is left to infer that no true system of moral worth exists among them.

Both the anticipation of Italian protagonists and the very crowding of Richardson's single-page list expand the horizons of the Richardsonian novel. The sheer number of "*Principal*" characters, fifty-one in all, exceeds the number that a reader of *Pamela*, or even *Clarissa*, might reasonably have expected from the intimacy of an epistolary fiction "edited" by Richardson. This relatively large number of protagonists, including "ITALIANS," announces to the reader that Richardson's novelistic project has shifted from strictly private and domestic concerns to those of a more social, even cosmopolitan, universe. Just as *Clarissa* moved the epistolary novel from the countryside of *Pamela* to the increasingly public, urban realm of London, so *Grandison* pushes the boundaries of the Richardsonian novel ever outward to include continental Europe.

Having abandoned titular sequencing altogether in arranging the English names within his list, Richardson returns to the conventional design of subscription lists in one curious way. In the light of that model, the two names printed in small capitals, "*Sir* CHARLES GRANDISON" and "*Miss* HARRIET BYRON," are politically evocative, for such lists occasionally used typography to highlight the importance of an individual subscriber. For example, the well-known subscription list for Alexander Pope's edition of *The Works of Shakespear* honors "THE KING" by placing him in over-sized, capital letters atop the list of other names (Figure 7.16).[37] By extending similar typographical distinction to his two main characters, Richardson plays about with the social hierarchy that his list's visual design otherwise rejects. For a printer-publisher-author who financed his own work at each stage of its production, this typographical crowning of characters who take the place of subscribers on the page asserts Richardson's own sovereignty as an author. As we know from his private correspondence, Richardson prided himself on his economic independence and freedom from patrons:

> I never sought out of myself for patrons. My own industry, and God's providence, have been my whole reliance . . . And it is a glorious privilege, that a middling man enjoys who has preserved his independency, and can occasionally (though not Stoically) tell the world, what he thinks of that world, in hopes to contribute, though but by his mite, to mend it.[38]

The typography of the list of "NAMES of the *Principal* PERSONS" in *Grandison* embodies the author's proud declaration and leaves Richardson unencumbered to "tell the world, what he thinks of that world."

The emphatic use of typography further guides the reader's perception of the book's characters and plot. Richardson's unique use of small capitals for the hero and heroine of the novel marks them as the capital couple, so to speak, of the ensuing story. The specter of a marriage between Charles and Clementina loses its force when the reader has already seen Harriet as Charles's only female equal among the story's principals. In apparent reaction to the wide-ranging interpretive responses to *Clarissa*, Richardson seems wary of trusting his readers to find such a marriage inappropriate and therefore underscores the "correct" interpretation with the layout and typography of the opening list. Unfortunately for Richardson, this project failed at least in part. As late as December of 1753, whilst an eager public still awaited *Grandison*'s concluding

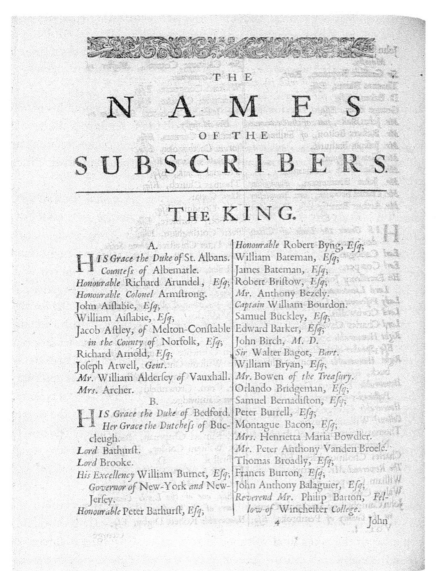

FIGURE 7.16
First page of the subscription list to Alexander Pope's *The Works of Shakespear* (London: Printed for Jacob Tonson, 1725).

volume (eventually published on 14 March 1754), Richardson continued to debate with Lady Bradshaigh her own wavering sympathies for the "two *angells*" as well as what she objected to as the hero's "divided love" for Harriet and Clementina.[39] Although Richardson relies on the so-called "accidentals" of typography throughout the novel to emphasize desired interpretations, not all readers were swayed by his emphatic use of type. At least one anonymous critic objected to the manner in which typographical gimmickry underlined *Grandison*'s didacticism:

You represent him ["your Grandison"] likewise to be a man universally learned, and tell us, at the same time, in capital letters, that SIR CH. GRAN. is a CHRISTIAN; and that too, in the strictest and most bigoted sense of the word; for he refuses the woman he loves, for a difference in religious principles.[40]

Richardson's orchestration of typographical accidentals throughout his novel, although it could not guarantee interpretive cohesion, reinforces the verbal text. Readers are rapidly conditioned to view typographical distinctions as significant, even if they do not agree with the reading that these distinctions assert.

Of course, by titling the list "NAMES of the *Principal* PERSONS," Richardson already distinguishes certain characters from the rest, establishing an artificial hierarchy internal to the novel that replaces "real" social status. For example, in the real world the title held by Lady Frampton, mentioned in the novel's initial letter but not the cast list, puts her on a social par with Lady Mansfield. The world of the novel, however, demands that the reader pay closer attention to Lady Mansfield than Lady Frampton, since only the former will, as the list indicates, play a significant role in the story. This means the readers can use the list as a means of determining the relative importance of a new character. Such a practice necessitates a fair amount of flipping back to the front of the first volume during the multi-volume reading process and blurs the distinction between the novel and its packaging. This mechanical tyranny, this physical oscillation between narrative and paratext, illustrates the degree to which graphic design governs the *Grandison* reading experience. The novel's extensive index, by demanding a non-linear approach, exerts an ever greater hold over the reading and interpretation of *Grandison*.

In each edition of *Grandison* printed under Richardson's supervision, the novel's index is approximately one hundred pages long and occupies roughly one quarter of the text's final volume (Figure 7.17).[41] Given the high cost of paper in the eighteenth century, the length of the index alone signals the importance that Richardson attached to it.[42] For a printer-publisher who cut and pasted extensively to save paper during the printing of *Clarissa*, because the paper saved was far more valuable than the increase in labor expended, the addition of this lengthy index to an already elephantine text demanded serious financial, as well as artistic, consideration.[43] Interestingly, Richardson did not aggressively advertise *Grandison*'s index, which suggests that he did not expect its presence to increase sales. The two contemporary book reviews of *Grandison* make no mention of the fact that Richardson would include an index in the last forthcoming volume.[44] If Richardson did not believe that this investment would pay off financially, why did he make it?

[305]

INDEX

Hiſtorical *and* Characteriſtical

TO THE

Six VOLUMES of this WORK.

A few only of the SENTIMENTS *with which this Work abounds, are inſerted in this* INDEX. *There is only room to refer to the reſt by Figures; under the proper Heads; as in* Advice *to Women,* Anger, *&c.*

A.

ABſence of Lovers, vol. iii. p. 114. Promotive of a cure for Love, vi. 226.

ADAM; his complaiſance to Eve, according to Milton, animadverted upon, iv. 336.

ADDISON, *Mr.* the fair Sex under great obligations to him, ii. 406.

Addreſs to men of ſenſe in the gay world, iii. 40 to 47.

Adventures of Love; women have often more courage in them than men, v. 287.

Adverſity is the trial of principle, iv. 196.

Advice or Cautions to women, i. 13. 17. 19. 26 to 29. 37. 82. 151. 300. 302. 326, 327. 411. | ii. 208. | iii. 358. | vi. 299. *See* Single *Women.*

Affectation, i. 50. 55, 56. | ii. 189. 399. | iii. 12.

Age, the preſent, its character, i. 253. 271. Much obliged to the Spectators, vi. 204.

Age of fancy, a dangerous time in a young woman's life, ii. 384. | iii. 316.

VOL. VI. X *Aged*

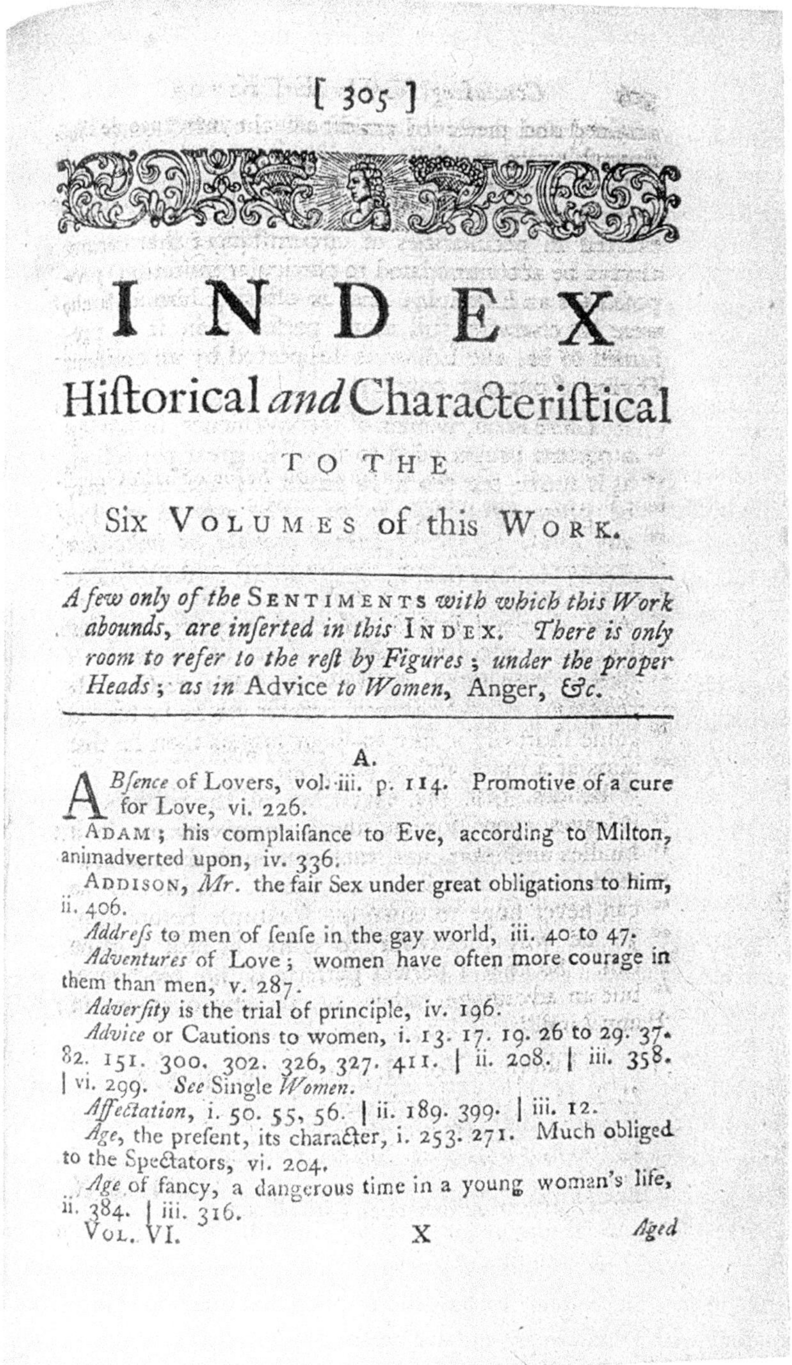

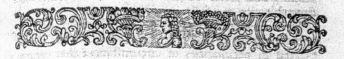

FIGURE 7.17 The first page of the index found in the second edition of Samuel Richardson's *The History of Sir Charles Grandison*, 6 vols. (1754), VI, 305.

Although her modern Oxford edition of *Grandison* lacks the index, Jocelyn Harris's account of it in her prefatory "Note on the Text" acknowledges its hermeneutic implications:

> It is notable . . . that the Index is not an entirely mechanical extrapolation, nor is it objectively compiled. Some of its interpretations are reminiscent of the revisions to later editions, especially where they concern such matters as Harriet's pertness, the behaviour of Charlotte, the debate on learning, and Sir Charles's patriotism, while the entry under the name of the Count of Belvedere suggests a significantly more visible character than appears in the book, presumably, that he may appear worthy of Clementina. Characters are simplified in didactic summary, and in short the compiling moralist of the Index goes far to repudiate the flexible creations of the novelist.[45]

Harris's observation that many of the entries resemble "revisions to later editions" highlights the manner in which Richardson invests in the corrective possibilities of the index.

Take the interpretive uncertainties that plague Richardson's fictional accounts of duelling together with the *Grandison* index's citation under that heading. Duelling was a practice that Richardson strongly opposed. His opposition is clearest in his "Six Letters upon Duelling," likely discards from his letter-writing manual *Familiar Letters*.[46] However, the "Six Letters" remained unpublished during Richardson's lifetime, possibly because of their radical opposition to a practice that the age still regarded in the fading light of aristocratic privilege. Viewing Richardson's novels through the lens of the "Six Letters" and their unequivocal opposition to duelling, Harris argues that his fictions "played a major part in disseminating the new *mentalité*" against the old aristocratic code of revenge. *Clarissa*, after all, is a story that begins and ends with a duel, framing the heroine's tragic victimization within the violent male world of aristocratic privilege gone awry. Yet, Harris agrees, Richardson's "decision to have Lovelace killed by private revenge presents a problem."[47] In point of fact, the villain meets a fitting death by the sword of Colonel Morden. And, as the duel takes place on French soil, the justice of Lovelace's fate avoids breaching English law. Morden performs his "duty" of avenging Clarissa with a grave dignity, reluctantly fulfilling a family obligation that Richardson himself defended in material now referred to as "Hints of Prefaces for *Clarissa*," arguing a precedent in the biblical story of Dinah (Gen. 34).[48] Harris agrees that while in the "Six Letters" Richardson implied that duelling is intolerable, "the analogy with Dinah seems to have persuaded him that revenge on behalf of a raped family member such as Clarissa was a justifiable exception."[49] In addition to muddying the moral waters by allowing for possible exceptions, Richardson's text also demonstrates a troubling familiarity with the code of duelling in order to avoid, understandably, the simple condemnation of either participant merely through a violation of that code. Moreover, although in fighting Lovelace Morden disobeys "the dear angel," his reluctance suggests he is free of the levity or bloodthirstiness that would cast doubt upon his decision. The brief report of the actual duel depicts Morden not as Lovelace's murderer but as the intermediary of divine justice:

> Sir, said the colonel, with the piety of a confessor (wringing Mr. Lovelace's hand), snatch these few fleeting moments, and commend yourself to God.
> And so he rode off. (Penguin edn, 1487)

True, we are told by Belford that Morden experiences second thoughts:

> altho' at *the time* he owns he was not sorry to be called upon, as he was, to take either the one course or the other; yet now, coolly reflecting upon his beloved cousin's reasonings against duelling; and upon the price it had too probably cost the unhappy man; he wishes he had more fully considered those words in his cousin's posthumous letter: "If God will allow him time for repentance, why should you deny it him?" (Penguin edn, 1494)[50]

Yet Belford's closing aside about Morden's change of heart could appear, in this context, a polite equivocation in keeping with the Colonel's aristocratic bearing.

Grandison again displays a certain ambiguity about this practice. Indeed, recalling Morden's sober decision to fight a duel, a reader might well interpret Sir Charles's refusal as evidence of cowardice. In order to counteract such a reading, the index entry under "Duelling" underscores Richardson's antipathy with a list within a list:

> *Duelling*, i. 291.354.361.367.368. Its barbarous rise, i. 373. The subject embellished by observations on the examples of that kind given — by the Horatii and Curiatii, i. 374. — by what passed between Tullus third king of Rome, and Albanus, ibid. — between Metellus and Sertorius, ibid. — between Augustus and Mark Antony, ibid. . . . between Marschal Turenne and the Elector Palatine, ibid. Sir Charles's syllogystical reasonings against it, i. 376, 377. The Council of Trent express against this barbarous practice, i. 378. The edict of Lewis the XIV. against it, one of the greatest glories of his reign, ibid.

By placing Sir Charles among this list of generals and kings Richardson encourages the reader to see him as part of an heroic, military tradition, despite (or rather precisely because of) his refusal to duel.[51] But whereas Richardson had responded in the third edition of *Clarissa* (1751) to the misreadings of Colonel Morden's duel with Lovelace with a neutralizing footnote, which, like an index, directs the reader to all previous passages which treat the practice of duelling, in *Grandison* he applies the index in its stead.[52] In fact, one reason that *Grandison* contains far fewer footnotes than *Clarissa* may be that nearly all such local correctives are collected in its closing volume's index rather than scattered throughout as notes. Ironically enough, this procedure supports rather than supplants the novel's mimetic conceit: armoured at the rear with an index, *Grandison*'s pages are blissfully free from the editorial intrusions and typographical bullets that suffused the pages of *Clarissa* (especially in the 1751 edition) with the decidedly graphic look of print that compromised with every interruption the conceit that we are reading a collection of private letters.

Just as the paratextual frame of *Grandison* affects the subjectivity of the reader, the index counterbalances the subjective narrations of the fictional characters, and polices the space between author and characters. For example, the index entry under "CHARLES I" underscores the historical parallel to the *Grandison* story, a parallel already present in the character's name and apparently prominent in Richardson's mind: "CHARLES I. fatal consequences of his marriage with a Popish Princess, iii. 158" (VI, 323).

Any readers searching for the title character under "Charles Grandison" or "Charles" rather than "Grandison, Charles" would come across this entry. The cited page refers to a discussion between Sir Charles and Father Marescotti, an Italian priest who points to the marriage of Charles I "to convince me [Grandison] of the unfitness of an alliance between families so very opposite in their religious sentiments" (III, 158). In the narrative, however, Sir Charles remains unconvinced by the historical example, arguing that mutual toleration can sustain such a marriage. Without recourse to the index, a naïve reader might choose to agree with Sir Charles, who is not merely the incontestable hero of the novel but articulates a position for which substantial support must have existed. And yet, the plot eventually undermines Sir Charles's message of toleration. Ultimately the hero will abandon his courtship of Clementina for the reason cited in the index: Sir Charles finally comes to realize that marrying a Roman Catholic would demand the sacrifice of his personal and political sovereignty. By underscoring the "fatal consequences" of such a union in the index, Richardson protects his own reading of this scene, rather than his character's. To use Harris's phrase, the "compiling moralist" again combats "the flexible creations of the novelist." Richardson's design of the index acts as a corrective to his epistolary fiction.

Richardson's indexing strategy may be contextualized within the reading culture of eighteenth-century England, particularly John Locke's theories of private reading. According to the instructions provided in *A New Method of a Common-Place-Book*, Locke encouraged readers to keep books in which, as Robert DeMaria, Jr., puts it, "they could organize all of their notes by carefully selected, generally predictable topics."[53] Rather than allow the reader to compose notes (mentally or literally) which derived from each individual text and his or her encounter with it, Locke insisted that a commonplace book track a standard and consistent series of issues through all types of text. Richardson literalizes Locke's suggestion of maintaining rigid personal categories of reading by designing the Lockean list as an integral part of his novel. In the packaging of *Grandison*, Richardson encourages his readers to view his novel only through the specific moral and social categories that he himself stipulates to be the important loci of meaning and utility.

In fact, a few years earlier, Richardson had already experimented with a Lockean list of sorts in *Clarissa* when he added the didactic *Collection of the Moral and Instructive Sentiments* to the novel. The *Collection* is a precursor to the more extensive index found in *Grandison* and functions as both a mild hermeneutic corrective and a commonplace book. In fact, Richardson deemed the *Collection*, first compiled as a paratext to the third and fourth editions of *Clarissa* in 1751, sufficiently successful to enhance it for separate publication as a free-standing compendium to his complete fictional *oeuvre* in 1755.[54] William Beatty Warner explains how the *Collection*, which Richardson referred to as an "index" in the preface to the 1751 *Clarissa*, promotes interpretive cohesion and corrects misinterpretations: "The index replays *Clarissa* as a coherent system, where 'characters' of fixed identity interact to trace a 'plot,' which expresses a certain 'theme.'"[55] Richardson dispenses moral, legal, and economic advice in the *Collection* on topics as various as "Oeconomy. Frugality. Housewifry." and "Rapes." He there directs the reader to illustrative examples of these lessons by volume and page number: "By Frugality we are enabled to be both just and generous, iv. 158." When *Clarissa* is approached through this catalogue of aphorisms, individual scenes become cases in a neatly organized book of manners, uniting the novel with its conduct-book precursors. Some citations may, in fact, be too "neat" – clearing away the nuanced moral dilemmas of the novel with sweeping generalizations. For example, Mrs. Howe's opinion that *Clarissa* will be accountable for Lovelace's future "mischiefs" if she "does not prosecute" – an opinion initially recounted in the novel with pained skepticism by her daughter – appears in the *Collection* under "Rapes" as a generally held principle: "The woman who, from Modesty, declines prosecuting a brutal Ravisher, and has his life in her hands, is answerable for all the mischiefs he may do in future, vi. 183." The *Collection* thus generalizes from a scene or statement, endorsing a specific interpretation after the event. Not all readers shared Richardson's apparent enthusiasm for the *Collection*; Samuel Johnson soon suggested he consider another type of indexing strategy – a scholarly *index rerum*.

Indeed, the most convincing evidence that the type of index found in *Grandison* springs from the contemporary habit of list-making and referencing may lie in the fact that the very idea for a scholarly index at the close of a novel originated, not with Richardson himself, but with the age's greatest lexicographer and compiler of reference books. As early as March of 1751, Samuel Johnson planted the seed for the *Grandison* index by requesting one for *Clarissa*, which he had then just finished perusing in an apparent gift copy of the about-to-be-released fourth edition in handsome octavo. Though he praises the "improved" appearance of the novel, which in the fourth edition (and the simultaneously published third in duodecimo) had been expanded and newly outfitted with the *Collection*, Johnson suggests also adding an *index rerum*:

9 March 1751

Dear Sir:

Though Clarissa wants no help from external Splendour I was glad to see her improved in her appearance but more glad to find that she was now got above all fears of prolixity, and confident enough of Success, to supply whatever had been hitherto suppressed. I never indeed found a hint of any such defalcation but I fretted, for though the Story is long, every letter is short.

I wish You would add an *Index Rerum* that when the reader recollects any incident he may easily find it, which at present he cannot do unless he knows in which volume it is told; for Clarissa is not a performance to be read with eagerness and laid aside for ever, but will be occasionally consulted by the busy, the aged, and the studious, and therefore I beg that this Edition by which I suppose Posterity is to abide, may want nothing that can facilitate its use.

SAM. JOHNSON[56]

This astonishing letter reveals that Johnson thinks of Richardson's novels as potential reference texts, as books to be "consulted." His judgment is unequivocal: "Clarissa is not a performance to be read with eagerness and laid aside for ever." Although it flatters Richardson that "though the Story is long, every letter is short," Johnson's request for a final index of things reveals a simple problem that plagued the new "species" of writing in general and Richardson's epistolary novels in particular: from the standpoint of consultation and utility the new genre was simply too long.[57]

Although the novel's growing popularity confirms that length was no impediment to pleasure, Johnson worries that the bulk of a novel frustrates rereading, and by extension reading for specific instruction. Johnson thinks that a comprehensive index would enable those who had already read this huge work once to cope with Richardson's prolixity and mine his novel for its utility as a reference work. Johnson signals that, armed with an *index rerum*, a reader could locate any vaguely remembered passage with relative ease. Apparently, to Johnson's way of thinking, the new edition's *Collection* did not yet measure up to this functional ideal. Of course, the *Dictionary* project, completed the year after *Grandison* but well under way by the time he advised Richardson on an index in 1751, shows that Johnson, whose entries under "Oats," "Tory," and "Grubstreet" are legendary instances of subjective definition, was himself a partisan maker of lists and compendia. In advising Richardson to add an index to a work of fiction, Johnson encouraged his friend to build not merely a streamlined memory-aid that objectively assists "the busy, the aged, and the studious" but a device that might allow the author to better manage posterity's memory of his own text.

With the *Collection* to *Clarissa* and the index to *Grandison*, Richardson had in mind not the first-time reader but, as Johnson envisioned, the re-reader of his novels. Richardson himself seems increasingly conscious of the distinction between influencing readers' anticipation of a text and guiding their recollection. At first, Richardson happily provided his novels with elaborate promissory tables of contents. For example, the lavishly illustrated sixth edition of *Pamela* in four volumes (1742) opens with what the book's title page has reason to boast is "An Ample TABLE of CONTENTS," since it offers detailed summaries of each of Pamela's ensuing letters and journal entries. A paragraph at the head of this list, which duly labels it a "copious INDEX," explains its two-pronged intention: "*to revive the Memory of the principal Matters in the Minds of those who have read them, and to give an easy and clear View of what they contain, to those who have not.*" For a first-time reader (admittedly this costly edition and its engraved plates aims at a collector's market) the clarity with which the list's plot summaries are rendered takes a bit of the sting out of the ensuing action. For example, take Mr. B's initial infiltration of the boudoir:

> XXV. *To the same*. [i.e. from Pamela to her parents] Her Master hides himself in their Closet, and overhears a Discourse against himself between Mrs. *Jervis* and her, as they are going to Rest. Being alarmed at the Rustling of his Gown, she, almost undress'd, goes towards the Closet; and he rushing out, she flies to the Bed of Mrs. *Jervis*, and falls into Fits.
> XXVI. *To the same*. Mrs. *Jervis*, resenting her Master's Conduct in her Apartment, gives him Warning. He agrees that they shall go away both together; and tells them, That he shall probably embrace a Proposal of Marriage that has been made him, and think no more of *Pamela*. Her Joy on hearing this. Hopes now, that all the Danger is over; but will not be too secure. (I, iv)

The list also fails to honor its mnemonic promise. If used by a re-reader to relocate a dimly remembered scene, the list's thirty-six pages of tightly spaced summary are far too cumbersome to serve as the kind of quick-find reference tool Johnson describes.

The preface to the 1751 edition of *Clarissa*, however, is testimony to Richardson's growing disaffection with such prefatory lists of contents. Here

Richardson explains why he has subdivided the old table of contents and moved each resulting précis to the back of the individual volumes of the new 1751 text:

> In the Second Edition an ample *Table of Contents* to the *whole* work was prefixed to the first volume: But that having in some measure anticipated the Catastrophe, and been thought to detain the Reader too long from entering upon the History, it has been judged adviseable to *add* (and that rather than *prefix*) to each Volume its *particular* contents; which will serve not only as an Index, but as a brief Recapitulation of the most material passages contained in it; and which will enable the Reader to connect in his mind the perused volume with that which follows; and more clearly shew the characters and views of particular correspondents. (x–xi)

Richardson has now come to judge the paratextual device of the prefatory table, though commonly found in contemporary fiction and non-fiction alike, as problematic.

Whereas in 1751 Richardson thought it advisable to move the table of contents to the end of the volumes, turning eventually to an *index rerum* in *Grandison*, other novelists manipulated to their own advantage the anticipation roused by the prefixed table of contents, often using a deceptive bill of fare. The convention of the summary chapter title is a prerequisite for this type of novelistic table, which gathers together verbatim the titles of succeeding chapters. For instance, the table of contents to Swift's *Travels* (1726) contains the formulaic constructions expected from a travel narrative: "The Author giveth some Account of himself and Family . . . He is shipwrecked, and swims for his Life" or "A great Storm described." Although Richardson feared that his epistolary summaries would reveal too much of the plot, Swift's table does not divulge the particular novelties of Gulliver's story. Without prior knowledge of Lilliput, Brobdingnag, or the Houyhnhnms, a reader can only guess at the oddly exotic names mentioned in the table. Similarly, the joke embedded in the summary "The Empress's Apartment on fire by an Accident; the Author instrumental in saving the rest of the Palace," is inaccessible to the first-time reader, who has yet to learn how Gulliver produced the flood that saved the palace. The *Travels*'s prefatory list assists readers in relocating specific episodes, although far less reliably than the extensive index of *Grandison*. However, while the *Travels*'s contents pages offer opaque summaries useful only to the informed reader, the lists fronting Fielding's *Joseph Andrews* (1742), lists similarly constructed from colorful chapter titles, deliberately misdirect the naïve reader and, ironically in light of Richardson's objections, heighten suspense. The prefixed chapter title "A dreadful Quarrel which happened at the Inn where the Company dines, with its bloody Consequences to Mr. Adams" gives little hint that the calamity involves a "Pan full of Hog's-Blood" which descends upon poor Adams, wounding only his pride. Fielding, who is highly conscious of chapters and their titles (Book 11 opens with a chapter about chapters, entitled "Of Divisions in Authors"), thus manipulates print convention by constructing a table that, like Richardson's index, will aid re-reading without spoiling the plot, all the while augmenting suspense and highlighting the genre's rapidly coalescing conventions. Charlotte Lennox's *The Female Quixote* (1752), although suffused with many of Henry Fielding's titulary habits, emphasizes misdirection rather than re-reading in its prefatory list of contents, where the reader is told that "A very mysterious Chapter" will be followed by one "Not much plainer than the former." The movement of *Clarissa*'s original table of contents to the back connects the playful table of contents in novels by Swift, Fielding, and Lennox, to the seemingly divergent index in Richardson's *Grandison*.[58] Kidgell redundantly names his six-page satirical index to *The Card* "An Index of the Contents," reiterating the link between an *index rerum* and a prefatory table of contents.

Eighteenth-century print culture offers other types of precursor and companion to Richardson's index, some of which may actually compromise the intended grandeur of *Grandison*'s packaging: the satirical index, pseudo-scholarly machinery, and "keys." John Gay's index to his urban pastoral *Trivia; or, the Art of Walking the Streets of London* (1716) engaged the Scriblerian campaign to spoof contemporary scholarship, ridiculing what Swift belittled as "the *back door*" to the "palace of learning" and Pope crisply dismissed as "Index-learning."[59] The Scriblerians also satirized the addition of pseudo-scholarly machinery, including indexes, to give modern productions a scholastic appearance.[60] Both Alexander Pope in his *Dunciad Variorum* (1729) and Thomas Parnell in *The Battle of the Frogs and Mice* (1717) used footnotes, framing commentaries, and glossaries to imitate and ridicule these features of the pseudo-scholarly book. Thus, while for Richardson an index acts as a sign of legitimacy and utility, for the Scriblerians it was, like the prefatory puff, "a repository of unearned, and hence illegitimate knowledge." While what Roger Lund describes as the "Scriblerian animus toward the index function" may appear unwarranted to us as the grateful heirs of the new information culture that emerged in the eighteenth century, nonetheless the satirical index may have endangered Richardson's index by aligning it with the parodic.[61] In the end, the novel's appropriation of indexes and lists as signs of authority shows it running the same risks as when it appropriated the frontispiece.

In prose fiction, the so-called "keys" to scandal sheets, political satires, and amatory fiction loosely based on actual situations offer yet another precursor to the *Grandison* index. Eliza Haywood's "key" to her *Memoirs of a Certain Island Adjacent to the Kingdom of Utopia* (1725) is representative.[62] In her key, inserted at the end of the text, Haywood anticipates the workings of the book trade in much the same manner as Richardson. Most keys, usually in the form

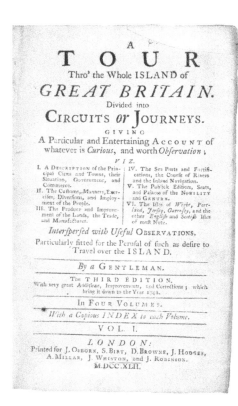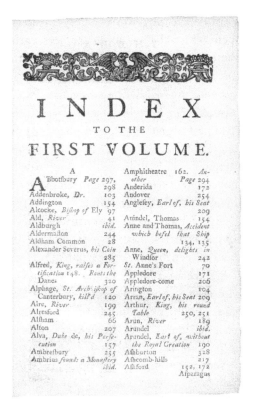

FIGURE 7.18 Title page and first page of index from an edition of Daniel Defoe's *A Tour Thro' the Whole Island of Great Britain* printed on Richardson's press, 4 vols. (London, 1742), 1, title and [357].

of pamphlets, were composed by someone other than the author and often printed by a rival publisher; all of them promised to expose the true identities and politics behind popular fictions.[63] Although separately published, a "key" often ended up bound with the work it purported to unlock, owing to the fact that individual consumers made most book-binding decisions, often bundling together short texts on related subjects. Haywood and Richardson both preempt this aspect of book production: they outfitted their original narratives with catalogues which elsewhere were published separately. As Johnson indicated when he asked for a post-publication index to *Clarissa*, contemporary publication conventions favored a separately published index not unlike the final version of the *Collection of Sentiments*.[64] Haywood, like Richardson with *Grandison*, provides the reader of her *Memoirs* with an immediate interpretive tool designed by the original author. Haywood's "key," though by no means as extensive or complicated as Richardson's index, anticipates the mechanisms of book production and offers interpretive guidance in ways that make it a literary precursor to the machinery in *Grandison*.

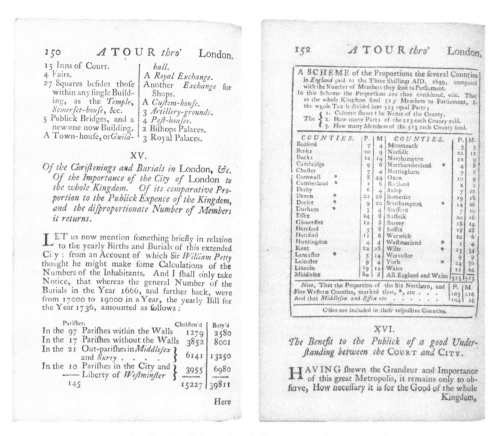

FIGURE 7.19 From Richardson's edition of Defoe's *Tour* (1742), II, 150 and 152.

Although eighteenth-century fiction abounds with indexes and index-like devices, eighteenth-century print culture provides even more examples of indexes in works of non-fiction. Lund claims that over the century, as the index proliferated in the new information culture, "readers would encounter new indexes of almost everything."[65] Certainly, indexes were commonplace. Yet they continued to be predominantly associated with the historical compendium and the scientific reference text. They also appeared as standard features of the collected works of classical writers, collected periodicals, scientific manuals, guide books, travelogues, and, of course, the Bible.[66] The rhetorical status of the index indicates the type of ambition Richardson harbored for the novel genre when he compiled one for *Grandison*. Richardson's own edition of Daniel Defoe's *A Tour Thro' the Whole Island of Great Britain* (1742) best exemplifies the archetypical eighteenth-century reference text. Advertised on the title page as outfitted "*With a Copious INDEX to each Volume*," Richardson's edition of Defoe's *Tour* includes indexes of up to a dozen pages in length that cite place names and persons mentioned in the central text of each volume (Figure 7.18). In addition, the *Tour* includes catalogues of all sorts: lists of architectural

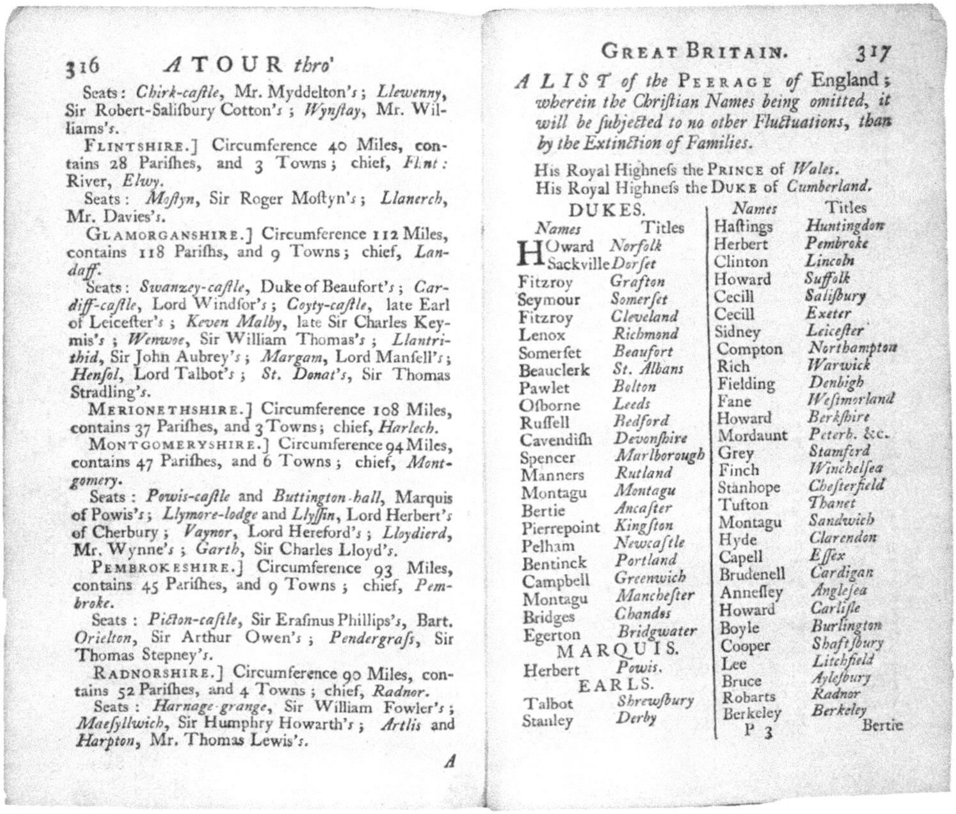

316 *A* TOUR *thro'*

Seats: *Chirk-caſtle*, Mr. Myddelton's; *Llewenny*, Sir Robert-Saliſbury Cotton's; *Wynſtay*, Mr. Williams's.

FLINTSHIRE.] Circumference 40 Miles, contains 28 Pariſhes, and 3 Towns; chief, *Flint*: River, *Elwy*.

Seats: *Moſtyn*, Sir Roger Moſtyn's; *Llanerch*, Mr. Davies's.

GLAMORGANSHIRE.] Circumference 112 Miles, contains 118 Pariſhs, and 9 Towns; chief, *Landaff*.

Seats: *Swanzey-caſtle*, Duke of Beaufort's; *Cardiff-caſtle*, Lord Windſor's; *Coyty-caſtle*, late Earl of Leiceſter's; *Keven Malby*, late Sir Charles Keymis's; *Wenwoe*, Sir William Thomas's; *Llantrithid*, Sir John Aubrey's; *Margam*, Lord Manſell's; *Henſol*, Lord Talbot's; *St. Donat's*, Sir Thomas Stradling's.

MERIONETHSHIRE.] Circumference 108 Miles, contains 37 Pariſhes, and 3 Towns; chief, *Harlech*.

MONTGOMERYSHIRE.] Circumference 94 Miles, contains 47 Pariſhes, and 6 Towns; chief, *Montgomery*.

Seats: *Powis-caſtle* and *Buttington-hall*, Marquis of Powis's; *Llymore-lodge* and *Llyſſin*, Lord Herbert's of Cherbury; *Vaynor*, Lord Hereford's; *Lloydierd*, Mr. Wynne's; *Garth*, Sir Charles Lloyd's.

PEMBROKESHIRE.] Circumference 93 Miles, contains 45 Pariſhes, and 9 Towns; chief, *Pembroke*.

Seats: *Picton-caſtle*, Sir Eraſmus Phillips's, Bart. *Orielton*, Sir Arthur Owen's; *Pendergraſs*, Sir Thomas Stepney's.

RADNORSHIRE.] Circumference 90 Miles, contains 52 Pariſhes, and 4 Towns; chief, *Radnor*.

Seats: *Harnage-grange*, Sir William Fowler's; *Maeſyllwich*, Sir Humphry Howarth's; *Artlis* and *Harpton*, Mr. Thomas Lewis's.

A

GREAT BRITAIN. 317

A LIST of the PEERAGE *of* England; *wherein the Chriſtian Names being omitted, it will be ſubjected to no other Fluctuations, than by the Extinction of Families.*

His Royal Highneſs the PRINCE of *Wales*.
His Royal Highneſs the DUKE of *Cumberland*.

DUKES.

Names	Titles
HOward	*Norfolk*
Sackville	*Dorſet*
Fitzroy	*Grafton*
Seymour	*Somerſet*
Fitzroy	*Cleveland*
Lenox	*Richmond*
Somerſet	*Beaufort*
Beauclerk	*St. Albans*
Pawlet	*Bolton*
Oſborne	*Leeds*
Ruſſell	*Bedford*
Cavendiſh	*Devonſhire*
Spencer	*Marlborough*
Manners	*Rutland*
Montagu	*Montagu*
Bertie	*Ancaſter*
Pierrepoint	*Kingſton*
Pelham	*Newcaſtle*
Bentinck	*Portland*
Campbell	*Greenwich*
Montagu	*Mancheſter*
Bridges	*Chandos*
Egerton	*Bridgwater*

MARQUIS.

Herbert	*Powis.*

EARLS.

Names	Titles
Talbot	*Shrewſbury*
Stanley	*Derby*
Haſtings	*Huntingdon*
Herbert	*Pembroke*
Clinton	*Lincoln*
Howard	*Suffolk*
Cecill	*Saliſbury*
Cecill	*Exeter*
Sidney	*Leiceſter*
Compton	*Northampton*
Rich	*Warwick*
Fielding	*Denbigh*
Fane	*Weſtmorland*
Howard	*Berkſhire*
Mordaunt	*Peterb. &c.*
Grey	*Stamford*
Finch	*Winchelſea*
Stanhope	*Cheſterfield*
Tufton	*Thanet*
Montagu	*Sandwich*
Hyde	*Clarendon*
Capell	*Eſſex*
Brudenell	*Cardigan*
Anneſley	*Angleſea*
Howard	*Carliſle*
Boyle	*Burlington*
Cooper	*Shaftſbury*
Lee	*Litchfield*
Bruce	*Ayleſbury*
Robarts	*Radnor*
Berkeley	*Berkeley*

P 3 Bertie

FIGURE 7.20 From Richardson's edition of Defoe's *Tour* (1742), IV, 316–17.

measurements, population statistics, names of hamlets and villages, even a list of members of the English peerage (Figures 7.19 and 7.20). The *Tour* is the type of reference text that must have instructed Richardson in the interpretive impact of both framing and listing: in *Grandison* Richardson co-opts such practices in order to claim for the novel a similar documentary authority and utility.[67]

At the same time, the addition of an *index rerum* to *Grandison* signals Richardson's growing faith in the new genre's cultural permanence. As Johnson foresaw, the index encourages a reader to return to the novel after having read it straight through. In this manner, the index combats not just local misinterpretation in the text, but the characterization of the genre itself as "short-lived." Contemporary critics often dismissed Richardson's epistolary novels as ephemeral, claiming that their novelty was their sole selling point:

> [W]hat recommends them to the notice of the present age is, their novelty, and their gratifying an idle and insatiable curiosity. In a few years that novelty

will wear off, and that Curiosity will be equally gratified by other compositions . . . Such, Sir, must be the fate of all works which owe their success to a present capricious humor, and have not real intrinsic worth to support them. Short-lived then as they are . . .[68]

Perhaps it was ambition, then, that launched the novel genre's first index. Richardson's investment in *Grandison*'s index formally insists that the fiction does contain "real intrinsic worth." As Johnson envisioned in his letter, the addition of an index declares that the novel shall occupy a long-lasting place in print culture as an important document for "Posterity." The index thus suggests a formal move to place the novel on the same shelf as other indexed books, and, by extension, to lend it an authoritative, referential status. In the words of an anonymous eighteenth-century critic of Richardson: "you have very pleasantly contrived to find a place there for your self in Homer's room."[69] This use of an index to ennoble the "new species of writing" parallels Henry Fielding's attempts to elevate the new genre to the level of a modern epic with classical references and allusions. With the *Grandison* index Richardson offers the epistolary novel as the literary touchstone of his time – a text worth consulting on 100 pages of cultural, social, and political issues, from *Adam* and *Addison* to *The World* and religious *Zeal*.

Coda

Soon after Laurence Sterne's death, the contents of his library were sold to Todd and Sotheran, at the sign of the Golden Bible in Stonegate, York.¹ Sterne's extensive book collection was speedily catalogued and offered for sale "*exceeding cheap*" on "*Tuesday, August 23, 1768.*"² The catalogue of this sale, although it neither precludes his having read books that he did not own nor guarantees his having read those that he did, is our most definitive record of Sterne's reading. Among the two-and-a-half thousand titles offered for sale from Sterne's library are hundreds of works of contemporary popular fiction. Richardson's novels, however, are conspicuously absent. Sterne apparently owned only a single volume of fiction by Richardson, for under the final category of "Odd Volumes Duodecimo," the sale catalogue lists the following lone volume of Richardsoniana: "Sir Charles Grandison, vol 7, *in Boards*, 1s." Sterne thus possessed an inexpensive copy of only the final volume of Richardson's last novel, the volume which houses what is the most extensive of the novel's early experiments with graphic design: the index.

Sterne's death in 1768 may have preempted additional volumes planned for *Tristram Shandy*, which as it stands resists closure. Wayne Booth once asked "Did Sterne Complete *Tristram Shandy*?"³ Maybe Sterne intended to follow Kidgell's example and annex a ludicrous index volume to *Tristram Shandy*, perhaps in the guise of Walter Shandy's *Tristrapaedia*. Walter shares with his times a pseudo-scientific impulse to index and collect smatterings of anecdotal knowledge into a coherent system. Walter's characteristically ineffectual plan to organize his own "scattered thoughts, counsels, and notions" into a "system of education" for his son Tristram, "so as to form an INSTITUTE for the government of [his] childhood and adolescence," adheres to the conduct-book model that operates in the *Grandison* index (v, xvi). It is tempting, therefore, to imagine a planned index as the most straightforward explanation for the mystery as to why Sterne owned a single volume of *Grandison* when he did not own (or no longer owned) the story to which it was a guide.[4] And yet, irrespective of whether or not it influenced Sterne, *Grandison's* index may indicate how far the novel had engaged Enlightenment empiricism and taxonomy.

And leaving guesswork aside, the material self-consciousness of *Tristram Shandy*, with its marbled, black, and be-dashed pages, seems of a piece with the graphic awareness of many earlier novelistic projects, including Richardson's. Indeed, in the larger context of the genre's radical experiments with print and graphic design, from front to end, frontispiece to index, Sterne's work appears far less experimental and even less original than history has credited. Without wishing to demote the playful genius of *Tristram Shandy*'s materiality, I have sought to promote the equally ingenious efforts of those many earlier novelists and proto-novelists who, along with their printers and publishers, smoothed the way for a Sterne. Unfortunately, the bulk of these graphic experiments in the evolution of the novel were, for a long time, lost under the crusty *terra firma* of traditional editorial practice, which buried, altered, or diminished every one of the novel's graphic dimensions I have discussed. Today, these practices are being called into question both from within the editorial community and from without. The bibliographical tide is turning to reveal new contours in the landscape of literary studies.

Ironically, the Web-based technology revolution may herald a return of the eighteenth-century book. *Project Gutenberg* was, for quite a while, the only viable model for the electronic duplication of old books: the project's many spin-offs (created in the mid-1990s rush to be among the first to market a literary database) offered searchable texts of books created from out-of-copyright editions (for legal reasons, pre-1923) that held little or no editorial authority.[5] A user of such databases had access to a work's verbal text (although of unreliable origins), but not to its appearance as a printed text. The recent changeover in some searchable online databases from word-processed (and ASCII-coded) texts to digitized images of the page-fields of books allows for an unprecedented access to the actual "look" of rare books and hand-press materials through the lens of the personal desktop.[6] In addition, many editorial projects are developing the rich potential of the electronic hypertext to offer a reader (in a manner that even Gabler could not have envisioned in the 1980s) a layered, synoptic edition of a text that manages to safeguard a book's original appearance in various editions simultaneously. Using and developing theories of hypertext editing, projects such as *The William Blake Archive*[7] and Jerome McGann's *Rossetti Archive*[8] are redirecting critical attention to both the area of graphic arts in early printed books and the impact of digital technology upon editorial theory. Recently, even some rare books libraries have begun building image databanks (modeled after the electronic collections of many art museums and galleries) out of their thrifty stockpiling of negatives from prior duplication requests.⁹ Although the resulting collection of images is eclectic, a user of such an imagebank has wide-ranging access to the visual diversity of the printed book, from *incunabula* to *Lolita*.

And not all efforts to resurrect old books are lofty editorial projects, created by ivory-tower bibliophiles supported by a high-tech staff. Just as the eighteenth-century's dominant desire for novelty witnessed a backlash of conservative thinking in, for example, the Scriblerian raillery against Grubstreet, so, too, has popular culture, awash in a sea of new technologies, recently shown a nostalgic longing for the age of paper. American novelist Nicholson Baker's *Double Fold: Libraries and the Assault on Paper* (Random House, 2001) emerges as perhaps the most fervent proponent for the book's return, arguing (with echoes of Eisenstein) that the innate value, meaning, and efficacy of an old printed newspaper or book cannot be adequately imparted to a microfilm or digital duplication.[10] Yet digital technologies and Web publishing are themselves rediscovering graphic design. Web designers have created scores of sites that offer the digital explorer dazzling arrays of type fonts, ornaments, and design ideas for desktop publishing or the setting up of their own Web site. Although many such sites haughtily convey the mistaken impressions that Bill Gates single-handedly invented the concept of graphic design and that Pica roman face or Caslon italic were forged in the smithies of Silicon Valley, many of them reinstate, for common use, graphic elements (such as old typefaces, printer's ornaments, the *hedera*, the pointing hand) that have remained hidden for centuries in the pages of hand-press books.

However, it is not merely bibliography that, by selectively applying new technology to its own specialist concerns, will benefit from its intersection with the digital age. The discourse of advanced technology may, in future, find it profitable to mine the language of bibliography. At present the "modernity" of digital technology remains largely unhistoricized. For example, not long after Paul Saenger argued for the significance of the inserting of white space between words, an invention he dated to medieval books, William Safire complained about the removal of silences between words on the medium of radio.[11] A new digital technology that could snip out the silences between spoken words on air – so as to increase advertisement space – was eliminating, Safire argued, the pregnant pause. Safire lamented in his regular *New York Times* "On Language" column that "cramming it together" was "the wave of the Future," unaware that Saenger had just shown that such squeezing was also in our past. Safire's concerns about high-tech radio editing could also have glossed Henry Fielding's elimination of his sister's dashes: "the silent squeeze also weakens discourse by removing dramatic pauses."[12] Although the Safire example is a bit cheeky, the fact is that observers of high technology frequently strain to articulate "new" problems, unaware that these have historical counterparts in the study of bibliography. Perhaps digital technology will soon discover that the history of the book contains some useful forerunners of the problems it faces.

In popular graphic design manuals such as *Homepage Usability: 50 Websites Deconstructed* (New Riders, 2001), by Jakob Nielsen and Marie Tahir, the medium of Web-design is itself becoming the subject of the same type of textual-studies-style scrutiny that I have tried to apply to the eighteenth-century novel. *Homepage Usability* reproduces fifty well-trafficked homepages from globally recognizable corporations such as Disney, Wal-Mart, CNN, and Ford, as well as a few smaller businesses (Job Magic in the UK) and institutions (the Art Institute of Chicago). It then deconstructs the "screen real estate" of each page and judges whether this or that feature on a page is easy to navigate. Each example in taxonomy is meant as a lesson in what to duplicate and what to avoid in one's own homepage. Nielsen and Tahir evaluate each page on whether it offers, like the title pages of books posted as advertisements in eighteenth-century London, content-rich information with clarity and precision at a glance. They estimate a homepage has only "10 seconds" to make an impression; I doubt the busy eighteenth-century Londoner awarded much additional time to a title page when passing a crowded show-board in Grubstreet. It is not merely the design industry's continued insistence upon the metaphor of the "page" for an electronic site that triggers my comparison. In essence, Nielsen and Tahir's considerations of the "usability" of such features as a page's Window Title, Tag Line, and URL are utterly in sync with my own deconstruction of the title, subtitle, and imprint of eighteenth-century title pages. In both cases the "page" is judged on how its verbal content and graphic design (layout, fonts, and "features") jointly impact the reader-consumer.[13] Because the industry's dominant medium of communication has shifted from paper to screen, the discipline of graphic design is undergoing a self-diagnostic – one that is not dissimilar to the current reconsiderations of "old" bibliographical concerns in our own literary discipline.

Not only may the modern novel and the study of its eighteenth-century beginnings yet be well served by the burgeoning digital-age revival in graphic design, graphic design may also glean something from the rhetoric of textual studies.

Notes

1 Expanding the literary text

1. For an example of this standard interpretation, see Irvin Ehrenpreis's benchmark discussion of this poem in *Swift: The Man, His Works, and the Age*, 3 vols. (Cambridge, MA: Harvard University Press, 1967), II, 384–87.
2. Donald F. Bond attributes to Sir Richard Steele the authorship of those first three paragraphs of Bickerstaff's that introduce Swift's poem. See Joseph Addison and Sir Richard Steele, *The Tatler*, ed. Donald F. Bond, 3 vols. (Oxford University Press, 1987), III, 224.
3. Bond's edition of *The Tatler* attributes *No. 21*'s article "From My Own Apartment" – which remarks on the increasing presence of the advertisements – to Swift (I, 164). In so doing Bond follows Herbert Davis who argued that "the reference in the Postscript to the Advertisements suggests the hand of Swift, as we know that he disapproved of their increasing prominence in the paper" (quoted by Bond, I, 164). The remaining central text of *No. 21* seems to be unproblematically attributed to Steele.
4. Swift in *Tatler No. 21*, Saturday, 28 May 1709; Addison and Steele, *The Tatler*, ed. Bond, I, 170.
5. *Ibid.*, 171.
6. See Marshall McLuhan, *The Gutenberg Galaxy: The Making of Typographic Man* (University of Toronto Press, 1962); Lucien Febvre and Henri-Jean Martin, *The Coming of the Book: The Impact of Printing (1450–1800)* (London and New York: Verso, 1990; first published, 1958; first English translation, 1976); and Elizabeth L. Eisenstein, *The Printing Press as an Agent of Change*, 2 vols. (Cambridge: Cambridge University Press, 1979).
7. Richard Cargill Cole, *Irish Booksellers and English Writers 1740–1800* (Atlantic Highlands, NJ: Humanities Press International, 1986); M. Pollard, *Dublin's Trade in Books 1550–1800* (Oxford: Clarendon Press, 1989); and S. Roscoe, *John Newbery and his Successors 1740–1814* (Hertfordshire: Five Owls Press, 1973) are but a few examples of the variety of new histories of eighteenth-century book production that mushroomed in the 1970s and 1980s. In addition, analytical and descriptive

bibliography, after nearly half a century of being underappreciated, experienced – in the wake of this new interest in the materiality of the book – something of a revival. See, for example, in the field of eighteenth-century studies: Nicolas Barker, "Typography and the Meaning of Words: The Revolution in the Layout of Books in the Eighteenth Century," in Giles Barber and Bernhard Fabian, eds., *Buch und Buchhandel in Europa im achtzehten Jahrhundert*, (Hamburg: Dr. Ernst Hanswedell & Co., 1981), 127–65, and D. F. McKenzie, *Bibliography and the Sociology of Texts*, The Panizzi Lectures Series (London: British Library, 1985).

8. See, for example, Alvin B. Kernan, *Printing Technology, Letters, and Samuel Johnson* (Princeton University Press, 1987); David F. Foxon, *Pope and the Early Eighteenth-Century Book Trade*, ed. James McLaverty, The Lyell Lectures, Oxford, 1975–6 (New York: Oxford University Press, 1991); and Julie Stone Peters, *Congreve, the Drama, and the Printed Word* (Stanford University Press, 1990).

9. See W. J. T. Mitchell, *Blake's Composite Art: A Study of Illuminated Poetry* (Princeton University Press, 1978).

10. Foxon's before-mentioned *Pope and the Early Eighteenth-Century Book Trade* exemplifies the frontline scholarship on the struggle between Pope and his printers and publishers to control the physical appearance of his texts.

11. Here are a few examples of the type of detailed attention that the graphic dress of *Tristram Shandy* has received in recent decades: W. G. Day, "*Tristram Shandy*: The Marbled Leaf," *The Library* 27 (1972), 143–45; R. B. Moss, "Sterne's Punctuation," *Eighteenth-Century Studies* 15.2 (Winter 1981–82), 179–200; Mark Loveridge, *Laurence Sterne and the Argument About Design* (Totowa, NJ: Vision and Barnes & Noble, 1982); Horst Meyer, "Das Geheimnis der marmorierten Seite: oder, *Tristram Shandy*s typographische Extravaganzen," *Antiquariat* (1986), A130–34; and Christopher Fanning, "On Sterne's Page: Spatial Layout, Spatial Form, and Social Spaces in *Tristram Shandy*," *Eighteenth-Century Studies* 10.4 (July 1998), 429–50.

12. See James McLaverty, *Pope, Print, and Meaning* (Oxford University Press, 2001), as well as J. Paul Hunter, "From Typology to Type: Print Technology and Ideology in *The Dunciad* and *Tristram Shandy*," in Margaret J. M. Ezell and Katherine O'Brien O'Keeffe, eds., *Cultural Artifacts and the Production of Meaning: The Page, the Image, and the Body* (Ann Arbor: University of Michigan Press, 1994), 41–69.

13. Joe Bray, Miriam Handley, and Anne C. Henry, eds., *Ma(r)king the Text: The Presentation of Meaning on the Literary Page* (Aldershot, Burlington USA, Singapore, Sidney: Ashgate, 2000). This collection offers a taste of the smorgasbord of papers given at an exceptionally lively 1998 Cambridge conference.

14. Gérard Genette, *Paratexts: Thresholds of Interpretation*, trans. Jane E. Lewin and foreword by Richard Macksey (Cambridge University Press, 1997). Genette's book was originally published in French as *Seuils* in 1987. In 1991, a partial translation by Marie Maclean became available as Genette, "Introduction to the Paratext," *New Literary History* 22 (1991), 261–73.

15. Genette, *Paratexts*, 2.

16. *Ibid.*

17. Jerome J. McGann, *A Critique of Modern Textual Criticism* (Chicago and London: University of Chicago Press, 1983).
18. G. Thomas Tanselle, "The Editorial Problem of Final Authorial Intention," *Studies in Bibliography* 29 (1976), 167–211. Tanselle rearticulated his notions of copy-text more fully in *A Rationale of Textual Criticism* (Philadelphia: University of Pennsylvania Press, 1992).
19. Hans Walter Gabler, "The Text as Process and the Problem of Intentionality," *Text* 3 (1987), 107–16, at 108.
20. James Joyce, *Ulysses: A Critical and Synoptic Edition*, prepared by Hans Walter Gabler with Wolfhard Steppe and Claus Melchior, 3 vols. (New York and London: Garland Publishing Inc., 1984).
21. Adrian Johns, *The Nature of the Book: Print and Knowledge in the Making* (Chicago and London: University of Chicago Press, 1998), 19.
22. *Ibid.*, 2.
23. *Ibid.*, 174.
24. Ralph Straus, *The Unspeakable Curll: Being Some Account of Edmund Curll, Bookseller to which is Added a Full List of his Books* (London: Chapman & Hall, 1927), 201.
25. Genette cites Voltaire's *Oeuvres Complètes*, put out by Baudoin in 1825, as "one of the first examples of a printed cover" (23).
26. John Carter, *ABC for Book Collectors*, revised by Nicholas Barker, 6th edn. (New Castle, DE: Oak Knoll Books, 1992), 203. In *A New Introduction to Bibliography* (New York and Oxford: Oxford University Press, 1972), Philip Gaskell describes the generic, unadorned appearance of such trade bindings: "Ordinary trade bindings of the seventeenth and early eighteenth centuries had very little decoration on the covers, and were rarely gilt" (152). Even when, in the latter part of the eighteenth century, trade bindings do become increasingly decorative (with gold-tooled fillets, lettering pieces, blind-tooled panels, and even paper labels), the consumer-determined final binding dominated: "[a] greatly increased proportion of books were retailed in paper wrappers and paper boards, uncut to allow for later rebinding in leather" (Gaskell, 152–53).
27. Of course this does not mean that prior to 1825 blank trade covers were entirely devoid of meaning: as Genette argues and Sterne's blank page confirms, "a mute fold, like every wasteful act, is a sign of distinction" (*Paratexts*, 27).
28. As a result, copies of eighteenth-century books in their original wrappers or trade bindings are, today, a rare find.
29. See Northrop Frye, *Anatomy of Criticism: Four Essays* (Princeton University Press, 1957); Ian Watt, *The Rise of the Novel: Studies in Defoe, Richardson, and Fielding* (London: Chatto & Windus, 1957); Benedict Anderson, *Imagined Communities: Reflections on the Origin and Spread of Nationalism* (London: Verso, 1983); and Michael McKeon, *The Origins of the English Novel, 1600–1740* (Baltimore: Johns Hopkins University Press, 1987).
30. Hunter, "From Typology to Type," 44.
31. Richard Macksey calls Sterne this in his introduction to Genette's *Paratexts* (xi).

32. Fielding's mock-errata, errata that "correct" the fiction's temporal details, testify to the fact that the early novel's rhetorical claims to stability and veracity were embedded in its production as a printed book well before Sterne makes similar points with *Tristram Shandy*. The text of Fielding's errata is reproduced at the head of this book. For an extended discussion of the printed marginalia in the third edition of *Clarissa*, see Florian Stuber's essay "Text, Writer, Reader, World," which serves as an introduction to *The Clarissa Project*'s eight-volume facsimile of the 1751 edition (New York: AMS Press, 1990). See also my essay "Richardson on the Margins: An Introduction to the Bradshaigh *Clarissa*," in *The Annotations in Lady Bradshaigh's Copy of* Clarissa, ed. Janine Barchas, with the editorial collaboration of Gordon D. Fulton, English Literary Studies Monograph Series 76 (Victoria, BC: University of Victoria, 1998), 9–42; esp. 18–24.

2 The frontispiece

1. Henry James, *The Portrait of a Lady*, ed. Nicola Bradbury with introduction by Graham Greene (Oxford University Press, 1987), 22.
2. The first edition of *Washington Square* (New York: Harper & Bros., 1881 [pub. 1880]) did bear a frontispiece. That American edition reproduced all the illustrations by George Du Maurier from the original serial publication in the *Cornhill Magazine*, including the image (refashioned as a frontispiece) of the protagonists' first meeting at a party. The above remarks in *Portrait* may, in fact, nod to James's encounter with the illustrated novel the year before. See Leon Edel and Dan H. Laurence, *Bibliography of Henry James*, 3rd ed. (Oxford: Clarendon Press, 1982), 50–54.
3. Ibid., 244.
4. Ibid., 244 and 245.
5. From James's famous preface to *Portrait* (*ibid.*, xxx).
6. See the transcript of *J. S. G. Boggs vs. Robert E. Rubin, Secretary of the Treasury, et al.*, United States Court of Appeals for the District of Columbia Circuit, argued 8 September 1998 and decided 6 November 1998 (No. 97-5313).
7. Piper traces the author-portrait tradition back to the fifth century BC, when statues of poets began to grace Greek temples. See David Piper, *The Image of the Poet: British Poets and their Portraits* (Oxford: Clarendon Press, 1982).
8. Ibid., 36.
9. For example, Piper describes how William Marshall's author portrait for Milton's *Poems* (1645) is a "Miltonic joke" on early frontispiece convention (35). The Greek inscription in this frontispiece derides the artistry of the portrait and was probably copied onto the plate by an engraver ignorant of its meaning.
10. Satires toyed with the iconography of the frontispiece genre, inverting the flagrant displays of aggrandizement to which such conventional portraiture was prone. For example, Jonathan Smedley's satiric attack on Pope and Swift, *Gullivariana: Or, A Fourth Volume of Miscellanies* (London: Printed for J. Roberts, 1728), fronts the text with an unflattering portrait of the two poets standing (Pope atop a table) in a landscape populated by satyrs and clowns sporting mock-Latin tags. A

constellation labeled "Stella!" hovers above this scene like a demonic flame. The engraving is signed "*Veritas Invenit. Justitia Sculpsit.*"

11. See, for example, Alison Conway, *Private Interests: Women, Portraiture, and the Visual Culture of the English Novel, 1709–1791* (Toronto and New York: University of Toronto Press, 2001).

12. This frontispiece first appeared in *The Works of Mrs. Eliza Haywood, Consisting of Novels, Letters, Poems, and Plays,* 4 vols. (London: Dan. Browne, junr., and S. Chapman, 1723–24); the Huntington Library's copy survives thus. The following year, the same London publishing team of Browne and Chapman used the plate once again in *Secret Histories, Novels and Poems,* 4 vols. (London: 1724–25). The portrait reappears as a frontispiece to subsequent editions of her works over the next few decades, implying that Haywood – who held close ties with the publishing industry – approved of the artist's rendering and the engraving's reuse. See Patrick Spedding, *A Bibliography of Eliza Haywood* (London: Pickering & Chatto, 2003/forthcoming).

13. At least one earlier book did use a genuine author portrait along with the term "novel" to promote itself, namely *The Unlucky Citizen Experimentally Described in the Various Misfortunes Of an Unlucky Londoner* (London: 1673). This visually innovative book by Francis Kirkman (*c.* 1632–80) is a partial account of the printing trade by a prominent publisher; it advertises the text on its title page as a novelty by claiming that it is "Intermixed with severall Choice Novels." It also bears a frontispiece portrait of the book's actual author, identified cryptically in the engraving as "F K Citizen *of London* / *Aetat*: 41, 1673." Kirkman's approximate age in 1673 corresponds neatly to the "41" of the frontispiece, which is presumably a genuine author portrait that works as a caste label for the book's benefit. It also has a second illustration, self-styled a "frontispiece," which is actually an allegorical storyboard of the book's episodic plot. Yet, though the text invokes the term "novel," this quirky and uneven seventeenth-century production hardly qualifies as a legitimate forerunner of the eighteenth-century genre.

14. *The Dunciad*, Book II, lines 151–58. For variants of these lines in different editions see *Volume V: The Dunciad*, ed. James Sutherland, in the Twickenham Edition of *The Poems of Alexander Pope*, ed. John Butt *et al.*, 11 vols. (London and New Haven, CT: Methuen and Yale University Press, 1963), V, 120.

15. The mention of a duodecimo format suggests that Pope was referring to the four-volume *Secret Histories, Novels, and Poems* (1724–25), because Haywood's *Works* (1723–24) were printed in octavo.

16. Although Vertue's engraving is the only known portrait of Haywood, the plate does exist in multiple states.

17. George Vertue (1684–1756) enjoyed a respectable reputation as an engraver of (mostly) portraits and a writer of art history. The "*Parmentier*" of the inscription is probably Jacques (a. k. a. "James") Parmentier (1658–1730), primarily a history and portrait painter who resided in London during the last decade of his life.

18. Other than what is usually inferred from Pope's mention, little is known about Elisha Kirkall (1682?–1742), except that he invented a short-lived method of

chiaroscuro engraving. The rather dark and unremarkable frontispiece for *Love in Excess* (1722) is typical of his style. In this frontispiece Kirkall shows the "dreadful view" that ends Part II of the novel: the stabbed bodies of Alovysa and the Baron lie on the floor of a dark, panelled chamber, while five stunned onlookers bear witness to their tragic death – Melliora (with candlestick), D'Elmont and Chevalier Brillian (both brandishing swords), and two manservants. I have not reproduced the Kirkall illustration here since it does not participate in the author-portrait tradition under discussion. For a readily available reproduction of the plate, please see the front matter to David Oakleaf's edition of Haywood's *Love in Excess*, 2nd edn. (Peterborough, ON: Broadview Press, 2000). For two further examples from Kirkall's *oeuvre* in a modern book, see plates 3 and 4 in Hanns Hammelmann and T. S. R. Boase, *Book Illustrators in Eighteenth-Century England* (New Haven, CT and London: Yale University Press, 1975), which depict scenes engraved for editions of Shakespeare's plays.

19. In a section on "The Portraits of Eliza Haywood" attached as an appendix to his bibliography, Spedding meticulously delineates the bibliographic facts. He convincingly outlines how scholars of Pope and Haywood, by taking Pope at his word, have perpetuated the myth of a portrait by Kirkall in the absence of any corroborating physical evidence.

20. For discussions of Vertue's portrait of Pope, see Maynard Mack, *Alexander Pope: A Life* (London: Norton, 1985), 331–33, quoted at 333; and James McLaverty, *Pope, Print, and Meaning*, 61–64. Mack's biography reproduces the original oil by Charles Jervas, now in the Bodleian Library, from which Vertue's engraving was copied, while McLaverty's book includes the Vertue engraving as an illustration to his discussion of the plate's centrality in the "projection of the author" (62). If the two Vertue portraits – the Haywood and Pope frontispieces – are placed side by side, their most prominent difference is their original size. The large Vertue engraving of Pope was, as early as 1715, advertised and sold separately; when the plate is reused as a frontispiece to the *Works* in 1717, the portrait "is so big that it has to be folded twice in order to fit into the quarto" (McLaverty, *Pope, Print, and Meaning*, 63). In spite of the discrepancy of format (which, ironically, lends the Haywood a comparative modesty), even a casual glance at the two plates notes similarities – similarities best described as shared echoes of Restoration portraiture's sensuality. The similarities in Haywood's frontispiece to his own Vertue portrait may have made Pope uncomfortable.

21. At the same time, and in all fairness to Parmentier and Vertue, it must be acknowledged that the engraving of Haywood, though tawdry, is not entirely devoid of artistic merit and draws upon an established tradition in Restoration portraiture for its intended effect. The image of the suggestively dishevelled Haywood seems perfectly in keeping with the heavy-lidded, languorous, fleshy, and ample-nosed portraits of the ladies of Charles II's court by, for example, Sir Peter Lely.

22. The beauty spot under Haywood's right eye, while present in some early copies of the plate, including one in the British Museum's Collection of Prints and Drawings where it is catalogued as an independent portrait (unattached to any

book), is lacking in others. It is this state of the plate that is reproduced at the front of *The Female Spectator: Being Selections from Mrs Eliza Haywood's Periodical, First Published in Monthly Parts (1744–6)*, ed. Gabrielle M. Firmager (London: Bristol Classical Press, 1993), should my reader wish to make a comparison. Further work on the dating of the various states of the plate – some of which might have circulated independently – must determine when this mark entered the portrait's history. If the beauty spot is a mark of one of the earliest states of the portrait, it must have been removed rather quickly. Certainly Pope, for whom such a spot would have been grist for the satirical mill, does not mention it in 1728.

23. James Sterling, *To Mrs. Eliza Haywood on Her Writings* (1732); quoted from Oakleaf's edition of Haywood's *Love in Excess*, which includes the full text of Sterling's panegyric at the back (278).

24. The plate is by Charles Grignion (1716–1810). Richardson's own printings of his fictions never included a frontispiece of their "editor." However, this engraved portrait of Richardson, copied after Joseph Highmore's portrait of the printer-author, did appear as an illustration in the *Royal Female Magazine* during January of 1760. It is this same image which subsequently reappears as a frontispiece portrait in editions of Richardson's works printed after his death in 1761.

25. There are a few notable exceptions to the neglect of frontispieces as literary text, among them Gary Spear, "Reading Before the Lines: Typography, Iconography, and the Author in Milton's 1645 Frontispiece: Papers of Renaissance Text Society, 1985–1991," in W. Speed Hill, ed., *New Ways of Looking at Old Texts*, Renaissance English Text Society special edn. (Binghamton, NY: Medieval and Renaissance Texts and Studies, 1993), 187–94. See also David Groves's short article "The Frontispiece to James Hogg's *Confessions*," *Notes and Queries* 235 (Dec. 1990), 421–22. Groves argues that the frontispiece to *The Confessions of a Justified Sinner* (a supposed "Fac Simile" of a diary entry by Robert Wringhim) is "an integral part of the novel" and "conveys Hogg's desire for authentic historical detail" (422). Most recently, James McLaverty discusses representations of the author in the works of Alexander Pope, mingling considerations of such graphics as the illustrative headpieces in *An Essay on Criticism* with the Vertue frontispiece portrait of Pope (*Pope, Print, and Meaning*, esp. 61–66.)

26. David Lenfest's "Checklist of Illustrated Editions of *Gulliver's Travels*, 1727–1914," *Papers of the Bibliographical Society of America* 62 (1968), 85–123, exemplifies the manner in which the history of the book's "illustrations" exclude consideration of the engravings of Gulliver in the first edition text. See also Elizabeth Duthie, "Gulliver Art," *The Scriblerian* 10.2 (Spring 1978), 127–31. An exception is Jeanne K. Welcher, "Eighteenth-Century Views of Gulliver: Some Contrasts between Illustrations and Prints," in Joachim Möller, ed., *Imagination on a Long Rein: English Literature Illustrated* (Marburg: Jonas Verlag, 1988), 82–93. While Welcher focusses on the Gulliveriana artwork found in later eighteenth-century editions, she acknowledges the first state of the first-edition portrait of Gulliver as an important textual feature (82–83). A more sustained treatment of the original Gulliver portraits is the chapter "Captain Gulliver and the Pictures" in Peter

Wagner, *Reading Iconotexts: From Swift to the French Revolution* (London: Reaktion, 1995), 37–74, esp. 44–46 and 60–62. Wagner convincingly argues that the *Travels*'s multiple frontispieces partake in the text's engagement with the features of travel literature. Still, Wagner ignores the Latin text of the frontispieces and seems unaware that the Faulkner edition of 1735 appeared in two formats, each bearing different portraits of Gulliver.

As to Swift's responsibility for the ironic Gulliver portrait, the signatures in the first edition's frontispiece indicate that John Sturt (1658–1730) designed the plate and a minor craftsman by the name of Sheppard engraved it. Although it is not definitively known at whose instigation the portrait was originally designed, the fact that Sturt also designed a frontispiece for use in the fifth edition of *A Tale of a Tub* (1710) improves the possibility that Swift knew (or knew of) the artist and guided his work on this project. In addition, and despite the fact that Motte made many unauthorized insertions and alterations to the first-edition text that infuriated the author, Swift never criticized the edition's frontispiece.

27. For a complete bibliographical description of the 1726 so-called A, AA, and B editions in which this plate appears in multiple states, see Dr. H. Teerink, *A Bibliography of the Writings of Jonathan Swift*, 2nd revised and corrected edn., ed. Arthur H. Scouten (Philadelphia: University of Philadelphia Press, 1963), 192–99.
28. Teerink argues for the existence of a "third state" of the 1726 portrait, from the same plate and with no significant changes to the image or inscription, but "retouched" and printed on "paper with horizontal chain lines" (193). Because the differences between the second and third state of the plate are bibliographic, rather than graphic, I do not consider this state separately in my discussion of the visual discrepancies in the portraits.
29. Persius, *Satura*, II, 73–74. *Juvenal and Persius*, trans. G. G. Ramsay, Loeb Classical Library (London: William Heinemann; Cambridge, MA: Harvard University Press, 1918), 340–41.
30. See Welcher, "Eighteenth-Century Views of Gulliver," 82.
31. The autobiographical portrait provides a detailed mathematical calculus of Gulliver's age. He is "Fourteen Years old" when he enters Cambridge, where he "resided three Years." At age 17 then, he is apprenticed to Mr. James Bates, with whom he "continued four Years" – making him 21 when he leaves for the Dutch city of Leyden. In Leyden he "studied Physick two Years and seven Months." "Soon after," he joins *The Swallow*'s crew as ship's surgeon for "three Years and a half." Gulliver is thus well into his 27th year when he marries Mary Burton. His "good Master *Bates* dying in two Years after," he is 29 when his business fails and he determines "to go again to Sea." After making "several Voyages, for six Years, to the *East* and *West-Indies*," Gulliver is 35 when he grows "weary of the Sea" and relocates his business to Wapping. "After three Years expectation that things would mend," Gulliver, now at least 38 years old, sets sail aboard the *Antelope* on 4 May 1699. Quoted from Jonathan Swift, *Gulliver's Travels*, ed. Albert J. Rivero (New York and London: W. W. Norton, 2002), 15–16. Rivero's edition is based upon the 1726 text.

32. Welcher's arithmetic is slightly off when she declares that "[t]he age, which comes as a surprise to the uncalculating reader, is right for Gulliver when his book was published" (82). Wagner also accepts Gulliver's age as noted in the inscription (46). Both critics do, however, recognize that 58 "was precisely Swift's age in 1726" and is "right for Swift" (Wagner, *Reading Iconotexts*, 46; Welcher, "Eighteenth-Century Views of Gulliver," 82).
33. Swift apparently contracted with Benjamin Motte to get the book out quickly. Irvin Ehrenpreis notes that the *Travels* appeared "on 28 October 1726 or soon after" – just one month shy of Swift's 59th birthday (*Swift*, III, 497).
34. In both formats, the *Travels* comprises the third volume in George Faulkner's four-volume edition of Swift's *Works* (1735). For a complete bibliographical description of the distinctions between the octavo and duodecimo formats, see Teerink, *Bibliography of the Writings of Swift*, 22–28 and 46–49.
35. Placed side by side, the two 1735 portraits may offer a temporal record of the narrator. If the octavo portrait depicts Gulliver at the start of his journey, bright-eyed with youthful optimism, the duodecimo portrait is that of the returned Gulliver, utterly transformed by his experiences and perched on the verge of insanity. I am grateful to Joe Branigan who, in reacting to a lecture I gave at the University of Delaware in January of 1997, first directed my attention to the temporal dimensions of the portraits.
36. Perhaps this frontispiece is a response to early contemporary criticism of Gulliver's lack of personal hygiene in the *Travels*. Smedley's previously mentioned *Gullivariana* (1728), for example, includes a parody of Swift's *Travels* that extrapolates from Gulliver's domestic routine to imagine his appearance: "[1714] THURSDAY. Wak'd with the Head-ach. Said no Prayers that Morning. Drest immediately. Look'd confounded *Rakish*" (144).
37. "Just one of the many, a virgin noble for ever, honoured the marriage torch and was shiningly false to her perjured father" (III, xi, 35). Trans. W. G. Shepherd, *Horace, The Complete Odes and Epodes* (New York: Penguin, 1985), 145.
38. Perhaps Swift anticipated and manipulated the standard publishing practice of issuing multiple formats directed at different sectors of the market. Faulkner's more lavish octavo edition includes a list of subscribers in the first volume and appears to have been the format issued to the book's subscription audience. The slightly smaller duodecimo edition (also printed on thinner paper) was presumably a cheaper version produced for general sale. The octavo's list of subscribers shapes a narrowly articulated community of readers, a community distinct from the unspecified audience of the cheaper duodecimo book. Given Swift's taste for raillery and satirical inversion, it comes as a surprise that the disheveled Gulliver does not front the loftier subscription format.
39. The youthful Gulliver's cleft chin, mouth, nose, and eyebrows – even his partly unbuttoned coat – correspond to Swift's own (compare Figures 2.6 and 2.8). In contrast, the tattered Gulliver in the less-expensive duodecimo edition lacks these resemblances to the portrait of Swift in the 1735 *Works*. Again, it remains possible to interpret the two Gulliver frontispieces as devices for differentiating between

40. Aaron Hill's remark on 26 December 1740, in a letter to Richardson, is the only extant mention of the Hogarth commission: "The designs you have taken for frontispieces, seem to have been very judiciously chosen; upon pre-supposition that Mr. Hogarth is able (and if any-body is, it is he) to teach pictures to speak and to think." Quoted from Barbauld, I, 56.
41. Although the exact number of copies of the first edition is unknown, Richardson himself declared that "a large impression" had been "carried off in less than Three Months" (*Pamela*, 2nd edn. (1741), I, xv). The second edition was released on 14 February 1741, only three months after the publication of the first. Continued high demand allowed Richardson to print five editions of *Pamela* in the year 1741. For a comprehensive table of the publication dates of all Richardson's editions of *Pamela* see William Merritt Sale, Jr., *Samuel Richardson: A Bibliographical Record of his Literary Career with Historical Notes* (New Haven, CN: Yale University Press, 1936), 13.
42. Citing possible "clues" in Richardson's correspondence, Eaves and Paulson stipulate that the two portraits were to depict "Pamela at the Pond" (the moment at which she contemplates suicide) and "Pamela and her bundles" (the scene in which she prepares to depart the Squire's house). See T. C. Duncan Eaves, "Graphic Illustration of the Novels of Samuel Richardson, 1740–1810," *Huntington Library Quarterly* 14 (1951), 349–83, at 351; and Ronald Paulson, *Hogarth, Volume II: High Art and Low, 1732–50* (New Brunswick, NJ: Rutgers University Press, 1992), 186–91, at 187. Thomas Keymer and Peter Sabor disagree, offering a slightly different interpretation of the same facts by suggesting that the subject of the "bundles" was intended as a replacement for a design of the pond scene. For this amendment as well as a neat summary of speculations by other critics, see Thomas Keymer and Peter Sabor, eds., *The Pamela Controversy: Criticisms and Adaptations of Samuel Richardson's* Pamela *1740–1750*, 6 vols. (London and Brookfield, VT: Pickering & Chatto, 2001), II, xxv–xxviii.
43. Hill to Richardson, 17 December 1740 (Barbauld, I, 54). If Richardson envisioned a traditional bust of Pamela to front his new edition, he might have had in mind something akin to Robert Feke's "Pamela Andrews," an early 1740s oil portrait. This portrait of a demure-yet-frank-eyed Pamela is reproduced in Keymer and Sabor, eds., *Pamela Controversy*, II, 349. A bust of this sort did, in fact, front an anonymous piece of illustrated Pamenalia entitled *The Life of Pamela* (London: Printed for C. Whitefield, 1741). Here a rather bland frontispiece portrait of the heroine, in ruffled finery, appears as a generically genteel addition to what is a piratical adaptation of Richardson's novel. The frontispiece is signed by engraver J[ohn] Carwitham.
44. *Pamela*, 2nd edn., 2 vols. (1741), I, xxxvi.
45. Eaves, *Graphic Illustration*, 350.
46. *Ibid.*, 352. In addition to the posthumous author portrait in the 1762 edition of Fielding's collected *Works*, Hogarth designed a lusty frontispiece for the 1731

edition of Fielding's burlesque *Tom Thumb*. See Robert Halsband, "Hogarth's Graphic Friendships: Illustrating Books by Friends," in James Engell, ed., *Johnson and his Age* (Cambridge, MA: Harvard University Press, 1984), 333–66.

47. Not until the publication of the costly sixth edition of *Pamela* in 1742, elaborately illustrated with twenty-nine copper-plate engravings by Francis Hayman and François Gravelot, would Richardson approve engravings for inclusion in his text. And after incurring a financial loss on that edition also, Richardson would never again resort to conventional illustration to enhance his novels.

48. Sterne, *Letters*, ed. Lewis P. Curtis (Oxford: Clarendon Press, 1935), 99. Sterne specified the scene he wished illustrated by the aging artist: "the loosest Sketch in Nature, of Trim's reading the Sermon to my Father &c; wd do the Business" (*ibid.*). Hogarth's comical design fronted the London publication of Sterne's first volume a month later in April of 1760. Because the frontispiece visually interprets a narrative event (as does the later one Hogarth made of the baptism for volume three) rather than depict the text's supposed author, *Tristram Shandy* does not participate in the portraiture dialogue under discussion. For separate considerations of these frontispiece illustrations see Halsband, "Hogarth's Graphic Friendships," and Melvyn New, "William Hogarth and John Baldessari: Ornamenting Sterne's *Tristram Shandy*," *Word and Image* 11.2 (April–June 1995), 182–95.

49. In *Imagining Monsters: Miscreations of the Self in Eighteenth-Century England* (University of Chicago Press, 1995), Dennis Todd describes how Mary Toft's claim to have given birth to seventeen rabbits flooded London with print merchandise capitalizing on the hoax.

50. See J. Paul Hunter, *Before Novels: The Cultural Contexts of Eighteenth-Century English Fiction* (New York: W. W. Norton, 1990).

51. This text exists in both an octavo and duodecimo version. Only the octavo edition of the anonymous *Life and Adventures of Mrs. Christian Davies, Commonly Called Mother Ross; Who, in Several Campaigns under King William and the Late Duke of Marlborough, in the Quality of a Foot-Soldier and Dragoon, Gave Many Signal Proofs of an Unparalleled Courage and Personal Bravery. Taken from her Own Mouth When a Pensioner of Chelsea-Hospital* . . . (London: Printed for C. Welch in Chelsea, 1740) contains the frontispiece portrait. The later portraits found in Hannah Snell's *The Female Soldier* closely mimic both the text and cursive script of this engraving's caption: "Christian Davis, commonly call'd Mother Ross."

52. Rudolf M. Dekker and Lotte C. van de Pol, *The Tradition of Female Transvestism in Early Modern Europe*, foreword by Peter Burke (London: Macmillan, 1989), 16.

53. Dianne Dugaw claims in her introduction to the Augustan Reprint Society's facsimile edition of *The Female Soldier* (London: 1750; Los Angeles: William Andrews Clark Memorial Library, 1989) that "while the outlines of her 'life and adventures' are highly conventionalized . . . Hannah Snell was a real person" (v).

54. As in the multi-formatted Faulkner editions of Swift's *Travels* and that of its Amazonian precursor *Mrs. Christian Davies*, consumers were presented with multiple versions of *The Female Soldier*. Because both versions bear the same synoptic title and identical 1750 imprint, the various formats have caused some

confusion. Snell's publisher and printer Robert Walker issued the text both as a cheap forty-six-page unillustrated version in duodecimo ("Price One Shilling" states the imprint) as well as "a more developed 187-page book which included engraved illustrations" printed in octavo (Dugaw, Introduction, v; she mistakenly calls the short, shilling-duodecimo an octavo). While *The Female Soldier* appeared in multiple formats, varying in length and literariness, the author portraits appear to have been included only in versions of the longer, book-length account. Dugaw glosses this format as more "novelistic" (v). The exclusivity of the frontispieces to the novelesque version confirms that, for reasons of generic aspiration and cost, only the novel appropriated the author portrait. The book-length "literary" version also includes two additional illustrative plates, though none are of our heroine/hero. Between pages 96 and 97 a bifolium is inserted with an engraving of "James Summs in prison" and, second, an engraving of "The Manner of execution of James Summs," who was, it seems, unceremoniously bagged and dropped in the harbor. My thanks to Bruce Whiteman, Head Librarian at the William Andrews Clark Memorial Library, for providing me with a description of the bifolium plates in the Clark's copy.

55. A rapidly produced Dutch translation of the novel entitled *De Vrouwelyke Soldaat of de Verbazende Levensgevallen van Anna Snell* (Amsterdam: Gerrit de Groot, 1750) contained a version of the full-length portrait, namely that in my Figure 2.9. The issue of *The Gentleman's Magazine* for July of 1750 featured, above that magazine's synopsis of Hannah Snell's new autobiography, a woodcut detail of the frontispiece shown in my Figure 2.10. Dekker and van de Pol reproduce these graphic borrowings in *The Tradition of Female Transvestism*, glossing the full-length portrait as a picture of "Hannah Snell, as she performed on stage in her male guise"(figs. 11–13, between pp. 48 and 49).

56. The authorship of this text has lately been disputed. Until recent decades it had been usual to attribute it to Defoe and only occasionally to William Bond, under whose name it appears in a subsequent edition, sporting a new title that enhances the uncanny and paranormal nature of Mr. Duncan's powers: *The Supernatural Philosopher: Or, The Mysteries of Magick . . . Unfolded by William Bond* (1728). Ralph Straus asserts in *The Unspeakable Curll* that "Defoe was employed to write an account of that popular entertainer Duncan Campbell" for Curll, whose name appears in the imprint (86). In their *Defoe De-Attributions: A Critique of J. R. Moore's Checklist* (London: Hambledon Press, 1994), P. N. Furbank and W. R. Owens question the traditional attribution to Defoe (126). They judge that Rodney Baine who, in his *Daniel Defoe and the Supernatural* (Athens, GA, 1968), 137–80, argued for William Bond as the more likely author, presented "convincing arguments" against Defoe's authorship. However, the fact that Michiel Van der Gucht (1660–1725) engraved both the *Campbell* frontispiece and the genuine, elegant portrait of Defoe affixed to his 1703 *Works* enhances Defoe's lingering association with this text. Incidentally, Van der Gucht was Vertue's master for a time (Vertue engraved the 1723 Haywood portrait) and also executed the frontispiece to *Rivella* (1714) discussed below.

57. Unlike the other frontispiece subjects under discussion, Mr. Duncan is not the supposed author of his own sensational life narrative. Although the title page is noncommittal on the subject of authorship, allowing for this tantalizing possibility, the central narrative is authored by a distinctly different persona and speaks of "Mr. Duncan" from start to finish in the third person. It is Defoe's lingering association with this particular text, as well as the similarities in visual approach to Snell's *Female Soldier*, that warrant a consideration of this portrait in a discussion of the novel's appropriation of frontispiece conventions.

58. Although Straus's attribution of this text to Defoe may have come under some scrutiny in recent years, the publication details he offers seem reliable. He confirms that both the first edition (printed in April) and the second (printed in August) boasted a frontispiece portrait and was priced at 5s. in octavo (*Unspeakable Curll*, 261–62).

59. In addition to the frontispiece, the second edition of *Duncan Campbell* is laden with graphic embellishments, including four engraved plates inserted into the central text. With the exception of a curious alphabet of hand signals through which Campbell gained literacy, these additional plates are hackneyed visual clichés: one illustrates a scene from his family history, depicting four men atop a rugged cliff-side assisting a troubled ship in the face of a strong gale (emitted from the puffed cheeks of a cherub in the plate's top right corner); another depicts one of Campbell's supposed bucolic visions, namely a "Grove" harboring a "Lamb" and two book-toting "Youths" upon whom beams a smiling baby-faced sun; the last offers another portrait, this time of the youthful Campbell "just ripening into Manhood." It shows an oval image of the soothsayer carried skyward by two angels and ribboned with the Latin inscription: "*TOTO NOTUS IN ORBE CAMPBELLUS*" (Campbell, known in all the world.) A further inscription in Greek ("held forth") and a quote from Ovid ("*Est Deus in nobis*") complete the hackneyed deification of the subject. The simplicity and iconographic restraint of the frontispiece portrait thus stand in striking contrast to the text's internal illustrations. The names of Thomas Hill (1661–1734) and Michiel Van der Gucht, listed on the frontispiece as its illustrating team ("T. Hill and M. V.dr Gucht"), also do not resurface in the signatures to the other plates (only the last of which is signed "J. Clark"). This lends further credence to the idea that the frontispiece was commissioned separately from the other plates, possibly under the author's directions. My guess is that, whosoever engineered the frontispiece, publisher Edmund Curll slapped on the additional illustrations; they smack of his penchant for popular kitsch.

60. Various works by Defoe can be linked to Richardson's printing workshop. See William M. Sale Jr.'s *Bibliographical Record*, 39–44, and *Samuel Richardson: Master Printer* (Ithaca, NY: Cornell University Press, 1950), 162–63, as well as Keith Maslen's *Samuel Richardson of London, Printer* (Dunedin, New Zealand: University of Otago English Department, 2001), 76–78. Richardson, who edited and reprinted various editions of the *Tour*, for example, may have gleaned something from Defoe's many experiments with graphic design (see also my

discussion of the index in *Grandison* in Chapter 7). Richardson's single documented assessment of Defoe, "an ingenious man, tho' a *dissenter*," confirms only cautious respect (*Clarissa*, 3rd edn. (1751), VII, 286–87).

61. For a general discussion of Edmund Curll's much-maligned business practices as well as his occasional conflict and association with Defoe, see Straus, *Unspeakable Curll*.

62. The frontispiece engraving of "The Famous ROXANA" appears in the first edition of the novel, entitled *The Fortunate Mistress: Or, a History of the Life and Vast Variety of Fortunes of Mademoiselle de Beleau . . . Being the Person known by the Name of the Lady Roxana, in the Time of King Charles II* (London, 1724). According to Rodney Baine, the frontispiece is a vital clue to the novel's contemporary setting. See his article "The Evidence from Defoe's Title Pages," *Studies in Bibliography* 25 (1972), 185–91. Baine argues that the frontispiece and its Turkish costume confirm that the title page, in which the compositor erroneously dates the text to the time of Charles II, has "misled" us about Defoe's intent. "Roxana's Turkish costume suggests that Defoe expected the alert reader to visualize present time, in the fringes of the court of George I, where Lady Mary Wortley Montagu had recently popularised Turkish dress for women"(190).

63. The first edition of *Moll Flanders* in 1722 does not bear a frontispiece according to *Defoe De-Attributions* by Furbank and Owens, the definitive bibliography of Defoe. Yet a first-edition copy in the Beinecke library's collection bears the frontispiece shown in Figure 2.14. Although I have been unable to determine the precise provenance of this frontispiece, it appears that *Moll Flanders* participates in the generic frontispiece portrait tradition through one of the book's many subsequent editions in the eighteenth century (the portrait mentions "this book"). Cognizant of this tradition, a prior owner of the Beinecke's copy bound the portrait with the novel's first edition. The Beinecke copy reminds us of the fact that consumers, rather than publishers, made most eighteenth-century binding decisions and thus influenced the paratextual apparatus with which individual copies of texts can appear. Further research may show that this frontispiece is an autonomous piece of print ephemera (though the inscription makes this unlikely) or an image commissioned by a savvy bookseller to slap on to a stock of yet-unsold copies of an edition of *Moll Flanders*, of which there were at least fifty-seven before 1828. For a checklist of these editions, see David Goldthorpe's "Textual Instability: The Fortunes and Misfortunes of *Moll Flanders*" (unpublished 1995 Ph.D. thesis, Open University, London). Regardless of its exact provenance, the image demonstrates the ubiquity of the novel's author-portrait tradition in eighteenth-century print culture. I am grateful to P. N. Furbank and David Goldthorpe for generously assisting me in my attempts to trace the image's provenance and for confirming that the image is not a part of an "authoritative" edition of *Moll Flanders*.

64. The work of Flemish engraver Michiel (or Michael) Van der Gucht (1660–1725) is occasionally confused with that of his two English-born sons, Jan (1697–1732?)

and Gerard (1697–1776) who followed their father's footsteps in the London trade.
65. Paula Backscheider, *Daniel Defoe, his Life* (Baltimore: Johns Hopkins University Press, 1989), 191.
66. *Ibid.*, 193.
67. David Blewett, *The Illustration of Robinson Crusoe, 1719–1920* (Gerrards Cross: Smythe, 1995), 27. Blewett's book's discussion of this complex frontispiece portrait is an expansion of his essay "The Illustration of *Robinson Crusoe*: 1719–1840," in Joachim Möller, ed., *Imagination on a Long Rein* (Marburg: Jonas Verlag, 1988), 66–81, esp. 66–67.
68. *Ibid.* Henceforth citations from Blewett's book will be noted parenthetically.
69. Although I cannot pin down the identity of "Clark," the "Pine" mentioned in the signature is most likely engraver John Pine (1690–1756), an intimate of Hogarth's and the well-known proprietor of a printshop in St. Martin's Lane.
70. Edward Kimber (1719–69) penned a few picaresque fictions modeled loosely upon Fielding's style of writing. Although *Joe Thompson* remains a minor fiction, the fact that it went into at least five editions by the mid-1780s suggests that it enjoyed a sizeable readership. Unfortunately the artist behind the *Joe Thompson* frontispiece remains unknown, as the engraving is unsigned.
71. See Straus, *Unspeakable Curll*, 192.
72. See Ronald Paulson's *Hogarth*, vol. II, *High Art and Low, 1732–1750* (New Brunswick, NJ: Rutgers University Press, 1992), 260–61.
73. Although the second edition of 1751 still sports the same frontispiece portrait as the first edition, by 1783 the frontispiece is replaced with four attendant illustrations of specific narrative moments, inserted into the central text as engraved plates.
74. Aileen Douglas contextualizes the popularity of this odd subgenre of the eighteenth-century novel within British consumerism in "Britannia's Rule and the It-Narrator," *Eighteenth-Century Fiction* 6.1 (1993), 65–82. She argues that the it-narrator is "emblematic of a burgeoning consumer culture" (68).
75. For a more complete account of the range of titles and subjects in the "it-narrator" mode, see Richard K. Meeker's bibliographic survey "Bank Note, Corkscrew, Flea and Sedan: A Checklist of Eighteenth-Century Fiction," *The Library Chronicle* 35 (1969), 52–57.
76. The engraving is signed "Boitard." It is doubtless the work of Louis Pierre Boitard (?–1758), a celebrated French-born book illustrator who worked his entire adult life in London.
77. Arthur H. Cash, "Historical Introduction" to John Wilkes and Thomas Potter, *An Essay on Woman by John Wilkes and Thomas Potter: A Reconstruction of a Lost Book*, ed. Arthur H. Cash (New York: AMS Press, 2000), 59. Although his gloss of *The Card* is limited to this quoted passage, Cash offers a concise and intriguing summary of nearly all that is known about the disreputable Kidgell – including his involvement in a conspiracy against John Wilkes, his role in a literary forgery,

his embezzlement of a trust fund, his attempts at blackmail, and his absconding to Holland in disgrace.

78. *The Cambridge Bibliography of English Literature*, ed. F. W. Bateson (Cambridge University Press; New York: Macmillan Co., 1941) considers *The Card* a "satire on Edward Young and Richardson's *Sir Charles Grandison*" (II, 545). Although Kidgell casts his satirical net widely, ridiculing, for example, the creations of various early novelists in his final ballroom scene where Roderick Random promenades with Mrs. Booby, Thomas Jones dances with Clarissa Harlowe, and David Simple partners with Betsy Thoughtless, Richardson appears to be his primary target (II, 294–95).
79. *The Oxford English Dictionary* attributes the first documented use of the modern slang meaning of "card" as applied to a person ("indicating some eccentricity or peculiarity") to Charles Dickens in 1836. Hence this denotation, although appropriate to Kidgell's choice of the *knave* of clubs, seems anachronistic here.
80. Review of *The Card*, *The Monthly Review* 12 (1755), 117–21, at 117.
81. *Ibid.*, 120.
82. The hand-painted colors of the frontispiece – yellow, blue, black, and red – match those found in contemporary decks. See the variety of color illustrations in W. Gurney Benham's *Playing Cards: History of the Pack and Explanations of its Many Secrets* (London: Spring Books, 1931).
83. Review of *The Card*, *The Monthly Review*, 120–21.
84. "Upon my life, *Sukey*, an humble Servant as cooing as a Dove, and as submissive as *Pompey* the Little, . . ." (Kidgell, *The Card*, II, 132).
85. For information on Kidgell's politics, see Cash's "Historical Introduction" to *An Essay on Woman*, esp. 58–62.
86. An anonymous London satire of 1643 on the struggle between King and Parliament couches politics in terms of a card game: *The Bloody Game at Cards. As It Was Played Betwixt the King of Hearts. And the Rest of His Suite, against the Residue of the Packe of Cards. Wherein Is Discovered Where Faire Play; Was Plaid and Where Was Fowle*. This Royalist satire sports a woodcut image of the King of Hearts on its heavily ornamented title page. For a more detailed discussion of the cultural weight of playing cards see Ronald Paulson's *Popular and Polite Art in the Age of Hogarth and Fielding* (Notre Dame, IN: University of Notre Dame Press, 1979).
87. Bickham's "Medley" offers particularly persuasive evidence for this popular political association with the Jack of Clubs since it is itself a pre-selected pastiche of different anti-Jacobite materials.
88. During the same year as the appearance of *Millenium Hall*, Sarah Scott publishes another Newbery book with a frontispiece portrait: *The History of Mecklenburgh, from the First Settlement of the Vandals in that Country, to the Present Time; Including a Period of about Three Thousand Years* (London: Printed for J. Newbery, 1762). *The History of Mecklenburgh* is not a prose fiction but a genuine chronological history of the settlement of a geographic region. This is precisely why the relationship between these two texts and their frontispieces is so striking.

Rather than the conventional map of the relevant region, *The History of Mecklenburgh* is fronted by an engraved portrait of "Charlotte, Queen of Great Britain, &c." By means of this portrait frontispiece, the history aims to excite the reader's curiosity in the persona of the new queen, the Princess of Mecklenburgh. Both 1762 texts by Scott deploy the frontispiece to elide personal and social history; both frontispieces are signed "*A. Walker del. et sculp.*" Anthony Walker (1726–65) was a London draughtsman and engraver who primarily rendered frontispieces from his own designs.

89. Apparently the catalyst for Manley's hastily written autobiographical fiction was Curll's rumoured publication of her biography penned by the hack writer Charles Gildon (1665–1724). For further discussion of the genesis of this text see Katherine Zelinsky's introduction to her edition of *The Adventures of Rivella* (Peterborough, ON: Broadview Press, 1999).

90. In her edition of *The Adventures of Rivella*, Zelinsky states that the autobiography "raises questions about its own truthfulness, obscuring clear distinctions between fact and fiction in its complex interplay of the discrete discursive modes and practices – historical, juridical, romantic, and otherwise – with which Manley constructs her own self-portrait" (Intro., 11). Criticism of Manley's text, which hitherto focussed on its accuracy of fact, has increasingly stressed its relationship to the emerging novel genre. See, for example, John J. Richetti, *Popular Fiction Before Richardson: Narrative Patterns 1700–1739* (Oxford: Clarendon Press, 1969); Lennard J. Davis, *Factual Fictions: The Origins of the English Novel* (New York: Columbia University Press, 1983); Janet Todd, "Life after Sex: The Fictional Autobiography of Delarivier Manley," *Women's Studies* 15 (1988), 43–55; and Rosalind Ballaster, *Seductive Forms: Women's Amatory Fiction from 1684 to 1740* (Oxford: Clarendon Press, 1992).

91. Although I cannot identify the former artist, the latter signature belongs, of course, to Michiel Van der Gucht, the engraver of both the 1720 portrait of *Duncan Campbell* – another Curll production – and the legitimate author portrait affixed to Defoe's 1703 *Works*.

92. Although it does not refer to or explain the presence of the frontispiece, the first paragraph of the central text describes the scene depicted in the plate (*Rivella*, Broadview Press edition, 43).

93. *Ibid.*, 18.

94. *Ibid.*

95. Hunter, *Before Novels*, 341.

96. See Philip Stewart's study of eighteenth-century book illustration entitled *Engraven Desire: Eros, Image and Text in the French Eighteenth Century* (Durham, NC and London: Duke University Press, 1992), esp. 7.

97. Of course, for nearly every such title about places and abstractions another novel named after an individual (*Emma* [1816], *Jane Eyre* [1847], or *David Copperfield* [1849–50]) can be found among nineteenth-century fiction. My claim is simply that the opposite is not true for the eighteenth century, when novels are almost exclusively named after their protagonists.

3 The title page

1. *Dunciad, Variorum*, ed., James Sutherland, Twickenham Edition, v, 64.
2. See Rodney M. Baine, "The Evidence from Defoe's Title Pages,"186. To Baine's evidence from Defoe I can add the rubricated title page of the 1741 edition of *Moll Flanders*.
3. Baine, "Evidence," 185.
4. McKerrow quoted in *ibid*.
5. Gaskell, *New Introduction to Bibliography*, 52.
6. Baine, "Evidence," 185.
7. Genette, *Paratexts*, 34.
8. *Crusoe*'s titular promises of exoticism and veracity are, of course, originally reinforced by the frontispiece portrait discussed in the previous chapter.
9. Virginia Woolf, "Robinson Crusoe," *The Common Reader: Second Series*, 5th impression (London: Hogarth Press, 1948; first published 1932), 51–58, at 54.
10. *Ibid*.
11. *Ibid*.
12. In *The Author's Farce* (1730), Henry Fielding identifies the crowded title page as a mark of hack writing. His caricature of the scribbler, Mr. Dash, defends his prolix titles: "It becomes an author to be diffusive in his title page. A title page is to a book what a fine neck is to a woman, therefore ought to be the most regarded as it is the part which is viewed before the purchase" (II, iii). Quoted from Charles B. Woods's edition of Fielding's play (London: Edward Arnold, 1966), 28. Interestingly, Fielding's jest takes the author's role in the title page's construction for granted.
13. The odd phrase "**Moll Flanders**, &c." quizzically suggests that this title has, in spite of its prolixity, already undergone a process of reduction. Why "etcetera," if not to intentionally tease with a hint at Moll's protean nature and many aliases?
14. Genette, *Paratexts*, 71.
15. Although the title pages of fictions by Manley, Haywood, Swift, and Defoe in the early decades of the century sport double-ruled borders, this typographical framing of the novel's title page appears to have fallen utterly out of fashion by mid-century.
16. *Moll Flanders* was advertised as published "this day" on 27 January 1722. See Furbank and Owens, *Defoe De-Attributions*, 199.
17. In *incunabula* a printer's mark or device served as the printer's imprint on a book, marking with image rather than word the publisher on the colophon (that precursor of the modern title page found at the end, rather than the beginning, of early printed books). "Although," writes John Carter in *ABC for Book Collectors*, "this practice declined towards the end of the seventeenth century, it has never died out" (76). Modern examples include the Borzoi of Alfred A. Knopf and the Penguin of Penguin Books, and can also appear on a book's spine. Although infrequent in early novels, the eighteenth-century title page can feature a device in conjunction with the printer's shop sign or street address of the imprint.

18. These items are quoted from the title pages to: Edward Kimber's *The Life and Adventures of Joe Thompson* (1750); William Bond's *The History of the Life and Adventures of Mr. Duncan Campbell* (1720); and Delarivier Manley's *Rivella* (1714). See Figures 2.16, 2.11, and 2.21 in the previous chapter.
19. For example, in *Samuel Richardson: Master Printer*, William M. Sale turns to a book's graphic evidence for such authorization. Sale synthesizes the evidence offered by the printer's ornaments that served as the unique (because hand-made) part of Samuel Richardson's stock-in-trade. By means of those ornaments that are shared between texts, Sale traces Richardson's involvement in the production of specific books. Sale's list of the books printed by Richardson as well as Sale's list of the ornaments used in his shop have been substantially expanded by Keith Maslen, deploying the same systematic ornament study, in his *Samuel Richardson of London, Printer*.
20. See, for example, the title page of *The Lover's Week: Or, the Six Days Adventures of Philander and Amaryllis* (1718) which simultaneously shields and gentrifies its author Mary Hearne with the attribution "Written by a Young LADY." The fact that this early novel, dedicated "To Mrs. Manley," controversially asserts a woman's right to take a lover outside of marriage may have contributed to the choice to publish anonymously. The book's dedication further titillates with the initials "M. H." Several decades hence, Sarah Fielding's *The Adventures of David Simple* (1744) deploys the similar attribution "By a Lady" on its title page – and without the need to shield the author from any controversy other than the life of dependency and genteel poverty that drove her to write. The tag "By an Adept" is found at least twice on title pages to novels by Charles Johnstone (1719?–1800?) – perhaps turning this variant into a recognizable brand or pseudo-pseudonym of sorts. See, for example, his it-narrated novel *Chrysal: Or, the Adventures of a Guinea* (1760) as well as his satiric *The Adventures of Anthony Varnish; Or, A Peep at the Manners of Society* (1786) which are both attributed to "an ADEPT."
21. As briefly noted in the previous chapter, *The Unlucky Citizen Experimentally Described in the Various Misfortunes Of an Unlucky Londoner* (1673) simultaneously discloses and disguises its author's identity. The book's two frontispieces, though one is a portrait, coyly refuse to name the pictured author, identifying him only as "F K." The book is, in fact, authored by bookseller Francis Kirkman. Because Kirkman's name does appear in nearly complete form within the book's imprint, the mystery of the author's identity is short-lived: "Printed by *Anne Johnson*, for *Fra. Kirkman* and are to be sold at his Shop in *Fan-Church street* over against the sign of the *Robin Hood* near *Aldgate* and by most other Booksellers, 1673."
22. *The Post-Man Robb'd of his Mail: or, the Packet Broke Open* (1719) cites its authorship as "By the beſt WITS of the preſent Age." Considered one of the forerunners of the epistolary novel, *The Post-Man* was actually penned and published by Charles Gildon, a hack writer in Curll's stable and known devotee to the reigning cult of novelty. The book's introduction is signed with added flourish "Sir Roger de Whimsey." Both these variations on anonymity seem calculated to evoke the general experimentality of Gildon's text, a text that in its comical

side-by-side publication of the Latin and English title pages of a "translated" subplot (inserted into the middle of the novel) strikes a Shandian note. The attention paid to title pages by means of this insertion highlights the titular self-consciousness of Gildon's text. Similarly, the attribution tag "By the MAKER" when reused in John Kidgell's *The Card* (1755) will evoke that novel's playful emphasis on the nature of the book as a physical object – exemplified in Kidgell's hand-colored frontispiece, unconventional illustration of a folded playing card, and printed musical interlude.

23. In October of 1748, after having read the anonymously published initial instalments to *Clarissa*, Lady Bradshaigh left two letters at Richardson's Salisbury Court address (the imprint on the novel's title page lists him as the publisher). In these letters she pleaded with him to alter his rumoured intentions to kill off his heroine in the next instalments (Barbauld, IV, 179–81). She even went so far as to threaten Richardson with an extraordinary "curse" if he "dare[d]" to "make Lovelace and Clarissa unhappy": "May the hatred of all the young, beautiful, and virtuous, for ever be your portion! and may your eyes never behold any thing but age and deformity!" (Barbauld, IV, 181). Lady Bradshaigh's epistolary siege upon Richardson is well known. She herself comically imagined the author's complaint at the barrage of her subsequent letters: "What! Every post! No respite! No quiet! No hopes of being relieved from the persecutions of this troublesome woman!" (Barbauld, IV, 202). Lady Bradshaigh, who signed her letters "Belfour," hid her own identity more effectively than anonymous publication hid Richardson's – forcing Richardson to place an advertisement in *The Whitehall Evening-Post* in order to write "Belfour" back. For further details of this first exchange see Thomas Keymer, "Richardson, Incognita, and the *Whitehall Evening-Post*: New Light on Richardson's Correspondence with Lady Bradshaigh and the Text of His First Letter," *Notes and Queries* 39.4 (Dec 1992), 477–80.

24. Ian Campbell Ross describes Sterne's transformation from "obscure incumbent of a Yorkshire parish to National celebrity" as "sudden" in his introduction to the 1983 Oxford edition of *Tristram Shandy* (vii). The first volumes of *Tristram Shandy* were offered for sale in London on 1 January 1760; by early March, Sterne could already boast of the many "civilities shewn" and "greatest honours paid" him by "the Great" (Sterne to Catherine Fourmantel, 8 March 1760; quoted in Ross's introduction, vii). Sterne also declared that he wrote "not to be *fed*, but to be *famous*" (vii). Sterne's utter delight in his own fame confirms that the anonymous publication of his novel was never intended to conceal his identity from public view.

25. Jane Barker, *A Patch-Work Screen for the Ladies; Or, Love and Virtue Recommended: in a Collection of Instructive Novels. Related after a Manner Intirely New, and Interspersed with Rural Poems, Describing the Innocence of a Country-Life. By Mrs. Jane Barker* (London: Printed for E. Curll; and T. Payne, 1723). The author attribution "By Mrs. Jane Barker" near the name of "E. Currll" in the imprint offers a titillating juxtaposition. By virtue of its plainness the author's name supports the title's claims to rustic "*Innocence*," while the imprint implies that it is financed by a bookseller notorious for his scandalous

productions. It is also possible that in the wake of the genuine success of her *Love Intrigues* (1713), which was attributed to "A Young Lady" and saw four editions by 1750, Barker had gained both the confidence and the stature to break through the barrier of paper anonymity. Both texts are Curll publications.

26. Not only do the explicit sequels to *David Simple*, such as *Familiar Letters* (1747) and *David Simple. Volume the Last* (1753), ride the coat-tails of Sarah Fielding's initial success in this manner. Her fictions *The Governess* (1747) and *The Lives of Cleopatra and Octavia* (1757) boast on their title pages of having been written "By the Author of DAVID SIMPLE." The title pages to all editions of *Clarissa* and *Grandison* printed on Richardson's press fix that author's brand in similarly circuitous fashion.

27. John Brewer, *Pleasures of the Imagination: English Culture in the Eighteenth Century* (London: HarperCollins, 1997), 142.

28. See my essay "Before Print Culture: Mary, Lady Chudleigh and the Assimilation of the Book," in Dennis Todd and Cynthia Wall, eds., *Serious Reflections on Occasional Forms: Essays on Eighteenth-Century Genre and Culture* (Delaware University Press, 2001), 15–35.

29. I cited this pamphlet in Chapter 2, note 86 as a gloss on Kidgell's *The Card*.

30. See the imprints of Defoe's *A New Voyage Round the World* (1725); Henry Fielding's *Joseph Andrews* (1742); and the fourth edition of Peter Longueville's *The Hermit: Or, the Unparallel'd Sufferings And Surprising Adventures of Mr. Philip Quarll* (1768), another castaway story cashing in on *Crusoe*'s long-lived success.

31. These formulas lack precision so that for the same printshop there might exist multiple articulations of the same address. For example, novels by Henry and Sarah Fielding locate the establishment of their shared publisher-printer, Andrew Millar, in different ways: "Printed for A. MILLAR, over-againſt *St. Clement's Church*, in the *Strand*" reads the imprint on *Joseph Andrews* (1742); "Printed for the AUTHOR: And Sold by A. MILLAR, opposite *Katharine Street*, in the *Strand*" announces the subscription edition of *Familiar Letters* (1747); both *The Governess* (1749) and *Amelia* (1752) direct their reader simply to "A. MILLAR, in the *Strand*." The sequential diminution of address suggests that as both the Fieldings and Millar gained stature, the need for greater exactness in the mention of location decreased. This might also impact on the novel genre's slow building of brand over time, decreasing the need for the gentrification of address. Of course, it is also possible that Millar moved or acquired additional shops in the Strand and found a less specific address more flexible. However, *A Dictionary of the Printers and Booksellers who were at Work in England Scotland and Ireland from 1725 to 1775*, ed. H. R. Plomer, G. H. Bushnell, and E. R. McC[lintock] Dix (London: Bibliographical Society, 1968) only repeats the addresses mentioned in the imprints above, taking them at face value and giving no further indication that Millar actually moved locations.

32. See Edward Long (1734–1813), *The Anti-Gallican; or, the History and Adventures of Harry Cobham, Esquire. Inscribed to Louis the XVth, by the Author* (London: "Printed for T. LOWNDS, at his Circulating Library in *Fleet-Street*," 1757). From

mid-century onwards, reflecting the popularity of the new lending libraries, various texts begin advertising their participation in circulating libraries in their imprints. The key phrase on the title page – rendered in legalistic black-letter type – "𝕭𝖆𝖗𝖗𝖞 𝕮𝖔𝖇𝖍𝖆𝖒, Esquire" similarly gentrifies both the title character and his accompanying text.

33. See, for example, the second edition of Delarivier Manley's anonymous *Secret Memoirs* (1709), where the imprint reads: "Printed for *John Morphew* near *Stationer's Hall*, and J. Woodward in *St. Chriſtopher's* Church-yard, in *Thread-needle-ſtreet*." See also the imprint upon Richard Griffith's anonymously published and highly experimental fiction *Something New* (1772): "Printed for the AUTHOR; And Sold by E. and C. Dilly, in the Poultry; and Meſſieurs Kincaid and Creech, Edinburgh." Dedicated "TO ALL THE WORLD," this experimental fiction privileges novelty over literary ambition. It not only takes Shandean liberties with aposiopesis and punctuation but closes each of its two volumes with a musical "dirge" – a chapter's-worth of musical notation. It is, of course, possible that this imprint, too, is as self-conscious about convention as the rest of the book. Alternatively, since "Printed for the AUTHOR" meant that publishers were unwilling to risk their own money, Griffith may have had no other option than a Cheapside bookseller.

34. Miss Bingley and her sister Mrs. Hurst tar "sweet" Jane Bennet's marital prospects with the brush of Cheapside: "But with such a father and mother, and such low connections, I am afraid there is no chance of it. I think I have heard you say, that their uncle ... lives somewhere near Cheapside." Jane Austen, *Pride and Prejudice*, ed. Donald J. Gray (New York and London: Norton, 1966), 24.

35. The address is from the 1687 title page to A. Lovell's English translation of Cyrano de Bergerac's travel fantasy, *The Comical History of the States and Empires of the World of the Moon*. The full imprint reads: "LONDON: Printed for *Henry Rhodes*, next door to the *Swan-Tavern*, near *Bride-Lane* in *Fleet-Street*, 1687." The vendor's uncultured address, in this instance, does not reflect a lack of aspiration. In his *Science Fiction Before 1900: Imagination Discovers Technology* (New York: Twayne, 1994), Paul K. Alkon characterizes Cyrano's fiction as a "daring social satire" and "an important archetype for the Swiftian and Voltarian philosophical tale of travel and ideas" (162).

36. See Johns, *The Nature of the Book*.

37. See, respectively, the imprints of Charles Gildon's *The Post-Man Robb'd of his Mail* (1719); Edward Kimber's *The Life and Adventures of Joe Thompson* (1750); the anonymous *The History of Betty Barnes* (1753); and William Goodall's *The Adventures of Capt. Greenland* (1752).

38. See the following editions of works by Ben Jonson: *The Characters of Two Royall Masques* (London: [by G. Eld] for Thomas Thorp, and are to be ſold [by L. Lisle] at the ſigne of the Tigers head in Paules Church-yard, 1608); *The Masque of Queenes Celebrated from the House of Fame . . .* (London: By N. Okes. for R. Bonian and H. Wally, and are to be ſold at the Spred Eagle in Poules Church-yard, 1609); *Bartholmew Fayre: A Comedie, Acted in the Yeare, 1614. By the*

Lady Elizabeths Seruants . . . The Diuell is an Asse: A Comedie Acted in the Yeare, 1616, by His Maiesties Seruants; The Staple of Newes: A Comedie Acted in the Yeare, 1625, by His Maiesties Seruants (London: Printed by I.B. for Robert Allot, and are to be ſold at the ſigne of the Beare, in Pauls Church-yard, 1631); and *The New Inne. Or, The Light Heart* (London: Printed by Thomas Harper, for Thomas Alchorne, and are to be ſold at his ſhop in Pauls Church-yeard, at the ſigne of the greene Dragon, 1631). For a time Jonson sold works out of his own residence in Lime Street, displaying the sign of the Snail in order to better attract customers: *The Arch's of Triumph Erected in Honor of the High and Mighty Prince. Iames . . .* (London: By Iohn Windet, printer to the honourable citie of London, and are to be ſold at the authors house in Lime-ſtreet, at the ſigne of the Snayle, 1604).

39. Peter W. M. Blayney, *The Bookshops in Paul's Cross Churchyard*, published as part of the series of Occasional Papers of the Bibliographical Society 5 (London: Bibliographical Society, 1990), 75.

40. See Straus, *Unspeakable Curll* (183) and Plomer *et al.*, eds., *A Dictionary of the Printers and Booksellers* (92–95). The change in signage coincided with a move in location, to Rose Street in Covent Garden.

41. Curll uses the printer's ornaments featuring "Pope's Head" in accordance with the print convention of the "device," or "printer's mark," in the imprint. When a printer works under the shop sign of a cameo of a famous author, the device on the title page might participate, almost like a mini-variant of the frontispiece, in the tradition of the author portrait. For example, bookseller-printer J. Tonson, whose 1729 edition of the collected *Spectator* directs one to the address "*Shakeſpear's-Head*, over against *Katherine-ſtreet* in the *Strand*," used a wood-relief mini-portrait of the Bard on the title pages of many of his books, including that one. The title page to Eliza Haywood's 1751 novel *The History of Miss Betsy Thoughtless* ("Printed by T. GARDNER, and ſold at his Printing-Office at *Cowley's* Head, facing St. *Clement's Church*, in the *Strand*; and by all Bookſellers in Town and Country") likewise features a prominent device depicting a mini-bust of Cowley. Later in the century, books bearing the imprint "Printed for T. BECKET and P.A. DE HONDT, at Tully's Head, in the Strand" might also bear on their title pages a small printer's ornament depicting a bust of Cicero in Romanesque profile; this is the case for their 1769 English edition of Rousseau's *Eloisa*.

42. Both *The Farther Adventures of Robinson Crusoe . . .* (1719) and the *Serious Reflections during the Life and Surprising Adventures of Robinson Crusoe . . .* (1720) are sold under the sign of "the *Ship*" by W. Taylor.

43. Genette, *Paratexts*, 65.

44. *Ibid.*, 95.

45. *Ibid.*, 146.

46. Hunter dates "common agreement about the meaning of the term" to the mid-1780s. See *Before Novels*, 26.

47. It should be noted that Margaret Anne Doody challenges this long-held assumption (variously articulated by critics of the novel from Ian Watt to Michael

McKeon) throughout *The True Story of the Novel* (New Brunswick, NJ: Rutgers University Press, 1996).
48. Hunter, *Before Novels*, 27.
49. Ibid., 25.
50. Genette, *Paratexts*, 55.
51. Sarah Scott's previously mentioned novel *Millenium Hall* is a notable exception to the increasing brevity of the novel's titular habits. Even in 1762 Scott fancies a rather lengthy summary title which, like Richardson's, defines her project outside of traditional genre indicators: *A Description of Millenium Hall, and the Country Adjacent: Together with the Characters of the Inhabitants, and such Historical Anecdotes and Reflections, as May excite in the Reader proper Sentiments of Humanity, and lead the Mind to the Love of Virtue. By a Gentleman on his Travels* (London: Printed for J. Newbery, 1762). The fact that *Millenium Hall* marks a turning point in the novel's concern from individual to group identity has already been noted and may partly explain this regression to an old-style title.
52. Like the term "novel," the term "history" was not a newcomer to fiction's title pages. Of course Aphra Behn had used a similar formula as early as 1688 with "OROONOKO: OR, THE Royal Slave. A TRUE HISTORY." I do not wish to ignore that the word "history" appears in titles to prose fictions at a much earlier date than the 1750s; I merely suggest that the term history develops adhesive properties as a generic label around this time. The modern Norton edition reproduces the original title page in its front matter.
53. Smollett appears particularly wedded to the term "adventures," from *The Adventures of Roderick Random* (1748) to *The Adventures of Sir Launcelot Greaves* (1762).
54. That Lennox's return to the label "Adventures" is self-consciously done, is evidenced by the Countess's ironic reflections in *The Female Quixote*: "The word Adventures carries in it so free and licentious a Sound in the Apprehensions of People at this Period of Time, that it can hardly with Propriety be apply'd to those few and natural Incidents which compose the History of a Woman of Honour." Quoted from World's Classics paperback edition, ed. Margaret Dalziel (Oxford University Press, 1989), 327.
55. This text has long been acknowledged as a precursor to Sterne's *Tristram Shandy*. Wayne Booth mentions this "comic novel" as "a possible 'source' . . . for some of the materials of *Tristram Shandy*" in his unpublished dissertation "*Tristram Shandy* and its Precursors: The Selfconscious Narrator" (University of Chicago, 1950). He also cites Helen Sard Hughes's early discussion of this work's connection to Sterne in "A Precursor of *Tristram Shandy*," *JEGP* 17 (1918), 227–51.
56. See Roscoe, *John Newbery and His Successors*. In 1762, Newbery also published Sarah Scott's *Millenium Hall* and her *History of Mecklenburgh*, with their innovative frontispieces (see the previous chapter's discussion). Perhaps Kidgell selected Newbery as *The Card*'s publisher because, as a printer of juvenile literature, he proved amenable to requests for graphic embellishments – even from writers of non-juvenile books.

57. Review of *The Card*, 117.
58. Genette, *Paratexts*, 71.
59. Ibid., 146. Although Genette does not further gloss the *Tom Jones* epigraph or seek to locate its source, Sheridan Baker notes in his Norton Critical Edition of *Tom Jones* (1973) that "Fielding's motto comes from Horace, who is paraphrasing the opening of the *Odyssey* (1, 1–3) in his *Ars Poetica*, 141–42" (4). Thus Fielding fronts his text with a phrase that is doubly borrowed and transmuted: he could be indicating to the educated reader, the layering, altering, and recycling of tradition that occurs in his version of the emerging genre of the novel.
60. The three parts of Haywood's *Love in Excess* all sport epigraphs gathered from English, rather than classical, sources. The first part is fronted by some lines of poet and playwright, George Granville, Baron Landsdowne (1667–1735): "—In vain from Fate we fly, / For first or last, as all must die, / So 'tis as much decreed above, / That first or last, we all must love." Ahead of the second part appeared some lines from Dryden's translation of Chaucer: "Each day we break the bond of humane laws / For love, and vindicate the common cause. / Laws for defence of civil rights are placed, / Love throws the fences down, and makes a gen'ral waste. / Maids, widows, wives, without distinction fall, / The sweeping deluge love comes on and covers all." On the final part a reader finds these lines from the epilogue to *The Spartan Dame*, a play by Thomas Southerne (1660–1746): "Success can then alone your vows attend, / When worth's the motive, constancy the end." Unlike the classical epigraphs found elsewhere, these contemporary materials about romantic love and faithfulness do not lend Haywood's text great literary authority. They do, however, announce the nature and subject of her amatory fiction.
61. Genette, *Paratexts*, 144–45.
62. "—Why friend," asks bookseller Bookweight when presented with a bill for mottoes gathered from Latin, English, and Greek source texts, "are your Latin mottos dearer than your Greek?" Mr. Index replies, "Yes marry are they, sir. For as nobody now understands Greek, so I may use any sentence in that language to whatsoever purpose I please" (*Author's Farce*, Act II, scene v; Woods's edn., 30).
63. Sterne continued his project well into the 1760s; all subsequent installments of *Tristram Shandy* feature a dizzying array of epigraphs of various languages and seriousness.
64. The title page of the first edition of *Roderick Random* (1748) can boast of a classical epigraph a year prior to the publication of *Tom Jones*: "*Et genus & virtus, nisi cum re, vilior alga est.* Hor" (Horace, *Sermones*, II, v, 8); this translates as "And yet birth and worth, without substance, are more paltry than seaweed." *Satires, Epistles and Ars Poetica*, trans. H. Rushton Fairclough, Loeb Classical Library (London: William Heinemann; New York: G. P. Putnam's Sons, 1926), 198–99. In Horace, the line is spoken by Ulysses in lamentation of his present poverty after his return home to Ithaca. If the source of the quotation is known by the reader, the epigraph hints at Roderick's sea voyage to rebuild his lost fortune.
65. The *Peregrine Pickle* title page sports this epigraph: "*Respicere exemplar vitae morumque jubebo / Doctum imitatorem, & veras hinc ducere voces.* / Hor" (Horace,

Ars Poetica, 317). The original Horace read "vivas" where *Peregrine*'s title reads "veras" and translates: "I would advise one who has learned the imitative art to look to life and manners for a model, and draw from thence <u>living</u> words" [my emphasis]. *Satires, Epistles and Ars Poetica*, trans. Fairclough, 476–77. With the slight change in wording, Smollett thus appears to stress the "truth" of his story, rather than the animated quality of his prose; ironically – and characteristically – he stresses veracity with a literary untruth, a misquotation. Again, this clever twist is only accessible to those who not only read Latin but who recognize the alteration of the original.

66. This text's tongue-in-cheek epigraphs read: "gressumque Canes comitantur berilem. Vir.Aen" (Virgil, *Aeneid*, VIII, 462) and "*mutato nomine de te Fabula narratur. Hor*" (Horace, *Sermones*, I, i, 69–70). There appears to be a misprint in the line from the *Aeneid*, where "berilem" is actually "erilem" and translates: "guardian dogs attend their master's steps." *Aeneid, 7–12*, trans. H. Rushton Fairclough, Loeb Classical Library (Cambridge, MA: Harvard University Press, 2000), 92–93. The Horace translates: "change but the name and the tale is told of you." *Satires, Epistles and Ars Poetica*, trans. Fairclough, 8–11. Thus the quotations are genuine (despite the misprint), although their new context opposite the frontispiece portrait of a lapdog ridicules the rhetorical gesture of the allusion.

67. "*Felices ter & amplius Quos irrupta tenet Copula*" (Horace, *Carmina*, I, xiii, 17–18). The lines translate: "Thrice happy and more are they whom an unbroken bond unites" (modern editions of Horace's *Ode* read "*inrupta*" where Fielding's title page has "*irrupta*"). Horace, *The Odes and Epodes*, trans. C. E. Bennett, Loeb Classical Library (London: William Heinemann; Cambridge, MA: Harvard University Press, 1914), 40–41. The ribald pun embedded in the Latin *copula* is clearly intentional in Fielding's epigraphic selection. Yet, lest the comedy of the cryptic quotation compromise the literary seriousness of his art, Fielding makes certain that it remains accessible only to those who can decipher its Latin meaning and recognize it as Horace's; indeed he does not even acknowledge his source. Recognition offers additional rewards, since the line is from an *Ode* on Jealousy, offering an early hint of the Achilles heel of Amelia's marriage. Below it Fielding expounds upon the sexual innuendo – at least for those with a knowledge of Greek: Γυναικὸς οὐδὲν χρῆμ' ἀνηρ ληίζεται Ἐσθλης ἄμεινον ὀνδὲ ρίγιον κακης. The quotation translates: "A man can possess nothing better than a virtuous woman, not anything worse than a bad one," from Simonides, *Iambics*, iii. I'm grateful to Ken Larsen for this translation.

68. "*Hominem pagina nostra sapit. Martial*" (Martial, *Epigramaton*, x, iv, 10); "My page smacks of humanity." Martial, *Epigrams*, ed. and trans. D. R. Shackleton Bailey, Loeb Classical Library (Cambridge, MA: Harvard University Press, 1993), 328–29. The context of the original Martial is one that asserts the realism of the writer's art: "You won't find Centaurs here or Gorgons or Harpies, my page ...." Thus Sarah Fielding and Jane Collier use the epigraph to mitigate the strangeness of their dramatic dialogue-turned-novel and reassert in

scholarly terms its participation in a genre committed to veracity and humanity.

69. The epigraph reads: "*Quicquid agunt Homines, Votum, Timor, Ira, Voluptas, Gaudia, Discursus, nostri Farrago Libelli.* Juv" (Juvenal, *Satires*, I, 85–86). The original lines from Juvenal read "*quidquid*" instead of "*quicquid*"; this may be a misprint on Kidgell's page. The quotation translates: "All the doings of mankind, their vows, their fears, their angers and their pleasures, their joys and goings to and fro, shall form the motley subject of my page." *Juvenal and Persius*, trans. G. G. Ramsay, Loeb Classical Library (London: William Heinemann; Cambridge, MA: Harvard University Press, 1918), 8–9. This much-quoted line from Juvenal (*The Tatler* also adopted it for some issues in 1709), licenses an anything-goes approach to the many eighteenth-century texts flying it as a banner. This may, in fact, be part of Kidgell's critique of the novel – that it has not been exclusive enough.

70. *Bates* plays a number of games with its epigraph: "*Sublatum ex occulis quaerimus.* Hor" (Horace, *Carmina*, III, xxiv, 32). As is, the quote translates into "we seek the one snatched from sight" and thus would appear to give mournful epigraphic testimony to the death of Mr. Bates, the subject of these memoirs. However, the original lines from Horace mourn the departure of a late-appreciated Virtue (gendered feminine), rather than a person, and are taken from a poem that ponders the curse of Mammon. Not only does the epigraph remove all mention of virtue but Mrs. Bates, in seeking to publish for money, risks aligning her book with the false god Horace counsels against. For the record, the epigraph misprints the original "*oculis*" as "*occulis*," and alters "*sublatam*" to "*sublatum.*" Although the first alteration (the addition of an extra "c") may be a misprint, the second change alters the gender of the subject, shifting the meaning of the original line to suit the occasion of Mr. Bates's absence.

71. A few experimental fictions continue this trend beyond the 1750s, including Richard Griffith's *Something New* (1772), which contains a self-reflexive epigraph taken from a story about the scattering of verses traced upon leaves blown about irrecoverably by the wind: "Nec revocare situs, aut jungere carmina curat; / Inconsulti abeunt. – VIRG" (Virgil, *Aeneid*, III, 451–52); "Nor to recover their places and unite the verses; inquirers depart no wiser than they came." *Eclogues; Georgics; Aeneid, 1–6*, trans. H. Rushton Fairclough and revised G. P. Goold, Loeb Classical Library (Cambridge, MA: Harvard University Press, 1999), 402–03. Although epigraphs continue to surface here and there upon the title pages of late-century fictions, including upon Richard Graves's *Columella; Or, the Distressed Anchoret. A Colloquial Tale* (1779) and Charles Johnstone's *The Adventures of Anthony Varnish* (1786), the reflexivity of the epigraph to *Something New* confirms that the genre's new-found self-consciousness largely prohibits a "straight" utilization of such caste labels after the visually explosive 1750s.

72. An earlier instance of the novel's use of an English epigraph is found on Mary Hearne's *The Lover's Week* (1718): "*The Cause of Love can never be assign'd; / 'Tis in no Face, but in the Lover's Mind.* / Dryden." The quotation is from Dryden's 1670

tragedy set in the ancient world, *Tyrannick Love, or the Royal Martyr* (Act III, scene 1). A post-1750s instance of English epigraph usage on the novel's title page is Susannah Minifie's (later Mrs. Gunning) *Family Pictures, A Novel* (in collaboration with Margaret Minifie, 1764) which sports a quotation from the final act of William Congreve's tragedy *The Mourning Bride* (1697): "Still in the paths of honour perſevere, / And not from paſt or preſent ills deſpair; / For bleſſings ever wait on virtuous deeds, / And though a late, a ſure reward ſucceeds. / CONGREVE."

73. The title page of Sarah Fielding's *The Governess* already strikes a more populist tone with its crowded and decidedly non-genteel mix of font and type than do her *David Simple* (1744), *The Cry* (with Jane Collier, 1754), or *The Lives of Cleopatra and Octavia* (1757). The text enhances its popular "look" with an extensive passage from Shakespeare's *A Midsummer Night's Dream* that occupies over a third of the title page – thus dominating it. The layout and epigraphic selection suggest that Sarah Fielding is marketing this text, a text apparently self-financed as evidenced in the imprint's phrase "Printed for the AUTHOR," to an audience different from her other projects. The added financial risk of self-publishing may have influenced her to use a non-elitist epigraph – an epigraph so different in kind from the Latin she deploys on *The Cry*.

74. The *Joe Thompson* title page borrows its epigraph from the opening lines to Pope's theatrical *Prologue to Mr. Addison's Tragedy of Cato* (1713): "*To wake the Soul, by tender Strokes of Art; / To raiſe the Genius, and to mend the Heart; / To make Mankind in conſcious Virtue bold, / Live o'r each Scene, and be what they behold. / For this* _____." As in *The Governess*, the jumbled pie of font and type on *Thompson*'s title page (though far less crowded than Sarah Fielding's) risks its association with popular productions of the press. That may, however, be the reaction (and audience) it aims to solicit. When the text is reprinted in 1783, however, the theatrical quotation from Pope still graces its title page.

75. Shakespeare again appears here. This time the quoted passage is from *Richard II*, Act V, scene v: "*The* Brain *I'll prove the* Female *to my* Soul! */ My* Soul *the* Father; *and theſe two beget / A* Generation *of ſtill* Breeding Thoughts, */ And theſe ſame* Thoughts *people* this little World, / *In Humours like the People of* This World."

76. See Edward Long's amusing *Anti-Gallican* of 1757. The combination of title, mock dedication (to Louis XV), and epigraphic quote gives evidence of the fact that this satire ridicules the novel's continental borrowings and affectations.

77. The title page of *Chrysal* bears the following epigraphic selection:

> _____*Hold the Mirror up to Nature,*
> *To ſhew Vice its own image, Virtue its own Likeneſs,*
> *And the very Age and Body of the Times*
> *His form and Preſſure.* SHAKESPEARE.
> Qui capit, ille facit.

78. Epigraphs used by other genres continue unimpeded throughout the century and beg the question of whether the novel genre has, at century's end, successfully transitioned from fledgling literature into the kind of literary authority cited on other books. I have not come across a citation from a novel on the title pages to other types of eighteenth-century publication. The closest the novel appears to come to entering print culture in the form of an epigraph and, in this manner, confirming its own canonicity is on the title page to the fourth edition of Sir Herbert Croft's *Love and Madness, A Story Too True* (Dublin, 1786), which sports the following excerpt of dialogue:

> GOVERNOR. "Who did the bloody Deed?
> OROONOKO. "The Deed was mine.
> "Bloody I know and I expect
> "Your Laws ſhould tell me ſo. Thus ſelf condemn'd
> "I do reſign myſelf into their hands.
> "The hands of Justice.   OR. 5. 3.

The title page quotes from the final conversation – moments after the murder of Imoinda – between the hero Oroonoko and the Governor; in its new context, the quoted passage glosses a popular fiction which was based upon the genuine murder of Martha Ray by James Hackman. Yet, even this minor sensational fiction does not borrow its authority directly from Aphra Behn's *Oronooko: Or, The Royal Slave. A True History* (1688). Instead, it quotes from Thomas Southerne's 1695 dramatic adaptation by the same name. Thus even here, the early novel's popularity is siphoned through drama's greater respectability before it can enter a title page as an epigraph.

79. Genette, *Paratexts*, 147.

4 '*Clarissa*'s musical score

1. Austen, *Pride and Prejudice*, ed. Gray, 119.
2. Jane Austen, *Emma*, ed. Stephen M. Parrish (New York and London: Norton, 2000), 179.
3. *Pride and Prejudice*, 121.
4. Jane Austen, *Persuasion*, ed. John Davie and intro. Claude Rawson (Oxford University Press, 1971; reissued with new intro., 1990), 48–49.
5. Ibid., 49.
6. The title character in *Emma* knows "the limitations of her own powers too well to attempt more than she could perform with credit" (147).
7. *Emma*, 147 and 149.
8. For example, a clear family resemblance can be found in Frances Burney's works. In *Evelina* (1778) the "uneducated and unprincipled" Madame Duval loudly fakes musical connoisseurship, boasting "music is my passion," while the heroine's finer appreciation is conveyed privately and indirectly: "There was an exceeding good concert, but too much talking to hear it well. Indeed I am quite astonished to find

how little music is attended to in silence; for though every body seems to admire, hardly any body listens." *Evelina*, ed. Edward A. Bloom (Oxford University Press, 1989), 93 and 105.
9. *Pamela*, first edition, I, 92–93; and II, 96–97.
10. *Pamela: Or, Virtue Rewarded. In a Series of Familiar Letters From a Beautiful Young Damsel to her Parents: And Afterwards in Her Exalted Condition . . . The Third and Fourth Volumes . . . By the Editor of the Two First* (London: Printed for S. Richardson: and sold by C. Rivington, 1742), IV, 109–14.
11. *Clarissa*, 3rd edn. (1751), VIII, 102. Unless otherwise noted, all quotations from *Clarissa* will henceforth refer to the 1751 third-edition text in eight volumes and will be cited parenthetically by volume and page number. The *Clarissa Project*'s eight-volume facsimile of this 1751 edition (New York: AMS Press, 1990) has made this important edition widely available; only this modern reproduction of the novel offers the engraved folding score in a manner faithful to its original appearance.
12. *The History of Sir Charles Grandison*, 6th edn., 7 vols. (London: Printed for J. and F. Rivington, 1770), II, 24.
13. See Richard Leppert's *Music and Image: Domesticity, Ideology and Socio-cultural Formation in Eighteenth-Century England* (Cambridge University Press, 1988). Leppert discusses how in eighteenth-century England "the culture demanded music as an appropriate mark of both femininity itself and female class status" (29).
14. For example, the four-volume Everyman's library edition (1932) shrinks the music and the lyrics of (only) stanza XIV onto a single, conventionally sized page of unadorned text (I, 277). The eight-volume Shakespeare Head Press edition (Oxford: Basil Blackwell, 1943) does include a rendition of the music in sheet form, although, in addition to differing in size and visual appearance, this does not fold dramatically outward as in Richardson's printings. In the Penguin edition of *Clarissa*, edited by Angus Ross, the music is removed from the central text and reproduced in an appendix on the last page of a reprinting which otherwise honors the first edition as its copy-text.
15. For example, in *Clarissa's Ciphers: Meaning and Disruption in Richardson's Clarissa* (Ithaca and London: Cornell University Press, 1982), Terry Castle's discussion of hermeneutic questions raised across "a number of sign systems" relies upon the Shakespeare Head Press edition and makes no mention of the heroine's musical notes (91). The folding score remains unnoticed by even those who write about Carter's *Ode*, Clarissa's musical playing, or song and dance in Richardson: see, Jocelyn Harris, *Samuel Richardson* (London: Cambridge University Press, 1987), 56–57; Martha Bowden, "Composing Herself: Music, Solitude and St. Cecilia in *Clarissa*," *1650–1850: Ideas, Aesthetics, and Inquiries in the Early Modern Era* 2 (1996), 185–201; and Margaret Anne Doody, *A Natural Passion: A Study of the Novels of Samuel Richardson* (Oxford: Clarendon Press, 1974), 352–64. In a subsequent essay, entitled "The Man-made World of Clarissa Harlowe and Robert Lovelace," Doody does note the musical score in *Clarissa*,

acknowledging the original material appearance of this "fold-out page of music." However, Doody's brief assessment of this page as "a present from Clarissa" does not fully explore this unusual textual moment. This essay by Doody is found in Valerie Grosvenor Myer, ed., *Samuel Richardson: Passion and Prudence* (Totowa, NJ: Barnes & Noble, 1986), 52–77, at 62–63. The tradition of Clarissa's music as a keepsake was, incidentally, revived by the Johnson Society of the Central Region at a meeting on 30 April 1999, where it offered attendees a pamphlet entitled *Ode to Wisdom: A Poem by Elizabeth Carter As Set to Music by Clarissa Harlowe*. This little-known pamphlet contains a useful brief introduction by John Dussinger and a handsome facsimile of the novel's engraved score.

16. See, Steven R. Price, "The Autograph Manuscript in Print: Samuel Richardson's Type Font Manipulation in *Clarissa*," in Paul C. Gutjahr and Megan L. Benton, eds., *Illuminating Letters: Typography and Literary Interpretation* (Amherst: University of Massachusetts Press, 2001), 117–35, esp. 129–34. Price stands out as acknowledging Clarissa's music as a striking visual phenomenon in the novel. Price argues for Richardson's mimetic use of typography and focuses on the manner in which the engraved script font of the plate of music "suggests actual handwriting" (133).

17. Richardson to Elizabeth Carter, 18 December 1747. The 1747–48 correspondence between Carter and Richardson does not appear in Barbauld or (fully) in Carroll; the latter includes only a paragraph from another letter dated 17 December 1748. The exchange was, however, reprinted in *The Monthly Magazine* 33 (1812), 533–35. I quote from this reprinting.

18. The musical score appears in all of Richardson's original editions of *Clarissa*: in the first edition (1748) the engraved folding leaf of music is bound to face page 50 in Volume II; in the second edition (1749) it faces page 48 in Volume II; and in the third (1751) and fourth (1759) page 54, again in Volume II. Richardson has the music re-engraved for inclusion in the fourth edition in octavo (1751), where it is re-sized to fit on page 362 of Volume I. For a complete collation of the contents of each edition see Sale's *A Bibliographical Record*, 45–58.

19. Angus Ross, from "Notes" to his 1985 Penguin edition of *Clarissa*, 1514, note L54.

20. See William M. Sale, Jr., "A Bibliographical Note on Richardson's *Clarissa*," *Library*, or *Transactions of the Bibliographical Society*, 2nd series, vol. XVI, (London: Humphrey Milford, 1936), 448–51.

21. Literary criticism appears to have been influenced on this point by Richardson's many biographers. Accounts of the publication history of *Clarissa* highlight Richardson's appropriation of Carter's *Ode* without remarking upon the uncommon decision to set it to music. See Alan Dugald McKillop, *Samuel Richardson: Printer and Novelist* (Chapel Hill: University of North Carolina Press, 1936), 141; T. C. Duncan Eaves and Ben D. Kimpel, *Samuel Richardson: A Biography* (Oxford: Clarendon Press, 1971), 214–16; and Sale, *A Bibliographical Record*, 52.

22. Elizabeth Carter to Samuel Richardson, 13 December 1747, reprinting of correspondence.

23. Samuel Richardson to Elizabeth Carter, 18 December 1747, reprinting of correspondence.

24. *Ibid*. In fact, Carter wrote an epitaph for Richardson. Anna Barbauld chooses to end her "Life," the introduction to the *Correspondence*, with this tribute (1, ccxii).
25. *Ibid*. Unfortunately, it is not known whom Richardson employed for the musical setting of the ode.
26. John Alcock, *Six Suites of Easy Lessons for the Harpsicord or Spinet, with a Trumpet Piece* (London: Printed for the author and sold by him in Plymouth: Mr. Walsh in Catherine Street in the Strand: Mr. Pierce in Crosby Square and at all the musick shops, 1741); William Babell, *Suits [sic] of the Most Celebrated Lessons Collected and Fitted to the Harpsicord or Spinet* (London: I. Walsh and I. Hare, 1717); Jean Philippe Rameau, *A Collection of Lessons for the Harpsicord. Opera Seconda* (London: Printed for I. Walsh, 1760); Jean Joseph Cassanea de Mondonville, *Six Sonatas or Lessons for the Harpsicord Which May Be Accompanied with a Violin or German Flute* (London: Printed for I. Walsh, 1753).
27. For an image of "Mad Paper X" see Figure 5.7.
28. References to the common method of sale for individual musical pieces can be found in advertisements or publication notes in music of the period. A song bound with *A Collection of the Choicest Songs and Dialogues* (London, 174? [Unique bound bundle of individual sheet music found in the Special Collections Research Center, the University of Chicago Library, under call number M1738.C79.]), "The Storm: or the Dangers of the Sea. Sung by Mr. Dodd," for example, bears the subscript "London: Printed and Sold by R. Falkener, No. 45 Salisbury-Court, Fleetstreet. Where may be had a choice collection of the most celebrated Songs, Catches, & c. at a PENNY a-page." Similarly the advertisement at the front of *The Musical Miscellany; Being a Collection of Choice Songs, Set to the Violin and Flute, By the most Eminent Masters* (London: Printed by and for John Watts, 1729–31) confirms the standard format of printed music in loose half-sheets: "A Collection of Choice Songs are here bound up together, the only Method of preserving them; and at so easy a Rate, that they will not cost the Purchasers half the Money they wou'd come to in loose Half Sheets" [my emphasis]. Although the unique, privately bundled *Collection* of sheet music in which these items are found is tentatively assigned a "1704?" date in the University of Chicago's library catalogue, it includes some pieces of music with publication dates ranging between 1735 and 1741, making it much more contemporary to the discussion of sheet music at the time of Clarissa's publication than would first appear. I have amended the date in my citations of this volume.
29. *The Musical Entertainer . . . Engraved by George Bickham, Junr.*, 2 vols. (London: Printed for and sold by Charles Corbett Bookseller, 1740). There exists a beautiful 1965 facsimile reprint of this important work, printed by Broude Bros. of New York.
30. Of the better-known mid-eighteenth-century periodicals, *The Gentleman's Magazine* contains perhaps the most numerous examples of letterpress music. For a typical collection of letterpress music, see *An Antidote against Melancholy. Being a Collection of Fourscore Merry Songs, Wherein those of the same Subject and Key are*

placed in agreeable Succession in Relation to the Different Measures of Time, After the Manner of Suits [sic] *of Lessons* (London: Printed for Daniel Brown, 1749). It is interesting to note that this particular collection of printed "merry songs" also conspicuously models itself, like Clarissa's music, after the more elevated genre of "suits of lessons."

31. "It was Mr. *Western's* Custom every Afternoon, as soon as he was drunk, to hear his Daughter play on the Harpsichord: for he was a great Lover of Music, and perhaps, had he lived in Town, might have passed for a Connoisseur: for he always excepted against the finest compositions of Mr. *Handel*. He never relished any Music but what was light and airy; and indeed his most favourite Tunes, were *Old Sir* Simon *the King, St.* George *he was for* England, *Bobbing* Joan, and some others" (*Tom Jones*, Book IV, ch. v). Quoted from Fielding, *The History of Tom Jones, A Foundling*, ed. Fredson Bowers, intro. Martin C. Battestin, and illustr. Warren Chappell, Wesleyan Edition (Wesleyan University Press, 1975), 169. Western's three favorite Restoration tunes are a predictable ensemble of patriotic ditty and bawdy ballad. For a discussion of these songs see W[illiam]. Chappell, *Old English Popular Music*, ed. H. Ellis Woolridge, 2 vols. (New York: J. Brussel, [c. 1961]), I, 280–82 and 312; II, 102–104. The collection *An Antidote against Melancholy* mentioned above, for example, contains a similar miscellany of songs fit for an afternoon of Fieldingesque revelry: "Here lies honest Stephen, with Mary his Bride," "Prithee Cloe, give o'er," and "The mighty State of Cuckoldom by Matrimony thrives."

32. This particular genre of all-verbal lyric books seems to bear evocatively georgic titles: *The Hive. A Collection of the Most Celebrated Songs* (London: Printed for J. Walthoe junr., 1724); *The Robin. A Collection of Six Hundred and Eighty of the most Celebrated English and Scotch Songs: None of Which are Contain'd in the Other Collections of the Same Size Call'd the Linnet and Thrush* (London: Printed for C. Hitch & I. Osborn, 1749).

33. I am grateful to Larry Zbikowski and Tom McGeary who generously aided me in identifying these particular musical characteristics.

34. Richardson's use of music to distinguish between different kinds of novel reader parallels Henry Fielding's use of classical allusions and quotations in *Tom Jones*. Just as Fielding encouraged with his epigraphs and classical allusions a cultural literacy requirement for readers of the "new species" of writing, the use of musical notation in *Clarissa* suggests that Richardson also imagined the ideal novel reader to have a specific, though distinct, level of cultural sophistication.

35. Roger Lonsdale in his biography of Charles Burney, the eighteenth-century musical historiographer who was (for a time) a music teacher in provincial King's Lynn during the early 1750s, consistently describes Burney's work explicitly in terms of gender and class: "his daily round of teaching the daughters of the aristocracy and the wealthy middle classes." See Lonsdale's *Dr. Charles Burney; A Literary Biography* (Oxford: Clarendon Press, 1965), 55. For a more recent discussion of gender, class, and musical education in eighteenth-century England consult Leppert, *Music and Image*.

36. Jocelyn Harris characterizes the maiden community depicted in Carter's *Ode to Wisdom* as akin to "Mary Astell's idea of a Protestant Nunnery [which] Richardson praised in *Grandison* (III, 9)" (*Samuel Richardson*, 56).
37. Leppert argues that music (particularly the musical education of girls) in eighteenth-century society remained "an essential component in maintaining the status quo to gender hierarchy" (*Music and Image*, 40). While music might, Leppert acknowledges, create a "compensatory space for women," it continues to be valued in society as a harmless pastime, an activity "viewed as non-developmental and expressive of stationary time" (40 and 29). Richardson, I believe, means to show in *Clarissa* that music can, in addition to dispelling boredom, serve a powerful communal function in women's lives.
38. A few pages later, while Clarissa pleads with her Aunt Hervey, Bella again flaunts her lack of interest, as opposed to her genuine friendship, by engaging in musical behavior: "Bella all the while humming a tune, and opening this book and that, without meaning; but saying nothing" (I, 310).
39. This particular letter of Anna's also opens with a musical metaphor that similarly aligns musical performance with female independence and stubborn self-sufficiency: "You plead generously for Mr. Hickman. Perhaps, with regard to him, I may have done, as I have often done in singing – Begun a note or key too high; and yet, rather than begin again, proceed, tho' I strain my voice, or spoil my tune" (III, 169).
40. For a more expansive discussion of Lovelace's "multiple assault on female friendship," see Janet Todd's chapter on *Clarissa*, "Sentimental Friendship," in her book *Women's Friendship in Literature* (New York: Columbia University Press, 1980), 9–68, esp. 61–63. Todd does not remark on the role of music in the novel's depiction of female friendships and maiden community.
41. With characteristic irony, Austen echoes this same sentiment in *Emma* where Mrs. Elton laments the lack of a female community of amateur musicians: "[F]or married women, you know – there is a sad story against them, in general. They are but too apt to give up music" (180).
42. For a broader contextualization of music's complex role in matrimony during the eighteenth century, see the chapter entitled "Music in Domestic Space: Domination, Compensation, and the Family" in Leppert, *Music and Image*, 176–200.
43. *Pamela*, 1st edn., II, 63.
44. See Richardson and Lady Bradshaigh, *The Annotations*, ed., Barchas, 53.
45. Apparently still unsatisfied with the "subtlety" of the songbird analogy, Richardson also adds Lovelace's observations on the grotesque practice of using "'burning knitting-needles to put out the eyes of the poor feather'd songster" (IV, 16). The decision to mark all "new" material with marginal bullets in the 1751 text, makes such a passage as this – and with it Lovelace's explicit cruelty – stand out.
46. Margaret Anne Doody glosses the "fold-out page" as precisely such an invitation: "The reader can remove it for the domestic music library. 'A present from Clarissa' this might be called, a piece of her making offered as a gift" ("The Man-made World," 63).

47. See Bowden, "Composing Herself."
48. Griffith, *Something New*, II, 253.
49. Ibid., 253.
50. Ironically, Kidgell's illustration does indeed document a lost cultural habit of eighteenth-century England. Additional evidence suggests that the practice of writing messages on the back of playing cards was of relatively long duration: William Hogarth in "The Toilette" (scene iv of his "Marriage à-la-mode" series of 1743–45) includes a scattering of similarly inscribed playing cards in a corner of the domestic scene. In *Marriage à-la-mode: A Re-view of Hogarth's Narrative Art* (Manchester University Press, 1983), Robert L. S. Cowley contextualizes this detail in the Hogarth print, asserting that "visiting cards were often improvised on the backs of playing cards" (112).
51. One anonymous critic argued that "[W]hat recommends them [Richardson's novels] to the notice of the present age is their novelty, and their gratifying an idle and insatiable curiosity. In a few years that novelty will wear off, and that Curiosity will be equally gratified by other compositions ... Such, Sir, must be the fate of all works which owe their success to a present capricious humor, and have not real intrinsic worth to support them. Short-lived then as they are ..." *Critical Remarks on Sir Charles Grandison, Clarissa and Pamela ... By a Lover of Virtue* (London: Printed for J. Dowse, 1754), 50.
52. A few critics have tried to bring Richardson's sense of graphic design to the fore. Although disappointing in the primacy of its discussions of material objects rather than the materiality of the text, Stephanie Fysh's *The Work(s) of Samuel Richardson* (Newark: University of Delaware Press, 1997) focusses needed attention on Richardson's overlapping careers as printer and author. In addition Richardson's use of attendant illustration serves as the subject of Janet Aikins's essay "Richardson's 'speaking pictures'" in Margaret Anne Doody and Peter Sabor, eds., *Samuel Richardson: Tercentenary Essays* (Cambridge University Press, 1989), 146–66. Aikins's discussion of a "powerful visual aesthetic" in *Pamela* pays close attention to the engravings by Hayman and Gravelot that Richardson commissioned for the sixth edition (1742) of this novel. Similarly, Murray L. Brown attends to Richardson's visual acumen as it applies to his use of verbal iconography and imagery ("Learning to Read Richardson: *Pamela*, 'Speaking Pictures,' and the Visual Hermeneutic," *Studies in the Novel* 25.2 [Summer 1993], 129–51).
53. At least one edition of *Tristram Shandy* includes a musical score. The paperback edition of *The Life and Opinions of Tristram Shandy, Gentleman*, ed. James Aiken Work (New York: Odyssey Press, 1940), devotes a page in the story's central text to the lyrics and musical score of "Lilliburlero" (70). Readers of this edition might have assumed that there was a "musical page" in Sterne's original work. In fact, there is no such musical score in the original printings of Sterne's novel. The fact that the music in the Odyssey edition does not appear inconsistent with the rest of Sterne's visually experimental text supports my claim that Richardson's musical page resembles Sterne's self-conscious application of graphic design.

5 The space of time

1. Gérard Genette, *Narrative Discourse, An Essay in Method*, trans. Jane E. Lewin, foreword, Jonathan Culler (Ithaca, NY: Cornell University Press, 1980), 218.
2. Genette, *Narrative Discourse*, 218.
3. *Ibid.*
4. Richardson to Aaron Hill, 20 January 1745/6. Quoted from Carroll, 63.
5. George Sherburn in his introduction to the Riverside Edition of *Clarissa* (Boston, MA: Houghton Mifflin, 1962), xii.
6. Mark Kinkead-Weekes, *Samuel Richardson: Dramatic Novelist* (Ithaca, NY: Cornell University Press, 1973), 421
7. Castle, *Clarissa's Ciphers*, 154.
8. In the 1950s and 1960s, before the advent of Deconstruction, a number of literary critics took the time-schemes in *Pamela* and *Clarissa* seriously, analyzing references to dates and times in Richardson's novels for historical specificity and evidence of character development. See Arthur Sherbo, "Time and Place in Richardson's Clarissa," *Boston University Studies in English* 3 (1957), 139–46; John Samuel Bullen, *Time and Space in the Novels of Samuel Richardson*, in the Utah State University Press Monograph Series 12.2 (Logan, UT: Utah State University Press, 1965); and Dorothy Parker, "The Time Scheme of *Pamela* and the Character of B.," *Texas Studies in Literature and Language* 11 (1969), 695–704. Sherbo, Bullen, and Parker each provide useful local observations about the temporal features of Richardson's fictions. None, however, remarks on Richardson's augmentation of his narrative's temporal dimensions through the physical features of his printed page.
9. Richardson to Sophia Westcomb, 1746(?); quoted in Carroll, 65.
10. Richardson to Sophia Westcomb, 15 September 1746; quoted in Carroll, 68. Glossing both these descriptions in *Reading* Clarissa: *The Struggles of Interpretation* (New Haven, CT and London: Yale University Press, 1979), William Beatty Warner notes that "[f]amiliar letter writing begins with the isolation of the writer from the mundane world, with its random interruptions, so all attention can be concentrated on the self"(99).
11. Because Richardson's use of the small printer's ornaments evolves from edition to edition, I introduce them here in the manner in which they appeared in the first edition of *Clarissa* (1748). However, unless otherwise indicated (as here), I will continue to quote from Richardson's third-edition text of *Clarissa* (1751) and parenthetically cite to the volume and page numbers from that eight-volume edition, an important edition made widely available in the AMS Press reprint.
12. Warner, *Reading Clarissa*, 99.
13. See Donnalee Frega, *Speaking in Hunger: Gender, Discourse, and Consumption in* Clarissa (Columbia, SC: University of South Carolina Press, 1998).
14. Every general rule has its exceptions. Three mid-century fictions are worth mentioning in this respect – one a work of historical fiction and two examples of science fiction in the epistolary form. An early example of the epistolary novel,

Marquise de Bressay's *Letters from Julia, the Daughter of Augustus, to Ovid. A Manuscript Discovered at Herculaneum* (London: Printed for Lockyer Davis, 1753), is an epistolary fiction set in ancient times. Conversely, the unattributed *Private Letters from an American in England to his Friends in America* (London: Printed for J. Almon, 1769) is remarkable for setting its epistolary tale in the future. "These letters," explains its advertisement leaf, "are supposed to be written towards the close of the eighteenth century, by a young American; who is stimulated by curiosity to pay a visit to the country of his ancestors." An extremely early epistolary science fiction is Samuel Madden's *Memoires of the Twentieth Century. Being Original Letters of State, under George the Sixth* ... (London: Printed for Messieurs Osborn and Longman, Davis, and Batley, 1733). The rarity of this particular work is compounded by the fact that it was soon suppressed and most copies destroyed. See William Harlin McBurney, *A Check List of English Prose Fiction, 1700–1739* (Cambridge, MA: Harvard University Press, 1960), 94.

15. *Pamela*, intro. William M. Sale, Jr. (New York and London: Norton, 1958; reissued 1993), 189–91.
16. Parker, "Time Scheme of *Pamela*," 696.
17. After a long absence from modern paperback editions, this pregnant pause of white space has been reinserted into the new Oxford World's Classics *Pamela*, ed. Thomas Keymer and Alice Wakely (Oxford University Press, 2001), 49. Hitherto editions such as the Norton and the Meridian Classic (New York: New American Library, 1980) did not reproduce this visual hiatus in the original text, rendering Pamela's narrative seamless precisely where the layout had originally signaled discontinuity (see pages 44 and 81 in the respective editions). The Meridian Classic paperback packages the novel with Fielding's scathing pamphlet attack and is entitled *Pamela, Samuel Richardson. Shamela, Henry Fielding*; it includes an introduction by John M. Bullitt.
18. One critic to note the significance of the layout of Pamela's letter is Ronald Paulson: "Pamela's interruption by the sudden arrival of Mr. B is a white gap on the page; . . . [This letter] is a symbolic visual object." Ronald Paulson, *Emblem and Expression: Meaning in English Art of the Eighteenth Century* (Cambridge, MA: Harvard University Press, 1975), 51. Paulson does not elaborate on the implications of this white space for an interpretation of the heroine's motivations.
19. Genette, *Narrative Discourse*, 218.
20. Price, "The Autograph Manuscript in Print," 128.
21. Ibid., 135.
22. Castle, *Clarissa's Ciphers*, 121.
23. *The Gentleman's Magazine* 19 (August 1749), 348–49; quoted in Thomas Keymer, "Jane Collier, Reader of Richardson, and the Fire Scene in *Clarissa*," in Albert Rivero, ed., *New Essays on Samuel Richardson* (New York: St. Martin's Press, 1996), 141–61, at 153–54. Albert von Haller's review has been reproduced in full in *Volume 1: Prefaces, Postscripts and Related Writings*, intro. Jocelyn Harris and ed. Thomas Keymer, of *Samuel Richardson's Published Commentary on Clarissa, 1747–65*, ed. Florian Stuber et al., 3 vols. (London: Pickering & Chatto, 1998), 140–46. It is possible to interpret the third edition of 1751, in which Richardson

omits the graphic distinction of Clarissa's two signatures, as a partial concession to Haller's objections.
24. Forster mss., xv, 2, fols. 33–34, Victoria and Albert Museum; quoted in Keymer, "Jane Collier, Reader," 155. See also *Volume 1, Published Commentary*, ed. Stuber *et al.*, at 143.
25. Arthur Sherbo, in his previously mentioned essay of 1957, enumerates all of the references in *Clarissa* to historical events and year-dates in an attempt to calculate what specific year Richardson has in mind for the setting of his story. Sherbo notes Richardson's "reluctance of the precise dating of the happenings in Clarissa," a reluctance best exemplified in the absence of a date on the heroine's coffin: "April X. [Then the year]" (142). Sherbo concludes that the "vagueness" of both time and place in the novel "strengthens the feeling of realism" (145). In his introduction to the 1985 Penguin edition of *Clarissa*, Angus Ross suggests that 1732 is "the most likely year" for the temporal setting of the novel (23). The particulars of that calendar year correspond neatly to the scarce mentions of specific days and months in the letters.
26. On several occasions the characters themselves gloss the temporal function of the printer's ornament with verbal text that accounts precisely for the time just spent away from their writing. These accounts suggest that the time intervals marked by the ornaments can range widely: from "ten minutes" (II, 247), to "about an hour" (I, 116), or even "two hours" (II, 6).
27. For an analysis of the relationship between new eighteenth-century technologies for counting time on clocks and the emergence of new paradigms for recounting it in prose see Stuart Sherman, *Telling Time: Clocks, Journals, and English Narrative Form, 1660–1795* (University of Chicago Press, 1996). Sherman argues for the presence of a "long-running cultural encounter between a particular mode of chronometry and a strikingly matched mode of writing." Although Sherman's study does not focus on either the works of Richardson or methods of printing, it points to the epistolary novel as one of the emerging genres which exhibit the dominant preoccupation with inhabiting and tracking time.
28. Book 2, chapter 1; Wesleyan Edition of Henry Fielding, *Joseph Andrews*, ed. Martin C. Battestin (Oxford: Clarendon Press, 1967), 89–92.
29. *Joseph Andrews*, Wesleyan Edition, 89.
30. *Ibid.*, 89–90.
31. Hunter, "From Typology to Type," 50.
32. *Ibid.*, 51.
33. *Clarissa*, 3rd edn., I, 52. The "place" is the Wood-house and the few "rotted" boards in its wall that allow for the clandestine exchange of letters between Clarissa and Lovelace through the boundary between the Harlowe estate and "the Green Lane."
34. In the first-edition text of this passage (II, 157) printer's ornaments are lacking altogether. This suggests that Richardson added them in the third edition to emphasize this transition.
35. Warner, *Reading* Clarissa, 207–208.
36. *Ibid.*, 207.

37. *Ibid.*, 208.
38. *Ibid.*
39. Anne C. Henry, "The Re-mark-able rise of '...': reading ellipsis marks in literary texts," in Bray, Handley, and Henry, eds., *Ma(r)king the Text*, 120–42. Henry's observations about *Clarissa* (131–34) are limited to the ellipsis marks in the first-edition text, although she does note that Richardson paid attention to "revising his ornaments through the four editions of *Clarissa*" (141, note 40). Interestingly, the tradition of ellipsis marks, and Richardson's small floral ornaments in particular, is receiving unprecedented attention. See also Christopher Flint, "In Other Words: Eighteenth-Century Authorship and the Ornaments of Print," *Eighteenth-Century Fiction* 14.3–4 (April–July 2002), 627–72.
40. I would like to thank the graduate students who engaged in a *Clarissa* seminar in 1999 at the University of Auckland, particularly Christine Summers, for making me aware of the possibility that the associative function of the *fleurons* in the first edition dissolves deliberately over the course of that work's seven volumes.
41. I have found only a single exception to this practice: Volume I, page 52. In this letter by Clarissa a similar pair of printer's flowers replaces her usual mark. The nearly identical appearance of this set of ornaments suggests a compositor's error, probably owing to that piece of type having found its way into the wrong compartment of the printer's wooden type case.
42. Again, I have found only one instance in the third edition where a letter by Anna is (mistakenly?) interrupted by a different marker, namely the pair of rosettes (above) associated with Clarissa (I, 70).
43. Belford's ornament first appears on page 251 of Volume VI, after which his letters frequently feature this temporal mark. On one occasion this same ornament, although arranged in a new configuration on the page, marks a temporal ellipsis in a letter by Mrs. Harlowe (VII, 36). Towards the end of that same volume, a different ornament surfaces in Belford's correspondence, although it must be said that it bears a close resemblance to that found in his prior letters (VII, 422–24). These minor violations of an otherwise consistent visual strategy only make sense (particularly because they are so slight) as compositor's errors and/or limitations owing to stock.
44. For example, in a letter by Mrs. Norton a distinct set of ornaments marks the news-break in her writing: "I am just now informed that your Cousin Morden is arrived from England" (VII, 110). Similarly, Colonel Morden is allocated his own mark of interruption in the final volume (VIII, 83).
45. Charlotte Brontë, *Jane Eyre*, 2nd edn., 3 vols. (London: Smith, Elder and Co., Cornhill, 1848), III, 43. Modern reprints of Frances Burney's *Evelina*, 3 vols. (1778) faithfully reproduce the rows of asterisks found in two locations in that novel's first-edition text. These lacunae, too, may mildly impune Evelina's promise of full disclosure.
46. This "fast-find" feature of the small printer's ornaments somewhat resembles the function of that edition's marginal "Dots." Like the "Dots" in the third edition, which "distinguished" newly added material, the ornaments visually sort the

authors of the letters. The fact that both of the visual features unique to the third edition, the marginalia and the printer's flowers, provide the reader with a visual "search" tool suggests that Richardson redesigned *Clarissa* according to the model of the reference text. His massive index to *Grandison* (see my final chapter) appears to grow out of this same desire for enhancing the novel's utility through design.

47. Lovelace's trite and unimaginative flower imagery (some of it borrowed from poetry by Dryden and Rowe) to describe Clarissa is quite extensive. For a representative sampling in Volume III, see pages 283, 285, 286, and 329.

48. Castle, 142–43; Margaret Anne Doody, *A Natural Passion*, 186, n1. While Castle and Doody ponder the semiotic significance of the "ornaments" in Clarissa's coffin text (images of "the head of a white Lily snapped short off," an urn, a winged hour-glass, and crowned serpent) they do not apply the same interpretive pressure to the actual ornaments found throughout the text of the novel (VII, 312).

49. According to the labels provided by Elizabeth Carroll Reilly in her *Dictionary of Colonial American Printers' Ornaments and Illustrations* (Worcester, MA: American Antiquarian Society, 1975), ornaments similar to the ones in Belford's letters are described as "Acorns" while those found in Anna's writing fall under the heading of "Stylized Plants." All the *fleurons* used by Richardson are, in fact, pieces of existing Caslon type. Richardson simply breaks up the rows of "Long Primer Flowers" usually reserved for decorative borders and, in the case of Lovelace's constellation, deploys his stock of asterisks in a unique manner. For an illustration of William Caslon's decorative borders, see Anne C. Henry, "The Re-mark-able rise of '. . .'," 131.

50. Several books on Richardson carefully reproduce printer's ornaments from *Clarissa* as decoration, without explicitly glossing these icons as part of his literary text. See the ornamentation in Margaret Anne Doody and Peter Sabor, eds., *Samuel Richardson: Tercentenary Essays* (Cambridge University Press, 1989) and Tassie Gwilliam's *Samuel Richardson's Fictions of Gender* (Stanford University Press, 1993).

51. In a paper entitled "Clarissa's Father's House" given at the Thirty-Sixth Annual Meeting of the Johnson Society of the Central Region in April 1995, Patricia Brückmann first directed my attention to the symbolism of the garden ornaments in the description of the Dover Street residence.

52. At least three critics have noted the allusion to Ovid in this ornament: John Carroll, "Lovelace as Tragic Hero," *University of Toronto Quarterly* 42.1 (1972), 14–25, at 19; Jocelyn Harris, "Richardson: Original or Learned Genius?" in Doody and Sabor, eds., *Tercentenary Essays*, 188–202, at 190; and Howard D. Weinbrot, "Clarissa, Elias Brand and Death by Parentheses," in *New Essays on Samuel Richardson*, 117–40, at 126. The same emblematic tailpiece also appears in Volumes VI and VIII of the third edition, though suggestively not in the volumes prior to the rape scene.

53. Jocelyn Harris, "Richardson: Original or Learned Genius?" 126.

54. M. B. Parkes, *Pause and Effect: An Introduction to the History of Punctuation in the West* (Berkeley and Los Angeles: University of California Press, 1993), 61.

6 Sarah Fielding's "David Simple"

1. Swift, "On Poetry: A Rapsody," lines 93–94; quoted from *The Writings of Jonathan Swift*, ed. Robert A. Greenberg and William B. Piper (New York and London: Norton, 1973), 569.
2. The first edition of the anonymously published *The Adventures of David Simple: Containing an Account of His Travels through the Cities of London and Westminster, in Search of a Real Friend. By a Lady* (London: Printed for A. Millar, 1744) appeared in May of 1744. The second edition appeared a few months later, in July: *The Adventures of David Simple: Containing an Account of His Travels through the Cities of London and Westminster, in Search of a Real Friend. By a Lady. The Second Edition, Revised and Corrected by Henry Fielding, Esq.* (London: Printed for A. Millar, 1744). This second edition replaces Sarah Fielding's original preface with one authored by her brother.
3. Appearing under the title *Adventures in Search of A Real Friend* (London: G. Virtue, 1822) this edition of *David Simple* claims Henry Fielding as its author. Amusingly, the name of the publisher encourages us to judge this misattribution as a mistake rather than a calculated marketing ploy.
4. Peter Sabor notes in the introduction to his University Press of Kentucky edition (Lexington, KY, 1998) of *The Adventures of David Simple and Volume the Last* that already the sales of the novel's first edition, "which at six shillings cost the same as *Joseph Andrews*, must have been brisk, since a second edition appeared only ten weeks later" (x).
5. Sabor, *ibid.*, xxvii.
6. Sarah Fielding, *The Adventures of David Simple*, ed. Malcolm Kelsall (Oxford University Press, 1969), in "Note on the Text," xx and xxi.
7. Robert S. Hunting echoes Henry Fielding's condescending assessment of Sarah Fielding's writing in his description of the substantive changes in the second edition: "changes actuated by Fielding's knowledge of law"; "elevation of diction"; "correction" of fact; and the insertion of a "more masculine" irony. See Hunting's article "Fielding's Revisions of *David Simple*," Boston University Studies in English 3 (1957), 117–21. Similarly, despite the implied focus of his 1939 Harvard dissertation entitled "The Life and Works of Sarah Fielding", Herman O. Werner, Jr. compares the two editions of *David Simple* in a lengthy appendix for the purposes of enumerating "any definite characteristics of [Henry] Fielding's writing illustrated therein" (Appendix B, 299). See also, Aurélien Digeon, "Autour de Fielding II: Fielding, conseiller littéraire de sa soeur, est portraituré par elle en retour," *Revue Germanique* 11 (1920), 353–62.
8. Peter Sabor's edition of *David Simple* faithfully reproduces her original punctuation (down to the lengths of the broken and unbroken dashes) and its subsequent visual design. Until the appearance of Sabor's edition in 1998, Henry Fielding's corrected edition had been the standard text of *David Simple* and the only one in print since 1744.
9. Henry Fielding, *Preface* to *David Simple*, second edition, vii.
10. Henry Fielding's use of the word "impression" here is, in fact, misleading. Henry

Fielding did not just "correct" his sister's text while it remained in standing type at the printer's. The bibliographical distinctions (such as catch-words, spacing, etc.) between Sarah and Henry Fielding's texts, indicate that the second edition is substantially reset. If a first edition text, perhaps with Henry Fielding's written-in corrections, was used as the copy-text for the printing of the second edition, that would explain why the page numbers of the second edition correspond so closely to those of the first – making it appear, at first glance, like a second impression.

11. Peter Sabor offers a meticulous list of the "Substantial Variants Between the First and the Second Edition" as Appendix II to his edition of *David Simple* (350–66). This lengthy list gives an accurate indication of the extent of Henry's interventions as well as the minuteness of each pernickety correction of diction and phraseology. Alterations in bibliographical accidentals (spelling, punctuation, capitals, italics) are not recorded on Sabor's list and would presumably increase its length much further.
12. Kelsall, ed., "Note on the Text," *Adventures*, xix.
13. Sabor, ed., introduction to *Adventures and Volume the Last*, xxix. Sabor notes that with these corrections "he is again making Sarah Fielding write more like himself."
14. See also note 10.
15. Kelsall, ed., "Note on the Text," xix.
16. *Ibid.*
17. See especially the chapter "The Technology of Printing and the Stabilization of the Symbols," in Parkes, *Pause and Effect*, 50–61.
18. Hunter, "Typology to Type," 49.
19. Gaskell, *New Introduction to Bibliography*, 339; my emphasis.
20. Shakespeare scholarship abounds with problematic variations in the punctuation of different plays, presumably as a result of the involvement of multiple compositors. See, for example, C[harlton] T. Hinman, *Printing and Proofreading of the First Folio of Shakespeare*, 2 vols. (Oxford: Clarendon Press, 1963), II, 250. Parkes neatly sums up Hinman's argument that "the distribution of work among compositors setting the first folio of Shakespeare's plays explains the presence of semicolons on some pages of *Hamlet* and *Henry VIII* but not others" (53).
21. Martin C. Battestin, "Fielding's Novels and the Wesleyan Edition: Some Principles and Problems," in G. E. Bentley, Jr., ed., *Editing Eighteenth-Century Novels* (Toronto: The Committee for the Conference on Editorial Problems, 1975), 9–30. Henry Fielding's orchestration of his own accidentals thus appears somewhat ironic in view of his objections to his sister's preferred use of the dash.
22. Page 32 of Volume II in the second edition of *David Simple* includes two notable exceptions to Henry Fielding's progressive elimination of his sister's dashes: on this page Henry Fielding adds two dashes which do not appear in the original text. I cannot explain this momentary lapse in Henry Fielding's otherwise-consistent editorial approach.
23. *David Simple*, 1st edn., II, 195. All further quotations from the text of *David Simple* refer to this, the first, edition and will be cited parenthetically by volume and page number.

24. This "realist" application of the dash appears the least problematic for Henry Fielding; when he leaves the original dashes intact they often serve to indicate such auditory pauses.
25. See, for example, John Mullan's discussion of this characteristic feature of sentimental fiction throughout *Sentiment and Sociability: The Language of Feeling in the Eighteenth Century* (Oxford: Clarendon Press, 1988).
26. Samuel Johnson, *Dictionary of the English Language* (London, 1755; Harlow: Longman Group, 1990).
27. Attempts at the formal codification of punctuation late in the century reflect these same dominant prejudices against the dash. Joseph Robertson, author of *An Essay on Punctuation*, describes the dash as "frequently used by hasty and incoherent writers, in a very capricious and arbitrary manner instead of the regular point" (2nd edn., 1786). Quoted in Vivienne Mylne, "The Punctuation of Dialogue in Eighteenth-Century French and English Fiction," *The Library* 1 (1979), 43–61, at 60.
28. Some of Henry Fielding's alterations of the verbal text of *David Simple*, namely his removal of Sarah's footnotes (notes which explicitly name the literary texts to which she alludes), corroborate the theory that his assessment of the reading level of the novel's audience differed from hers. For his part, Henry Fielding felt that when quoting authors such as Shakespeare or Pope, one need not insult the reader with a footnote.
29. Hunter, *Before Novels*, 336.
30. *The Life, Travels, and Adventures of Christopher Wagstaff, Gentleman, Grandfather to Tristram Shandy. Originally published in the latter end of the last century* (London: Printed for J. Hinxman, 1762).
31. Ian Watt, "The Comic Syntax of *Tristram Shandy*," in Howard Anderson and John S. Shea, eds., *Studies in Criticism and Aesthetics, 1660–1800: Essays in Honor of Samuel Holt Monk* (Minneapolis: University of Minnesota Press, 1967), 315–31, at 320.
32. This is not to say that Sarah Fielding and Laurence Sterne share the same hermeneutic assumption about the ability of print to accurately mimic conversation. As Roger Moss points out, Sterne's unpredictable punctuation challenges a reader's belief in the "direct correlation between the physical facts of language (pauses, breathing, tone) and their spatial representation" on the printed page. Moss, "Sterne's Punctuation," 184. Unlike *Tristram Shandy*, *David Simple* does not seek to expose the limitations of the print medium, but rather to exploit its range of verbal and visual possibilities.
33. Watt, "Comic Syntax ," 320.
34. Those who, in the latter end of the century, continued to see the dash as a telltale mark of amateurish writing thought Sterne's work particularly objectionable. Indeed, in *Elements of Punctuation*, David Steele's discussion of the "needless" use of the dash singles out Sterne for criticism: "for I know of no other author, whose works have been so terribly be-dashed, or who has been generally considered more unintelligible" (London, 1786), 58, n. a; quoted in Mylne, "Punctuation of Dialogue," *Library*, 60.

35. Malcolm Kelsall also appears to recognize a Richardsonian characteristic in Sarah Fielding's use of the dash: "Above all, Henry dashed out Sarah's dashes. These corrections are minute, but frequent. One wonders what he would have done with Richardson" (Kelsall, ed., "Note on the Text," xxiii).
36. Mylne, "Punctuation of Dialogue," *Library*, 60.
37. Price, "Samuel Richardson's Type Font Manipulation," esp. 122–28, quoted at 124 and 127.
38. Parkes, *Pause and Effect*, 93.
39. In *Samuel Richardson's Theory of Fiction* (The Hague and Paris: Mouton, 1971), Donald L. Ball locates the dash as a "device" Richardson first employs in *Pamela* "to increase conversational effect" (Appendix B, 295).
40. In his "Note on the Text" to the Oxford World's Classics *Pamela*, Thomas Keymer tempers a recognition of the expressive length-variations in the Richardsonian dash with pragmatism: "the first edition's use of many fractionally different dash-lengths, and its occasional alternative use of strings of hyphens suggests nothing more interesting than that Richardson's employment of dashes as an author had overrun his stock of them as a printer" (xxxvi).
41. Mylne, "Punctuation of Dialogue," *Library*, 60–61.
42. Vivienne Mylne, "Prévost's Translation of Dialogue in Richardson's *Clarissa*," *Franco British Studies* 1 (Spring 1986), 1–11, at 1.
43. Joe Bray, "'Attending to the *Minute*': Richardson's Revisions of Italics in *Pamela*," in Bray, Handley, and Henry, eds., *Ma(r)king the Text*, 105–19.
44. The overall division of Sarah Fielding's novel into stylistically distinct halves might explain why she follows the Richardsonian model of punctuation in the second volume more closely than in the first. While the first half of *David Simple* follows a panoramic Fieldingesque pattern, the second narrows its subject to four characters and their first-person narratives – making it stylistically more Richardsonian in both scope and sentiment.
45. For a detailed analysis of this verbal–visual transformation see Mylne, "Prévost's Translation," *Franco-British Studies*.
46. Mylne, "Punctuation of Dialogue," *Library*, 61; "Prévost's Translation," *Franco-British Studies*, 1.
47. Mylne, "Punctuation of Dialogue," *Library*, 61.
48. *The Correspondence of Henry and Sarah Fielding*, ed. Martin C. Battestin and Clive T. Probyn (Oxford: Clarendon Press, 1993), 144–49.
49. Battestin and Probyn appear, in fact, to take this view. In a footnote to this letter in the *Correspondence* they point a reader to the *Preface* in the second edition of *David Simple* for "HF's accurate description of his sister's grammatical 'carelessness'" (150, n.7).
50. In fact, Fredson Bowers, in his "Textual Introduction" to the Wesleyan Edition of *Joseph Andrews*, ed. Martin C. Battestin (Oxford: Clarendon Press, 1967), holds that for this novel the "first edition represents for the accidentals" the "supreme authority" as a copy text ([xxxix]–xlvii, at xli). Bowers explains that "when [Henry] sent the marked-up pages of the first edition to the press as copy for the second printing, there is no evidence that in any major respect he

altered the accidentals that had passed his scrutiny in the original proof sheets" (xl).
51. See Appendix v to the Wesleyan Edition of *Joseph Andrews* (385).
52. The plate is reminiscent of the continental illustrations of Fielding which exploited the novelist's flair for creating compromising narrative situations for his female characters. For example, Philip Stewart describes a 1750 plate by Gravelot which illustrates the scene in *Tom Jones* where Tom rescues Mrs. Waters, "stripped half naked," from Northerton who is using a garter to tie her to a tree. "There too," notes Stewart, "the woman's breasts, of which Fielding makes much, are exposed to Tom's gaze" (*Engraven Desire*, 356, n.16). According to Stewart, Gravelot's illustration appeared in *Histoires de Tom Jones*, 4 vols. (Amsterdam, 1750), II, 124.
53. See Stewart's discussion of "tandem editions of Boccaccio in Italian and French in 1757" (*ibid.*, 323–33).

7 The list and index

1. George C. Williams, *Adaptation and Natural Selection* (Princeton University Press, 1966), quoted in Richard Dawkins, *The Extended Phenotype* (Oxford University Press, 1982), 59.
2. Robert Irwin, "Your Novel Needs Indexing," in John Fowles and A. L. Kennedy, eds., *New Writing 9* (New York: Vintage, 2000), 60–79. With his tongue, if not firmly at least frequently, in his cheek, Irwin cites an impressively (and surprisingly) long list of indexes in modern novels, from George Gissing's *The Private Papers of Henry Ryecroft* (1903) to Alain de Botton's *Kiss and Tell* (1995).
3. Irwin, "Your Novel," 72.
4. Eaves and Kimpel, *Samuel Richardson*, 11. Richardson's apprenticeship lasted from 1 July 1706 to 2 July 1713.
5. Prompted by the Dublin piracy of *Grandison* in November 1753, Richardson hurriedly printed the first and second editions – a duodecimo edition in seven volumes and a more luxurious octavo edition in six volumes – concurrently over the next five months. Richardson employed the services of several other printing shops for the rapid production of these first two editions. Such collaboration was not uncommon and would not have undermined Richardson's ultimate control over the visual design of *Grandison*. Richardson printed a third, revised edition in duodecimo in March 1754, and was near completing a fourth edition (also in duodecimo) when he died in July 1761. The paratextual frame of catalogues under discussion is present in every edition printed before his death. For further details about *Grandison*'s production and publication history see Sale, *Bibliographical Record*, 65–93 and Jocelyn Harris, "The Reviser Observed: The Last Volume of *Sir Charles Grandison*," *Studies in Bibliography* 29 (1976), 1–31.
6. Jonathan Swift, *Gulliver's Travels*, ed. Albert J. Rivero, 233.
7. C. J. Rawson, *Gulliver and the Gentle Reader: Studies in Swift and our Time* (London and Boston, MA: Routledge and Kegan Paul, 1973), 101 and 102.
8. Some authors, such as Alexander Pope and Samuel Richardson, were attentive to the placement of even capital letters in the printing of their texts. See Stuber,

"Introduction: Text, Writer, Reader, World," in *The Clarissa Project*, esp. 19–21, and Foxon, *Pope and the Early Eighteenth-Century Book Trade*. This means, of course, that there is nothing to prevent the supposition that Swift, too, crowds this list with capital letters deliberately. Like the conventions of punctuation, the placement of capitals was not regulated by strict grammatical rules and allowed for manipulation by a meticulous author – if aided and abetted by the book's printing house.

9. Kevin L. Cope, "Richardson the Advisor," in *New Essays on Samuel Richardson*, ed. Albert J. Rivero (New York: St. Martin's Press, 1996), 27–28. Cope's citations refer to the following editions: *Pamela*, ed. George Saintsbury (London: Dent, 1914; reprinted 1955) and *Clarissa, or the History of a Young Lady*, ed. Angus Ross (Harmondsworth: Penguin, 1985).

10. *Clarissa*, ed. Angus Ross, 1385, 1383, and 1384. References in this chapter are to this Penguin edition.

11. For a sample of the monstrosities on display in the curiosity cabinets of eighteenth-century Europe, see Barbara Maria Stafford, *Artful Science: Enlightenment and the Eclipse of Visual Education* (London and Cambridge, MA: MIT Press, 1994), particularly the engraving from Georges-Louis Leclerc's *Histoire Naturelle* (1749) entitled "Pickled Monsters," which illustrates the keeping of small deformed animals and body parts in liquid spirits (261). For a discussion of the related popular interest in displaying monsters at fairs, see Dennis Todd, *Imagining Monsters*, esp. 145–48.

12. The comparison to Swift is one that Richardson makes himself in a footnote to *Clarissa* a few pages hence. There he compares his description of the dying Sinclair (another catalogue of disconnected bodily parts) to the grotesque inventory of the female body in Swift's *The Lady's Dressing Room* (Penguin edn., at 1388). For an extended discussion of this allusion to Swift see Jocelyn Harris, "Grotesque, Classical and Pornographic Bodies in Clarissa," in Albert J. Rivero, ed., *New Essays on Samuel Richardson*, 101–16.

13. Nigel Dennis, "Swift and Defoe," in Robert A. Greenberg and William B. Piper, eds., *The Writings of Jonathan Swift* (New York and London: Norton, 1973), 661–69, at 663.

14. Henry Fielding, *Joseph Andrews*, 2 vols. (London, 1742), II, 33. In this instance, the graphic effect is accurately rendered in the printing of many modern editions: see, for example, the Wesleyan Edition of *Joseph Andrews*, 204, or the World Classics paperback edition derived from Battestin's earlier Wesleyan Edition and published as *Joseph Andrews and Shamela*, ed. Douglas Brooks-Davies (1980; Oxford University Press, 1990), at 181–82.

15. Richardson's letter-writing manual serves the same basic reference function as legal form books: both types of "collection" offer a representative selection of contemporary forms of address appropriate to a wide variety of occasions, in order to instruct the reader in the local application of a formalized discourse. Legal form books gather together a selection of representative examples of documents of all kinds, including articles of agreement, summaries of cases, and

wills, usually "digested" in alphabetical order. Many such form books also list short definitions of legal terminology – even calendars of court proceedings. The titles of a few of these legal reference collections offer an idea of both function and audience: *The Attorney's Compleat Pocket Book, Containing Above Four Hundred of Such Choice and Approved Precedents, in Law, Equity, and Conveyances, as an Attorney May Have Occasion for When Absent from His Office*, 5th edn., 2 vols. (London: Printed by His Majesty's Law Printer for J. Worrall, 1764); William Bohun, *The Practising Attorney; Or, Lawyer's Office: Containing, the Business of an Attorney In All Its Branches*, 2nd edn. ([London] In the Savoy: Printed by E. and R. Nutt, and R. Gosling, 1726); and Robert Gardiner, *Instructor Clericalis: Directing Clerks Both in the Court of the King's Bench and Common Pleas, in the Abbreviation and Contraction of Words*, 5 vols. (London: Printed by J. Walthoe, 1715–27). Lest anyone think that these books were consulted only by travelling lawyers and clerks, and thus largely unknown to both Richardson and his readers, the following title makes clear that form books were also aimed at the informed consumer: *Law Quibbles; Or a Treatise of the Evasions, Tricks, Turns, and Quibbles Commonly Used in the Profession of the Law, to the Prejudice of Clients, and Others*, 4th edn. ([London] In the Savoy: Printed by E. and R. Nutt, 1736). Despite such differences in titles and implied audience, all such legal form books contain similar information presented in the codified manner of an indexed manual.

16. Perhaps the most famous examples of Grubstreet's interest in the law is that specimen of Scriblerian satire dubbed *Straddling versus Stiles*, authored by the group in 1716. This mock report of a fictional lawsuit is filled with not only comically verbose legalese but also with the typographical gimmickry (black letter font etc.) evocative of the many eighteenth-century pamphlets and magazine reports of legal cases.

17. For a discussion of the related discourse of "curiosities," see Barbara M. Benedict, *Curiosity: A Cultural History of Early Modern Inquiry* (University of Chicago Press, 2001). The rise of the auction house (both Christie's and Sotheby's are eighteenth-century institutions) also derives from the age's proclivity for collections and collecting. This phenomenon, too, may have its links to the novel. See Cynthia Wall, "The English Auction: Narratives of Dismantlings," *Eighteenth-Century Studies* 31.1 (Fall 1997), 1–25.

18. See Hunter, *Before Novels* (esp. chapter 8) and his essay "Robert Boyle and the Epistemology of the Novel," *Eighteenth-Century Fiction* 2.4 (July 1990), 275–92. Although Hunter does not discuss collecting *per se*, he offers a partial trace of the impact of the scientific discourse of empiricist observation upon the genre of the novel.

19. See John Elsner, "A Collector's Model of Desire: The House and Museum of Sir John Soane," in John Elsner and Roger Cardinal, eds., *The Cultures of Collecting* (Cambridge, MA: Harvard University Press, 1994), 155–76. Sir John Soane (1753–1837) started construction on three houses on the north side of Lincoln's Inn Fields in 1792. The 1833 Act of Parliament that established Soane's residence as

a public museum stipulated that the location and arrangement of the collection be preserved and maintained.

20. Virginia Woolf, *Orlando: A Biography* (San Diego, New York, and London: Harcourt Brace, 1992), 208.
21. Alexander Pope, *The Rape of the Lock*, canto 1, line 138; Twickenham Edition of *The Poems of Alexander Pope*, in *Volume II: Rape of the Lock*, ed. Geoffrey Tillotson, 156.
22. McKeon, *Origins of the English Novel*, 20.
23. See Hunter, *Before Novels*.
24. On the relationship of the novel to the anthology, see Leah Price, *The Anthology and the Rise of the Novel: From Richardson to George Eliot* (Cambridge University Press, 2000).
25. Barbara M. Benedict, *Making the Modern Reader: Cultural Mediation in Early Modern Literary Anthologies* (Princeton University Press, 1996), 4.
26. For mention of the "visual or perceptual lists" often found in the novel's descriptions of location, see Cynthia Wall, "Details of Space: Narrative Description in Early Eighteenth-Century Novels," *Eighteenth-Century Fiction* 10.4 (July 1998), 387–405, esp. 395–96.
27. See Sale's *Master Printer* and Maslen's *Samuel Richardson of London, Printer* for inventories of plays printed on Richardson's press.
28. At least one of Richardson's contemporaries found the dramatic design unusual enough to warrant a spoof, because John Kidgell, in *The Card* (1755), imitates Richardson's list of principal persons down to the sub-heading "ITALIANS" at the bottom. Reviewed as a satirical "attack . . . chiefly leveled at the exceptional parts in the plan, characters and style of the history of *Sir Charles Grandison*," Kidgell proves that Richardson's new printerly machinery caught the attention of fellow novelists. Review of *The Card*, 117.
29. See Mark Kinkead-Weekes, *Samuel Richardson: Dramatic Novelist* (Ithaca: Cornell University Press, 1973). This is not the only study to examine the long-acknowledged dramatic features of Richardson's texts. For a comprehensive list of the range of criticism on this topic, see note 64 in Jocelyn Harris, "Introduction" to *Volume 1: Prefaces, Postscripts and Related Writings*, ed. Keymer, in Richardson, *Published Commentary*, ed. Stuber *et al.*, 1: vii–xcv, at xci–xcii.
30. The argument in *Clarissa* between Anna and Mrs. Howe over Antony Harlowe's proposal of marriage to the latter is an extreme example. This debate is recounted by Anna as a "*dialogue*" and thus claims the dramatic style of presentation as Anna's own. The whole argument is printed as a scene between speakers "M." and "D.," abbreviations for mother and daughter evocative of the conventions of a printed play (3rd edn., IV, 162–63). Although the accompanying figure is taken from the novel's third edition, all editions of *Clarissa* printed by Richardson feature this graphic layout; it is also faithfully approximated in Angus Ross's Penguin paperback, which takes the first edition as its copy text (626–30).
31. In the introduction to her edition of *The History of Sir Charles Grandison* (1972; Oxford University Press, 1986), Jocelyn Harris gathers up all the "techniques of

the stage" found in the novel, from the list of *dramatis personae* to the novel's use of stage directions and attention to costume (xv–xvi).
32. Richardson in the margins of Lady Bradshaigh's first-edition copy of *Clarissa* (III, 100). See Barchas, "Richardson on the Margins," *Annotations*, 61. As I explained in my edition of the annotations, I read such bursts of feeling as evidence of Richardson's discomfort with the epistolary genre's indeterminacy. Thomas Keymer in his *Richardson's* Clarissa *and the Eighteenth-Century Reader* (Cambridge University Press, 1992), on the other hand, attributes to Richardson pedagogical intent that, Keymer argues, mitigates this discomfort.
33. McKeon, *Origins of the English Novel*, 21.
34. For further discussion of Richardson's supposed "xenophobic" tendencies, see Ewha Chung, *Samuel Richardson's New Nation: Paragons of the Domestic Sphere and "Native" Virtue* (New York: Peter Lang, 1998), 132.
35. See Sale (*Master Printer*, 111–18), for a list of works printed by subscription on Richardson's press. Richardson's own novels were all self-financed and never printed by the subscription method. Hence none of his novels ever bore a formal subscription list.
36. Richardson to M. Defreval, 21 January 1750 (Barbauld, v, 273).
37. Since the model typified by Pope's list of subscribers continued to serve as the design standard, Richardson – and his readers – would surely have been familiar with the common practice of using larger type for uniquely important political subscribers. A subscription list such as, for example, the one in Sarah Fielding's *Familiar Letters* (1747), might also typographically distinguish those who paid extra for an edition on special paper: "*Those marked with an Asterisk* are Subscribers for Royal Paper.*" This practice does not appear to gloss the *Grandison* list.
38. Richardson to M. Defreval, 21 January 1750 (Barbauld, v, 273).
39. For a discussion of Richardson's frantic period of revision, possibly in standing type, of the novel's final volume and a correspondence with, among others, Lady Bradshaigh that may have influenced the nature of his revisions, see Harris, "The Reviser Observed," quoted at 14 and 4.
40. Anonymous, *Critical Remarks on Sir Charles Grandison*, 20. This text has been reprinted as Volume XIII of *Richardsoniana* in the series The Life and Times of Seven Major British Writers (New York: Garland, 1975).
41. For a detailed bibliographical description of the contents of these three *Grandison* editions see Sale, *A Bibliographical Record*, 65–85; and Harris "The Reviser Observed."
42. Citing evidence from Richardson's accounting records, William Sale claims that it was not unusual for the paper expense of printing a book to amount to three-fifths of the total printing cost (*Master Printer*, 25).
43. See Sale's article "A Bibliographical Note on Richardson's *Clarissa*," which describes Richardson's laborious rearrangement of signatures and cancellation of leaves to save paper in the third and fourth volumes of the first edition of *Clarissa*.

44. Reviews of *Grandison*, *Gentleman's Magazine* 23 (November 1753), 543; and *Monthly Review* 10 (January 1754), 70–71. Richardson's advertising campaign was limited to the notice announcing the publication of the final volumes of the octavo and duodecimo editions in the *Public Advertiser* (14 March 1754). This conventional announcement amounts to a quasi-facsimile description of the title pages of the final volumes which includes brief mention of the fact that "to these volumes are added *An Historical and Characteristical Index*."
45. Jocelyn Harris, "Note on the Text," *Grandison*, xxxvii. Ironically, in the light of Richardson's own financial disincentives, the choice to omit the index from the Oxford edition was entirely a concession to cost.
46. See the first volume of the *Published Commentary*, intro. Harris and ed. Keymer, 276–85. The "Six Original Letters upon Duelling" were first published in the opening volume of the short-lived *Candid Review and Literary Repository* (March 1765), 227–31.
47. Harris, "Introduction" to vol. 1 of *Published Commentary*, lxxviii and lxxxi. For her extensive discussion of duelling in Richardson's fictions, see lxxvi–lxxxiv.
48. The "Hints of Prefaces" are letters and materials found among the Richardson manuscripts in the Forster Collection at the Victoria and Albert Museum under that heading (FM xv, 2, ff. 50–57). A transcript is supplied in vol. 1 of *Published Commentary*, 312–36.
49. Harris, "Introduction," *Published Commentary*, lxxxiii.
50. Admittedly, some of Richardson's readers recognized the barbarity of duelling even in this scene. In her marginal annotations Lady Bradshaigh records her reaction: "A most enormous blot in Col.^{l} Mordens character" (Barchas, *The Annotations*, 139).
51. This is not to say, of course, that Richardson's index always succeeds in making readers "see" either the barbarity of duelling or the heroism inherent in Charles's refusal. John Kidgell's hero in *The Card*, for example, accepts a challenge to a duel "(and not a Box of the Ear instead of it*) . . . [Footnote] *A Method of duelling peculiar to his cousin *Grandison*" (II, 94).
52. The corrective footnote in the third edition of *Clarissa* reads:

> - (*a*) Several worthy persons have wished, that the heinous Practice of
> - Duelling had been more forcibly discouraged, by way of Note, at the
> - Conclusion of a Work, designed to recommend the *highest and most important Doctrines of Christianity*. It is humbly presumed, that those persons have not sufficiently attended to what is already done on that subject in Vol. II. p. 60. and in Vol. VIII. Letters x. xxxvii. xxxviii. xxxix.* (VIII, 276)

53. Robert DeMaria, Jr., "Samuel Johnson and the Reading Revolution," *Eighteenth-Century Life* 16 (November 1992), 86–102. For DeMaria's more

extended treatment of how the personal reading history of Samuel Johnson functions as a lens through which to view the different habits and philosophies of private reading operating in eighteenth-century England, see his *Samuel Johnson and the Life of Reading* (Baltimore: Johns Hopkins University Press, 1997).

54. In 1755 Richardson offered to the public his *A Collection of the Moral and Instructive Sentiments, Maxims, Cautions and Reflections Contained in the Histories of Pamela, Clarissa, and Sir Charles Grandison* as a free-standing index-like compendium to all three of his novels. The 1755 *Collection* has been reprinted as the third volume of *Published Commentary on* Clarissa, with an introduction by John Dussinger and afterword by Ann Jessie Van Sant.

55. William Beatty Warner, *Reading Clarissa*, 194.

56. Quoted from *Letters of Samuel Johnson*, ed. Bruce Redford, 5 vols. (Princeton University Press, 1992), I, 47–48.

57. Johnson was not the only one to express concern about Richardson's prolixity. *The Monthly Review* 10 (January 1754) wryly notes before having seen the completed work of *Grandison* that certain readers already "cry out for an abridgement to seven tedious volumes," 70.

58. The "ludicrously detailed table of contents" to the anonymous *The Country Gentleman's Companion . . . By a Country Gentleman, From His Own Experience*, 2 vols. (London: Printed for the author, 1753) offers a contemporary example of a self-consciously exhaustive table of contents which, by virtue of its location at the back, approximates the function of an index because it guides re-entry to the text. Stephen Weissman, "Occasional List No. 107. Rare Books and Manuscripts. Part VI: Sk to Z" (New York: Ximenes Rare Books, 1994), item 51 in this sale catalogue.

59. Swift, *A Tale of a Tub*, 8th edn. (Dublin: Printed by S. Powell, 1741), section VII; and Pope, *Dunciad*, Book I, line 279.

60. The previously mentioned duodecimo edition of *Life and Adventures of Mrs. Christian Davies* (London: Printed for and sold by R. Montagu, 1740) provides a good example of a Grubstreet index. A Defoe-esque account of one woman's escapades as a soldier, this novel is indexed according to the battles and cities mentioned in it. The index thus lends this minor work of autobiographical fiction the appearance of a genuine military history.

61. Roger D. Lund, "The Eel of Science: Index Learning, Scriblerian Satire, and the Rise of Information Culture," *Eighteenth-Century Life* 22.2 (May 1998), 18–42, at 19 and 21.

62. Eliza Haywood, *Memoirs of a Certain Island Adjacent to the Kingdom of Utopia*, 2 vols. (London: Printed and sold by all the booksellers of London and Westminster, 1725).

63. Again, the Scriblerians pose an exception to the conventional workings of the book trade: in response to absurd, anti-Catholic readings of Pope's *Rape of the Lock* the group quickly produced their own "papist" reading, entitled "A Key to the Lock" (1714).

64. In his correspondence, Richardson suggests that the *Collection of Sentiments* was, in fact, conceived as a text which could be read and used independently: "I have taken much pains in the table of sentiments I mentioned. Many of my friends wish to see it printed by itself, as a collection of maxims, aphorisms, &c. which they think would be of service to the world, independent of the history, as they relate to life and manners." Richardson to M. Defreval, 21 January 1750 (Barbauld, v, 274).
65. Lund, "Eel of Science," 25.
66. For example, the popular family bible, S. Smith, ed., *The Compleat History of the Old and New Testament, Or, a Family Bible with Critical and Explanatory Annotations, Extracted from the Writings of the Most Celebrated Authors . . . Together with Maps, Cuts, & Curiously Design'd and Engrav'd in Copper. By S. Smith . . .* , 2 vols. (London, Printed by W. Rayner, 1735–37), contains an extensive apparatus which includes "The HISTORY of the Lives, Actions . . . of Jesus and Apostles and answers to objections" as well as "An Index to the Holy Bible" arranged alphabetically by place names and names of biblical characters. As numerous biblical scholars have noted, indexes to bibles were (and still are) extremely powerful means of controlling interpretation. Just as Richardson did not invent indexing, neither did he invent the interpretive application of an index. As with his use of the folding illustration and running marginal annotations in the 1751 *Clarissa*, Richardson mines print culture for useful forms, selecting for fictional adaptation those printed designs that will serve his purpose.
67. The fact that the *Tour* is organized as an epistolary narrative makes it a particularly close textual kin of *Grandison* with its reference-text machinery.
68. Anonymous, *Critical Remarks on* Sir Charles Grandison, 5.
69. Ibid., 53.

Coda

1. See the prefatory comments by Charles Whibley to *A Facsimile Reproduction of a Unique Catalogue of Laurence Sterne's Library* (New York: Edgar H. Wells & Co., 1930), 9.
2. *Ibid.* From the 1930 facsimile of the catalogue's original title page.
3. Wayne Booth, "Did Sterne Complete *Tristram Shandy*?," *Modern Philology* 48 (1951), 172–78.
4. Novels, admittedly, quickly disappear from shelves. Thus it is possible that the final volume of *Grandison* was a chance survivor from a complete set. Yet, even if Sterne retained the isolated index volume after he discarded, lost, or gifted the other six, this too implies particular interest.
5. See: http://www.gutenberg.net/.
6. A good example of the modified Web-based procedure is *Early English Books Online* (Bell and Howell Information [formerly UMI], 1999) http://www.umi.com/eebo/. It is, at present, a database of roughly 125,000 historical literary works, digitalized from the pre-existing *Early English Books* microfilm collection published by UMI. Although there are still teething problems, *EEBO* offers subscribers digital page-by-page access to titles listed in

Pollard & Redgrave's *Short-Title Catalogue* (1475–1640), Wing's *Short-Title Catalogue* (1641–1700), and the *Thomason Tracts* (1640–61).

7. *The William Blake Archive* is remarkable for its ability to search within a literary text for the images embedded in its original illustrations (i.e. under "cloud," "cherub," or "worm"). See: http://www.blakearchive.org/.

8. See: http://jefferson.village.virginia.edu/rossetti/index.html/.

9. Yale's Beinecke Library's collection of digital images is, among image databases of rare book collections, possibly the most impressive one to date. Using the thousands of photo negatives that the library had kept through the years from prior requests for duplication from their collections, the Beineke has built a formidable e-library of images. Via the Beinecke library's main Web site (http://www.library.yale.edu/beinecke/) one can search by author, title, and key word (though not yet by image type, as in the Blake archive) thousands of still photographs, pages of manuscripts, and pages of books from their collection. A search can bring up 300 thumbnail pictures, each of which can be opened to reveal a full-screen image. Since past user-demand, rather than a systematic editorial procedure, generated the images selected for inclusion in the database, the resulting shape of the Beinecke's nascent image bank remains, of course, spotty and chaotic.

10. Better known for his radically original fiction writing, Nicholson Baker has, starting with a *New Yorker* article about the evils of dumping old card catalogues in 1994, taken on what he sees as the modern library's "assault on paper" in favor of microfilm and digital scanning. His title, *Double Fold*, refers to the "acid test" routinely performed by various libraries on twentieth-century wood-pulp books and periodicals to ascertain whether a volume has become too brittle for use. In the double-fold test you simply dog-ear a page and fold it back and forth a number of times (the number depends upon the library's local standard) to see if it breaks off. No lead-pencil Luddite, Baker is in favor of digital technology and the photo-duplication of fragile texts; he simply argues that the charm, cultural evidence, and graphic value of old newspapers deserve preservation and that the "brittle" pages of these texts are actually not deteriorating as fast as claimed. He asks that libraries continue to warehouse these still-useful items rather than discard them for pulping.

11. See Paul Saenger, *Space Between Words: The Origins of Silent Reading* (Stanford University Press, 1997). At the time of publication, Saenger was Curator of Rare Books at the Newberry Library, Chicago.

12. William Safire's newspaper column was entitled "Squeezewords: Cramming it Together as the Wave of the Future," *New York Times Magazine* (6 February 2002), section 6, page 28.

13. Jakob Nielsen and Marie Tahir, *Homepage Usability: 50 Websites Deconstructed* (Indianapolis: New Riders, 2001).

Works cited

Anthologies and reference texts are listed under the editor's name, where known. Otherwise such collections are listed by title. Titles and imprint information to early editions have been listed in accordance with modern convention that abbreviates both. The following entries have been grouped under five headings: "Periodicals and Reviews," "Early Editions"; "Modern Editions"; "Critical and Secondary Works"; and "Websites."

Periodicals and Reviews

Reprinting of the 1747–8 correspondence between Elizabeth Carter and Samuel Richardson. *The Monthly Magazine* 33 (1812), 533–35.
Review of *The Card*. *The Monthly Review* 12 (1755), 117–21.
Review of *Clarissa*. *The Gentleman's Magazine* 19 (August 1749), 348–49.
Reviews of *Grandison*. *The Gentleman's Magazine* 23 (November 1753), 543.
  The Monthly Review 10 (January 1754), 70–71.

Early Editions

Addison, Joseph, and Sir Richard Steele. *Spectator*. 9th edn. 8 vols. London: Printed for J. Tonson, 1729.
  The Tatler. No. 238. London: 17 October 1710.
Alcock, John. *Six Suites of Easy Lessons for the Harpsicord or Spinet, with a Trumpet Piece*. London: Printed for the author, 1741.
An Antidote against Melancholy. Being a Collection of Fourscore Merry Songs, Wherein Those of the Same Subject and Key Are Placed in Agreeable Succession in Relation to the Different Measures of Time, After the Manner of Suits [sic] of Lessons. London: Printed for Daniel Brown, 1749.
Anonymous. *The Bloody Game at Cards. As It Was Played betwixt the King of Hearts. And the Rest of His Suite, against the Residue of the Packe of Cards. Wherein Is Discovered Where Faire Play; Was Plaid and Where Was Fowle*. London: [s.n.] 1643.

Critical Remarks on Sir Charles Grandison, Clarissa and Pamela . . . By a Lover of Virtue. London: Printed for J. Dowse, 1754.

The Country Gentleman's Companion. In Two Volumes . . . Contains, I. Of the Horse in General. II. Of Riding in General . . . XVIII. Of Taking All Sorts of Fish. By a Country Gentleman, from His Own Experience. 2 vols. London: Printed for the author, and sold by T. Trye . . . , 1753.

[formerly attributed to Sarah Fielding]. *The History of Betty Barnes*. 2 vols. London: Printed for D. Wilson and T. Durham, 1753.

[formerly attributed to Daniel Defoe]. *Life and Adventures of Mrs. Christian Davies, Commonly Called Mother Ross; Who, in Several Campaigns under King William and the Late Duke of Marlborough, in the Quality of a Foot-Soldier and Dragoon, Gave Many Signal Proofs of an Unparalleled Courage and Personal Bravery. Taken from her Own Mouth When a Pensioner of Chelsea-Hospital*. London: Printed for C. Welch in Chelsea, 1740.

[formerly attributed to Daniel Defoe]. *Life and Adventures of Mrs. Christian Davies, Commonly Called Mother Ross . . .* London: Printed for and sold by R. Montagu, 1740.

The Life and Memoirs of Mr. Ephraim Tristram Bates, Commonly called Corporal Bates, a broken-hearted soldier. London: Printed by Malachi ****, for Edith Bates . . . and sold by W. Owen, 1756.

The Life of Pamela. Being a Full and Particular Relation of the Birth and Advancement of that Fortunate and Beautiful Young Damsel. London: Printed for C. Whitefield, 1741.

Private Letters from an American in England to his Friends in America. London: Printed for J. Almon, 1769.

The Attorney's Compleat Pocket Book, Containing Above Four Hundred of Such Choice and Approved Precedents, in Law, Equity, and Conveyances, as an Attorney may have Occasion for When Absent from His Office. 5th edn. 2 vols. London: Printed by His Majesty's Law Printer for J. Worrall, 1764.

Babell, William. *Suits [sic] of the Most Celebrated Lessons Collected and Fitted to the Harpsicord or Spinet*. London: I. Walsh and I. Hare, 1717.

Barker, Mrs. Jane. *Love Intrigues: Or, the History of the Amours of Bosvil and Galesia as related to Lucasia, in St. Germains Garden. A Novel. Written by a Young Lady*. London: Printed for E. Curll; and C. Crownfield, at Cambridge, 1713.

A Patch-Work Screen for the Ladies; Or, Love and Virtue Recommended: in a Collection of Instructive Novels. Related after a Manner Intirely New, and Interspersed with Rural Poems, Describing the Innocence of a Country-Life. By Mrs. Jane Barker. London: Printed for E. Curll; and T. Payne, 1723.

Bickham, George. *The Highlanders Medley, or the Duke Triumphant*. [engraving, 1746].

Bohun, William. *The Practising Attorney; or, Lawyer's Office: Containing, the Business of an Attorney In all its Branches*, 2nd edn. [London] In the Savoy: Printed by E. and R. Nutt, and R. Gosling, 1726.

Bond, William [also attributed to Daniel Defoe]. *The History of the Life and Adventures of Mr. Duncan Campbell*. 2nd edn. London: Printed for E. Curll, 1720.

[attributed to Defoe]. *The Supernatural Philosopher: Or, The Mysteries of Magick . . . Unfolded by William Bond*. London, 1728.

Brontë, Charlotte. *Jane Eyre*. 2nd edn. 3 vols. London: Smith, Elder and Co., Cornhill, 1848.

A Collection of the Choicest Songs and Dialogues. London, 174? Unique. [Unique bound bundle of individual sheet music found in the Special Collections Research Center, the University of Chicago Library, under call number M1738.C79.]

Coventry, Francis. *The History of Pompey the Little: Or The Life and Adventures of a Lap-Dog*. London: Printed for M. Cooper, at the Globe in Paternoster Row, 1751.

Croft, Sir Herbert. *Love and Madness, A Story Too True. In a Series of Letters, Between Parties Whose Names Would Perhaps Be Mentioned Were They Less Known or Less Lamented*. 4th edn. Dublin: Printed for the proprietor, 1786.

de Bergerac, Cyrano. *The Comical History of the States and Empires of the World of the Moon*. Trans. A. Lovell. London: Printed for Henry Rhodes, 1687.

de Bressay, Marquise. *Letters from Julia, the Daughter of Augustus, to Ovid. A Manuscript Discovered at Herculaneum*. London: Printed for Lockyer Davis, 1753.

de Mondonville, Jean Joseph Cassanea. *Six Sonatas or Lessons for the Harpsicord Which May Be Accompanied with a Violin or German Flute*. London: Printed for I. Walsh, 1753.

Defoe, Daniel. *The Farther Adventures of Robinson Crusoe: Being the Second and Last Part of his Life* . . . London: Printed for W. Taylor, 1719.

The Fortunate Mistress: Or, a History of the Life and Vast Variety of Fortunes of Mademoiselle de Beleau . . . Being the Person known by the Name of the Lady Roxana, in the Time of King Charles II. London: Printed for T. Warner . . . , 1724.

The Fortunes and Misfortunes of the Famous Moll Flanders, &c. London: Printed for and sold by W. Chetwood . . . , 1722.

Jure Divino: A Satyr. In Twelve Books. By the Author of the True-Born-Englishman. London: [s.n.], 1706.

The Life and Strange Surprizing Adventures of Robinson Crusoe, of York, Mariner. London: Printed for W. Taylor, 1719.

A New Voyage Round the World, by a Course Never Sailed Before. London: Printed for A. Bettesworth . . . , 1725.

Serious Reflections During the Life and Surprising Adventures of Robinson Crusoe: with His Vision of the Angelick World. London: Printed for W. Taylor, 1720.

A Tour Thro' the Whole Island of Great Britain. 3rd edn. 4 vols. London: Printed for J. Osborne . . . , 1742.

[*Works*] *A True Collection of the Writings of the Author of The True Born English-man. Corrected by Himself*. London: Printed, and are to be sold by most booksellers in London and Westminster, 1703.

Donaldson, William. *The Life and Adventures of Sir Bartholomew Sapskull, Baronet. Nearly Allied To Most of the Great Men in the Three Kingdoms. By Somebody*. 2 vols. London: Printed for J. Williams, 1768.

Dunton, John. *The Life, Travels, and Adventures of Christopher Wagstaff, Gentleman, Grandfather to Tristram Shandy. Originally published in the latter end of the last century*. London: Printed for J. Hinxman, 1762.

Dunton, John. *A Voyage Round the World: Or, a Pocket-Library, Divided into Several Volumes. The First of which contains the Rare Adventures of Don Kainophilus, from his cradle to his 15th year . . . Recommended by the Wits of Both Universities.* London: Printed for Richard Newcome, [1691].

Fielding, Henry. *Amelia. By Henry Fielding, Esq.* 4 vols. London: Printed for A. Millar, 1752.

The History of the Adventures of Joseph Andrews, and of His Friend Mr. Abraham Adams. London: Printed for A. Millar, 1742.

The History of Tom Jones, A Foundling. In Six Volumes. By Henry Fielding, Esq. 6 vols. London: Printed for A. Millar, 1749.

The Tragedy of Tragedies; Or the Life and Death of Tom Thumb the Great. As it is Acted at the Theatre in the Hay-Market. With the Annotations of H. Scriblerus Secundus. London: Printed, and sold by J. Roberts, 1731.

The Works of Henry Fielding, Esq; with the Life of the Author. 4 vols. London: Printed for A. Millar, 1762.

Fielding, Sarah. *The Adventures of David Simple: Containing an Account of His Travels through the Cities of London and Westminster, in Search of a Real Friend. By a Lady.* 2 vols. London: Printed for A. Millar, 1744.

The Adventures of David Simple: Containing an Account of His Travels through the Cities of London and Westminster, in Search of a Real Friend. By a Lady. The Second Edition, Revised and Corrected by Henry Fielding, Esq. 2nd edn. 2 vols. London: Printed for A. Millar, 1744.

The Adventures of David Simple. Volume the Last, in Which His History is Concluded. London: Printed for A. Millar, 1753.

Familiar Letters between the Principal Characters in David Simple, and Some Others. 2 vols. London: Printed for the author and sold by A. Millar, 1747.

The Governess; Or, Little Female Academy. Being a History of Mrs. Teachum, and Her Nine Girls. London: Printed for the Author; and sold by A. Millar, 1749.

The Lives of Cleopatra and Octavia. By the Author of David Simple. London: Printed for the author, and sold by Andrew Millar . . . , 1757.

and Jane Collier. *The Cry.* 3 vols. London: Printed for R. and J. Dodsley, 1754.

Gardiner, Robert. *Instructor Clericalis: Directing Clerks both in the Court of the King's Bench and Common Pleas, in the Abbreviation and Contraction of Words.* 5 vols. London: Printed by J. Walthoe, 1715–27.

Gildon, Charles. *The Post-Man Robb'd of his Mail: Or, the Packet Broke Open.* London: 1719.

Goodall, William. *The Adventures of Capt. Greenland.* London: Printed for R. Baldwin, 1752.

Graves, Richard. *Columella; Or, the Distressed Anchoret. A Colloquial Tale.* London: J. Dodsley, 1779.

Griffith, Richard. *Something New.* 2 vols. London: Printed for the Author, 1772.

Hawkins, William. *Henry and Rosamond. A Tragedy*. London: Printed for William Owen, 1749.

Haywood, Eliza. *The History of Miss Betsy Thoughtless*. 4 vols. London: Printed by T. Gardner, 1751.

Lasselia: Or, the Self-Abandon'd. A Novel. Written by Mrs. Eliza Haywood. London: 1724.

Memoirs of a Certain Island Adjacent to the Kingdom of Utopia. 2 vols. London: Printed and sold by all the booksellers of London and Westminster, 1725.

Secret Histories, Novels and Poems. In four volumes. Written by Mrs. Eliza Haywood. 4 vols. London: Printed for Dan. Browne, junr., and S. Chapman, 1724–25.

A Spy Upon the Conjurer: Or, A Collection of Surprising Stories, with Names, Places, and Particular Circumstances Relating to Mr. Duncan Campbell, Commonly Known by the Name of the Deaf and Dumb Man. London: Sold by Mr. Campbell at the Green-Hatch, 1724.

The Works of Mrs. Eliza Haywood, Consisting of Novels, Letters, Poems, and Plays. 4 vols. London: Dan. Browne, junr., and S. Chapman, 1723–24.

Head, Richardson. *The English Rogue Described, in the Life of Meriton Latroon, A Witty Extravagant: Comprehending the Most Eminent Cheats of Both Sexes*. London: Printed for Francis Kirkman, 1672.

Hearne, Mary. *The Lover's Week: Or, the Six Days Adventures of Philander and Amaryllis*. London: Printed for E. Curll . . . , 1718.

The Hive. A Collection of the Most Celebrated Songs. London: Printed for J. Walthoe, junr., 1724.

Hooke, Robert. *Micrographia: Or Some Physiological Descriptions of Minute Bodies Made by Magnifying Glasses*. London: Printed for John Martyn, 1667.

James, Henry. *Washington Square*. New York: Harper & Bros., 1881 [pub. 1880].

Johnstone, Charles. *The Adventures of Anthony Varnish; Or, A Peep at the Manners of Society*. London: Printed for William Lane, 1786.

Chrysal: Or, the Adventures of a Guinea . . . By an Adept. London: Printed for T. Becket, 1760.

Jonson, Ben. *The Arch's of Triumph Erected in Honor of the High and Mighty Prince. Iames. The First of That Name. King, of England and the Sixt of Scotland*. London: By Iohn Windet, 1604.

Bartholmew Fayre: A Comedie, Acted in the Yeare, 1614 . . . The Diuell is an Asse: A Comedie Acted in the Yeare, 1616 . . . ; The Staple of Newes: A Comedie Acted in the Yeare, 1625. London: Printed by I.B. for Robert Allot, 1631.

The Characters of Two Royall Masques. London: [by G. Eld] for Thomas Thorp, 1608.

The Masque of Queenes Celebrated from the House of Fame: By the Most Absolute in All State, and Titles. Anne Queene of Great Britaine, &c. With Her Honourable Ladies. At White Hall, Febr. 2. 1609. London: By N. Okes. for R. Bonian and H. Wally, 1609.

The New Inne. Or, The Light Heart. London: Printed by Thomas Harper, 1631.

Kelly, William Fitzmaurice. *Love and Artifice, Or A Compleat History of the Amour Between Lord Mauritio and Emilia*. Printed for E. Curll, 1734.

Kidgell, John. *The Card*. 2 vols. London: Printed for the Maker, 1755.

Kimber, Edward. *The Life and Adventures of Joe Thompson. A Narrative Founded on Fact*. London: Printed for John Hinton . . . and W Frederick, 1750.

Kirkman, Francis. *The Unlucky Citizen Experimentally Described in the Various Misfortunes Of an Unlucky Londoner*. London: Printed by Anne Johnson, for Fra. Kirkman, 1673.

Law Quibbles; or a Treatise of the Evasions, Tricks, Turns, and Quibbles Commonly Used in the Profession of the Law, to the Prejudice of Clients, and Others, 4th edn. [London] In the Savoy: Printed by E. and R. Nutt, 1736.

Lennox, Charlotte. *The Female Quixote; Or, the Adventures of Arabella*. 2 vols. London: Printed for A. Millar, 1752.

Long, Edward. *The Anti-Gallican; or, the History and Adventures of Harry Cobham, Esquire. Inscribed to Louis the XVth, by the Author*. London: Printed for T. Lownds, 1757.

Longueville, Peter. *The Hermit: Or, the Unparallel'd Sufferings And Surprising Adventures of Mr. Philip Quarll*. 4th edn. London: Printed for J. Wren . . . , 1768.

Madden, Samuel. *Memoires of the Twentieth Century. Being Original Letters of State, under George the Sixth* . . . London: Printed for Messieurs Osborn and Longman, Davis, and Batley, 1733.

Manley, Delarivier. *The Adventures of Rivella; or, the History of the Author of the Atalantis*. London: [s.n.], 1714.

—— *A Secret History of Queen Zarah, and the Zarazians; Being a Looking-glass for ____ _____ In the Kingdoms of Albigion*. 2 vols. Albigion [i.e. London: s.n.], 1705.

—— *Secret Memoirs and Manners of Several Persons of Quality, of Both Sexes. From the New Atalantis, an Island in the Mediteranean*. 2 vols. Printed for John Morphew . . . and J. Woodward, 1709.

Minifie, Susannah, later Mrs. Gunning [in collaboration with Margaret Minifie]. *Family Pictures, A Novel. Containing Curious and Interesting Memoirs of Several Persons of Fashion in W_____re. By a Lady*. 2 vols. London: Printed for W. Nicoll and T. Durham, 1764.

The Musical Miscellany; Being a Collection of Choice Songs, Set to the Violin and Flute, By the most Eminent Masters. London: Printed by and for John Watts, 1729–31.

Pope, Alexander. *The Works of Shakespear. In Six Volumes. Collated and Corrected by the Former Editions, by Mr. Pope*. 6 vols. London: Printed for Jacob Tonson, 1723–25.

Rameau, Jean Philippe. *A Collection of Lessons for the Harpsicord. Opera Seconda*. London: Printed for I. Walsh, 1760.

Richardson, Samuel. *Clarissa. Or, the History of a Young Lady*. 1st edn. 7 vols. London: Printed for S. Richardson, 1748 [pub. 1747–48].

—— *Clarissa. Or, the History of a Young Lady*. 2nd edn. 7 vols. [only vols. 1–4 were reprinted for this edn.] London: Printed for S. Richardson, 1749.

Clarissa. Or, the History of a Young Lady. 3rd edn. 8 vols. London: Printed for S. Richardson, 1751.

A Collection of the Moral and Instructive Sentiments, Maxims, Cautions and Reflections Contained in the Histories of Pamela, Clarissa, and Sir Charles Grandison. London: Printed for S. Richardson, 1755.

The History of Sir Charles Grandison. 2nd edn. 6 vols. London: Printed for S. Richardson, 1754.

The History of Sir Charles Grandison. 6th edn. 7 vols. London: Printed for J. and F. Rivington, 1770.

Pamela: Or, Virtue Rewarded. In a Series of Familiar Letters From a Beautiful Young Damsel to Her Parents. 1st edn. 2 vols. London: Printed for C. Rivington . . . and J. Osborn, 1741 [pub. 1740].

Pamela: Or, Virtue Rewarded. In a Series of Familiar Letters From a Beautiful Young Damsel to Her Parents. 2nd edn. 2 vols. London: Printed for C. Rivington . . . and J. Osborn, 1741.

Pamela: Or, Virtue Rewarded. In a Series of Familiar Letters From a Beautiful Young Damsel to Her Parents. 6th edn. 4 vols. London: Printed for S. Richardson, 1742.

Pamela: Or, Virtue Rewarded. In a Series of Familiar Letters From a Beautiful Young Damsel to Her Parents: And Afterwards in Her Exalted Condition . . . The Third and Fourth Volumes . . . By the Editor of the Two First. 2 vols. London: Printed for S. Richardson, and sold by C. Rivington, 1742.

The Correspondence of Samuel Richardson. Ed. Anna Laetitia Barbauld, 6 vols. London: R. Phillips, 1804.

"Six Original Letters upon Duelling." *Candid Review and Literary Repository* 1 (March 1765), 227–31.

The Robin. A Collection of Six Hundred and Eighty of the most Celebrated English and Scotch Songs: None of Which are Contain'd in the Other Collections of the Same Size Call'd the Linnet and Thrush. London: Printed for C. Hitch & I. Osborn, 1749.

Rousseau, Jean-Jaques. *Eloisa, or a Series of Original Letters Collected and Published by J. J. Rousseau. Translated from the French.* 4th edn. 4 vols. London: Printed for T. Becket and P. A. De Hondt, 1769.

Scott, Sarah. *A Description of Millenium Hall, and the Country Adjacent: Together with the Characters of the Inhabitants, and such Historical Anecdotes and Reflections, as May excite in the Reader proper Sentiments of Humanity, and lead the Mind to the Love of Virtue. By a Gentleman on his Travels.* London: Printed for J. Newbery, 1762.

The History of Mecklenburgh, from the First Settlement of the Vandals in that Country, to the Present Time; Including a Period of about Three Thousand Years. London: Printed for J. Newbery, 1762.

Short Airs and Lessons for the Harpsicord or Spinet by Several Hands. London: [17–].

Smedley, Jonathan. *Gullivariana: Or, A Fourth Volume of Miscellanies.* London: Printed for J. Roberts, 1728.

Smith, S., ed. *The Compleat History of the Old and New Testament, or, a Family Bible with Critical and Explanatory Annotations, Extracted from the Writings of the*

Most Celebrated Authors . . . Together with Maps, Cuts, & Curiously Design'd and Engrav'd in Copper. By S. Smith. 2 vols. London: Printed by W. Rayner, 1735–37.

Smollett, Tobias. *The Adventures of Sir Launcelot Greaves.* 2 vols. London: Printed for C. Coote, 1762.

— *The Adventures of Peregrine Pickle. In Which are included, Memoirs of a Lady of Quality.* 4 vols. London: Printed for the Author, 1751.

— *The Adventures of Roderick Random.* 2nd edn. 2 vols. London: Printed for J. Osborn, 1748.

Snell, Hannah. *The Female Soldier; Or, The Surprising Life and Adventures of Hannah Snell.* Octavo edn. London: Printed for and sold by R. Walker, 1750.

Sterne, Laurence. *The Life and Opinions of Tristram Shandy, Gentleman. Vol. III.* 2nd edn. London: Printed for R. and J. Dodsley, 1761.

— *Tristram Shandy.* 2 vols. Reprinted edn. London: Printed for T. Caddel, 1780.

Swift, Jonathan. *A Tale of a Tub.* 8th edn. Dublin: Printed by S. Powell, 1741.

— *Travels into Several Remote Nations of the World. In Four Parts. By Lemuel Gulliver.* London: Printed for Benj. Motte, 1726.

— *Works.* 4 vols. Dublin: Printed for George Faulkner, 1735. [Octavo and duodecimo editions.]

Young, Edward. *The Brothers. A Tragedy. Acted at the Theatre Royal in Drury-Lane.* London: Printed for R. Dodsley, 1753.

Modern Editions

Addison, Joseph, and Sir Richard Steele. *The Tatler.* Ed. Donald F. Bond. 3 vols. Oxford University Press, 1987.

Austen, Jane. *Emma.* Ed. Stephen M. Parrish. New York and London: Norton, 2000.

— *Persuasion.* Ed. John Davie. Intro. Claude Rawson. Oxford University Press, 1971; reissued with new intro., 1990.

— *Pride and Prejudice.* Ed. Donald J. Gray. New York and London: Norton, 1966.

Behn, Aphra. *Oroonoko.* Ed. Joanna Lipking. New York and London: Norton, 1997.

Burney, Frances. *Evelina.* Ed. Edward A. Bloom. Oxford University Press, 1989.

Carter, Elizabeth. *Ode To Wisdom: A Poem by Elizabeth Carter. As Set to Music by Clarissa Harlowe.* Urbana-Champaign: University of Illinois and Johnson Society of the Central Region, 30 April 1999.

Fielding, Henry. *Adventures in Search of A Real Friend.* London: G. Virtue, 1822. [False attribution and title; actually Sarah Fielding's *David Simple.*]

— *The Author's Farce.* Ed. Charles B. Woods. London: Edward Arnold, 1966.

— *The History of Tom Jones, A Foundling.* Ed. Fredson Bowers. Intro. Martin C. Battestin. Illustr. Warren Chappell. Wesleyan Edition. Wesleyan University Press, 1975.

— *Joseph Andrews and Shamela.* Ed. Douglas Brooks-Davies. Oxford University Press, 1980; reprinted 1990.

— *Joseph Andrews.* Ed. Martin C. Battestin. Wesleyan Edition. Oxford: Clarendon Press, 1967.

— *Tom Jones.* Ed. Sheridan Baker. New York and London: Norton, 1973.

and Sarah Fielding. *The Correspondence of Henry and Sarah Fielding*. Ed. Martin C. Battestin and Clive T. Probyn. Oxford: Clarendon Press, 1993.

Fielding, Sarah. *The Adventures of David Simple and Volume the Last*. Ed. Peter Sabor. Eighteenth-Century Novels by Women Series. Lexington, KY: University Press of Kentucky, 1998.

The Adventures of David Simple. Ed. Malcolm Kelsall. Oxford University Press, 1969.

Haywood, Eliza. *The Female Spectator: Being Selections from Mrs Eliza Haywood's Periodical, First Published in Monthly Parts (1744–6)*. Ed. Gabrielle M. Firmager. London: Bristol Classical Press, 1993.

Love in Excess. Ed. David Oakleaf. 2nd edn. Peterborough, ON: Broadview Press, 2000.

Horace. *Horace, The Complete Odes and Epodes*. Trans. W. G. Shepherd. New York: Penguin, 1985.

Horace: The Odes and Epodes. Trans. C. E. Bennett. Loeb Classical Library. London: William Heinemann; Cambridge, MA: Harvard University Press, 1914.

Satires, Epistles, and Ars Poetica. Trans. H. Rushton Fairclough. Loeb Classical Library. New York: G. P. Putnam's Sons, 1926.

James, Henry. *The Portrait of a Lady*. Ed. Nicola Bradbury. Intro. Graham Greene. Oxford University Press, 1987.

Johnson, Samuel. *Dictionary of the English Language*. Facsimile of 1755 London edn. Harlow: Longman Group, 1990.

Letters of Samuel Johnson. Ed. Bruce Redford. 5 vols. Princeton University Press, 1992.

Johnson Society of the Central Region. *Ode to Wisdom: A Poem by Elizabeth Carter As Set to Music by Clarisa Harlowe*. Intro. John Dussinger. Urbana-Champaign: Johnson Society of the Central Region/ University of Illinois, 1999.

Juvenal. *Juvenal and Persius*. Trans. G. G. Ramsay. Loeb Classical Library. London: William Heinemann; Cambridge, MA: Harvard University Press, 1918.

Lennox, Charlotte. *The Female Quixote*. Ed. Margaret Dalziel. World's Classics edn. Oxford University Press, 1989.

Manley, Delarivier. *The Adventures of Rivella*. Ed. Katherine Zelinsky. Peterborough, ON: Broadview Press, 1999.

Martial. *Epigrams*. Ed. and trans. D. R. Shackleton Bailey, Loeb Classical Library. Cambridge, MA: Harvard University Press, 1993.

The Musical Entertainer . . . Engraved by George Bickham, Junr. 2 vols. London: Printed for and sold by Charles Corbett Bookseller, 1740; New York: Broude Bros., 1965. [Facsimile reprint.]

Persius. *Juvenal and Persius*. Trans. G. G. Ramsay. Loeb Classical Library. London: William Heinemann; Cambridge, MA: Harvard University Press, 1918.

Pope, Alexander. *The Poems of Alexander Pope*. Twickenham Edition. Ed. John Butt *et al*. 11 vols. London and New Haven, CT: Methuen and Yale University Press, 1963.

Richardson, Samuel. *Clarissa, or the History of a Young Lady*. Ed. Angus Ross. Harmondsworth: Penguin, 1985.

Clarissa. Ed. George Sherburn. Riverside Edition. Boston, MA: Houghton Mifflin, 1962.

Clarissa. Shakespeare Head Press Edition. 8 vols. Oxford: Basil Blackwell, 1943.

Clarissa. Intro. John Butt. 4 vols. Everyman's Library Edition. London and New York: J. M. Dent & Sons, 1932.

The History of Sir Charles Grandison. Ed. Jocelyn Harris. Oxford University Press, 1986 (first pub. 1972).

Pamela. Ed. Thomas Keymer and Alice Wakely. Oxford World's Classics. Oxford University Press, 2001.

Pamela. Intro. William M. Sale, Jr. New York and London: Norton, 1958; reissued 1993.

Pamela, Samuel Richardson. Shamela, Henry Fielding. Intro. John M. Bullitt. Meridian Classic Edition. New York: New American Library, 1980.

Pamela. Ed. George Saintsbury. London: Dent, 1914; reprinted 1955.

Samuel Richardson's Published Commentary on Clarissa, 1747–65. Ed. Florian Stuber et al. 3 vols. London: Pickering & Chatto, 1998.

Selected Letters of Samuel Richardson. Ed. John Carroll. Oxford: Clarendon Press, 1964.

and Lady Bradshaigh. *The Annotations in Lady Bradshaigh's Copy of* Clarissa. Ed. Janine Barchas, with collaboration of Gordon D. Fulton. English Literary Studies Monograph Series 76. Victoria, BC: University of Victoria, 1998.

Snell, Hannah. *The Female Soldier*. Duodecimo edn. 1750. Augustan Reprint Society, Facsimile edn. Intro. Dianne Dugaw. Los Angeles: William Andrews Clark Memorial Library, 1989.

Sterne, Laurence. *Letters*. Ed. Lewis P. Curtis. Oxford: Clarendon Press, 1935.

The Life and Opinions of Tristram Shandy, Gentleman. Ed. Ian Campbell Ross. World's Classics Series. Oxford University Press, 1983.

The Life and Opinions of Tristram Shandy, Gentleman. Ed. James Aiken Work. New York: Odyssey Press, 1940.

Swift, Jonathan. *Gulliver's Travels*. Ed. Albert J. Rivero. New York and London: W. W. Norton, 2002.

The Writings of Jonathan Swift. Ed. Robert A. Greenberg and William B. Piper. New York and London: Norton, 1973.

Virgil. *Aeneid, 7–12; Appendix Vergiliana*. Trans. H. Rushton Fairclough. Revised G. P. Goold. Loeb Classical Library. Cambridge, MA: Harvard University Press, 2000.

Eclogues; Georgics; Aeneid, 1–6. Trans. H. Rushton Fairclough. Revised G. P. Goold. Loeb Classical Library. Cambridge, MA: Harvard University Press, 1999.

Whibley, Charles, ed. *A Facsimile Reproduction of a Unique Catalogue of Laurence Sterne's Library*. New York: Edgar H. Wells & Co., 1930.

Wilkes, John, and Thomas Potter. *An Essay on Woman by John Wilkes and Thomas Potter: A Reconstruction of a Lost Book*. Ed. Arthur H. Cash. New York: AMS Press, 2000.

Woolf, Virginia. *Orlando: A Biography*. San Diego, New York, London: Harcourt Brace, 1992.

Critical and Secondary Works

Aikins, Janet. "Richardson's 'Speaking Pictures.'" In Margaret Anne Doody and Peter Sabor, eds., *Samuel Richardson: Tercentenary Essays*. Cambridge University Press, 1989, 146–66.

Alkon, Paul K. *Science Fiction Before 1900: Imagination Discovers Technology*. New York: Twayne, 1994.

Anderson, Benedict. *Imagined Communities: Reflections on the Origin and Spread of Nationalism*. London: Verso, 1983.

Backscheider, Paula. *Daniel Defoe, his Life*. Baltimore: Johns Hopkins University Press, 1989.

Baine, Rodney M. *Daniel Defoe and the Supernatural*. Athens, GA: University of Georgia, 1968.

"The Evidence from Defoe's Title Pages." *Studies in Bibliography* 25 (1972), 185–91.

Baker, Nicholson. *Double Fold: Libraries and the Assault on Paper*. New York: Random House, 2001.

Ball, Donald L. *Samuel Richardson's Theory of Fiction*. The Hague and Paris: Mouton, 1971.

Ballaster, Rosalind. *Seductive Forms: Women's Amatory Fiction from 1684 to 1740*. Oxford: Clarendon Press, 1992.

Barchas, Janine. "Before Print Culture: Mary, Lady Chudleigh and the Assimilation of the Book." In Dennis Todd and Cynthia Wall, eds., *Serious Reflections on Occasional Forms: Essays on Eighteenth-Century Genre and Culture*. Delaware University Press, 2001, 15–35.

Barker, Nicolas. "Typography and the Meaning of Words: The Revolution in the Layout of Books in the Eighteenth Century." In Giles Barber and Bernhard Fabian, eds., *Buch und Buchhandel in Europa im achtzehnten Jahrhundert*. Hamburg: Dr. Ernst Hanswedell & Co., 1981, 127–65.

Battestin, Martin C. "Fielding's Novels and the Wesleyan Edition: Some Principles and Problems." In G. E. Bentley, Jr., ed., *Editing Eighteenth Century Novels*. Toronto: The Committee for the Conference on Editorial Problems, 1975, 9–30.

Benedict, Barbara M. *Curiosity: A Cultural History of Early Modern Inquiry*. University of Chicago Press, 2001.

Making the Modern Reader: Cultural Mediation in Early Modern Literary Anthologies. Princeton University Press, 1996.

Benham, W. Gurney. *Playing Cards: History of the Pack and Explanations of its Many Secrets*. London: Spring Books, 1931.

Blayney, Peter W. M. *The Bookshops in Paul's Cross Churchyard*. In series Occasional Papers of the Bibliographical Society. No. 5. London: Bibliographical Society, 1990.

Blewett, David. *The Illustration of* Robinson Crusoe, *1719–1920*. Gerrards Cross: Smythe, 1995.

"The Illustration of *Robinson Crusoe*: 1719–1840." In Joachim Möller, ed., *Imagination on a Long Rein*. Marburg: Jonas Verlag, 1988, 66–81.

Boggs, J. S. G., vs. Robert E. Rubin, Secretary of the Treasury, et al. United States Court of Appeals for the District of Columbia Circuit. Argued 8 September 1998 and decided 6 November 1998. Case no. 97–5313.

Booth, Wayne. "Did Sterne Complete *Tristram Shandy?*" *Modern Philology* 48 (1951), 172–78.

"*Tristram Shandy* and its Precursors: The Selfconscious Narrator." Unpublished dissertation, University of Chicago, 1950.

Bowden, Martha. "Composing Herself: Music, Solitude and St. Cecelia in *Clarissa*." *1650–1850: Ideas, Aesthetics, and Inquiries in the Early Modern Era* 2 (1996), 185–201.

Bowers, Fredson. "Textual Introduction." In the Wesleyan Edition of *Joseph Andrews*, ed. Martin C. Battestin. Oxford: Clarendon Press, 1967, [xxxix]–xlvii.

Bray, Joe. "'Attending to the *Minute*': Richardson's Revisions of Italics in *Pamela*." In Bray, Handley, and Henry, eds., *Ma(r)king the Text: The Presentation of Meaning on the Literary Page*. Aldershot, Burlington USA, Singapore, Sidney: Ashgate, 2000, 105–19.

Bray, Joe, Miriam Handley, and Anne C. Henry, eds. *Ma(r)king the Text: The Presentation of Meaning on the Literary Page*. Aldershot, Burlington USA, Singapore, Sidney: Ashgate, 2000.

Brewer, John. *Pleasures of the Imagination: English Culture in the Eighteenth Century*. London: HarperCollins, 1997.

Brown, Murray L. "Learning to Read Richardson: *Pamela*, 'Speaking Pictures,' and the Visual Hermeneutic," *Studies in the Novel* 25.2 (Summer 1993), 129–51.

Bullen, John Samuel. *Time and Space in the Novels of Samuel Richardson*. In Utah State University Press Monograph Series 12.2. Logan, UT: Utah State University Press, 1965.

Carroll, John. "Lovelace as Tragic Hero." *University of Toronto Quarterly* 42.1 (1972), 14–25.

Carter, John. *ABC for Book Collectors*. Revised Nicholas Barker. 6th edn. New Castle, DE: Oak Knoll Books, 1992.

Cash, Arthur H. "Historical Introduction." In *An Essay on Woman by John Wilkes and Thomas Potter: A Reconstruction of a Lost Book*. Ed. Arthur H. Cash. New York: AMS Press, 2000, 1–68.

Castle, Terry. *Clarissa's Ciphers: Meaning and Disruption in Richardson's* Clarissa. Ithaca and London: Cornell University Press, 1982.

Chappell, W[illiam]. *Old English Popular Music*. Ed. H. Ellis Woolridge. 2 vols. New York: J. Brussel, [c. 1961].

Chung, Ewha. *Samuel Richardson's New Nation: Paragons of the Domestic Sphere and "Native" Virtue*. New York: Peter Lang, 1998.

Cole, Richard Cargill. *Irish Booksellers and English Writers 1740–1800*. Atlantic Highlands, NJ: Humanities Press International, 1986.

Conway, Alison. *Private Interests: Women, Portraiture, and the Visual Culture of the English Novel, 1709–1791*. Toronto and New York: University of Toronto Press, 2001.

Cope, Kevin L. "Richardson the Advisor." In Albert J. Rivero, ed., *New Essays on Samuel Richardson*. New York: St. Martin's Press, 1996, 27–28.

Cowley, Robert L. S. *Marriage à-la-mode: A Re-view of Hogarth's Narrative Art*. Manchester University Press, 1983.

Day, W. G. "*Tristram Shandy*: The Marbled Leaf." *The Library* 27 (1972), 143–45.

Davis, Lennard J. *Factual Fictions: The Origins of the English Novel*. New York: Columbia University Press, 1983.

Dawkins, Richard. *The Extended Phenotype*. Oxford University Press, 1982.

Dekker, Rudolf M., and Lotte C. van de Pol. *The Tradition of Female Transvestism in Early Modern Europe*. Foreword. Peter Burke. London: Macmillan, 1989.

DeMaria, Robert, Jr. *Samuel Johnson and the Life of Reading*. Baltimore: Johns Hopkins University Press, 1997.

"Samuel Johnson and the Reading Revolution." *Eighteenth-Century Life* 16 (November 1992), 86–102.

Dennis, Nigel. "Swift and Defoe." In Robert A. Greenberg and William B. Piper, eds., *The Writings of Jonathan Swift*. New York and London: Norton, 1973, 661–69.

Digeon, Aurélien. "Autour de Fielding II: Fielding, conseiller littéraire de sa soeur, est portraituré par elle en retour." *Revue Germanique* 11 (1920), 353–62.

Doody, Margaret Anne. *The True Story of the Novel*. New Brunswick, NJ: Rutgers University Press, 1996.

"The Man-made World of Clarissa Harlowe and Robert Lovelace." In Valerie Grosvenor Myer, ed., *Samuel Richardson: Passion and Prudence*. Totowa, NJ: Barnes & Noble, 1986, 52–77.

A Natural Passion: A Study of the Novels of Samuel Richardson. Oxford: Clarendon Press, 1974.

and Peter Sabor, eds. *Samuel Richardson: Tercentenary Essays*. Cambridge University Press, 1989.

Douglas, Aileen. "Britannia's Rule and the It-Narrator." *Eighteenth-Century Fiction* 6.1 (1993), 65–82.

Duthie, Elizabeth. "Gulliver Art." *The Scriblerian* 10.2 (Spring 1978), 127–31.

Eaves, T. C. Duncan. "Graphic Illustration of the Novels of Samuel Richardson, 1740–1810." *Huntington Library Quarterly* 14 (1951), 349–83.

and Ben D. Kimpel. *Samuel Richardson: A Biography*. Oxford: Clarendon Press, 1971.

Edel, Leon, and Dan H. Laurence. *Bibliography of Henry James*. 3rd ed. Oxford: Clarendon Press, 1982.

Ehrenpreis, Irvin. *Swift: The Man, his Works, and the Age*. 3 vols. Cambridge, MA: Harvard University Press, 1967.

Eisenstein, Elizabeth L. *The Printing Press as an Agent of Change*. 2 vols. Cambridge University Press, 1979.

Elsner, John. "A Collector's Model of Desire: The House and Museum of Sir John Soane." In John Elsner and Roger Cardinal, eds., *The Cultures of Collecting*. Cambridge, MA: Harvard University Press, 1994, 155–76.

Fanning, Christopher. "On Sterne's Page: Spatial Layout, Spatial Form, and Social Spaces in *Tristram Shandy*." *Eighteenth-Century Studies* 10.4 (July 1998), 429–50.

Febvre, Lucien, and Henri-Jean Martin. *The Coming of the Book: The Impact of Printing (1450–1800)*. London and New York: Verso, 1990; first published, 1958; first English translation, 1976.

Flint, Christopher. "In Other Words: Eighteenth-Century Authorship and the Ornaments of Print." *Eighteenth-Century Fiction* 14.3–4 (April–July 2002), 627–72.

Foxon, David F. *Pope and the Early Eighteenth-Century Book Trade*. Ed. James McLaverty. The Lyell Lectures, Oxford, 1975–6. New York: Oxford University Press, 1991.

Frega, Donnalee. *Speaking in Hunger: Gender, Discourse, and Consumption in* Clarissa. Columbia, SC: University of South Carolina Press, 1998.

Frye, Northrop. *Anatomy of Criticism: Four Essays*. Princeton University Press, 1957.

Furbank, P. N., and W. R. Owens. *Defoe De-Attributions: A Critique of J. R. Moore's Checklist*. London: Hambledon Press, 1994.

Fysh, Stephanie. *The Work(s) of Samuel Richardson*. Newark: University of Delaware Press, 1997.

Gabler, Hans Walter. "The Text as Process and the Problem of Intentionality." *Text* 3 (1987), 107–16.

Gaskell, Philip. *A New Introduction to Bibliography*. New York and Oxford: Oxford University Press, 1972.

Genette, Gérard. *Narrative Discourse, An Essay in Method*. Trans. Jane E. Lewin. Foreword Jonathan Culler. Ithaca, NY: Cornell University Press, 1980.

  Paratexts: Thresholds of Interpretation. Trans. Jane E. Lewin. Foreword Richard Macksey. Cambridge University Press, 1997.

  "Introduction to the Paratext." Trans. Marie Maclean. *New Literary History* 22 (1991), 261–73.

Goldthorpe, David. "Textual Instability: The Fortunes and Misfortunes of *Moll Flanders*." Unpublished 1995 Ph.D. thesis, Open University, London.

Groves, David. "The Frontispiece to James Hogg's *Confessions*." *N&Q* 235 (Dec. 1990), 421–22.

Gwilliam, Tassie. *Samuel Richardson's Fictions of Gender*. Stanford University Press, 1993.

Halsband, Robert. "Hogarth's Graphic Friendships: Illustrating Books by Friends." In James Engell, ed., *Johnson and his Age*. Cambridge, MA: Harvard University Press, 1984, 333–66.

Hammelmann, Hanns, and T. S. R. Boase. *Book Illustrators in Eighteenth-Century England*. New Haven, CT and London: Yale University Press, 1975.

Harris, Jocelyn, ed. *The History of Sir Charles Grandison*. Oxford University Press, 1986 (first pub. 1972).

  Samuel Richardson. London: Cambridge University Press, 1987.

  "Grotesque, Classical and Pornographic Bodies in Clarissa." In Albert J. Rivero, ed., *New Essays on Samuel Richardson*. New York: St. Martin's Press, 1996, 101–16.

"Introduction" to *Volume 1: Prefaces, Postscripts and Related Writings*, ed. Thomas Keymer. In *Samuel Richardson's Published Commentary on* Clarissa, *1747–65*, ed. Florian Stuber *et al*. 3 vols. London: Pickering & Chatto, 1998, I, vii–xcv.

"The Reviser Observed: The Last Volume of *Sir Charles Grandison*." *Studies in Bibliography* 29 (1976), 1–31.

"Richardson: Original or Learned Genius?" In Margaret Anne Doody and Peter Sabor, eds., *Samuel Richardson: Tercentenary Essays*. Cambridge University Press, 1989, 188–202.

Henry, Anne C. "The Re-mark-able Rise of '. . .': Reading Ellipsis Marks in Literary Texts." In Joe Bray, Miriam Handley, and Anne C. Henry, eds., *Ma(r)king the Text: The Presentation of Meaning on the Literary Page*. Aldershot, Burlington USA; Singapore, Sidney: Ashgate, 2000.

Hinman, C[harlton] T. *Printing and Proofreading of the First Folio of Shakespeare*, 2 vols. Oxford: Clarendon Press, 1963.

Hughes, Helen Sard. "A Precursor of *Tristram Shandy*." *JEGP* 17 (1918), 227–51.

Hunter, J. Paul. *Before Novels: The Cultural Contexts of Eighteenth-Century English Fiction*. New York: W. W. Norton, 1990.

"Robert Boyle and the Epistemology of the Novel." *Eighteenth-Century Fiction* 2.4 (July 1990), 275–92.

"From Typology to Type: Print Technology and Ideology in *The Dunciad* and *Tristram Shandy*." In Margaret J. M. Ezell and Katherine O'Brien O'Keeffe, eds., *Cultural Artifacts and the Production of Meaning: The Page, the Image, and the Body*. Ann Arbor: University of Michigan Press, 1994, 41–69.

Hunting, Robert S. "Fielding's Revisions of *David Simple*." Boston University Studies in English 3 (1957), 117–21.

Irwin, Robert. "Your Novel Needs Indexing." In John Fowles and A. L. Kennedy, eds., *New Writing 9*. New York: Vintage, 2000, 60–79.

Johns, Adrian. *The Nature of the Book: Print and Knowledge in the Making*. Chicago and London: University of Chicago Press, 1998.

Joyce, James. *Ulysses: A Critical and Synoptic Edition*. Prepared by Hans Walter Gabler, with Wolfhard Steppe and Claus Melchior. 3 vols. New York and London: Garland Publishing Inc., 1984.

Kernan, Alvin B. *Printing Technology, Letters, and Samuel Johnson*. Princeton University Press, 1987.

Keymer, Thomas. *Richardson's* Clarissa *and the Eighteenth-Century Reader*. Cambridge University Press, 1992.

"Jane Collier, Reader of Richardson, and the Fire Scene in *Clarissa*." In Albert Rivero, ed., *New Essays on Samuel Richardson*. New York: St. Martin's Press, 1996, 141–61.

"Richardson, Incognita, and the *Whitehall Evening-Post*: New Light on Richardson's Correspondence with Lady Bradshaigh and the Text of His First Letter." *Notes and Queries* 39.4 (Dec 1992), 477–80.

and Peter Sabor, eds. *The Pamela Controversy: Criticisms and Adaptations of Samuel Richardson's* Pamela *1740–1750*. 6 vols. London and Brookfield, VT: Pickering & Chatto, 2001.

Kinkead-Weekes, Mark. *Samuel Richardson: Dramatic Novelist*. Ithaca: Cornell University Press, 1973.

Lenfest, David. "Checklist of Illustrated Editions of *Gulliver's Travels*, 1727–1914." *Papers of the Bibliographical Society of America* 62 (1968), 85–123.

Leppert, Richard. *Music and Image: Domesticity, Ideology and Socio-cultural Formation in Eighteenth-Century England*. Cambridge University Press, 1988.

Lonsdale, Roger. *Dr. Charles Burney: A Literary Biography*. Oxford: Clarendon Press, 1965.

Loveridge, Mark. *Laurence Sterne and the Argument About Design*. Totowa, NJ: Vision and Barnes & Noble, 1982.

Lund, Roger D. "The Eel of Science: Index Learning, Scriblerian Satire, and the Rise of Information Culture." *Eighteenth-Century Life* 22.2 (May 1998), 18–42.

McBurney, William Harlin. *A Check List of English Prose Fiction, 1700–1739*. Cambridge, MA: Harvard University Press, 1960.

McGann, Jerome J. *A Critique of Modern Textual Criticism*. Chicago and London: University of Chicago Press, 1983.

McKenzie, D. F. *Bibliography and the Sociology of Texts*. The Panizzi Lectures Series. London: British Library, 1985.

McKeon, Michael. *The Origins of the English Novel, 1600–1740*. Baltimore: Johns Hopkins University Press, 1987.

McKillop, Alan Dugald. *Samuel Richardson: Printer and Novelist*. Chapel Hill: University of North Carolina Press, 1936.

McLaverty, James. *Pope, Print, and Meaning*. Oxford University Press, 2001.

McLuhan, Marshall. *The Gutenberg Galaxy: The Making of Typographic Man*. University of Toronto Press, 1962.

Mack, Maynard. *Alexander Pope: A Life*. London: Norton, 1985.

Maslen, Keith. *Samuel Richardson of London, Printer*. Dunedin, New Zealand: University of Otago English Department, 2001.

Meeker, Richard K. "Bank Note, Corkscrew, Flea and Sedan: A Checklist of Eighteenth-Century Fiction." *The Library Chronicle* 35 (1969), 52–57.

Meyer, Horst. "Das Geheimnis der marmorierten Seite: oder, *Tristram Shandys* typographische Extravaganzen." *Antiquariat* (1986), A130–34.

Mitchell, W. J. T. *Blake's Composite Art: A Study of Illuminated Poetry*. Princeton University Press, 1978.

Moss, Roger B. "Sterne's Punctuation." *Eighteenth-Century Studies* 15.2 (Winter 1981–2), 179–200.

Mullan, John. *Sentiment and Sociability: The Language of Feeling in the Eighteenth Century*. Oxford: Clarendon Press, 1988.

Mylne, Vivienne. "Prévost's Translation of Dialogue in Richardson's *Clarissa*." *Franco British Studies* 1 (Spring 1986), 1–11.

"The Punctuation of Dialogue in Eighteenth-Century French and English Fiction." *The Library* 1 (1979), 43–61.

New, Melvyn. "William Hogarth and John Baldessari: Ornamenting Sterne's *Tristram Shandy*." *Word and Image* 11.2 (April–June 1995), 182–95.

Nielsen, Jakob, and Marie Tahir. *Homepage Usability: 50 Websites Deconstructed*. Indianapolis: New Riders, 2001.

Parker, Dorothy. "The Time Scheme of *Pamela* and the Character of B." *Texas Studies in Literature and Language* 11 (1969), 695–704.

Parkes, M. B. *Pause and Effect: An Introduction to the History of Punctuation in the West*. Berkeley and Los Angeles: University of California Press, 1993.

Paulson, Ronald. *Emblem and Expression: Meaning in English Art of the Eighteenth Century*. Cambridge, MA: Harvard University Press, 1975.

Hogarth. 3 vols. New Brunswick, NJ: Rutgers University Press, 1991–93.

Popular and Polite Art in the Age of Hogarth and Fielding. Notre Dame, IA: University of Notre Dame Press, 1979.

Peters, Julie Stone. *Congreve, the Drama, and the Printed Word*. Stanford University Press, 1990.

Piper, David. *The Image of the Poet: British Poets and their Portraits*. Oxford: Clarendon Press, 1982.

Plomer, H. R., G. H. Bushnell, and E. R. McC[lintock] Dix, eds. *A Dictionary of the Printers and Booksellers Who Were at Work in England, Scotland and Ireland From 1725 to 1775*. London: Bibliographical Society, 1968.

Pollard, M. *Dublin's Trade in Books 1550–1800*. Oxford: Clarendon Press, 1989.

Price, Leah. *The Anthology and the Rise of the Novel: From Richardson to George Eliot*. Cambridge University Press, 2000.

Price, Steven R. "The Autograph Manuscript in Print: Samuel Richardson's Type Font Manipulation in *Clarissa*." In Paul C. Gutjahr and Megan L. Benton, eds., *Illuminating Letters: Typography and Literary Interpretation*. Amherst: University of Massachusetts Press, 2001, 117–35.

Rawson, C[laude] J. *Gulliver and the Gentle Reader: Studies in Swift and our Time*. London and Boston, MA: Routledge and Kegan Paul, 1973.

Reilly, Elizabeth Carroll. *Dictionary of Colonial American Printers' Ornaments and Illustrations*. Worcester, MA: American Antiquarian Society, 1975.

Richetti, John J. *Popular Fiction Before Richardson: Narrative Patterns 1700–1739*. Oxford: Clarendon Press, 1969.

Roscoe, S. *John Newbery and His Successors 1740–1814*. Hertfordshire: Five Owls Press, 1973.

Saenger, Paul. *Space Between Words: The Origins of Silent Reading*. Stanford University Press, 1997.

Safire, William. "Squeezewords: Cramming it Together as the Wave of the Future." In *New York Times Magazine* (6 February 2002), sec. 6, 28.

Sale, William Merritt, Jr. *Samuel Richardson: A Bibliographical Record of His Literary Career with Historical Notes*. New Haven, CT: Yale University Press, 1936.

Samuel Richardson: Master Printer. Ithaca, NY: Cornell University Press, 1950.

"A Bibliographical Note on Richardson's *Clarissa*." *Library*, or *Transactions of the Bibliographical Society*. 2nd series. Vol. XVI. London: Humphrey Milford, 1936, 448–51.

Sherbo, Arthur. "Time and Place in Richardson's Clarissa." *Boston University Studies in English* 3 (1957), 139–46.

Sherman, Stuart. *Telling Time: Clocks, Journals, and English Narrative Form, 1660–1795*. University of Chicago Press, 1996.

Spear, Gary. "Reading Before the Lines: Typography, Iconography, and the Author in Milton's 1645 Frontispiece. Papers of Renaissance Text Society, 1985–1991." In W. Speed Hill, ed., *New Ways of Looking at Old Texts*. Binghamton, NY: Medieval and Renaissance Texts and Studies, 1993, 187–94.

Spedding, Patrick. *A Bibliography of Eliza Haywood*. London: Pickering & Chatto, 2003/forthcoming.

Stafford, Barbara Maria. *Artful Science: Enlightenment and the Eclipse of Visual Education*. London and Cambridge, MA: MIT Press, 1994.

Stewart, Philip. *Engraven Desire: Eros, Image and Text in the French Eighteenth Century*. Durham, NC and London: Duke University Press, 1992.

Straus, Ralph. *The Unspeakable Curll: Being Some Account of Edmund Curll, Bookseller to which is Added a Full List of his Books*. London: Chapman & Hall, 1927.

Stuber, Florian. "Introduction: Text, Writer, Reader, World." In Florian Stuber *et al.* eds., *The Clarissa Project, Volumes 1–8*. New York: AMS Press, 1990, I, 1–53.

Tanselle, G. Thomas. *A Rationale of Textual Criticism*. Philadelphia: University of Pennsylvania Press, 1992.

"The Editorial Problem of Final Authorial Intention." *Studies in Bibliography* 29 (1976), 167–211.

Teerink, Dr. H. *A Bibliography of the Writings of Jonathan Swift*. 2nd revised and corrected edn. Ed. Arthur H. Scouten. Philadelphia: University of Pennsylvania Press, 1963.

Todd, Dennis. *Imagining Monsters: Miscreations of the Self in Eighteenth-Century England*. University of Chicago Press, 1995.

Todd, Janet. *Women's Friendship in Literature*. New York: Columbia University Press, 1980.

"Life after Sex: The Fictional Autobiography of Delarivier Manley." *Women's Studies* 15 (1988), 43–55.

Wagner, Peter. *Reading Iconotexts: From Swift to the French Revolution*. London: Reaktion, 1995.

Wall, Cynthia. "Details of Space: Narrative Description in Early Eighteenth-Century Novels." *Eighteenth-Century Fiction* 10.4 (July 1998), 387–405.

"The English Auction: Narratives of Dismantlings." *Eighteenth-Century Studies* 31.1 (Fall 1997), 1–25.

Warner, William Beatty. *Reading* Clarissa: *The Struggles of Interpretation*. New Haven, CT and London: Yale University Press, 1979.

Watt, Ian. *The Rise of the Novel: Studies in Defoe, Richardson, and Fielding*. London: Chatto & Windus, 1957.

"The Comic Syntax of *Tristram Shandy*." In Howard Anderson and John S. Shea, eds., *Studies in Criticism and Aesthetics, 1660–1800: Essays in Honor of Samuel Holt Monk*. Minneapolis: University of Minnesota Press, 1967, 315–31.

Welcher, Jeanne K. "Eighteenth-Century Views of Gulliver: Some Contrasts Between Illustrations and Prints." In Joachim Möller, ed., *Imagination on a Long Rein: English Literature Illustrated*. Marburg: Jonas Verlag, 1988, 82–93.

Weinbrot, Howard D. "Clarissa, Elias Brand and Death by Parentheses." In Albert Rivero, ed., *New Essays on Samuel Richardson*. New York: St. Martin's Press, 1996, 117–40.

Weissman, Stephen. "Occasional List No. 107. Rare Books and Manuscripts. Part VI: Sk to Z." New York: Ximenes Rare Books, 1994.

Werner, Herman O., Jr. "The Life and Works of Sarah Fielding." Unpublished dissertation. Harvard University, 1939.

Woolf, Virginia. "Robinson Crusoe." In *The Common Reader: Second Series*. 5th impression. London: Hogarth Press, 1948 (first pub. 1932), 51–58.

Websites

http://www.blakearchive.org/. The William Blake digital archive.

http://www.gutenberg.net/. Homepage of Project Gutenberg, "Fine Literature Digitally Re-Published."

http://jefferson.village.virginia.edu/rossetti/index.html/. The Complete Writings and Pictures of Dante Gabriel Rossetti, "A Hypermedia Research Archive."

http://www.library.yale.edu/beinecke/. Yale's Beinecke Library's collection of digital images can be reached via the "Research Workstation" link on this site.

http://www.umi.com/eebo/. This Early English Books Online (EEBO) resource can only be utilized by members of subscribing institutions. The 125,000 works in this database, governing texts printed between 1475 and 1700, are presented as images which may be viewed online or downloaded in PDF format for viewing offline.

Index

The visual artists, designers, illustrators, and engravers – many of them little-known craftsmen – have been distinguished by an asterisk (*).

accidentals (*see also* punctuation, printer's ornaments, and typography) 6, 61, 149, 154, 157, 162, 169, 170, 176, 198, 199–200, 259
Addison, Joseph 85, 213, 240, 244, 245
advertising 3–6, 60–91, 174, 200, 216, 217, 249
Aikins, Janet 252
Alcock, John 249
Alkon, Paul K. 239
Anderson, Benedict 14
anonymity, attribution, pseudonymity 27, 30, 53, 56, 58, 67–70, 80, 81, 83, 87, 153, 233, 239
aposeopesis (*see* lacunae)
Aristotle 76
Astell, Mary 251
Athena 96, 105
Austen, Jane 59, 71, 79, 92–93, 94, 99, 106, 108, 251

Babell, William 249
Backscheider, Paula 42
Baine, Rodney M. 60, 61–91, 229, 231, 235
Baker, Nicholson 216
Baker, Sheridan 242
Ball, Donald L. 261
Ballaster, Rosalind 234
Barbauld, Anna Laetitia 248
Barker, Jane 70
Barker, Nicolas 219, 220

Barth, John 18
Barthelme, Donald 18
Bates, Ephraim Tristram 81–83, 87, 90, 144, 147
Battestin, Martin C. 157, 171, 250, 261
Behn, Aphra 241, 246
Benedict, Barbara M. 264, 265
Betty Barnes 239
Bickham, George 54, 101, 104
bindings 14, 17, 66, 174, 210, 231
Bindon, Francis 48
Blake, William 6, 8–9, 215
Blayney, Peter W. M. 74
Blewett, David 42–47
Boccaccio, Giovanni 262
Boggs, J. S. G. 20–21
Bohun, William 264
Boitard, Louis Pierre* 51, 232
Bond, Donald F. 218
Bond, William 229
Booth, Wayne 214, 241
Bowden, Martha 111, 247
Bowers, Fredson 250, 261
Bradshaigh, Lady Dorothy 68, 110, 199, 266, 267
Bragg, Benjamin 42
Bray, Joe 169, 219
Brewer, John 238
Brontë, Charlotte 144, 234
Brontë, Emily 59
Brown, Murray L. 252

Browne, Sir Thomas   166
Brückmann, Patricia   257
Bullen, John Samuel   253
Bullitt, John M.   254
Bunyan, John   47
Burney, Charles   250
Burney, Frances   246, 256

Campbell, Duncan   37–41, 42, 47, 56, 69, 72, 236
Carroll, John   248, 253, 257
Carroll, Lewis   174
Carter, Elizabeth   97–98, 105, 116, 248
Carter, John   220, 235
Carwitham, John*   227
Cash, Arthur H.   232, 233
Caslon, William   257
Castle, Terry   119, 121, 132, 149, 247
Cave, Edmund   132
Cervantes (*see also* Lennox's, *Female Quixote*)   79, 156
Chambers, Ephraim   186
Chappell, Warren   250
Chappell, William   250
chapter divisions   134–135, 208–209
children's literature   83
Chaucer   186, 242
Chung, Ewha   266
Cicero   240
"Clark & Pine"* (*see also* Pine, John*)   43, 47
Cleland, John   59
coffee houses and taverns   3, 69, 71–72, 181, 182
Cole, Richard Cargill   218
Collier, Jane (*see also* Fielding, Sarah)   132, 190
Congreve, William   77, 89, 219, 245
Conway, Alison   222
Cope, Kevin L.   177
Coventry, Francis   15, 27, 50, 51, 53, 80, 87
Cowley, Abraham   240
Cowley, Robert L. S.   252
Croft, Sir Herbert   246
Curll, Edmund   13–14, 15, 40, 41, 56, 60, 61, 70, 74, 75, 229, 230, 234, 236

Darwin, Charles   173
Davies, Mrs. Christian (a.k.a. "Mother Ross")   36, 228, 268

Davis, Herbert   218
Davis, Lennard J.   234
Day, W. G.   219
de Bergerac, Cyrano   239
de Botton, Alain   262
de Bressay, Marquise   254
Defoe, Daniel   13, 15, 18, 21, 27, 36, 60, 72, 75–76, 77, 80, 135, 184, 234, 238
    and Duncan Cambell   37, 41
    fondness for paratexts   41–42, 48, 56, 57
    use of lists and inventories   179, 182, 187
    Works:
    Jure Divino   42, 46
    Moll Flanders   42, 45, 64, 178
        lists and bills   179
        title page   63–64, 65–67, 71
    Robinson Crusoe   7, 12, 42–48, 56, 63, 75, 77
        inventories   179
        maps   99
        title page and title   62–63, 65–67, 76, 78
    Roxana   42, 44
    Tour   210, 211–212, 230
Defreval, M.   266, 269
Dekker, Rudolf M.   228, 229
DeMaria, Robert, Jr.   204
de Mondonville, Jean Joseph Cassanea   249
Dennis, Nigel   179
device or printer's mark   75, 240
Dickens, Charles   59, 85, 233
Dickinson, Emily   6
Diderot, Denis   186
Digeon, Aurélien   258
dogs   1, 48–49, 50, 51, 80, 142, 143, 144, 243
Doody, Margaret Anne   149, 240, 247, 251, 257
Douglas, Aileen   232
drama and the printed play   14, 46, 70, 89, 98, 108, 165, 168, 175, 189–191, 219, 242, 243, 245, 246, 259
Dryden, John   13, 89, 242, 244, 257
duelling   202–204
Dugaw, Dianne   228, 229
Du Maurier, George*   221
Dunton, John   164, 166, 167, 168
Dussinger, John   248
Duthie, Elizabeth   224

eating and fasting   3, 82, 105, 120, 121–125, 178, 180, 181, 182
Eaves, T. C. Duncan   35, 248, 262
Ehrenpreis, Irvin   218, 226
Eisenstein, Elizabeth L.   8, 12, 216
electronic text (*see* web-based publishing)
Ellman, Lucy   174
Elsner, John   264
engravers (*see also* entries under individual artists)   11
Ephraim Tristram Bates (see *Bates*)
Epictetus   85
epigraphs   76, 85–90, 104, 171, 250

Fanning, Christopher   219
Faulkner, George   30, 31, 32, 33, 34, 99, 228
Febvre, Lucien   8
Feke, Robert*   227
Fielding, Henry   15, 36, 70, 77, 80, 86, 88, 89, 179, 213, 228, 232
  and sister Sarah (*see* Fielding, Sarah)
  definition of genre   77
  Hogarth's portrait of   24–27, 59
  rivalry with Richardson   170–171
  Works:
    Amelia   87, 238
    Author's Farce   61–91, 166, 235
    Joseph Andrews   16, 77, 119, 180, 182
      chapter divisions   134–135, 208–209
      economic rhetoric of list-making   180–182
      illustrated   171–172
      title and title page   79, 238
    Shamela   35, 128, 233
    Tom Jones   59, 77, 85, 86, 157, 233, 250, 262
Fielding, Sarah   15, 152, 179
  and brother Henry   15
    his editorship of *David Simple*   153–170, 216
  and Jane Collier   80, 87, 88, 190, 192
  Works:
    Cleopatra and Octavia   238
    Countess of Dellwyn   170
    David Simple   7, 70, 153–165, 174, 233, 236
    Familiar Letters   181, 238, 266
    The Cry   87, 88, 165, 190, 192
    The Governess   89, 238

Flaubert, Gustave   186
Flint, Christopher   256
fonts (*see* typeface)
food (*see* eating)
Fowles, John   18
Foxon, David F.   219, 263
Frega, Donnalee   123, 125
Frye, Northrop   14
Fulton, Gordon D.   221
Furbank, P. N.   229, 231, 235
Fysh, Stephanie   252

Gabler, Hans Walter   10–11, 215
Gardiner, Robert   264
Gaskell, Philip   61, 157, 220
Gay, John   209
Genette, Gérard   9–10, 11, 27, 47, 61, 66–91, 118, 128, 220
Gildon, Charles   234, 236, 239
Gissing, George   262
Goldthorpe, David   231
Goodall, William   89, 239
Granville, George   242
Gravelot, François*   66–91, 97, 228, 252, 262
Graves, Richard   244
Griffith, Richard   112, 113, 239, 244
Grignion, Charles*   25–27
Groves, David   224
Grubstreet   13, 14, 22, 41, 42, 60, 71, 85, 166, 167, 168, 184, 207, 216, 217, 268
Gunning, Susannah (*see* Minifie)
Gutenberg   12, 218
Gwilliam, Tassie   257

Halsband, Robert   228
Hammelmann, Hanns   223
Handel, George Frideric   93, 250
Handley, Miriam   219
Harris, Jocelyn   149, 190, 202, 204, 247, 251, 254, 257, 262, 263, 265, 266
Hawkins, William   189
Hayman, Francis*   61–91, 97, 228, 235, 252
Haywood, Eliza   13, 15, 68, 75, 77, 79–80, 89, 135, 235
  frontispiece portrait of   22–24, 27, 229
  ridiculed in *Dunciad*   22

Haywood, Eliza (*cont.*)
  Works:
    Betsy Thoughtless 59, 233, 240
    Love in Excess 77, 85
    Memoirs of a Certain Island 209–210
    Spy upon the Conjurer (*see also* Campbell, Duncan) 69, 72
Head, Richardson 187
Hearne, Mary 236, 244
Henry, Anne C. 139, 219, 257
Hill, Aaron 35, 119
Hill, Thomas* 230
Hinman, Charlton T. 259
Hobbes, Thomas 179
Hogarth, William* 24, 25, 48–49, 110, 180, 232, 252
  and Henry Fielding 25–27, 35
  and Richardson 35–36, 47, 91, 235
  and Sterne 36
Hogg, James 224
Holland 4, 37, 225, 233
Homer 89, 176, 186, 213, 242
Hooke, Robert 72, 73, 85, 177
Horace 31, 82, 83, 85, 86, 87, 90, 242, 243, 244
Hughes, Helen Sard 241
Hulett, J.* 171–172
Hunter, J. Paul 16, 36, 58, 77, 80, 134–135, 219, 240, 259, 260, 264, 265
Hunting, Robert S. 258

illustrators, engravers (*see* individual entries under artist's name)
imprints 65, 66, 67, 70–76, 83, 235, 237
Irwin, Robert 262
italics (*see* accidentals)
it-narrators, objects that narrate 50, 53, 55, 89, 188, 236

James, Henry 19–20, 90
Jervas, Charles* 223
Johns, Adrian 12, 72, 85
Johnson, Samuel 13, 80, 186, 219
  on punctuation 165–166
  suggests index for *Clarissa* 205–207, 210, 213
  Work:
    Dictionary 51, 85, 165, 186, 206
Johnstone, Charles 89, 236, 244

Jonson, Ben 74
Joyce, James 10, 186
Juvenal 2, 46, 52, 84, 90, 244

Kelly, William Fitzmaurice 75
Kelsall, Malcolm 154, 156, 261
Kernan, Alvin B. 219
Keymer, Thomas 227, 237, 254, 255, 261, 266
Kidgell, John 15, 50–55, 83–84, 87, 89–90, 112–116, 209, 214, 237, 265, 267
Kimber, Edward 15, 48–50, 89, 236, 239
Kimpel, Ben D. 248, 262
Kinkead-Weekes, Mark 119, 190
Kirkall, Elisha* 22, 23–24
Kirkman, Francis* 222, 236

lacunae, ellipsis marks, aposiopesis 67, 128, 135, 139, 141–145, 158
law, lawyers, legal documents 25, 58, 82, 93, 131, 132, 156, 176, 182–184, 185, 202, 215, 258
Leclerc, Georges-Louis 263
Lely, Sir Peter* 223
Lenfest, David 224
Lennox, Charlotte 80, 209
Leppert, Richard 247, 250, 251
Lewis, Matthew 89
Linnaeus, Carolus 186
Lintot, Bernard 60–61
Locke, John 204–205
Long, Edward 89, 238
Longueville, Peter 238
Lonsdale, Roger 250
Loveridge, Mark 219
Lund, Roger D. 209, 211

McBurney, William Harlin 254–257
McGann, Jerome J. 10, 215
McGeary, Tom 250
McKenzie, D. F. 219
McKeon, Michael 14, 77, 186, 194, 240
McKerrow 61
McKillop, Alan Dugald 248
McLaverty, James 219, 223, 224
McLuhan, Marshall 8
Mack, Maynard 223
Macksey, Richard 16
Madden, Samuel 254

Magritte, René 84
Manley, Delarivier 13, 15, 27, 58, 68, 135, 235, 236, 239
   Queen Zarah 68
   Rivella 56–58, 229, 236
maps and mapmakers 28, 41, 99, 234
Ma(r)king the Text 9
Martial 88, 243
Martin, Henri-Jean 8
Maslen, Keith 230, 236, 265
Meeker, Richard K. 232
Melville, Herman 186
Messier, Charles 186
Meyer, Horst 219
Millar, Andrew 25, 48, 71, 86, 157, 158, 161, 170, 171, 172, 210
Milton, John 221, 224
Minifie, Susannah (later Mrs. Gunning) 245
Mitchell, W. J. T. 219
Montagu, Lady Mary Wortley 231
Moss, Roger B. 219, 260
Motte, Benjamin 28, 29, 31, 226
Mullan, John 260
museums 177, 186, 215, 217
music 7, 91, 92–116, 120, 237, 239
   in Austen 92–93
   in Fielding 101
   in Richardson 93, 95
   lesson books 100
   musical miscellanies 102, 103, 104, 105
Mylne, Vivienne 168, 169, 260

Nabokov, Vladimir 174, 186, 216
New, Melvyn 228
Newbery, John 52, 83, 84, 233, 241
Nielsen, Jakob 217

ornaments (*see* printer's ornaments)
Ovid 148, 149, 227–230, 257
Owens, W. R. 229, 231, 235

Parker, Dorothy 253, 254
Parkes, M. B. 151, 156, 168, 259
Parmentier, Jacques* 22–24, 223
Parnell, Thomas 209
Paulson, Ronald 35, 232, 233, 254

Persius 29
Peters, Julie Stone 219
Pine, John* 43, 47
Piper, David 21
playing cards 37–54, 71, 112, 114, 252
plays (*see* drama)
Pollard, M. 218
Pope, Alexander 8–9, 49, 60–61, 71, 74, 75, 85, 89, 186, 198, 199, 209, 214–215, 219, 221, 224, 245, 260, 262, 268
   Dunciad and portraits of "Eliza" 22–24, 41
pornography 171, 262, 263
Prévost, Abbé (a.k.a. A. F. Prévost d'Exiles) 169
Price, Leah 265
Price, Steven R. 94, 131, 168
printer's ornaments (*see also* tailpieces) 7, 117, 119–152
printer's mark (*see* device)
Probyn, Clive T. 261
pseudonymity (*see* anonymity)
punctuation 7, 9, 14, 51, 61, 129, 151–152, 153–170

Rabelais, François 176, 186
Radcliffe, Anne 89
Rameau, Jean Philippe 249
Rawson, Claude 176
Redford, Bruce 268
Reilly, Elizabeth Carroll 257
Richardson, Samuel 13, 15, 53, 77, 90–91, 157, 236
   and epistolary technique 118–119
   and innovative punctuation 164, 168–170
   and interpretive control 11, 36, 41, 47, 128, 191–193, 198–200, 202, 204
   as "editor" 68, 70, 153
   as indexer and list-maker 108, 109, 177–179, 188–213
   as printer of works by others 168, 174, 189, 195, 211
   frontispiece portrait of 25–27, 59
   Works:
      Clarissa 59, 121, 122, 123, 124, 130, 131, 139, 140, 141, 142, 143, 144, 150, 173, 177, 191, 194, 195, 196, 197, 233
      and music 7, 93, 94–116, 131–132
      and time 120–125, 128–151

Richardson, Samuel (*cont.*)
    lists of *dramatis personae* 191–193, 197–198
    tables of contents 207–208
    third edition's marginal dots 16, 108, 110, 204, 256, 267
    title 79
    Collection of Moral and Instructive Sentiments 108, 109, 205, 206, 210
    Familiar Letters 184, 202
    Grandison 54–55, 116, 137, 138, 177, 188, 201, 214, 233, 251
        and its title 79
        and music 93, 107, 109, 112
        and paratexts 175, 179, 184, 257
            index 200–213, 214
            list of *dramatis personae* 188–200
    Pamela 14, 59, 78, 97, 126, 127, 129, 177, 183, 191, 197–198
        and legal form books 182–184
        and music 93, 97, 109, 112
        and time 125–128, 133, 134, 135
        failed Hogarth commission 35–36, 37, 91
        table of contents 207
Richetti, John J. 234
Rivero, Albert J. 225
Robertson, Joseph 260
Roscoe, S. 218, 241
Ross, Angus 97, 247, 255, 265
Ross, Ian Campbell 237
Rossetti, Dante Gabriel 215
Rousseau, Jean-Jaques 240
Rowe, Nicholas 257
Royal Society 73, 177, 186
rubrication 60–61

Sabor, Peter 153, 154, 156, 227, 258, 259
Saenger, Paul 216
Safire, William 216–217
Sale, William Merritt, Jr. 97, 227, 230, 236, 248, 262, 265, 266
science fiction 253
science and fiction 72, 85, 173, 175, 176–177, 184, 186
Scott, Sarah 55–56, 57–59, 241
Scott, Sir Walter 79, 89
sentimental fiction 163, 164
sexual ambiguity & transvestitism 36–37, 195
Shakespeare, William 89, 158, 198, 199, 223, 240, 245, 259, 260
Sherbo, Arthur 253, 255
Sherburn, George 119
Sherman, Stuart 255
shop signs and street addresses 66, 71, 73–76, 235, 236
Simonides 243
Smedley, Jonathan 221, 226
Smith, Adam 173
Smollett, Tobias 15, 50, 88, 179, 184, 187
    Works:
        Peregrine Pickle 80, 87
        Roderick Random 86, 87, 180, 233
        Sir Launcelot Greaves 89
Snell, Hannah 15, 36–37, 38, 39, 40–41, 56, 80, 81, 230
Soane, Sir John (*see also museums*) 186
Southerne, Thomas 242, 246
Spear, Gary 224
Spedding, Patrick 222, 223
Stafford, Barbara Maria 263
Steele, David 260
Steele, Sir Richard 1, 85, 240, 244
    Works:
        Tatler No. 21 5
        Tatler No. 238 1–6
Sterling, James 224
Sterne, Laurence 8–9, 15, 152
    and Hogarth 36
    his library copy of *Grandison* 214
    Tristram Shandy 9, 17, 59, 70, 80, 85, 86, 87, 146, 168, 186, 220
        asterisks 144
        flamboyant graphics 15–16, 96, 112, 116
        forerunners 94, 144, 166, 215, 237, 239, 241
        legalese 184
        planned index 214–215
        punctuation 164
Stewart, Philip 234, 262
Straus, Ralph 220, 229, 230, 231, 232, 240
Stuber, Florian 221, 262
Sturt, John* 225
subscription 31, 195–196, 199, 226

Swift, Jonathan   6, 13, 15, 21, 52, 57, 89, 221, 235, 239
  genuine portraits of the Dean   34, 48
  on punctuation   153, 166
  Works:
  City Shower   1–6, 11
  Gulliver's Travels   85, 228
    chapter titles and suspense   208
    frontispiece portraits   7, 20, 27, 28–34, 37, 41, 47, 48
    lists and scientific empiricism   176, 177
    maps   28, 99
    narrative reliability   12, 31
  Tale of a Tub   143, 145, 209

Tahir, Marie   217
tailpieces and head pieces   149–151, 193
Tanselle, G. Thomas   10
taverns (*see* coffee houses)
Teerink, H.   225, 226
Thackeray, William   85
theatre (*see* drama)
time and temporal cohesion   46, 47, 118–152
Todd, Dennis   228, 263
Todd, Janet   234, 251
Toft, Mary   36
Tonson, Jacob   199
typeface and typography   4, 7, 48, 61, 65, 66, 67, 83, 131, 147, 184, 198–200, 204, 216, 239, 245, 248, 257

Updike, John   174

van de Pol, Lotte C.   228, 229
Van der Gucht, Gerard*   232
Van der Gucht, Jan*   231
Van der Gucht, Michiel*   42, 56, 229, 230
Vauxhall   100
Vertue, George*   22–24, 34, 229
Virgil   186, 243, 244
Voltaire   220, 239
von Haller, Albrecht   132

Wagner, Peter   224, 226
Wagner, Richard   120, 140
Wakely, Alice   254
Walker, Anthony*   55, 234
Wall, Cynthia   264, 265
Warner, William Beatty   137, 205, 253
Watt, Ian   14, 77, 166–167, 240
Watteau, Jean Antoine*   110
web-based publishing, web-page design, and electronic text   215–217
Weinbrot, Howard D.   257
Weissman, Stephen   268
Welcher, Jeanne K.   224, 225, 226
Werner, Herman O., Jr.   258
Westcomb, Sophia   120
Whibley, Charles   269
Wilde, John   174
Wilkes, John   232
Williams, George C.   173
Woolf, Virginia   174, 186
  on Defoe   62–63

Young, Edward   189, 190, 233

Zbikowski, Larry   250
Zelinsky, Katherine   57, 234

Lightning Source UK Ltd.
Milton Keynes UK
UKHW03f0520220518
322939UK00008B/56/P